AF477995

Strategic Culture and Weapons of Mass Destruction

Initiatives in Strategic Studies: Issues and Policies

James J. Wirtz
General Editor

Jeffrey A. Larsen
T.V. Paul
Brad Roberts
James M. Smith
Series Editors

INITIATIVES IN STRATEGIC STUDIES provides a bridge between the use of force or diplomacy and the achievement of political objectives. This series focuses on the topical and timeless issues relating to strategy, including the nexus of political, diplomatic, psychological, economic, cultural, historic, and military affairs. It provides a link between the scholarly and policy communities by serving as the recognized forum for conceptually sophisticated analyses of timely and important strategic issues.

Nuclear Transformation: The New U.S. Nuclear Doctrine
Edited by James J. Wirtz and Jeffrey A. Larsen

Proliferation of Weapons of Mass Destruction in the Middle East: Directions and Policy Options in the New Century
Edited by James A. Russell

The Last Battle of the Cold War: The Deployment and Negotiated Elimination of Intermediate Range Nuclear Forces in Europe
Maynard W. Glitman

Critical Issues Facing the Middle East: Security, Politics and Economics
Edited by James A. Russell

Militarization and War
Julian Schofield

Global Politics of Defense Reform
Edited by Thomas Bruneau and Harold Trinkunas

Perspectives on Sino-American Strategic Nuclear Issues
Edited by Christopher P. Twomey

Strategic Culture and Weapons of Mass Destruction: Culturally Based Insights into Comparative National Security Policymaking
Edited by Jeannie L. Johnson, Kerry M. Kartchner, and Jeffrey A. Larsen

STRATEGIC CULTURE AND WEAPONS OF MASS DESTRUCTION

CULTURALLY BASED INSIGHTS INTO COMPARATIVE NATIONAL SECURITY POLICYMAKING

Edited by

*Jeannie L. Johnson, Kerry M. Kartchner,
and Jeffrey A. Larsen*

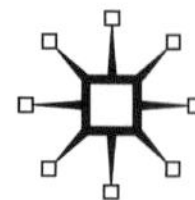

STRATEGIC CULTURE AND WEAPONS OF MASS DESTRUCTION
Copyright © Jeannie L. Johnson, Kerry M. Kartchner, and
Jeffrey A. Larsen, 2009.

First published in 2009 by
PALGRAVE MACMILLAN®
in the United States—a division of St. Martin's Press LLC,
175 Fifth Avenue, New York, NY 10010.

Where this book is distributed in the UK, Europe and the rest of the world,
this is by Palgrave Macmillan, a division of Macmillan Publishers Limited,
registered in England, company number 785998, of Houndmills,
Basingstoke, Hampshire RG21 6XS.

Palgrave Macmillan is the global academic imprint of the above companies
and has companies and representatives throughout the world.

Palgrave® and Macmillan® are registered trademarks in the United States,
the United Kingdom, Europe and other countries.

ISBN-13: 978–0–230–61221–1
ISBN-10: 0–230–61221–0

Library of Congress Cataloging-in-Publication Data is available from the
Library of Congress.

A catalogue record of the book is available from the British Library.

Design by Newgen Imaging Systems (P) Ltd., Chennai, India.

First edition: January 2009

10 9 8 7 6 5 4 3 2 1

Printed in the United States of America.

Jeannie dedicates this book to Steve, who makes her contribution to this and all other work possible.

Kerry dedicates this book with devotion to the incomparable women at the center of his life: Michelle, Brittany, and Chelsea, and their remarkable mother, Sophie; and to his new son-in-law, Trevor.

Jeff expresses his hopes for a world in which his children Heather, Peter, Andrew, and Carolyn can safely pursue their love of foreign cultures and appreciate the wonderful babble of strange tongues in distant lands.

PART III: THE WAY AHEAD

Figures

FOREWORD

When in the late 1980s I put forward a research proposal on culture as a variable in nuclear strategy (a subject that was going to occupy me for eight years), I met with general incomprehension on both sides of the Atlantic, and I suspect that I got the money for the project for reasons other than my persuasiveness on the importance of the subject. Perhaps crucially, I lacked some of the now current vocabulary to describe what I was trying to examine, namely how different "cultures" contributed to the preferences in nuclear strategy that others—with the exception of Colin Gray[1]—were still trying to explain solely in terms of the logic of geography, targeting, payloads, reach, and so on. I did not use the word "culture" but "mentality," a term inherited from the French school of *Annales* historians such as Fernand Braudel, Michel Vovelle, and so on who applied anthropological methodology to historical research in the early 1960s,[2] long before anybody had heard of Clifford Geertz. "The past is another country" sums up this approach nicely, a second wave of which was exported by anthropologists to other disciplines in the 1980s (the Geertz generation), bringing in a rich harvest from the 1990s onward, but now under the heading "culture."

One early offshoot was discussion of "strategic culture," a term I did not espouse at the time as those who defined it and were using it in the 1970, 1980s, and early 1990s tended to focus too narrowly, in my view, on military culture, or on the culture of government decision makers—a small elite contributing to a discourse on defense (the "strategic community").[3] In this book, however, the term strategic culture as defined by Jeannie Johnson, Kerry Kartchner, and Jeffrey Larsen is used in a much larger definition that I find extremely useful for the analysis of the subject at hand. It focuses on government policies on weapons of mass destruction (WMD) against a more general background of a society's culture. Regimes—even totalitarian regimes—cannot operate without taking into account culture and public opinion; trying to do so would be like playing a piece of music without instruments. They have to play on a register of emotions, metaphors, myths, *idées reçues,* and "lessons from the past," which are current in the culture in which they operate. But they themselves are part of such a culture; they themselves carry within themselves all these ideas, convictions, beliefs, and points of reference. A culture extremely centered on one leader will not tend to collective decision making or even consultation on the use of nuclear weapons. A culture with good historical experience of coalitions will have a greater trust in an ally than one with experiences of abandonment, emphasized in popular lore. It is therefore extremely useful, in this context, to consider not only the subculture(s) of the armed forces or the strategic community, but also that of the society as a whole. I cannot say how pleased I am to see that this argument has been taken up by these researchers, hopefully striking the mortal blow to the assumption that decision making on political issues, including defense, including WMD, can be predicted by an a-cultural, "objective" games theory or "Realist" theory of all being after "power" and oil and nothing else. I am still amazed that these theories ever reigned supreme in the aftermath of World War II, when, in the eyes of the world, a German regime—with the general support of its population—staked its cards on becoming "world power or going under," when the latter could not possibly have been in its interest, with a net effect of loss of life and treasure that could not have been greater had somebody deliberately set out to harm Germany. But past and contemporary times are replete with examples of behavior—including self-sacrificial behavior, right down to suicide bombers—that cannot be explained merely in terms of the quest for power or riches.

Let us stick, then, to strategic culture. But instead of reiterating or maladroitly summarizing what the contributors are saying so competently and aptly in their respective case studies, I shall add a few points—ideas, admonitions, perhaps insights—and identify problems to stretch the agenda of future research in this subject.

While as human beings we are part-rational, part-irrational, as researchers we tend toward comprehensive rationality. Our basic school training in mathematics, the natural sciences, or philosophy leads us to look out for and expect to find coherent logical patterns. Our first realization must be that cultures are not based on coherent logical patterns. Although the search for logical explanations and the solution of apparent contradictions has kept generations of Talmud and ecclesiastical scholars busy, the reality is that the multiauthored Hebrew Bible, New Testament, or the Koran, the constituent texts of Buddhism, or even monographs such as *Das Kapital* are not fully logically coherent. Cultures are even less so, as we have layers of different great texts and traditions overlaying each other, layers of different religions, and different values and customs. From its creation, Christianity had to compete with the classical heritage, outstandingly symbolized by the Iliad's warrior hero stories, every aspect of which clashed profoundly with the teachings of Jesus and his disciples, but which next to the Bible is the most ubiquitous influence on art in Christian Europe, right into art found in the papal palaces, picture galleries, and manuscript collections. But classical traditions and Christianity were not the only influence on Medieval Europe. The Crusades, for example, have been described as attempts by the Roman Church to marry the values of a largely pacific religion with the warrior culture of the mainly Germanic tribes that had taken over Europe in the Great Migrations, and who in the absence of other enemies tended to wage war on each other—which did not fit Christian values.[4] (Consequently, successive popes tried to channel this warrior spirit outward, away from causing ravages within their Christian flock.) And so on. We should therefore not expect to encounter any logical coherence in another culture. There may be some, but it is quite unpredictable where we will find it. We should thus talk about *clusters* of beliefs particular to a culture, but rarely if ever about belief *systems*.

Another *déformation professionelle* hampers our work, and that is, that as good students, we have been taught to deduce "right answers" logically, mathematically. As avid readers of detective novels, we are furthermore persuaded that there are "normal" reactions to certain events, while what intuitively (and in the confines of our own cultural experience) we identify as "abnormal" reactions usually indicate the culprit. Famously, this theme is treated by Albert Camus in his *L'Etranger*, and by Heinrich Böll in his *Lost Honour of Katharina Blum*.[5] In both cases, an individual is brought before a court as a chief suspect in a crime because their lifestyle, and their emotional reactions to certain events, do not conform to what is generally regarded as "the norm" (not to mention that aberrant word, "natural") in that society. We thus have a strong tendency to project our own feelings—or what we imagine would be our reactions to certain events we have not actually experienced ourselves—on to others. We try to deduce logically what another's motives might be in doing a certain thing by trying "to put ourselves in their place." This basis of empathy, however, in many respects a particularly precious part of humanity, may blind us to cultural and individual differences. To give just one example, on his first visit to German Chancellor Angela Merkel, French President Nicolas Sarkozy offered to discuss the European sharing of French nuclear weapons, a subject proposed by the French repeatedly since the late 1950s. As the French assume everybody must surely aspire to having them, as to the French they are the ultimate symbol of sovereignty, Sarkozy assumed the Germans wanted them to, especially now that Germany is a sovereign country once more. He was surprised to find that (East German) Merkel, coming from a culture where all war and is seen as an absolute evil and nuclear weapons as very problematic, and where the military is as best accepted as a deterrent and peacekeeping force, showed no interest whatsoever in such a symbol.[6]

Next we must emphasize the existence, side by side, of different subcultures within a culture, sharing common points of reference, but perhaps disagreeing profoundly about some of their implications. What is vaguely termed the Left and the Right in politics tends to be associated with the prioritization of different values (though one would not know this looking at the domestic politics of, say, Tony Blair's Labour Party), and the browbeating of the trade unions by Margaret Thatcher in the 1980s will be a point of reference for both "sides" of the political spectrum in Britain, but will be interpreted differently. Similarly, the Vietnam War is seen differently by different subcultures within the United States—one social group tending toward the opinion that the United States should not have got involved in the first place, and that its defeat was morally predetermined; another—including especially the military—tending more to the judgment that the United States should simply have fought the war differently.

The term subculture can be applied to very different groupings, from a political party and its supporters, to people with common political leanings that few articulate but that many would "feel" they agree with (without being members of a particular party, but perhaps strongly guided by a family tradition), to specific organizations such as the military with its own culture(s). It is here that I want to draw attention to the fruitful contributions that the study of organizational cultures and the concept of "group think" can make to our analysis of strategic cultures.[7] What a group thinks depends to a significant extent on what it is customary for this group to think, what other members of the group think when a new member joins, to what extent the conformity in thinking is rewarded by factors such as advancement within the group, and so on. Some stress similarities between professional groups in different countries—military men, for example, may claim that they reached a surprising degree of mutual understanding and camaraderie with military professionals they encountered from adversary countries. Certain professional commonalities exist, but there are also blatant differences in organizational ethos and culture between different countries. French civil servants, especially those trained in the elite school *Ecole Normale d'Administration* or ENA (hence popularly called the *énarques*) think of themselves as the salt of the earth, and it is a privilege for the citizen to be allowed to talk to them, as anybody who has had dealings with French civil servants will tell you. The situation is very different in Britain where civil servants seem to be imbued with a greater sense of being at the service of the public (an ethos that is sadly now giving way to Continental-style red tape and a culture of libel that has spread from across the Atlantic). Diplomats also fall into quite distinct groups. While it is no longer true that most British diplomats have all studied "Greats" (classics) at Oxbridge, a particularly large proportion of British diplomats are language students, a vital selection principle, as particularly the English are so abysmally bad at languages. In Germany, by contrast most diplomats and senior civil servants in other ministries are by training lawyers, with all the consequences one can safely deduce from this.

Such cultural differences within a profession are even more striking when you look at armed forces. Anybody knows that there are particular cultures associated with army, navy, air force and marines. But even these differ from country to country. For example, the brainwashing and mental conditioning the U.S. Marines receive in their training is likely to be unparalleled in any other Western democracy. For another difference, while in Britain the Army and Navy look down on the Royal Air Force as newcomers without tradition, in France, a country where progress, innovation, and technology are valued much more than in Britain, they have been seen as the armed forces of the future, where the cleverest officers would go. More striking still is the difference of ethos in different countries. In Britain and France, people join the armed forces because they seek adventure and yearn to go abroad. In Germany, since 1955, men have joined the armed forces because it was a secure job in which they knew they would never be sent abroad. Not surprisingly, the "transformation" of NATO with its new missions since 1991 is something that is hard to swallow for them. These differences in ethos between these countries' armed forces strongly reinforce the cultural differences with regard to the legitimacy of the use of the armed forces; see the discrepancies over action in Afghanistan, 2002–2008.

Finally, one should underscore the benefit that bureaucratic politics analysis can bring to a researcher into a foreign culture. The rivalry between different parts of a state, different organizations within government, different sections of one ministry even, and generational conflicts, albeit to varying degrees, are probably a phenomenon applicable the world over. To fire off just a few tenets to complement those put forward so persuasively by the great path-blazers in this discipline, from Cyril Northcote Parkinson to Morton Halperin and Graham Allison:[8]

- Multilateral decisions are, to varying degrees, compromises driven by political considerations about how to satisfy the divergent interests of the parties involved in the decision making rather than by the logic of seeking the objectively best solution to the problem about which the decision is purportedly made. If the (compromise) decision turns out to be of useless or even negative effect, the parties to the decision making will disown it, arguing that they had to compromise on their own original negotiating position that would have provided the right solution, and on this basis they may demand to be put in sole charge of decision-making the next time. Collective decisions thus contain their own contradiction. If the (compromise) decision works, all parties will claim to have been the original proponents of this wonderful decision. Success has many fathers, but failure is an orphan.

- The successful bureaucrat (and to some extent, the successful officer) who will go far in life is the one who does not anger and upset his superior, does not defer too many decisions upward, does not come up with "ideas above his/her pay grade" (thus showing up the superior who has not had this idea), does not rock the boat, does not blatantly and visibly break rules (however nonsensical or inapplicable these may be to the case in question). It is thus rare that very original thinkers with much personal courage and initiative arrive at the top of any bureaucracy.

Instead, they tend to be cautious types, rarely inclined to risk their career over a point of principle or ethics.[9]

- Most people dislike both their predecessors in their posts and their successors, as their performances are invariably measured against the successes and styles of their predecessors/successors. "Your predecessor would not have done this" or "would not have proceeded in this way" is a disabling argument used by the (always considerable) forces of inertia within any bureaucracy, and it does not engender tender feelings toward this predecessor in those confronted with this argument.

The list could go on, and this book lends itself to many more such generalizations. All that remains for me is to encourage the reader to turn with excitement and curiosity to the following pages, which contain a great treasure of insights into the meaning of strategic culture and into the cultures of eight countries and one terrorist movement. These are insights that any analyst should take on board, especially any analyst with the responsibility of advising decision makers or forming public opinion on the subject.

BEATRICE HEUSER
Reading, UK, January 2008

NOTES

1. Colin S. Gray, *Nuclear Strategy and National Style* (Lanham, MD: Hamilton Press, 1986).

2. For an overview, see Stuart Clark, *The Annales School: A Critical Assessment* (London: Routledge, 1999).

3. Most famously Jack Snyder, *Soviet Strategic Culture: Implications for Limited Nuclear Options* (Santa Monica, CA: RAND, 1977); Ken Booth, *Strategy and Ethnocentrism* (London: Croom Helm, 1979); Yitzhak Klein, "A Theory of Strategic Culture," *Comparative Strategy*, Vol. 10 (1991), pp. 3–23. The exception is Carnes Lord, "American Strategic Culture," *Comparative Strategy*, Vol. 5, No. 3 (1986), pp. 269–93.

4. Jonathan Riley-Smith, *What Were the Crusades?* (Basingstoke: Macmillan, 1992).

5. Albert Camus, *L' Etranger (The Outsider)*, 1942, available from Penguin Classics; and Heinrich Böll, *Lost Honour of Katharina Blum* (New York: Penguin Twentieth Century Classics, 1974).

6 Ralf Beste and Stefan Simons, "Thanks but No Thanks: Sarko's Nuke Offer Bombs with Berlin," www.spiegel.de/international/europe/0,1518,506124,00.html of September 17, 2007. See Beatrice Heuser, *Nuclear Mentalities? Strategies and Belief Systems in Britain, France and the FRG* (London: Macmillan, July 1998); and Heuser, *NATO, Britain, France and the FRG: Nuclear Strategies and Forces for Europe, 1949–2000* (London: Macmillan, 1997).

7. Irving L. Janis, *Group Think: Psychological Studies of Policy Decisions and Fiascoes* 2nd edn. (Boston: Houghton Miflin, 1982).

8. Cyril Northcote Parkinson, *Parkinson's Law* (J. Murray, 1958); Morton H. Halperin, with the assistance of Priscilla Clapp and Arnold Kanter, *Bureaucratic Politics and Foreign Policy* (Washington, DC: Brookings Institution, 1974); Graham Allison, *Essence of Decision* (Boston: Little Brown, 1971).

9. For officers, see Norman Dixon, *On the Psychology of Military Incompetence* (1976, this edition London: Pimplico, 1994); but I owe this idea primarily to Admiral Chris Parry.

Acknowledgments

Many of the contributions to this volume are the product of an eighteen-month project undertaken by the Advanced Systems and Concepts Office (ASCO) of the Defense Threat Reduction Agency. We gratefully acknowledge the support of this office. In particular, we thank Dick Gullickson, Dave Hamon, Jennifer Perry, and Mike Urena for their support and efforts on behalf of this project. One of our editors, Kerry Kartchner, was the lead for this project at ASCO. The editors wish to express their appreciation to the participants in various conferences and symposia associated with this project, the first phase of which culminated in a conference held in Monterey, California, in September 2005. This phase was ably managed and hosted by the Center for Contemporary Conflict at the Naval Postgraduate School and its staff, including Anne Clunan, Peter Lavoy, Elizabeth Stone, and Christopher Twomey, The objective of this first phase of the project was to validate strategic culture as an analytical tool for understanding present and prospective decisions regarding weapons of mass destruction. For their thoughtful and provocative presentations, interventions, comments, and other contributions, we would like to thank William D. Casebeer, Steve Coll, Michael C. Desch, Kevin Farrell, Theo Farrell, Hugh Gusterson, Robert Hickson, Darryl Howlett, Feroz Hassan Khan, Vali Nasr, and Andrew Scobell.

In 2006 ASCO asked Science Applications International Corporation (SAIC) to build on the successful foundation of this first phase of the project. We wish to thank the following analysts at SAIC for their effective management of the second phase, in which the analytical tools validated in the first phase were systematically applied to a series of case studies: Lew Dunn, Paul Bernstein, and Thomas Skypek. A second of our editors, Jeff Larsen, managed the project at SAIC. This phase included three conferences at which we asked the authors to present a series of commissioned case studies that considered the role of strategic culture in explaining state decisions to acquire, proliferate, or use a weapon of mass destruction. Those case studies make up the bulk of this volume. The first workshop was held in McLean, Virginia, in February 2006, and included nearly all members of the project, including the editors and authors in this book. The second conference was a two-day affair held at Deer Valley Lodge in Park City, Utah, in May 2006. It was hosted by the third member of our editorial troika, Jeannie Johnson, ably assisted by Cindy Nielsen of Utah State University. A number of additional strategic culture experts joined our group for that event, including Richard Delewski, Darryl Howlett, Richard Love, Brent Talbot, Amin Tarzi, and Christopher Twomey.

The USAF Institute for National Security Studies hosted a two-day workshop on strategic futures and al Qaeda's strategic culture in June 2006 in McLean, Virginia. Thanks to James Smith for inviting several of our authors to participate in that event.

Colin Gray hosted the final conference of the project, held at Reading University in Great Britain in August 2006. The purpose of this conference was to present our project findings to an international audience in order to minimize ethnocentrism. Among the participants in this event, we thank Simon Anglim, Jeremy Black, Stewart Brewer, J.H. Choi, Tony Coates, Christopher Coker, Theo Farrell, Babak Ganji, Andrew Garner, Bastien Giegerich, Sebastian L.v. Gorka, Darryl Howlett, Keith Payne, Glen Segell, Geoffrey Sloan, Mark Smith, Jeremy Stocker, and Rashed Uz Zaman for their contributions.

The editors express special appreciation to the authors whose contributions to the project were chosen for inclusion in this volume. They were selected from among dozens of essays, reports, presentations, and papers prepared over the course of the first and second phases of this project. Their perspectives have been vetted at the Park City and Reading conferences, and reviewed for both the DTRA project and this book.

In some cases, new materials were prepared specifically for this book following the completion of the DTRA/ASCO sponsored project. In this category, we thank Huiyan Feng and Jerry Mark Long for their case studies. Bradley Thayer of the National Institute for Public Policy contributed to the analytical framework that formed the comparative basis for our case studies. The editors also thank the publishers of the Canadian *International Journal* for permission to reprint David Haglund's essay "What Good is Strategic Culture?" which originally appeared in its summer 2004 edition.

While we are anxious to recognize the many constructive contributions of the earlier mentioned proponents of strategic cultural analysis, the editors of the present volume assume responsibility for whatever errors or flaws remain. We appreciate the willingness of DTRA/ASCO to share their project results with a broader audience. The papers prepared for that study have been cleared for public release. Nevertheless, the views expressed in this book are those of the authors or editors alone, and should not be construed to represent the views or policies of SAIC, the Defense Threat Reduction Agency, the U.S. Department of State, or any other U.S. government agency.

Contributors

Joseph S. Bermudez, Jr. is a senior analyst for Jane's Information Group based in Longmont, Colorado.

Fritz W. Ermarth is a private consultant, former senior policy analyst with Science Applications International Corporation in McLean, Virginia, and a career intelligence officer.

Huiyun Feng is an assistant professor of political science at Utah State University, Logan, Utah. She received her PhD from Arizona State University. Her research interests include foreign policy decision making, East Asian security, Chinese politics, and strategic culture.

Gregory F. Giles is a senior director with Hicks and Associates in McLean, Virginia. For nearly two decades he has been advising U.S. government clients and has testified before Congress on weapons of mass destruction threats and responses. He received his master's degree in International Affairs from Columbia University.

Colin S. Gray is professor of international politics and strategic studies and director of the Center for Strategic Studies at Reading University (UK). Previously, he served as professor in the Department of Politics, University of Hull (UK). He is the cofounder and former president of the National Institute for Public Policy in Fairfax, Virginia.

David G. Haglund is the Sir Edward Peacock Professor of political studies at Queen's University (Kingston, Ontario). His research focuses on transatlantic security and Canadian and American international security policy. He received his PhD in international relations from the Johns Hopkins School of Advanced International Studies. He coedits the *International Journal*.

Jeannie L. Johnson is a lecturer in the political science department at Utah State University, Logan, Utah. Her previous work includes posts in the intelligence community and academic contributions to the Defense Department. She holds an MA in political science and is pursuing her PhD from the University of Reading.

Rodney W. Jones is president of Policy Architects International, Reston, Virginia, and formerly served in the U.S. Arms Control and Disarmament Agency and *on the U.S. delegation to* the START negotiations. Born in India, he has published extensively on South Asian politics and nuclear and security issues. His PhD is from Columbia University where he has served as associate professor of political science.

Murhaf Jouejati is a professor of Middle East Studies at the National Defense University's NESA Center for Strategic Studies. Previously, he was the director of the Middle East studies program at the George Washington University's Elliott School of International Affairs. He holds a PhD in political science from the University of Utah.

Kerry M. Kartchner is senior advisor for strategic planning in the Bureau of International Security and Nonproliferation at the U.S. Department of State. He also teaches strategic culture at Missouri State University's Graduate Department of Defense and Strategic Studies in Fairfax, Virginia. He previously taught at the Naval Postgraduate School, and served as chief of strategy and policy studies at the Defense Threat Reduction Agency's Advanced Systems and Concepts Office. He holds a PhD from the University of Southern California.

Jeffrey S. Lantis is associate professor of political science at The College of Wooster and has served as a Fulbright Senior Scholar at the Australian National University in 2007. His specializations include international security and foreign policy analysis. He is author of numerous books, journal articles, and book chapters on strategic culture, transatlantic relations, and foreign policy decision making. He holds a PhD in political science from The Ohio State University.

Jeffrey A. Larsen is president of Larsen Consulting Group and a senior scientist with Science Applications International Corporation in Colorado Springs, Colorado. He also serves as an adjunct professor of international relations in the graduate programs of the University of Denver and Northwestern University, and as president of the International Security and Arms Control section of the American Political Science Association. He was NATO's 2005–6 Manfred Wörner Fellow, and holds a PhD in politics from Princeton University.

Jerry Mark Long is director, Middle East studies, and an associate professor in the Honors College at Baylor University in Waco, Texas. Dr. Long's current research interest is in formulating a national security policy to counter Islamic fundamentalism.

Thomas G. Mahnken is Deputy Assistant Secretary of Defense for policy planning in the Office of the Secretary of Defense. At the time he contributed to this volume, he was a visiting fellow at the Philip Merrill Center for Strategic Studies at the Johns Hopkins University and a professor at the U.S. Naval War College in Newport, Rhode Island. He received his PhD in international relations from the Johns Hopkins School of Advanced International Studies.

Willis Stanley is director of regional studies at the National Institute for Public Policy in Fairfax, Virginia. He earned an MA from George Washington University.

Part I

Strategic Culture Today

1

Introduction

Jeannie L. Johnson, Kerry M. Kartchner,
and Jeffrey A. Larsen

This book applies strategic cultural insights to policymaking, especially policies for combating the proliferation of weapons of mass destruction (WMD). It seeks to capitalize on the rising interest in exploring alternative analytical tools needed to confront the dynamic challenges of international security in the twenty-first century, where traditional approaches have become increasingly inadequate. Strategic culture is not a new concept, having been the subject of at least three (and possibly four) previous "waves" or "generations" of scholarship.[1] However, for all the previous thinking and debate over the concept, Colin Gray, a self-professed first-generation strategic culturalist, can still refer to the concept as "the startling familiar yet strangely under-explored notion of strategic culture."[2]

Background

In early 2006 the Advanced Systems and Concepts Office (ASCO) of the U.S. Defense Threat Reduction Agency (DTRA) commissioned a study of comparative strategic cultures with the goal of creating a college-level curriculum based on that methodological approach. This was led by the editors of the current book, and most of the chapters herein were commissioned for that study. The study's sponsor at ASCO was Dr. Kerry Kartchner, and the project lead at Science Applications International Corporation (SAIC) was Dr. Jeffrey Larsen. Three major workshops were held over the course of six months in Washington, DC, Park City, Utah, and Reading, UK. In early 2007 nine case studies and nine essays were posted on the DTRA web page for use by academics seeking readings directly addressing the issue of WMD decision making.[3]

Given the study's—and this book's—focus on weapons of mass destruction, and deriving some policy relevant insights from the study of strategic culture, the project directors posed the following questions to our authors to address with respect to each of the case studies:

- Does strategic culture shape a nation's decision to acquire WMD?
- Does strategic culture affect a nation's (or a group's) propensity to proliferate WMD to other nations or groups?

- Could strategic culture help determine a nation's willingness to use WMD against others?
- Are there cultural factors that promote or discourage a nation's tendencies to comply with or violate international norms regarding WMD?

Focusing on decisions related to WMD serves several useful purposes. In addition to testing the utility of strategic culture in helping explain international security behaviors, it narrows the scope of the research to a more manageable level, and gives structure to the questions investigated by our authors. In addition, the combined data of our completed case studies have helped illuminate which variables within strategic culture tend to play a strong role across regime types, allowing for some refinement in our research design. Finally, this exercise was reflective of the tasks policymakers face when approaching specific international relations problems. Strategic culture is a wide lens, but must prove that it can be focused on particular and specific security decisions in order to be useful.

When a nation state or a group considers what its actions and policies are going to be regarding WMD, it faces a range of choices. It can renounce pursuing the acquisition of WMD, and submit to international standards and regimes of nonproliferation. Or, it can choose to pursue acquiring the technology to lay the basis for a future decision to develop nuclear, chemical, or biological weapons without actually proceeding to the manufacture of such weapons, but only to give it the option of doing so if circumstances change in the future. For the purpose of setting forth a framework for assessing the possible impact of strategic culture on these types of decisions, there are four key "decision matrices" that this project is concerned with exploring[4]:

1. Strategic culture and compliance or noncompliance with international nonproliferation regimes and norms. Does strategic culture strengthen or undermine international or domestic norm-adherence policies and behavior?
2. Strategic culture and the acquisition of WMD. Does strategic culture inform or determine incentives for acquiring WMD?
3. Strategic culture and the proliferation of WMD. Does strategic culture promote or inhibit tendencies to proliferate WMD?
4. Strategic culture and the use of WMD. Does strategic culture influence decisions to use WMD, either in the sense of wielding WMD for deterrence and coercive purposes, or in the sense of actually conducting attacks with WMD?

Our authors were asked to think about the factors shaping the strategic culture under study, and to profile its resultant characteristics. Areas of specific evaluation included geography, shared narratives, relationships to other groups, threat perception, ideology and religion, economics, and type of government and leadership style. Authors were asked to probe further by asking:

- How should the given culture be described?
- What are the sources of the current or dominant culture?
- Are there single or multiple strategic cultures within the state?
- Is the culture evolving at an observable rate? What is causing the culture to evolve? What is the rate of the culture's evolution?
- Who maintains the culture? Who are the "keepers of the culture"?
- What does the given culture say about conflict, the international system, the utility of violence, and the laws of war?

- How important is strategic culture in the formation of security policy relative to other factors?
- What does the given strategic culture have to say about conflict and human nature? What does it say about the enemy?

One of the most difficult challenges in this project was assessing the importance of strategic culture relative to other factors. Case study and essay authors were asked to make a preliminary assessment of the explanatory power of strategic culture versus other intervening variables or theories in several ways: shaping the group's external and internal threat perceptions; the group's self-characterization, its role and self-perceived relationship to the overall international system; its security policies, including (but not limited to) decisions to acquire, use, proliferate, or constrain WMD, or to comply/violate international norms related to WMD; and, its conceptualized relationships to other groups (e.g., alliances).

REVIVAL OF THE CONCEPT

At least three factors underlie the current interest in reviving strategic culture as a field of study: the inadequacy of traditional analytical approaches, the shock of 9/11, and calls to develop and establish new frameworks to guide policymaking in the post–Cold War and post-9/11 security environments.

First, old tools and former analytical models, while still relevant, do not adequately or fully account for the dynamics of a new security environment. Jeff Lantis points out that cultural approaches have been used for hundreds of years, and he provides an overview of improvements that have strengthened the discipline in recent decades. Still, as he points out, there remains substantial room for refinement of the concept and its methodologies. For example, strategic culture still lacks a falsifiable middle range theory.

Second, the field was impacted by the surprise attacks on 9/11. The shock of being attacked with such devastating consequences on one's homeland aroused a great deal of introspection and searching for answers, especially among American scholars. For the field of international security September 11 has become a defining moment. While the horrifying events of that day did not by themselves precipitate renewed interest in exploring strategic culture, they gave impetus and urgency to the need to expand and deepen the study of strategic cultures, and to begin earnestly finding ways to apply strategic culture to policymaking. There are several reasons 9/11 had this effect. The horror of the act forced many in the West to wonder, "why do they hate us? What could have compelled these terrorists to undertake such actions?" As answers began to form, some began to speculate that there were ancient blood feuds on a grand scale that must be playing out, that maybe we had been caught up in a civil war within the Islamic civilization. If so, we needed to understand what that war was about, and why and how we had become entangled in it. For some, there were other questions lurking beneath the surface: had America brought this on itself?[5] Many asked whether there was something about our very culture that these terrorists hated. The events of 9/11 thus served as a catalyst for poignant introspection of our own culture.

Furthermore, like the citizens of most cultures, Americans tend to be ethnocentric. They believe that they have a superior culture, and that this culture has provided the nation with everything it needs to prosper and to understand the world and its place in it. All cultures condition their members to think certain ways, while at the same time providing preset responses to given situations. Thus culture bounds our perceptions and the range of options we have for responding to events. However, when a society experiences a severe shock or major disaster, it forces that culture to become more open-minded, as it becomes momentarily susceptible to new explanations, new paradigms, new ways of thinking, all in search of understanding and mitigating the shock that has befallen them. The events of 9/11 did that to America. Americans found themselves looking outside their own culture to better understand the cultures they must engage in the global community, including those cultures that may have less than benign intentions toward the United States or the West.

It became apparent in the aftermath of 9/11 that other cultures could produce men who were capable of doing things Americans could not even imagine. What else might they be capable of? What else could they be planning? The United States needed to rethink its assessment of possible threats. Those responsible for policymaking, or for analyzing or teaching national security affairs tried to explain these events and to determine how to deter or prevent future attacks. They confronted the imperative of understanding other cultures in a way sufficient to shape an adequate response. Americans began to ask themselves what they needed to know about these other cultures to successfully deter, dissuade, or, if necessary, defeat them.[6]

Third, several official studies and commissions have underscored the need for greater cultural awareness and sensitivity, and have challenged the policymaking community to establish new approaches based on cultural understanding and insights. To cite just one example, the 2004 Defense Science Board Study on Strategic Communications concluded that understanding the strategic cultural context for U.S. actions is vital to effectively implement and safeguard U.S. national security and foreign policy.[7] It found that hostility to U.S. national security goals and policies was undermining U.S. power, influence, and strategic alliances, and that much of this hostility was driven by a lack of understanding on the part of U.S. policymakers of the cultural and regional context for U.S. actions.

THE ANALYTICAL PROMISE OF STRATEGIC CULTURE

A key tenet of realism and its various sub-theories is that state actors behave rationally. Strategic culture seeks to amplify and contextualize this largely correct assumption. Most actors are, in fact, rational, but in order to project behavior on that premise, one must understand rationality within a cultural context. Agents within national populations, political administrations, and security related institutions are "rationally bounded" in their decision-making. According to Valerie Hudson "rationality itself may mean different things in different cultures." Hudson cites other studies showing that "differences in moral reasoning based on culture may skew traditional assumptions of rational-choice theory."[8] This has important implications for deterrence, and for understanding different motivations that various cultures may have for adhering to or rejecting international WMD norms, or for acquiring, proliferating, or employing WMD. For example, if one's deterrence threats are considered "irrational" by the targeted society, they may not be considered credible, or they may be misconstrued. They may not even be considered threats, or may be considered challenges to be confronted, thus having the exact opposite effect of that desired.

While some national decision-making cultures may be objectively deficient in terms of the processes or accuracy of input information, much of what distinguishes "rational" decisions from one society to another are value preferences. Values weighed by a rational actor in a cost/benefit analysis are often ideational as well as material, and cannot be accurately assessed without a substantive knowledge of the actor's preferences. Strategic culture's mantra, therefore, emphasizes that this body of knowledge, complex and messy as it is to obtain, is a necessary pursuit.

There are numerous reasons for studying strategic culture, some of which have already been noted. Such a study can help one better understand his own cultural identity, and his national roles and responsibilities toward other cultures, including recognizing and discerning the advantages and disadvantages of one's own cultural ethnocentricities. It can help us better understand the context in which our own policies operate, and to appreciate the consequences of those policies. It can lead to greater understanding of a prospective adversary's culture and how it defines victory, defeat, loss, and suffering, and how such meanings differ from one's own, in order to know, when necessary, what is required to impose defeat, loss, or sufficient suffering on such a society (for deterrence, dissuasion, or defense purposes).

Strategic culture can also allow us to more accurately evaluate and interpret our intelligence and threat assessments of dangers emanating from within other cultures (or dangers that are conditioned by other cultures), including our ability to detect cross-cultural deception, and to improve our ability to recognize cultural early warning signs of developing or emerging threats or crises (such as sudden shifts in the cultural symbols employed by cultural elites). It allows us to improve the effectiveness of our strategic communications, so as to ensure that our messages are being received and understood correctly; or to counter an adversary's propaganda, or properly interpret our own strategic communications.

On a larger scale, taking a strategic cultural perspective allows us to more fully appreciate the requirements for underwriting and promoting U.S. global responsibilities in a multicultural context. We may be able to assimilate foreign immigrants into our domestic cultural milieu in ways that do not set the stage for internal threats to arise, and we may be able to develop better cross-cultural crisis management techniques and approaches. It should allow us to negotiate across cultures more effectively. Finally, it may allow us to better forecast the implications of cultural change and evolution for strategic planning purposes.

The concept of "strategic culture" is undergoing a revival because it has become essential to better understand the reasons, incentives, and rationales for acquiring, proliferating, and employing WMD by diverse actors under circumstances that differ significantly from those for which previous analytical constructs now seem inadequate or irrelevant. If the United States and its allies are to assure prospective friends and partners in the common battle against WMD proliferation that their respective guarantees of extended security are credible, if they are to effectively dissuade potential proliferators from engaging in counterproductive acquisition of WMD, and if they are to deter and, if necessary, defeat those actors who rebuff these assurances and dissuasions, they need to understand the strategic cultural context for these objectives.

The term "WMD" has come to mean many different things, and is used in a number of different ways. However, for the purposes of this book we use Paul Bernstein's definition: weapons of mass destruction are "nuclear chemical, biological and radiological weapons, and their associated means of delivery, primarily but not limited to ballistic missiles."[9]

METHODOLOGY ISSUES

There are many methodological and epistemological challenges to using culture as an analytical adjunct to policymaking. The primary problem faced by strategic culture analysts is reducing the wide range of variables that may be termed "cultural" and presenting strategic culture analysis as a usable model. Studies under the rubric of strategic culture range the spectrum, from those focusing primarily on organizational culture within particular security bureaucracies, to others taking in the entire spectrum of ideational and material influences on a country. Aspects of national and organizational culture that may play a strong role in security policy within one regime may not necessarily match those factors that play the primary role in another.

No pretense at exhaustive or definitive resolution to these many challenges is attempted; they are addressed in greater detail in Jeffrey Lantis' excellent chapter. However, a few key epistemological issues need to be introduced.

Definitional issues loom large in scholarly debates about strategic culture. "Strategic culture" is an amalgam of two concepts, each distinct in its own right. To begin with, it is necessary to define both "culture" and "strategic."[10] Both are powerful and complex concepts and do not yield easily to facile delineations. The definitions upon which the case studies and essays in this book are based have been chosen for their adequacy pending further academic inquiry and refinement.

There are dozens of definitions of culture, mostly derived from the fields of anthropology, archeology, history, psychology, sociology, and modern popular cultural studies. Among the most pertinent definitions is the following from an 1865 publication cited by David Haglund: "that complex whole which includes knowledge, belief, art, morals, law, custom, and any other capabilities and habits acquired by man as a member of society."[11] From a seminal "third generation" strategic culture textbook, we find this definition. Culture is:

> a broad label that denotes collective models of nation-state authority or identity, carried by custom or law. Culture refers to both a set of evaluative standards (such as norms and values) and a set of cognitive standards (such as rules and models) that define what social actors exist in a system, how they operate, and how they relate to one another.[12]

The concept of culture is often used heuristically in three different senses, and is used in each sense to describe different ways in which culture relates to behavior.[13] First, culture can be considered a "shared system of meaning," with language and terms that are understood and agreed within a given culture, and that are used for identifying and defining what is considered rational. It is a way of interpreting the world, a way of relating to the community and its members, and the relationship of the community to other communities. It is based on "evolving meanings conditioned by historical precedent and contemporary experience."

Culture may be seen as a "collection of value preferences," specifying what a group, state, or society considers its appropriate security objectives and desires. Strategic culture in this sense contributes to defining the appropriate "ends" of a group or nation's national security policy. Culture shapes what constitutes allowable or optimal behavior; that is, it provides a "template for human action," relating ends and means in an appropriate and culturally sanctioned manner. In other words, this aspect of culture relates the meaning of the first aspect of culture (a system of shared meaning), with the objectives representing the collective value preferences, and helps determine appropriate means for achieving those ends. As Hudson explains: "What culture provides its members is a repertoire or palette of adaptive responses from which members build off-the-shelf strategies of action…We may not be able to predict choice and construction of a particular response by a particular member of the culture, but we can know what is on the shelf ready and available to be used or not."[14] Taken together, these three definitions are roughly analogous to the strategist's typology of ends, means, and strategies. That is, culture defines the ends, culture defines the means, and culture bounds the strategies for relating ends to means.

Strategic is defined as relating to the military means of assuring the survival, perpetuation, and prospering of a society's institutions, structures, and value preferences. It involves long-term planning perspectives, and the coordination of the full range of a nation's capabilities. Drawing on definitions from official military sources, strategic should be considered anything related to the advancement of a nation's interests, plans, policies, doctrines, activities, perspectives, or objectives, through coordination or synchronization with the actions and resources of all instruments of national power, including military, diplomatic, economic, cultural, intellectual, and informational.[15] In shorthand terms, it is how a nation relates means to ends. In certain cases, it refers to anything that perpetuates, or threatens, the survival of the nation.

There are a number of worthy definitions of strategic culture found throughout the three generations of scholarship. For the purposes of establishing a framework for comparing cultures across established criteria, we asked our authors to work with a specific definition of strategic culture, and to offer suggestions within their case studies regarding the applicability and utility of this definition for their respective cultures. Our definition is as follows: "*Strategic culture is that set of shared beliefs, assumptions, and modes of behavior, derived from common experiences and accepted narratives (both oral and written), that shape collective identity and relationships to other groups, and which determine appropriate ends and means for achieving security objectives.*"

Beyond definitional issues, there are other questions of methodology that would be addressed in any study based on strategic culture, including causality, stasis, and relevance. Culture as an explanation is seldom direct and seldom operates alone; it is linked to other variables and approaches. How do we ensure we are measuring cultural predispositions or orientations correctly? This is abstract, and the researcher is one level removed from the data. Cultures change, and subsets may arise at various times; how can we identify the real underlying culture? How do we assess and measure change, including the rate of change, of a culture? Has the rise of globalization and interdependence diminished the cultural distinctions between societies?[16] Colin Gray notes that "culture is learned, not genetically inherited. So it can change."[17] Yaacov Vertzberger explains usefully that "the impact of culture is uneven over time. Nations go through periods when cultural values assert themselves over considerations of power and other periods when the preoccupation with power relegates culture to a minor role in their external affairs."[18]

POLICY IMPLICATIONS: STRATEGIC CULTURE AND WMD

When it comes to identifying the policy implications of strategic culture, the central question remains unchanged: Does (strategic) culture matter? There is a healthy and proactive debate on this question within the field of cultural studies.[19] The question has been more specifically addressed thus: To what extent does culture shape behavior and define values in discernible and measurable ways that can serve policy relevant purposes? Which behaviors and values are most subject to cultural influence, or find their origins most firmly rooted in cultural grounds? The question can also be more narrowly defined: When, and under what strategic/military circumstances, does culture matter? According to Michael Desch, in an essay written for the first phase of the comparative strategic cultures project upon which the present book is based, there are three international circumstances where cultural explanations may usefully supplement (but not supplant) other analytical perspectives:

- Cultural variables may explain the lag between structural change and alterations in state behavior.
- Cultural variables may account for why some states behave irrationally and suffer the consequences of failing to adapt to the constraints of the international system.
- In structurally indeterminate situations, domestic variables such as culture may have more independent impact.[20]

While Desch and others argue that strategic culture can only supplement and not replace the dominant realist theory of state behavior, some additional hypotheses examined in the chapters of this book suggest that strategic culture can be more salient relative to other considerations (economics, geography, ideology, leadership style), when the following conditions exist:

- There is a strong sense of danger to the group's existence, identity, or value structure. It believes its culture is under threat.
- There is a strong "messiah complex," or sense of mission, associated with the group's identity, and its relationship to other groups.
- There is a preexisting strong cultural basis for group identity.
- The group's leadership frequently resorts to citing cultural symbols in support of its national security aspirations and programs.
- There is a high degree of homogeneity within the group that is centered on "shared narratives."
- Historical experiences strongly predispose the group to perceive threats and to respond with violent (military) means.
- Scriptural justifications are cited by the cultural elite; for example, if significant views are expressed among the "keepers of the culture" that using nuclear weapons or other WMD could be justified by the culture's shared oral or written "narrative."
- Fatalistic assumptions dominate internal policy debates and external strategic communications; for example, if the culture assumes that a wider conflict with other civilizations is inevitable. Or, if some even believe that such a conflict should be instigated, and that the instigating culture would even emerge from it better off.
- Attitudes toward nuclear weapons are characterized by a certain "nuclear naiveté"; for example, if the culture's leaders do not appreciate how profoundly destructive a nuclear war would be, and appear casual in their threats to acquire, proliferate, or use nuclear weapons, or other weapons of mass destruction. Such attitudes

may also be reflected in policies, statements, or doctrines that view such weapons as instruments of coercion, crisis manipulation, diplomatic blackmail, regional dominance, or as weapons of first rather than last resort.
* Other cultures are demonized; for example, if the culture believes its principal enemy is "the Great Satan" and deserves to be annihilated.

About the Book

In the first essay of this volume, Jeffrey Lantis offers a look at the evolution of strategic culture as a mode of analysis. While academics may find the lack of a unified approach distressing, policymakers may discover the varied options useful. The cultural study appropriate for a soldier on the ground is quite different in subject matter and depth than the cultural education necessary for strategic decision-makers.

David Haglund's essay is reprinted from *International Journal*. We chose to include it here in its entirety because we have neither found any better description of the definitional challenges facing the field, nor a better rationale for the crucial importance of strategic culture in understanding today's world. His modest purpose, as he puts it, matches that of this volume: to "argue that categories of analysis associated with the concept of strategic culture can be, and should be, of interest to a variety of scholars who are motivated to understand how and why states end up making certain choices in grand strategy."[21]

Kerry Kartchner begins our exploration of case studies by focusing the lens of strategic culture on the specific question of WMD decision options facing nation states. He offers a framework for examining culture-based WMD questions across nation states and demonstrates how it might be used.

A set of nine case studies provide a narrowed, practical application of strategic culture as a theoretical paradigm. The cases included here investigate the influence of culture on state decisions to adhere to WMD related international norms, or to acquire, proliferate, or use biological, chemical, or nuclear weapons. Our case studies were not necessarily selected on the basis of their salience to expanding the horizons of strategic culture as a field of study per se, but for their relevance to policy issues surrounding WMD, for their ability to be researched, for their potential contribution to the development of a basic strategic culture curriculum of study, and for their potential significance in addressing certain methodological issues.

The United States and Russia were included for the strength of their standing as baseline cases; these complex cultural analyses were ably conducted by Thomas Mahnken and Fritz Ermarth, respectively. The United States was selected as a baseline case, and one that would touch on WMD use, international norms, and an extended period of nonuse. Russia and China add to the baseline dimension. These two states provide highly researchable cases, since area experts, government specialists, and academicians have devoted extensive time and resources to understanding their WMD histories, inner workings, and decision-making structures during the Cold War. China in particular has drawn the strong interest of strategic culture analysts and their critics, as Huiyan Feng demonstrates.

Israel is a unique case study given its policy of nuclear "strategic ambiguity." Investigating why some countries decide to overtly declare their nuclear programs—in violation of current international norms (India, North Korea)—and why others choose a path of ambiguity, is an intriguing question for Greg Giles. Given the dangers in its neighborhood, and its opportunities for nuclear use, Israel's decision to keep these weapons under wraps is remarkable.

An obvious choice for inclusion are two nuclear aspirants currently making headlines—Iran and North Korea. Their flouting of international norms, propensities toward proliferation, and heated rhetoric vis-à-vis the United States make them hard to ignore. Both are secretive and coy regimes and posed significant challenges for our authors. Willis Stanley captures the long, proud history of Iran, and Joseph Bermudez tackles the cult of personality that controls North Korea.

India shares the world's most dangerous nuclear border with its neighbor Pakistan. In addition to evaluating scenarios for nuclear use between these two countries, we asked Rodney Jones to examine the cultural factors behind India's decision to buck the international system by acquiring weapons in the first place.

We also selected two cases that represent potential nuclear aspirants—one state and one non-state actor. Although Syria does not have the material capability to pursue a full WMD arsenal at this time, it may someday seek nuclear weapons. Dealings in its neighborhood suggest that a WMD-stocked Middle East is one possible future scenario. Murhaf Jouejati evaluates the strategic culture of a country sitting on the sidelines, determining whether to get in the game. His interpretation may tell us something about how domestic beliefs and processes influence this critical decision.

Our final case study steps outside the normal parameters of strategic culture studies and investigates the applicability of this mode of analysis to a non-state actor—al Qaeda. Osama bin Laden has made clear that he is interested in acquiring a nuclear weapon and has gone to great lengths to forge Islamic justification for its use against the United States, according to Mark Long.[22] Given the proliferation of non-state security concerns, one test for the utility of strategic culture as a foreign policy forecasting tool will be its ability to shed light on the preferences and modes of strategic behavior of actors outside the traditional nation state.

Following the case studies, Colin Gray, one of the founders of the strategic culture discipline, sums up the utility of strategic culture as a mode of analysis and cautions practitioners on the possible pitfalls of its overuse. His seminal essay "Out of the Wilderness: Prime Time for Strategic Culture" explains the origins of the field, defines what strategic culture is and what it portends to do, describes why strategic culture matters to policymakers, and provides a litany of potential pitfalls a strategic culturalist may fall into—or have to explain to nonbelievers.

In the final chapter, Jeannie Johnson recommends a strategic culture framework designed to create a common baseline for academic research, with an eye toward utility for intelligence analysts, diplomats, military planners, and policymakers.

Notes

1. David G. Haglund argues that while the strategic culture scholarship of the 1970s is frequently considered the "first generation," the idea was initially explored in the 1920s and 1930s. See "What Good Is Strategic Culture? A Modest Defence of an Immodest Concept," *International Journal*, Vol. 59, No. 3 (Summer 2004), pp. 479–502, reprinted with permission as chapter two.
2. Jeffrey Lantis reviews the history of this school of thought in chapter 3. See also Colin Gray, "Strategic Culture as Context: The First Generation of Theory Strikes Back," *Review of International Studies*, Vol. 25 (1999), pp. 49–69.
3. The papers and case studies from SAIC's 2006 Comparative Strategic Cultures Curriculum Project can be found at http://www.dtra.mil/ASCO/comparativestrategiccultures.cfm.

In addition to essays and case studies, the website includes annotated bibliographies, conference reports, and a suggested syllabus for teaching an upper division course in strategic culture.

4. We use the term "decision matrices" because, of course, in any given case, it may not be a question of a single decision, but a series of decisions that eventually lead to a significant policy direction. Even the term "decision" may not be accurate in all cases, especially where there is little or no evidence of a specific decision, but where this analysis may be more concerned with general behaviors, certain actions, or stated or implicit policies that are reflected in how a nation or group acts toward or thinks about WMD, or may be expected to act, based on the hypotheses developed in this essay.

5. One of the editors of this book arrived in Beijing the day after 9/11, and thus had the unique experience of seeing the immediate reaction to these events through the perspective of Chinese officials, academics, and public audiences with whom he interacted over the next few days. He found that the general public, and many of the academics, were convinced that "America had brought this on itself."

6. The possibility of having to defeat a society or culture has become especially salient as the war in Iraq lingers years longer than anticipated. Defeating a society or culture short of completely obliterating it requires knowing when that culture or society will accept that it has been defeated, and come to terms with the victor. Not convincing that society or culture that it has been defeated in terms that it will understand may lead to having to defeat them over and over again.

7. This report can be found at http://www.acq.osd.mil/dsb/reports/2004–09-Strategic_Communication.pdf (accessed July 31, 2007).

8. Hudson cites two books by Amartya Sen, *Choice, Welfare, and Measurement* (Cambridge, MA: MIT Press, 1982); and *On Ethics and Economics* (New York: Basil Blackwell, 1987).

9. Paul Bernstein, "Weapons of Mass Destruction: A Primer," October 31, 2006, available at http://www.dtra.mil/ASCO/comparativestrategiccultures.cfm (accessed December 28, 2007). Bernstein further refers to a monograph by W. Seth Carus, *Defining "Weapons of Mass Destruction,"* National Defense University Center for the Study of Weapons of Mass Destruction, *Occasional Paper 4*, January 2006.

10. Haglund further explores the etymology and marriage of these two concepts in chapter two.

11. Haglund cites anthropologist Edward B. Tylor, *Early History of Mankind and the Development of Civilization*, 2nd ed. (London: John Murray, 1870), originally published in 1865.

12. Peter J. Katzenstein, "Introduction," in Peter J. Katzenstein, ed., *The Culture of National Security: Norms and Identity in World Politics* (New York: Columbia University Press, 1996), p. 6.

13. This typology is borrowed from Valerie M. Hudson, "Culture and Foreign Policy: Developing a Research Agenda," in Valerie M. Hudson, ed., *Culture and Foreign Policy* (Boulder: Lynne Rienner, 1997), pp. 7–9. See also the compilation of essays in a special edition of the journal *Political Psychology* by Valerie M. Hudson and Martin W. Simpson III, "Special Section on Culture and Foreign Policy," *Political Psychology*, Vol. 20, No. 4 (1999), pp. 667–801.

14. Hudson, *Culture and Foreign Policy*, p. 9.

15. *DOD Dictionary of Military and Associated Terms*, as amended through June 13, 2007, available at http://www.dtic.mil/doctrine/jel/doddict/(accessed August 1, 2007).

16. Michael J. Mazaar reviews the debate over whether distinct cultural identities are being homogenized by globalization in "Culture in International Relations," *The Washington Quarterly*, Spring 1996, available at http://www.globalpolicy.org/globaliz/cultural/cultur2.htm (accessed August 1, 2007).

17. Colin S. Gray, *Another Bloody Century: Future Warfare* (London: Weidenfeld and Nicolson, 2005), p. 88.

18. Yaacov Y.I. Vertzberger, *The World in Their Minds: Information Processing, Cognition, and Perception in Foreign Policy Decisionmaking* (Palo Alto, CA: Stanford University Press, 1990), pp. 381–82, fn. 7.

19. This question is directly confronted in, for example, Lawrence E. Harrison and Samuel P. Huntington, eds., *Culture Matters: How Values Shape Human Progress* (New York: Basic Books, 2000).
20. Michael Desch, "Culture Versus Structure in Post-9/11 Security Studies," *Strategic Insights*, Vol. 4, No. 10 (October 2005), available at http://www.ccc.nps.navy.mil/si/2005/Oct/deschOct05.asp (accessed August 1, 2007).
21. Haglund, chapter 2.
22. An extensive discussion of this is found in Michael Scheuer's book, *Imperial Hubris* (Dulles, VA: Potomac Books, 2004).

2

What Good Is Strategic Culture?

David G. Haglund

Oscar Wilde famously referred to fox-hunting as the "unspeakable in pursuit of the inedible." With apologies to Wilde, those of us bounding off over conceptual hedges in quest of strategic culture might be called the unintelligible in pursuit of the incomprehensible. For no matter how achingly compelling is the need to render our concepts sharp "tools" for analysis, we unfailingly get entangled in constant wrangling over their very definition, with the result being that the passage of time often results in spreading confusion instead of enlightenment. This is so, notwithstanding the expressed hope of many that the same passage of time might reasonably be expected to generate a "literature" capable of penetrating and dispelling the conceptual fog, by speaking definitional truth to us.

But if the literature on strategic culture is to resemble that on every other political concept, it will be apparent that not only is the body of writing on our topic often bereft of literary merit, but it will inevitably produce noteworthy, unavoidable, and ongoing dissension in the analytical ranks: truths perhaps, when taken singly and contemplatively, but no overarching truth. Still, our failure to come to agreement over the term's meaning and applicability should be neither surprising nor particularly discouraging; it simply illustrates we are dealing with an interesting concept that, as with all such concepts, can be used to advantage if used carefully.

Strategic culture might not be a metaconcept in the way, say, that "power" is, but there is utility in the comparison. Consider that power is supposed to be one of the key notions at our disposal when we wax theoretical about international relations and foreign policy, and yet what strikes the student of power analysis is how much basic disagreement there can be over this word's meaning. If power is nothing other than aggregate capability, as many structural realists insist it is,[1] then certain claims about the "structure" of the international system (and *mutatis mutandis,* as we shall see below, strategic culture) become possible to make. Among the most important such claims is the one that enables us to discern a systemic pecking order predicated upon "relative capability," so that we are enabled to develop such other important concepts as unipolarity, bipolarity, or multipolarity in a bid to *describe* and comprehend that system. But if you follow the injunction of others, and regard power as simply being another way of saying "influence," then all descriptive bets are off, and theories about how and why states act become increasingly complicated, because they are dependent upon a myriad of situationally specific contexts.[2]

The point is not that there is something abnormal about the way the debate rages over the mega-concept, power; to the contrary, the debate is completely normal, and indeed, necessary, for unless there is healthy and substantial scholarly divisiveness about concepts, there can be no advance of theoretical knowledge in social science.[3] And while it is perhaps possible to imagine consensual understanding enveloping some political concepts, the cases when such occurs must be rare, and a concept about which we can say there exists basal agreement is probably not a very important tool for anyone's use.

Thus, if strategic culture is to follow the normal trajectory of political concepts (and here we should note it is still in its relative infancy, having been apparently first employed *under that name* only in the late 1970s),[4] then we can expect not only that debates about its meaning will be ceaseless, but that it will be prone, as are all concepts, to expansion. Churchill's quip about democracy being the worst form of government except for all the rest serves as a useful reminder about how unexceptional conceptual discord really is. And no less exceptional, even though one might wish it to be otherwise, is conceptual expansion.[5] This is so not only because of the very ambiguity of the concepts we deploy (no mean consideration in itself), but also because of the impact of changing conditions on the words we use to describe and understand the conditions. One political philosopher, T.D. Weldon, insists that because circumstances change, we must continually adjust the manner in which we express them. The adjustment can take two forms: we can either invent a new concept, or we can expand a familiar word or concept. "Usually," says Weldon, "the second method is preferred, partly because it avoids more confusion than it creates, indeed it seldom confuses anybody but political philosophers, and partly because the extended use has often come to be adopted uncritically in the natural course of events."[6]

Actually, our concept may just be in the early stages of expansion, given its relative youth, but its two "parent" elements are considerably older, and have probably spent more time than was good for them on the stretching rack. Thus, its nominal infancy to the contrary notwithstanding, strategic culture comes to us with a family history of conceptual confusion, one that has left its mark.

TOWARD A DEFINITION OF STRATEGIC CULTURE?

Ample foretaste of the debate about what strategic culture is to signify has been provided by earlier discussions over "culture" as a social variable, for as Raymond Williams has noted, the word ranks as one of the two or three most difficult in the English language (and he could have added, in any other language).[7] If things were not murky enough as a result of the nominative half of our concept, what shall we say of its modifier, "strategic"? Put this adjective and this noun together, and you get a sense of why Alastair Iain Johnston should have complained about how "remarkably undefined" is our concept.[8]

How could it be otherwise, in view of the parental elements' own definitional promiscuity? Let us take the modifier, strategic, for starters, as it is probably the less unruly parent. Although many seem to think that the root formation of strategic, "strategy," must be about things martial—and by extension, so too must strategic culture[9]—this does not have to be the case. Strategy can be about military matters, and often is, but those who insist it must *always* be called to the colors do it, and us, a disservice. The term actually connotes much more: used most commonly (as in the "strategic planning" that is all the rage in academic—and other—administrative circles these days) it simply seeks to establish a "rational" link between ends and means. Thinking or acting strategically stands for the attempt to correlate, in a manner that can pass basic cost–benefit muster, your goals with the resources at your disposal to meet those goals, and vice versa. As John Lewis Gaddis explains, "by 'strategy,' I mean quite simply the process by which ends are related to means, intentions to capabilities, objectives to resources."[10]

Things begin to get more complex when we couple the adjective with its noun, for unless we know what is meant by "culture," we are at a complete loss to determine its relationship to strategy. To be sure, culture has become a very popular notion in the human (or social) sciences, never more so than over the past dozen or so years, for reasons I relate in the section that follows. It has been a decade since two sociologists told us that now that culture's ship had come in, the time was ripe for social scientists to do an "inventory of its cargo."[11] But before we could take a peek inside the cargo hold, we had first to locate its hatch, meaning that we needed to come to some understanding of the basic structure of this vessel called culture. This was all the more necessary because the concept's earlier career had been such as to lead to its being branded, with reason, a "semantic monstrosity."[12]

If it had stood for anything consistently since Giovanni Andres introduced it, back in 1781, under the name *coltura* (by which he meant to imply the conditions of human attainment preserved in writing), it was the notion of extension, or growth. And grow it did: in less than a century it was expanded from the written to all other forms of registering the achievements of humanity, so that the anthropologist, Edward B. Tylor, could conceive of it in a seminal 1865 work as "that complex whole which includes knowledge, belief, art, morals, law, custom, and any other capabilities and habits acquired by man as a member or society."[13]

Culture did not only possess importance as a register of civilization's noblest accomplishments (its "high," or big-C, variant); it was also beginning to take on an epistemological function, helping those who engaged in studying collective life to develop ways of thinking about what was important in group cognition. An early discipline to feel the effects of culture's epistemological role would be history, where the "new history" of the late nineteenth and early twentieth century ("old," actually, from today's standpoint) stood out against dominant perspectives associated with Leopold von Ranke's "scientific" approach to history, and Edward Freeman's notion of history as merely being the record of "past politics."[14]

The old "new" history faced an uphill climb, especially in America in the first half of the twentieth century, where it seemed downright antediluvian to argue against a hard-headed economic interpretation of history propagated by the Progressive (or Wisconsin) school, for whom class interests provided the most elegant and satisfactory answer to the large questions about America's past. But after the Second World War, it became not just possible but well-nigh obligatory for American history and politics to be examined under a new, cultural, lamp—one that shone light into such heretofore under-analyzed collective categories as ethnicity and social–psychological propensities toward irrationality. And though it might not have been easy a half-century ago to identify what culture *was,* it was more than possible to signal two areas of enquiry that properly belonged to the new cultural history: ideas and ethnicity. Thus intellectual history and ethnocultural studies began to emerge as important sub-disciplines in their own right, each subsumed under the broader, cultural, rubric.[15]

What was occurring in history was also taking place in most of the other human sciences, with anthropologists among the most noteworthy contributors. And if no one could define culture to everyone's satisfaction, the name of one anthropologist in particular would become a consensus repeater on most lists of authorial "must reads." This was Clifford Geertz, whose 1973 book, *The Interpretation of Cultures*, quickly established itself as the *locus classicus* in the field of cultural studies. What Geertz did was to propose that we regard culture as consisting in "socially established structures of meaning in terms of which people do...things."[16]

Geertz's book, which has been adjudged "phenomenally influential,"[17] not only contributed to culture's growing popularity in social sciences outside of anthropology (with economics and psychology being notable holdouts), it also provided the opportunity for analysts of international security with a fascination for the emerging notion of strategic culture to contemplate actually *defining* their concept. For sure, definitional consensus would, in the nature of things, remain elusive, but some analysts began taking their cues from the cognitive instructions implicit in Geertz's work. More and more, and again following Geertz, culture was being conceived as a system of symbols by which collectivities transmit knowledge across time and space. As William Sewell put it, culture was nothing other than the "semiotic dimension of human social practice in general."[18]

It was this recognition of the symbolic content of culture that Alastair Iain Johnston seized upon in offering what is, to date, the most ambitious and sophisticated attempt at defining strategic culture. Its Geertzian pedigree is obvious, for as Johnston defines it, strategic culture consists in

> an integrated system of symbols (i.e., argumentation structures, languages, analogies, metaphors, etc.) that acts to establish pervasive and long-lasting grand strategic preferences by formulating concepts of the role and efficacy of military force in interstate political affairs, and by clothing these conceptions with such an aura of factuality that the strategic preferences seem uniquely realistic and efficacious.[19]

Lest it be thought that his reference above to "military force" makes his construct a narrowly bounded one, Johnston goes on to stipulate that the "grand strategic preferences" at whose service strategic culture must be placed entail more than purely military considerations, and include *all* those economic and political, as well as military, aspects of national power that must be brought to bear upon the task of accomplishing "national goals."

It may not be particularly easy to put into application Johnston's definition of our concept (notwithstanding that it may be the most elegant one going); still, it is not so difficult to detect what he had in mind in choosing to argue that strategic culture deserves to be taken seriously. First on his target list are those who minimize, or dismiss outright, ideational factors when they theorize "explanatory" variables in international security. Most visible in his cross hairs is the group he calls the "neorealists," i.e., the structural realists who he says are oblivious of the role of culture and history when they conceive the basis of state action. There is clearly something to the allegation, and even if it was Kenneth Waltz who primarily served to inspire his critique, Johnston's admonition could apply equally well to Robert Kagan's recent invocation of strategic culture as a quintessentially "dependent variable" (my words, not Kagan's) in international security matters. To Kagan, strategic culture certainly may exist, but it stands for effect not cause, being entirely explicable in terms of something else—relative capability. This accounts for America's being "from Mars" and quick to countenance martial solutions to security challenges, while Europe is (mainly) "from Venus," and reluctant to frame responses in the same way as its whilom friend across the Atlantic.[20]

The structural realists may be Johnston's principal objects of pursuit, but they are not his only quarry. He is also concerned with improving upon the work of two prior "generations" of strategic culturalists. In particular, he chides (a) the "first generation" of strategic culturalists, chiefly area-studies specialists of the Cold War period with an interest in the Soviet Union, for their indifference to specifying their variables, and (b) the "second generation," Gramscians of the late Cold War/early post–Cold War period, for their laziness in tracing the manner in which they would link their causes and effects.[21]

In the end, and despite his criticism of "positivists," Johnston remains at one with them on the importance of establishing reliable causality, though he recognizes the complexity of the challenge. Accordingly, he makes a determined effort to demonstrate how it is that the past continues to influence contemporary strategic choices (in his case, Chinese), in such a way as to constrain, or bound, rationality in state decisionmaking.[22] The irony is that Johnston's methodological rigor aligns him with his principal theoretical foes, the structural realists, with whom he shares a conviction that a certain kind of causal "explanation" is possible and therefore desirable, and distances him from so many of those who have otherwise themselves taken the cultural "turn" in international security, and who see it as their primary task to "understand" not "explain" strategic reality in any reliably causal manner.

TURN, TURN, TURN: THE RE-EMERGENCE OF CULTURE IN SECURITY STUDIES

What has been called the cultural (also sociological, as well as historical) "turn" in the human sciences was primarily a result of forces internal to the various disciplines and fields of inquiry involved, and reflected nothing so much as the latest phase in a continuous agreement to disagree over the very purpose of those sciences. But in international security studies, there was also an important external stimulus at work, which did much to fortify the recent re-emergence of culture as a category of importance. In this section I address these two sources of change, starting with the explanation/understanding debate, which was itself a legacy of the earlier "turn" at the end of the nineteenth century that resulted in the "new" (i.e., old) cultural history—a turn that witnessed, and was a manifestation of, the emergence of the hermeneutical tradition associated with Wilhelm Dilthey, who had an enormous influence upon the thinking of Max Weber.[23]

When Alastair Iain Johnston criticized what he termed the first-generation's inability or unwillingness, or both, to distinguish between cause and effect, he touched an epistemological nerve. Colin Gray's rebuttal of the charge constituted something of a *tu quoque*,[24] for Gray presumed to tar Johnston with the same "positivist" allegation Johnston had brought to bear against those "ahistorical, aculturalist" structuralists who had spurred him to action. Gray's rejoinder made two significant points: (1) not all realists (in whose ranks Gray included himself) were ahistorical or aculturalist; and (2) it was wrong to assume that strategic culture could be a causal variable, the best that could be hoped for being to regard it as "context," a category transcending both cause and effect. Gray essayed his own concise definition of the concept: "Strategic culture is the world of mind, feeling, and *habit in behaviour.*"[25]

In his response to Johnston, Gray staked out his own position on the explanation/ understanding debate, one that put him close to the interpretivist side of the house and at some philosophical distance from the alleged "positivism" of his fellow-travelling realists. (Not only this, but Gray, who had developed a reputation during the Cold War as an anti-Soviet hawk, also found reason to heap praise upon the leading Marxian scholar of culture, Raymond Williams!) Ultimately, however, there remained an ineradicable Forrest Gump aspect to Gray's use of strategic culture as context rather than causality, his insistence that "culture is as culture does"[26] sounding more than vaguely reminiscent of Tom Hanks's film recitation, "stupid is as stupid does."

Perhaps strategic-culture-as-context underspecifies *too* much, but there really need be nothing stupid about denying that the search for reliable causality must be the *sine qua non* of social science, nor can the rejection of such causality be taken to be synonymous with the rejection of theory; indeed, what Gray was chiefly articulating was a case for an hermeneutical approach to strategic culture. In so doing, he made explicit appeal to the contributions of two theorists of international relations, Martin Hollis and Steve Smith. (In the event, he would have been better off relying upon only half of the tandem, as the two authors end up on different pages when it comes to assessing the relative merits of a Weberian *Verstehen*,[27] whose earmark is the attempt to understand action from the perspective of the intentional actor, and a more structural *Erklären*,[28] predicated upon the kind of causal explanations from without that one finds—or expects to find—in the natural sciences; Hollis plumps for the former, Smith for the latter.)[29]

Be that as it may, the debate between enthusiasts of *Verstehen* and advocates of *Erklären* is an old one in the history of ideas, with echos going back far longer than a century, and detectable even today in the manner in which the concept, strategic culture, gets used. *Erklären* is associated with a Galilean approach to causal explanation in science (as in, "this took place because *that* did"), while *Verstehen* makes appeal to an Aristotelian approach, stressing teleological accounts (as in, "this happened so that *that* should occur"). But it was only in the late nineteenth century that the social sciences experienced their own "great awakening," with the emergence of a "positivism" displaying clear affinities to the Galilean tradition. Opposed to this would surface an antipositivism, a philosophy of science at times labelled "idealism," but one that would be better remembered as "hermeneutics." It was the German philosopher, Johann Gustav Droysen, who coined the distinction between *Verstehen* and *Erklären*, with the former being said (by him) to be the method of the historical sciences, and the latter that of the natural sciences.[30]

The battle begun a century ago continues today, and the Johnston-Gray tussle over the definition of strategic culture reflects a more general split among social scientists, who cannot seem to decide whether they should follow Émile Durkheim down the path of positivism, or Max Weber along the road to interpretivism. This debate has possibly outlived its usefulness, as more than one philosopher of science is prepared to tell you that the distinction between explanation and understanding can be overdrawn, and perhaps should be laid to rest, in favour of agreement that what we are really trying to generate, or must at least content ourselves with, is some modicum of "explicative understanding."[31] If this is so, then both Durkheim and Weber are after the same thing, and the path of positivism turns out to be a wide one, indeed.

In the two sections that follow, I am going to advert to this debate in illustrating what I take to be the two principal ways in which strategic culture might be invoked in the analysis of foreign policy. But in what remains of this section, I wish to turn to the other relevant feature of the recent cultural turn in international security, namely the structural earthquake set off by the ending of the Cold War, disappearance of the Soviet Union, and collapse of the bipolar era.

The ending of bipolarity obviously made life more complicated for those who had assimilated what Kenneth Waltz had to say about the basic stability of bipolarity.[32] Not that everyone was in agreement with Waltz during the Cold War, not even all realists,[33] but at least there was for a time a certain *descriptive* merit in taking as seriously as Waltz did the implications of the bipolar world—implications that ceased to be worth thinking about once their structural precondition disappeared. Many assumed that the (temporary?) derailing of structural realism à la Waltz meant the end of realist hegemony in international relations theory, hence the emphasis upon the "turn" the discipline was ostensibly in the process of making, away from realism and toward some other body of theory, constructivism to be precise.

So the turn was argued to be very much a "constructivist" one, in which "cultural" variables were going increasingly to make themselves felt in states' decisionmaking, post-bipolarity. And with culture's appearance as a variable to reckon with came another concept that was bound to be important: "identity."[34] This latter concept would be elevated to a central position in constructivist accounts of international outcomes, occupying for these theorists a position as central as that held by "power" for a certain kind of realist theoretician; identity would be the core organizing concept for realism's challenger, structuring cognition and prefiguring "interests."[35] If some might have raised the quibble that this new core concept was itself riddled with ambiguity,[36] the rejoinder came quickly that power's ambiguity had never stopped structural realists from placing *it* upon their theoretical pedestal.

Lost sight of as a result of the brouhaha attending the constructivist challenge to realist primacy were three matters that would have implications for the way in which we might employ strategic culture. First, culture was not a particularly novel variable in international security. Secondly, not all constructivists could be said to be anti-positivists. And thirdly, not all realists could be accused of being "aculturalists."

Regarding the first of these matters, it cannot even be said that *strategic* culture, albeit under some other label, had been unexplored theoretically prior to the decade in which it received its name, that of the 1970s. We can accept that culture and conflict have been intermeshed for as long as there has been strife among social groupings, but the systematic, scientific, study of the relationship between culture and conflict really began to take off during the Second World War, stimulated by funding provided by an American government eager to acquire operational insight into the national (strategic–cultural) "character" of its German and Japanese enemies. To this end, theory was essential. Johnston's three generations might be accurately enumerated insofar as concerns discussions of strategic culturalists so named, but it is apparent, as Michael Desch has shown, that there was at least one significant previous generation of "culturalists" who sought to demonstrate how and to what effect culture and strategic outcomes could be interrelated. Like Molière's M. Jourdain, this generation was speaking prose—the prose of strategic culture—without realizing it. Thus, the real first-generationers in the field of security studies were those cultural anthropologists motivated in the 1940s to demonstrate how "national character" had an impact upon a state's development of strategic will.[37]

Desch's other two generational cohorts, the second and third, correspond roughly to Johnston's first and third generations, and what is particularly worthy of note is

Desch's contention that what he calls the third (i.e., post–Cold War) generation is, by dint of the emphasis it places upon "ideational" variables, less attached to positivist approaches to the study of security than are competing paradigms within the field, such as realism. However, if what Desch intends to demonstrate is that realism "explains" strategic outcomes better than cultural accounts, then it must be because of something other than realism's positivist epistemology (if it indeed has such an epistemology). What I think Desch really meant to suggest is that *structural* realist, and not all realist, accounts trump culturalist ones, with the latter able, at best, to supplement realism: "In short, the new strategic culturalist theories will not supplant realist theories in national security studies because, by themselves, they have very limited explanatory power."[38]

Two things need to be said about this. First, it simply is not correct to argue that constructivist accounts that elevate ideational factors to the role of "explanatory" (or "independent") variables must be anti-positivist. Not all constructivists deserve to be placed outside the positivist pale, even if they might themselves insist upon the relegation. What is at issue here, and was demonstrated by the rejoinders Desch's article attracted,[39] is not necessarily whether causal "explanation" is desirable (or possible), but rather what sorts of explanation have greater persuasiveness, those derived from assessments of relative capability, or those embedded in national and international norms and discourses? While it would be wrong to argue all constructivists are positivists, it is equally fallacious to claim none (or at most, only a few) are.

At the very least, those constructivists who insist upon the autonomous, causal, prowess of ideas and discourse can be taken as positivists even within a restrictive understanding of positivism that emphasizes a nomothetic, or "covering-law" conception of explanation. But if David Dessler is to be believed, the positivist strain in constructivism extends more broadly, including those favouring, as did Weber, a "particularistic" and narrative-dependent rendering of causation. Whether we are prepared to include even Weber in the ranks of the positivists (a companionship that would have surprised him probably as much as Durkheim), it still can be said that constructivism per se need not be antithetical to the quest for reliable causality.[40]

By the very same token, Colin Gray is right to object to the dismissal of realists as "acultural, ahistorical" automatons. It is ironic enough to find constructivist tents pitched inside positivist epistemological campgrounds; even more ironic is the discovery of realists grazing in the pastures of interpretivism. For what else can this variety of realist be said to be doing when state action is ascribed to endogenous, identity derived categories, rather than deduced from assessments of a systemic structure revealed through relative capability? Adrian Hyde-Price and Lisbeth Aggestam are on the mark when they note that realists of a non-structural kidney have been enjoying "a renewed burst of life, particularly as the limitations of Waltzian parsimony become ever clearer."[41] Some have seen fit to label this more reflective theoretical orientation "neoclassical" realism.[42] It is usually a bad idea to attach the prefix "neo-" to otherwise serviceable concepts, as witnessed by the tortured semantic career of "neorealism," which not only never *was* required as a means of conveying the meaning amply supplied by "structural" realism, but which completely reversed the original sense some did propose to attach to the "neorealism" that first appeared on the scene in the early 1980s, as an inventory of the accoutrements of sound policy in an era of "complex interdependence"—i.e., an inventory that denied the utility of an aggregate construct of power![43]

Strategic Culture as Context: History, Identity, Character

Whether the above-mentioned variant of realism actually requires being called "neoclassical" need not distract us from pondering how the relative demise of structuralism should have stimulated a resurgence of interesting work on the part of traditional (or "classical") realists. This is not to say that constructivists were themselves absent from the renewal process; quite the contrary, it is simply to claim that they did not own the process, and to remark a (generally unappreciated) synthesis of constructivism and classicalism.[44] And if Gideon Rose might be scolded for abetting the neologists, he certainly deserves praise for drawing to our attention the preferred methodology of this genre of non-structural realists, who he instructs us place a premium upon "theoretically informed narratives, ideally supplemented by explicit counterfactual analysis, that trace the ways different factors combine to yield particular foreign policies."[45]

Here is a clue to the first of two ways in which strategic culture conceived as context can be put to work. What culture-as-context analysts seek to do is explicate foreign policies in terms either of (1) how particular states have acted in the past (i.e., their previous behavior is argued to have great bearing on their current and future options), or (2) how states are thought by their own and other peoples as being likely to act based on the "way they are" (i.e., their identity, or character, is said to predispose them toward certain policies). Analysts who employ strategic culture as a means of accounting for behavior's impact often turn to historical sociology for guidance; those who prefer to put the emphasis upon conceptions attending identity also avail themselves of approaches with a long-established pedigree, subsumed under the rubric national character. If both approaches are similar in dating from the first half of the twentieth century, a difference worth noting is that historical sociology has regained scholarly respectability after having been for some years in eclipse,[46] while national character studies, under that name, remain controversial, though when repackaged under the label "national identity" they not only become respectable, they become the vogue.[47]

Whatever else might divide them, strategic culturalists are dissatisfied with structuralist accounts of foreign policy choice; they may or may not be in agreement as to the attainability of reliable causality, but they do accept that cultural context, and therefore history, should "matter." *How* history should matter, no one can say exactly, but many analysts have been turning to narrative to supply explicative energy.[48] Their turn to narrative has led them to focus on the process (or phenomenon) known as "path dependence." Path dependence, as Paul Pierson observes, stands in contradistinction to certain assumptions of rational-choice theory that claim "large" causes should result in "large" outcomes.[49] As such, path dependence will have an ever-more congenial ring in the ears of some strategic culturalists, whose anti-structuralist epistemology, coupled with their conviction that patterns of behavior are "culturally" significant variables, will entice them to search for the cultural origins and character of path-dependent foreign policy choices.

It is, of course, one thing to invoke path dependence as the mechanism by which history can be said to continue to matter in the shaping of foreign (including security) policy, for instance in the general, and common-sensical, observation that choices made long in the past can go on limiting policy options in the future.[50] Yet it is quite another thing actually to tease out, or "trace,"[51] the process(es) by which path dependence manages to yield the context called strategic culture.

Strategic culturalists exploring the behavioral component of context will find them-selves being drawn ever closer to historical sociology, and will as a result have to come to grips with concepts closely related to path dependence. Among these latter, two stand out: temporal sequencing, and contingency. For path dependence can-not mean sensitive dependence upon "initial conditions"; rather, it must suggest a break point after which the ability of those initial conditions to shape the future altered substantially.[52] Some will label that break point "contingency," by which they will mean the development required to have set in train a new inertia, one in which the "path" led either to the efficient reproduction of cooperation (sometimes called "self-reinforcing sequences") or the reverse, the efficient reproduction of con-flict and discord (called "reactive sequences").[53] Which it is to be, and why, can be expected to provide work for strategic culturalists who take their concept to mean the "context" revealed by behavior, and who understand strategic culture as virtually indistinguishable from a country's historical record.

But as I said earlier, other strategic culturalists have taken contextual clues from elsewhere, and have not relied upon the behavioral record as evidenced in history. Not that they hold the past per se to be without instruction; rather they prefer to delve into "national character" as the source of whatever is deemed to be cultural in foreign policy. But they usually do not identify the object of their intellectual curiosity by that name. So what do they call it? In a word, "identity," a category that is held by constructivist and classical realist alike to endow meaning to "interest"—including and especially the "national interest." To be sure, there is nothing about identity that requires that its group, or societal, referent be the state or nation; col-lective identity accounts of international security phenomena are certainly not rare, or insignificant, and they might feature, *inter alia*, such transnational variables as religion or liberal-democracy, to take two common referents. But when it comes to the strategic culture of any particular country, the group referent reduces to the state or nation, and even to subnational identity groupings.[54] Interestingly, for all the attention accorded these days to identity, even and especially the "national" variant thereof, there is a marked reluctance of scholars openly to embrace the erstwhile con-cept of "national character," held by some to be a retrogressive notion that smacks of "essentialist," or "primordialist" categories.[55] If what is being alleged is that national character has been found guilty by prior association with "hereditarian" or racist assumptions about international relations, then one can easily see why it should have fallen out of favor; but if it is being avoided in name (though not in practice) because it is, as are most political concepts, ambiguous and even self-contradictory, then the shunning becomes less easy to justify, given the generic problems associated with political concepts, and especially given that national character's replacement by national identity merely substitutes one essentially contested category for another, in the process violating Ockham's razor.[56]

It can come as no surprise that even those social scientists who continue to employ the concept by its name disagree over its definition. Indeed, some will willingly concede that it resists defining—but is nevertheless too important to discard! One such scholar is Arthur Schlesinger, Jr., for whom national character raises important questions about the ability of America's creedal (constitutional) identity to withstand the challenge of a contemporary ethnic politics subsumed under the name "multiculturalism."[57] Although Schlesinger's pessimism on this score may not be justified, he is certainly correct in noting the important part played by ethnicity in discussions about national character. What this implies for analysts who interpret strategic culture as context is, or should be, apparent: the impact of ethnicity as a conditioning element in foreign policy making is a worthy object for their scholarly attentions. They might not think of themselves in this connection, but analysts who attempt to come to grips with the impact of ethnic diasporas in liberal-pluralist (or other kinds of) societies can be said to be working in the field of strategic culture.[58]

Attempts to assess the impact of a country's ethnic mix on its grand strategy do not exhaust the category of national character, of course. A major alternative manner in which the category is applied relates to the social-psychological variable known as "modal personality." Unlike ethnicity-based approaches to national character, studies that rely upon modal personality (i.e., a statistical notion for expressing personalities that appear with great frequency among members of a particular society) concentrate upon three major sources of evidence of a national character: personality assessments of individuals, psychological analyses of collective adult phenomena, and psychological assessments of child-rearing practices.[59]

Then there are, of course, those "non-ethnic" attributes of identity/character that can and do attest to how countries see themselves and others, and as I argue later, these too form part of the strategic-cultural approach to foreign policy, for they go to the very means by which collective cognition is enshrined and transmitted.

STRATEGIC CULTURE AS COGNITION: SYMBOLISM, MYTH, METAPHOR

There are enough similarities between strategic culture as context and strategic culture as cognition for anyone to make too big a fuss about their analytical separability; nevertheless, there is at least one difference worth noting, and it speaks to the very core of the explicative enterprise. Recall the thrust of Johnston's criticism of Gray, namely that his use of strategic culture was hopelessly muddled, as it so blurred the distinction between independent and dependent variables as to eliminate any prospect of strategic culture being of anyone's use in trying to sort cause from effect. I have hinted that this criticism has merit only to the extent one is committed to the notion of reliable causality; the more Laodicean the analyst is regarding the attainability of reliable causality, the less problematical becomes strategic culture as context. After all, and heretical though it might sound to some, if taxonomy and the kind of systematic understanding conveyed through interpretation are themselves part of the explicative enterprise, then even culture as context can serve us profitably, by helping us see things in foreign policy we might otherwise have missed.

Some are unhappy with this thought, which seems to them to be defeatist, going as it does against the grain of aspiring to the kind of knowledge that presumably can only be ours if we distinguish our "variables" in a credible manner. And it is in this respect that the second major category of strategic culture comes into play. It is no coincidence that the causal ambitiousness of Alistair Iain Johnston should have led him to a Geertzian approach to his topic (even though many will tell you, perhaps wrongly, that Geertz himself was agnostic on the issue of reliable causality).[60] But it is not just, or even perhaps chiefly, to Geertz that Johnston is indebted, for his approach to the subdisciplinary derivative, strategic culture, puts it squarely into alignment with an earlier tradition that had arisen in the main body of the discipline of political science, the tradition of "political culture," which we are about to see has remarkable affinities with our category in this section, strategic culture as cognition.

If the basic problem with culture as context is definitional fuzziness, culture as cognition holds out the promise of definitional clarity. Once the definition has been sufficiently "precised," why not envision using it as an independent variable? And what could be better than "political culture" to blaze the trail for strategic culture, for did not the career of the former concept demonstrate that it slew the very same definitional dragon whose breath has been heating up the debate over the latter concept? Why not turn to political culture as a means of "operationalizing" strategic culture?

The argument, on the surface, is not a bad one: for just as strategic culture is, political culture used to be itself subject to a variety of definitions; indeed, one critic observed that there were almost as many different meanings of political culture as there were political scientists professing an interest in it.[61] When it first burst on the scene in political science, during the 1930s and 1940s, it was as a result of the same interdisciplinary transfusion process that would bring culture into the purview of those who contemplated strategy, and it was again the anthropologists who were making the initial running. What happened in the subfield of strategy also occurred in the discipline more broadly: culture was often equated with "character" in the early days, but the more the latter was dissected the more it grew suspect as a useful category. By 1956, some two decades earlier than in the case of strategic culture, "political culture" got its name, yet even though Gabriel Almond might have told us what we should call it, he could not decree what it meant. Debate continued as to whether it was to signify the "generalized personality" of a people, or the collectivity's history, or something else altogether. By the late 1960s, political culture was well on the way to the conceptual dustheap.[62]

Political culture's rebound owed a bit to changes in the international system attending the Cold War's end, but it was primarily discontent on the part of some analysts with rational-choice modelling and game theory that gave the concept a new lease on life in the 1980s and 1990s.[63] For while the concept might have taken a nose-dive in the late 1960s and early 1970s, its core question—namely how to tap the subjective orientations of societies' members so as to account for political differences cross-nationally—never had gone out of fashion.[64] What had changed in the period between the decline and re-emergence of political culture was that a new element had been injected into the discussions of political scientists when they pondered how to assess "culture." That element was symbolism.

Symbolism helped resuscitate political culture in two ways. First, it solved the "level-of-analysis" problem hobbling political culture, for much of the early work by Almond and his associates relied upon survey data that, while it might indicate much of value about the perceptions and psychological state of *individuals*, seemed incapable of generating usable knowledge about the cognitive patterns of collectivities. Individuals, after all, had personalities, but only collectivities could be said to possess cultures, and the trick was to find a way to go from the individual to the collective level of analysis if culture was to mean anything. Symbolism provided the answer, enabling theorists to explore the social ideas of individuals.[65]

Symbolism could do this because of its second major contribution, which was to draw us to the cognitive devices that social groupings rely upon, as Lowell Dittmer phrased it, to "transmit meanings from person to person despite vast distances of space and time." Dittmer invited us to think of those devices, which include but are not limited to imagery and metaphor, as being identical to what the poet, T. S. Eliot, called "objective correlatives," namely mechanisms for the efficient expression of feelings. In this regard, symbols become a "depository of widespread interest and feeling." And for Dittmer, the task of those who would employ political culture must be nothing other than the systematic, scientific analysis of society's key symbols.[66] For, as Michael Walzer nicely put the same thought, symbols and images tell us "more than we can easily repeat."[67]

From this, it will be apparent how strategic culture as cognition might serve in shaping a research agenda, and this is so whether or not one believes in reliable causality. What I mean is that even if this category of strategic culture proves incapable of serving as anyone's independent variable, it can still do valuable scientific duty as a "specifying," or conditioning element, in explicative understandings of strategy, just as political culture supplies a conditioning element in political choice.[68] Analysts whose interest in strategic culture is situated primarily in the cognitive category might, for instance. be drawn to efforts at explicating strategic choice through the study of such nonliteral forms of communication as myth and metaphor, to take just the two most obvious such examples.[69]

CONCLUSION

This "modest" defence of strategic culture has not rested upon any particularly ambitious vision of the concept. Nor has it depended in any way upon the concept's being invested in redemptive qualities. Although some analysts do proclaim an interest in "culture" because of a dissatisfaction with realism, I am not of those who desire our concept to assume the outsized proportions necessitated by a liberationist agenda. Instead, I have sought to argue that categories of analysis associated with the concept of strategic culture can be, and should be, of interest to a variety of scholars who are motivated to understand how and why states end up making certain choices in grand strategy.

I have made two major claims in this chapter. First, I have noted that strategic culture shares with other concepts the quality of being contentious: here, the primary epistemological contest pits those who have faith in reliable causality against those who show a more agnostic disposition. There can be merit in both stances.

Secondly, I have sought to embed the roots of strategic culture in two different (but not totally so) substrata. Strategic culture as *context* is in turn divisible into (a) national historical behavior, and (b) national character and identity. As *cognition*, strategic culture is descended from the cognate concept of political culture, and as such has its most salient quality in the dimension of symbolism.

Strategic culture may be, to some. a "theory," but if it is such an entity I confess to being too obtuse to grasp it. Instead, I propose we think of strategic culture as a research program, one in which certain topics would seem natural objects of our curiosity. I conclude by nominating three such topics, though others could easily be added to the list: (1) path dependence and "rational" strategic choice; (2) ethnicity and foreign policy; and (3) the key symbols (especially myths and metaphors) of grand strategy.

NOTES

This chapter is reprinted with permission from *International Journal* (Summer 2004), pp. 479–502. The author wishes to acknowledge with gratitude research funding provided by the Social Sciences and Humanities Research Council of Canada (project no. 410–2001–1075: "Culture stratégique et grande stratégie au Canada, 1870–2000"), as well as to express his thanks to Stéphane Roussel for the inspired leadership he gave the project.

1. On the necessity for structural realists to conceive of power as "aggregate capability," see John J. Mearsheimer, *The Tragedy of Great Power Politics* (New York: W.W. Norton, 2001), p. 60.

2. For a vigorous rejection of the understanding of power as aggregate capability, see David A. Baldwin, *Paradoxes of Power* (Oxford: Basil Blackwell, 1989), esp. chapter 4: "Power Analysis and World Politics: New Trends versus Old Tendencies."

3. Some would disagree, and insist that unless we can come to agreed working definitions, we can never assign a value to our terms, thus cannot hope to measure them "scientifically." This insistence strikes me as being, in its own way, unscientific, if by the term science we simply mean the systematic organization and use of knowledge in a given area of inquiry. For a refreshingly catholic view of such a way to organize thinking about foreign policy, see James N. Rosenau, *The Scientific Study of Foreign Policy*, rev. and enl. ed. (London: Frances Pinter, 1980).

4. Jack Snyder is often credited with being the first writer explicitly to employ the rubric, in his *The Soviet Strategic Culture: Implications for Nuclear Options* (Santa Monica: RAND Corporation, 1977).

5. For a cautionary reminder, see Giovanni Sartori, "Concept Misformation in Comparative Politics," *American Political Science Review*, Vol. 64 (December 1970), pp. 1033–53. But for a tacit recognition that the problem may be immune to resolution, see David Collier and James E. Mahon, "'Conceptual Stretching' Revisited: Adapting Categories in Comparative Analysis," *American Political Science Review*, Vol. 87 (December 1999), pp. 845–55.

6. T.D. Weldon, *The Vocabulary of Politics* (Harmondsworth: Penguin Books, 1953), pp. 26–27.

7. Williams, cited by William H. Sewell, Jr., "The Concept(s) of Culture," in *Beyond the Cultural Turn: New Directions in the Study of Society and Culture*, ed. Victoria E. Bonnell and Lynn Hunt (Berkeley: University of California Press, 1999), pp. 35–61. For an extensive catalogue of culture's many, and at times contradictory, meanings, see A.L. Kroeber and Clyde Kluckhohn, *Culture: A Critical Review of Concepts and Definitions* (New York: Vintage Books, 1963).

8. Alastair Iain Johnston, *Cultural Realism: Strategic Culture and Grand Strategy in Chinese History* (Princeton: Princeton University Press, 1995), p. 1.

9. For such a bounded application of strategic culture, see Yitzhak Klein, "A Theory of Strategic Culture," *Comparative Strategy* 10 (January–March 1991): 3–23. Sometimes, an even more limiting modifier than strategic is chosen, as in the case of the debate over French military doctrine during the interwar period. For that debate, see Elizabeth Kier, "Culture and Military Doctrine: France between the Wars," *International Security*, Vol. 19 (Spring 1995), pp. 65–93; Kier, *Imagining War: French Military Doctrine between the Wars* (Princeton: Princeton University Press, 1997); and Douglas Porch, "Military 'Culture' and the Fall of France in 1940: A Review Essay," *International Security* Vol. 24 (Spring 2000), pp. 157–80.

10. John Lewis Gaddis, *Strategies of Containment: A Critical Appraisal of Postwar American National Security Policy* (Oxford: Oxford University Press, 1982), p. viii.

11. Ronald Jepperson and Ann Swidler, "What Properties of Culture Should We Measure?" *Poetics* Vol. 22 (1994), pp. 359–71, quote at pp. 359–60.

12. Donald R. Kelley, "The Old Cultural History," *History of the Human Sciences* Vol. 9 (August 1996): 101–26, quote at p. 101.

13. Ibid., p. 109. Edward B. Tylor's book was entitled *Early History of Mankind and the Development of Civilization* (2nd ed., London: John Murray, 1870; originally published in 1865); the earlier work by Giovanni Andres was called *The Origin, Processes, and Current State of All Literature* (*Dell'origine, progressi e stato attuale d'ogni letteratura*), 7 vols. (Parma, Italy: Stamperia reale, 1782–99).

14. Kelley, "Old Cultural History," 114–16.

15. Robert Kelley, *The Cultural Pattern in American Politics: The First Century* (New York: Alfred A. Knopf, 1979), pp. 6–9.

16. Quoted in ibid., p. 12.

17. Victoria E. Bonnell and Lynn Hunt, "Introduction," in *Beyond the Cultural Turn*, pp. 1–32, quotation on p. 3.

18. Sewell, "Concept(s) of Culture," p. 48.

19. Johnston, *Cultural Realism*, pp. 36–37. Also see his "Thinking about Strategic Culture," *International Security*, Vol. 19 (Spring 1995), pp. 32–64.

20. Robert Kagan, *Of Paradise and Power: America and the New World Order* (New York: Alfred A. Knopf, 2003).

21. Examples, respectively, of first- and second-generationers, as Johnston interprets them, are Colin S. Gray, "Strategic Culture as Context: The First Generation of Theory Strikes Back," *Review of International Studies*, Vol. 25 (January 1999), pp. 49–69; and Bradley Klein, "Hegemony and Strategic Culture: American Power Projection and Alliance Defence Politics," *Review of International Studies*, Vol. 14 (April 1988), pp. 133–48.

22. Johnston, *Cultural Realism*, pp. 1–2, 37–39.

23. Kelley, "Old Cultural History," p. 117.

24. Latin for "You, too" or "You, also." The editors.

25. Gray, "Strategic Culture as Context," p. 58 (emphasis in original).

26. Ibid., p. 69.

27. German for understanding and interpretation of meaning. The editors.

28. German verb, meaning "to explain." The editors.

29. Martin Hollis and Steve Smith, *Explaining and Understanding International Relations* (Oxford: Clarendon Press, 1990), pp. 72–74, 206–15.

30. Georg Henrik von Wright, *Explanation and Understanding* (Ithaca: Cornell University Press, 1971), pp. 4–6.

31. Ibid., pp. 134–35. Also see Richard Biernacki, "Method and Metaphor after the New Cultural History," in *Beyond the Cultural Turn*, pp. 62–92; and Patrick L. Gardiner, *The Nature of Historical Explanation* (Oxford: Oxford University Press, 1952).

32. Kenneth N. Waltz, *Theory of International Politics* (Reading, MA: Addison-Wesley, 1979).

33. See Robert Gilpin, *War and Change in World Politics* (Cambridge: Cambridge University Press, 1981), for a reminder that bipolarity might just be unstable and very dangerous.

34. Jeffrey Checkel, "The Constructivist Turn in International Relations Theory," *World Politics*, Vol. 50 (January 1998), pp. 324–48; Sujata Chakrabarti Pasic, "Culturing International Relations Theory: A Call for Extension," in Yosef Lapid and Friedrich Kratochwil, ed., *The Return of Culture and Identity in IR Theory* (Boulder, Co: Lynne Rienner, 1997), pp. 85–104.

35. Ted Hopf, "The Promise of Constructivism in International Relations Theory," *International Security*, Vol. 23 (Summer 1998), pp. 171–200.

36. For the argument that "identity" is simply too loose and self-contradictory a category to provide guidance for serious analysis, see Rogers Brubaker and Frederick Cooper, "Beyond 'Identity,'" *Theory and Society*, Vol. 29 (February 2000), pp. 1–47.

37. On the prominence of anthropologists among this pioneering generation of strategic culturalists, see E. Adamson Hoebel, "Anthropological Perspectives on National Character," *Annals of the American Academy of Political and Social Science*, Vol. 370 (March 1967), pp. 1–7.

38. Michael C. Desch, "Culture Clash: Assessing the Importance of Ideas in Security Studies," *International Security*, Vol. 23 (Summer 1998), pp. 141–70, quote at p. 170.

39. For some examples of the criticisms unleashed in his direction, see the separate contributions of John S. Duffield, Theo Farrell, and Richard Price, under the heading "Isms and Schisms: Culturalism versus Realism in Security Studies," *International Security*, Vol. 24 (Summer 1999), pp. 156–72.

40. See David Dessler, "Constructivism within a Positivist Social Science," *Review of International Studies*, Vol. 25 (January 1999), pp. 123–37.

41. Adrian Hyde-Price and Lisbeth Aggestam, "Conclusion: Exploring the New Agenda," in Aggestam and Hyde-Price, ed., *Security and Identity in Europe: Exploring the New Agenda* (New York: St. Martin's press, 2000), pp. 234–62, quote at p. 240.

42. See, for an intelligent application of the neologism, Gideon Rose, "Neoclassical Realism and Theories of Foreign Policy," *World Politics,* Vol. 51 (October 1998), pp. 144–72.

43. In what has to be the best example of the international relations conceptual equivalent of Gresham's Law, neorealism was debased to such an extent that it would soon come to stand for the virtual opposite of what it had originally been intended to represent. That the debasing was in some large measure the doing of Robert Keohane, one of pioneers of "complex interdependence" theory, only adds to the curiosity. For early applications of neorealism as a means of assessing the relative merits of a variety of "power assets" (including "soft power" ones) in an era in which *aggregate* capability was said to have lost relevance, see Robert Lieber, *No Common Power* (Glenview, ILL: Scott Foresman, 1988); Richard Feinberg, *The Intemperate Zone: The Third World Challenge to US Foreign Policy* (New York: W.W. Norton, 1983); and David B. Dewitt and John J. Kirton, *Canada as a Principal Power* (Toronto: John Wiley and Sons, 1983). The work most often associated with the transformation of the concept was Robert Keohane, ed., *Neorealism and its Critics* (New York: Columbia University Press, 1986), which really was a debate about the pros and cons of structural realism, the label Kenneth Waltz chose for his theory.

44. It is unappreciated in large measure due to the mistaken assumption of so many that realism must be all about either "security" (as those structuralists sometimes labelled "defensive realists" stress) or "power" (said to be the stellar variable for structuralists called "offensive realists"). But as Randall Schweller reminds us, structural realists, whether defensive or offensive, seem to have forgotten classical realism's roots, which reveal a myriad of objects of states' desire—including prestige, status, leadership, and market share (objects, he goes on to note, that probably ensure states will be more predisposed to competition than to cooperation). See Randall L. Schweller, "Realism and the Present Great Power System: Growth and Positional Conflict Over Scarce Resources," in Ethan B. Kapstein and Michael Mastanduno, eds., *Unipolar Politics: Realism and State Strategies After the Cold War* (New York: Columbia University Press, 1999), pp. 28–68.

45. Rose, "Neoclassical Realism," pp. 152–53.

46. On the rise, decline, and re-emergence of historical sociology, see Harry Elmer Barnes, *Historical Sociology: Its Origins and Development* (New York: Philosophical Library, 1948); and Dennis Smith, *The Rise of Historical Sociology* (Cambridge: Polity Press, 1991).

47. On the current fashionable status of identity, see Glenn Chafetz, Michael Spirtas, and Benjamin Frankel, "Introduction: Tracing the Influence of Identity on Foreign Policy," *Security Studies,* Vol. 8 (Winter 1998/99–Spring 1999), pp. vii–xxii.

48. See John Gerard Ruggie, "Peace in Our Time? Causality, Social Facts and Narrative Knowing," *American Society of International Law: Proceedings 89th Annual Meeting* (1995), pp. 93–100; and Ian Lustick, "History, Historiography, and Political Science: Multiple Historical Records and the Problem of Selection Bias," *American Political Science Review,* Vol. 90 (September 1996), pp. 605–18.

49. Paul Pierson, "Increasing Returns, Path Dependence, and the Study of Politics," *American Political Science Review,* Vol. 94 (June 2000), pp. 251–68.

50. See Theda Skocpol, "Sociology's Historical Imagination," in Theda Skocpol, ed., *Vision and Method in Historical Sociology* (Cambridge: Cambridge University Press, 1984), pp. 1–21.

51. On the methodological bona fides of "process tracing," see Stephen Van Evera, *Guide to Methods for Students of Political Science* (Ithaca, NY: Cornell University Press, 1997), pp. 64–67.

52. See Jack A. Goldstone, "Initial Conditions, General Laws, Path Dependence, and Explanation in Historical Sociology," *American Journal of Sociology,* Vol. 104 (November 1998), pp. 829–45.

53. James Mahoney, "Path Dependence in Historical Sociology," *Theory and Society* Vol. 29 (August 2000), pp. 507–48.

54. See Rodney Bruce Hall, *National Collective Identity: Social Constructs and International Systems* (New York: Columbia University Press, 1999); and William Bloom, *Personal*

Identity, National Identity and International Relations (Cambridge: Cambridge University Press, 1990).

55. This critique is made by Paul A. Kowert, "National Identity: Inside and Out," *Security Studies*, Vol. 8 (Winter 1998/99–Spring 1999), pp. 1–34.

56. For a sharp critique of those who would steer clear of national character while embracing other vague categories, see Dean Peabody, *National Characteristics* (Cambridge: Cambridge University Press, 1985).

57. Arthur M. Schlesinger, Jr., *The Disuniting of America: Reflections on a Multicultural Society* (New York: W.W. Norton, 1998), p. 169. Also see, on this theme, Samuel P. Huntington, "The Hispanic Challenge," *Foreign Policy, Vol.* 141 (March/April 2004), pp. 30–45.

58. For an example, see Tony Smith, *Foreign Attachments: The Power of Ethnic Groups in the Making of American Foreign Policy* (Cambridge, MA: Harvard University Press, 2000).

59. See Alex Inkeles and Daniel J. Levinson, "National Character: The Study of Modal Personality and Sociocultural Systems," in Gardner Lindzey and Elliot Aronson, ed., *The Handbook of Social Psychology*, 2nd ed *Group Psychology and Phenomena of Interaction* (Reading, MA: Addison-Wesley, 1969), 4: 418–506. Also see Geoffrey Gorer, *The American People: A Study in National Character* (New York: W.W. Norton, 1948).

60. Geertz is often associated with the argument that the best we can hope for is "thick description" of social reality, but one writer claims he nevertheless often strayed into the realm of implicit causality. Says this writer, the "riddle of what constitutes an adequate explication and how to distinguish causal claims from interpretive ones has vexed the best minds in philosophy for more than a century." Biernacki, "Method and Metaphor," pp. 72–73.

61. William M. Reisinger, "The Renaissance of a Rubric: Political Culture as Concept and Theory," *International Journal of Public Opinion Research*, Vol. 7 (Winter 1995), pp. 328–52.

62. Lucian Pye, "Political Culture Revisited," *Political Psychology*, Vol. 12 (September 1991), pp. 487–508.

63. Ronald Inglehart, "The Renaissance of Political Culture," *American Political Science Review* 82 (December 1988), pp. 1203–30.

64. Reisinger, "Renaissance of a Rubric," p. 331.

65. See, for the level-of-analysis problem, David J. Elkins and Richard E.B. Simeon, "A Cause in Search of Its Effect, or What Does Political Culture Explain?" *Comparative Politics*, Vol. 11 (July 1979), pp. 127–45; and Ruth Lane, "Political Culture: Residual Category or General Theory?" *Comparative Political Studies*, Vol. 25 (October 1992), pp. 362–87.

66. Lowell Dittmer, "Political Culture and Political Symbolism," *World Politics* Vol. 29 (July 1977), pp. 552–83.

67. Michael Walzer, "On the Role of Symbolism in Political Thought," *Political Science Quarterly*, Vol. 82 (June 1967), pp. 191–204, quote at p. 196.

68. As argued by Edward W. Lehman, "On the Concept of Political Culture: A Theoretical Reassessment," *Social Forces*, Vol. 50 (March 1972), pp. 361–70.

69. Examples would include Cyril Buffet and Beatrice Heuser, eds., *Haunted By History: Myths in International Relations* (Providence: Berghahn Books, 1998); and David G. Haglund, "The North Atlantic Triangle Revisited: (Geo)Political Metaphor and the Logic of Canadian Foreign Policy," *American Review of Canadian Studies*, Vol. 29 (Summer 1999), pp. 215–39.

3

Strategic Culture: From Clausewitz to Constructivism

Jeffrey S. Lantis

Cultural approaches to strategic studies have existed in various forms for hundreds of years. The argument that culture influences national security policy is grounded in classic works, including the writings of Thucydides and Sun Tzu. Clausewitz advanced these ideas by recognizing war and war-fighting strategy as "a test of moral and physical forces." The goal of strategy was much more than defeat of the enemy on the battlefield—it was the elimination of the enemy's morale.[1] In the twentieth century, national character studies linked Japanese and German strategic choices in World War II to deeply rooted cultural factors. Russell Weigley's 1973 classic *The American Way of Warfare* further underlined the importance of cultural roots of strategic dispositions. Jack Snyder's work on Soviet nuclear strategy during the Cold War directed scholarly attention to the key link between political and military culture and strategic choice.

Recent events have renewed scholarly interest in the role of culture in international security. Scholars and practitioners have begun to interpret challenges such as democratization in Iraq, U.S.–China trade disputes, nuclear tensions with Iran, and the war on terror through the lens of national identity and culture. Contemporary scholarship claims that a focus on strategic culture offers valuable perspective on military doctrine and critical choices such as nuclear strategy and the use of force.

This essay charts the evolution of the theory of strategic culture through several generations of scholarly work inside, and outside, the discipline. Particular attention is devoted to the relationship between strategic culture and policies on weapons of mass destruction (WMD). Key questions include: What are the ideational foundations of national security policy? Do cultural theories, newly inspired by constructivism, provide the most accurate explanations of security policy? Is strategic culture really "semi-permanent," as its supporters suggest, or can strategic culture evolve? Who are the "keepers" of strategic culture? And how universal is strategic culture? I conclude that while contemporary works on strategic culture offer promise, there remains substantial room for development of more reflexive models. A multifaceted approach may allow us to recognize greater nuances in competing systems and further energize our potential for accurate threat assessment.

Early Origins of the Cultural Approach

The "national character studies" of the 1940s and 1950s represented some of the first social scientific efforts to draw connections between culture and state behavior, based largely on anthropological models.[2] This work defined the roots of a nation's character, or culture, in language, religion, customs, socialization, and the interpretation of common memories.[3] Indeed, national character studies became popular tools for threat assessment during World War II. These studies drew intense criticism, however, because of concerns about stereotyping and the reification of the concept of culture.[4]

Prominent sociologists and anthropologists including Margaret Mead, Mary Douglas, and Claude Levi-Strauss, nevertheless, continued to probe links between culture and behavior. In *The Interpretation of Cultures* (1973), one of the most influential anthropological works on the subject, Clifford Geertz defined culture as "an historically transmitted pattern of meanings embodied in symbols, a system of inherited conceptions expressed in symbolic form by means of which men communicate, perpetuate, and develop their knowledge about and attitudes towards life."[5] He provided a useful model of culture and suggested ways that patterns of meanings could lead to distinct behaviors.

Political scientists Gabriel Almond and Sidney Verba launched a high-profile study of the concept of political culture in the 1960s, defining it as "that subset of beliefs and values of a society that relate to the political system."[6] Political culture, they argued, includes a commitment to values such as democratic principles and institutions, ideas about morality and the use of force, the rights of individuals or collectivities, and predispositions toward the role of a country in global politics. Political culture manifests itself on at least three levels: "the cognitive, which includes empirical and causal beliefs; the evaluative, which consists of values, norms and moral judgments; and the expressive or affective, which encompasses emotional attachments, patterns of identity and loyalty, and feelings of affinity, aversion, or indifference."[7] Talcott Parsons described culture as comprised of "interpretive codes" including language, values, and even substantive beliefs such as support for democracy or the futility of war.[8]

By the 1980s, interdisciplinary studies linking culture and politics had grown in popularity.[9] Sociologist Ann Swidler proposed a more complex model of connections between culture and state behavior, mediated by cultural "strategies of action." Swidler defined culture quite broadly as consisting of "symbolic vehicles of meaning, including beliefs, ritual practices, art forms, and ceremonies, as well as informal cultural practices such as language, gossip, stories, and rituals of daily life."[10] Building on the arguments of Max Weber and Parsons, she contended that interest-driven strategies are significant mediating conditions for state behavior.[11]

But while sociological models of culture became increasingly complex, subsequent studies of political culture yielded little theoretical refinement during this period. Critics argued that the approach was epiphenomenal and subjective, and that proponents of political culture made exaggerated claims about its explanatory power.[12] Cultural interpretive arguments remained alive in area studies, but fell out of favor in political science with the behavioral revolution.

Strategic Culture and Cold War Nuclear Policy

In 1977, Jack Snyder brought the political cultural argument into the realm of modern security studies by developing a theory of strategic culture to interpret

Soviet nuclear strategy. Snyder suggested that elites articulate a unique strategic culture related to security–military affairs that is a wider manifestation of public opinion, socialized into a distinctive mode of strategic thinking. He contended, "as a result of this socialization process, a set of general beliefs, attitudes, and behavior patterns with regard to nuclear strategy has achieved a state of semi-permanence that places them on the level of 'cultural' rather than mere policy."[13] Snyder applied his strategic cultural framework to interpret the development of Soviet and American nuclear doctrines as products of different organizational, historical, and political contexts, along with technological constraints. The result was his prediction that the Soviet military exhibited a preference for the preemptive, offensive use of force and the origins for this could be found rooted in a Russian history of insecurity and authoritarian control.

Snyder's contributions resonated with other security policy analysts, and subsequent work on strategic culture such as Ken Booth's *Strategy and Ethnocentrism* (1979) continued to explore the ideational foundations of nuclear strategy and superpower relations. Colin Gray suggested that distinctive national styles, with "deep roots within a particular stream of historical experience," characterize strategy-making in countries such as the United States and the Soviet Union. He defined strategic culture as "modes of thought and action with respect to force, which derives from perception of the national historical experience, from aspirations for responsible behavior in national terms" and even from "the civic culture and way of life." Thus, strategic culture "provides the milieu within which strategy is debated" and serves as an independent determinate of strategic policy patterns.[14]

In simple terms, this "first generation" of work on strategic culture described a synergistic link between strategic culture and WMD policy. Snyder and Gray argued that culture was a semi-permanent influence on policy shaped by elites and socialized into distinctive modes of thought. Nuclear strategy of potential adversaries could be predicted. Snyder's approach described a Soviet preference for the offensive, preemptive use of force and explained modernization initiatives in the nuclear infrastructure to support this orientation. The result of this study was new attention by scholars to the potentially predictive power of strategic culture.

However, critics asserted that the operationalization of strategic culture was problematic and subjective. They suggested that strategic cultural models were tautological as it would be nearly impossible to separate independent and dependent variables in a reliable way. Skeptics also charged that strategic cultural interpretations were by definition unique, drawing upon narrow and contextual historiography as much as anthropology. Furthermore, both supporters and detractors believed that the concept of strategic culture was fairly static, focusing on enduring historical orientations with strong predictive capability. Writing in 1988, Gray said that "social science has developed no exact methodology for identifying distinctive national cultures and styles." Literature on the "academically unfashionable subject of national character" was anecdotal at best, yet he believed that learning about the "cultural thoughtways" of a nation was crucial to understanding a country's behavior and its role in world politics.[15] Finally, structural realists had no room for so-called thick descriptive studies and were quick to sweep the concept of strategic culture to the side in their drive for more powerful and parsimonious models. Yitzhak Klein argued that only a "comparative, in-depth study of the formation, influence, and process of change in the strategic cultures of the major powers in the modern era" could make a useful contribution to studies of war and peace.[16] With the abrupt end of the Cold War—and, perhaps ironically, the nonuse of nuclear weapons by the superpowers—the concept of strategic culture at once fell into disfavor.

Strategic Culture Rediscovered: The Rise of Constructivism

In the 1990s, a new generation of scholarly work reasserted the utility of cultural interpretations.[17] Theoretical work on strategic culture, domestic structures, and organizational culture advanced significantly in this period, intersecting ever more frequently with the rise of constructivism. In a pathbreaking 1992 work, Alexander Wendt argued that state identities and interests can be seen as "socially constructed by knowledgeable practice."[18] According to Peter Katzenstein, Robert Keohane, and Stephen Krasner, constructivism recognizes the importance of "inter-subjective structures that give the material world meaning," including norms, culture, identity, and ideas on state behavior or on international relations more generally.[19] Constructivists argue that "national identities are social–structural phenomena," which provide a "logic of appropriateness" regarding policy choices.[20] Ted Hopf believes that the paradigm offers "a promising approach for uncovering those features of domestic society, culture, and politics that should matter to state identity and state action in global politics."[21]

The constructivist research program devotes particular attention to identity formation, with connections to organizational process, history, tradition, and culture. According to Valerie Hudson, constructivism

> views culture as an evolving system of shared meaning that governs perceptions, communications, and actions...Culture shapes practice in both the short and long term. At the moment of action, culture provides the elements of grammar that define the situation, that reveal motives, and that set forth a strategy for success.[22]

But constructivists focus primarily on social structures at the systems level, with special attention to the role of norms in international security.[23] Norms are defined as "intersubjective beliefs about the social and natural world that define actors, their situations, and the possibilities of action."[24] Nina Tannenwald's studies of the nuclear taboo and the norm of nonproliferation, along with Legro's work on military restraint during World War II, have generated a great deal of scholarly attention.[25]

Although the central tenets of constructivism were familiar to many—Geertz's work clearly had a significant influence on contemporary thinking, for example— this was successfully framed as a paradigmatic challenge to neorealism. One of the most controversial prongs of this challenge was the assertion by some constructivists that their approach would, assuredly, supplant neorealism as the dominant paradigm in the discipline. While this has not been accomplished, the rise of constructivism has clearly energized a new wave of strategic cultural research.

Third Generation Studies

Alastair Johnston's *Cultural Realism: Strategic Culture and Grand Strategy in Chinese History* (1995) is often cited as the quintessential third generation work on strategic culture. The study set out to investigate the existence and character of Chinese strategic culture and causal linkages to the use of military force against external threats. Johnston takes the concept of strategic culture seriously as an "ideational milieu that limits behavioral choices," from which "one could derive specific predictions about strategic choice." But Johnston chose several unconventional approaches for his cultural study. First, he selected the intriguing period of the Ming dynasty (1368–1644) as the focus for his contemporary theoretical test. Second, he adopted a methodological approach that offered a clear separation between the independent variable, cultural orientations, and the dependent variable, military strategy. He said, "China has exhibited a tendency for the controlled, politically driven defensive and minimalist use of force that is deeply rooted in the statecraft of ancient strategists and a worldview of relatively complacent superiority."[26] Ultimately, Johnston concluded that there were two Chinese strategic cultures in action: "one a symbolic or idealized set of assumptions and ranked preferences, and one an operational set that had a nontrivial effect on strategic choices in the Ming period."[27] Perhaps ironically, these cultures actually exhibit some classic elements of realpolitik.

Specialized studies of German and Japanese strategic culture also reflect third generation approaches.[28] Thomas Berger's *Cultures of Antimilitarism: National Security in Germany and Japan* (1998) focused on "antimilitarist political-military cultures" to explain patterns in those countries' foreign policy behaviors.[29] Berger noted that while Japan's economic and technological power placed it in a position to become an economic and perhaps even military superpower at the end of the Cold War, the persistent postwar culture of antimilitarism truly defined Japanese security policy in the 1990s. According to Berger, cultural beliefs and values act as a distinct national lens to shape perceptions of events and even channel possible societal responses. In this sense, he states, "cultures enjoy a certain degree of autonomy and are not merely subjective reflections of concrete 'objective' reality."[30] In a similar vein, Thomas Banchoff developed a consciously constructivist, "path-dependent" model of foreign policy whereby he argues that decisions taken at critical historical junctures have shaped the development of foreign policy over time.[31] John Duffield adds that far from setting off in adventurous new directions, "Germany has exercised considerable restraint and circumspection in its external relations since 1990."[32] To Duffield, "[t]he overall effect of national security culture is to predispose societies in general and political elites in particular toward certain actions and policies over others. Some options will simply not be imagined...some are more likely to be rejected as inappropriate or ineffective than others."[33] In a more recent work, Akan Malici employs a congruence procedure to convincingly argue that German elites subscribe to a "culture of reticence" in security affairs.[34]

Contemporary studies of military organizational cultures offer promise as well. Kier described the significance of organizational culture in the development of French military doctrine.[35] Steven Rosen provided a compelling account of the ways that the military and organizational cultures in India have shaped strategy over time. To Rosen, military culture is comprised of the "beliefs and assumptions that frame...choices about international military behavior, particularly those concerning decisions to go to war, preferences for offensive, expansionist or defensive modes of warfare, and levels of wartime casualties that would be acceptable."[36] According to these studies, organizational culture can be interpreted as an independent or intervening variable that directly influences strategic choice.

Another important dimension of third generation work, the study of security norms, lies at the intersection of culturalist and constructivist research. Norms are defined by Katzenstein, Ronald Jepperson, and Alexander Wendt as standards "of right or wrong, a prescription or proscription for behavior for a given identity."[37] One of the areas of normative study most closely related to WMD and threat assessment is focused on the nonnuclear norm or taboo.[38] To address the puzzle of why nuclear weapons were never employed by the superpowers during the Cold War, strategist Thomas Schelling first raised the concept of a "nuclear taboo" in the 1960s. He described an emerging tradition of nonuse of nuclear weapons: "a jointly recognized expectation that [nuclear weapons] may not be used in spite of declarations of readiness to use them, even in spite of tactical advantages in their use."[39]

In more recent, provocative works, Tannenwald, Richard Price, and T.V. Paul characterize a taboo as "a particularly forceful kind of normative prohibition that is concerned with the protection of individuals and societies from behavior that is defined or perceived to be dangerous…something that is not done, not said, or not touched."[40] The nuclear taboo literature places special emphasis on the power of morality and related norms in shaping state behavior. As Tannenwald argues, "nuclear weapons have come to be defined as abhorrent and unacceptable weapons of mass destruction" over the past fifty years. This moral opprobrium has become so acute that the use of nuclear weapons today is "practically unthinkable."[41] These optimists claim that taboos represent "bright line" norms that have significant constitutive effects.[42]

Strategic Culture and WMD Policy

Generations of scholarship have produced greater understanding of ties between culture and state behavior. Strategic cultural studies have provided rich descriptions of particularistic cultures and identities, and researchers have acknowledged important links between external and internal determinants of national security policy. Cultural studies have been informed by cross-disciplinary linkages to anthropology, historical research, sociology, and psychology. Inspired by constructivism, scholars have begun to explore ways in which strategic culture is shaped and may evolve over time. As a result, even skeptics have acknowledged that contemporary works on culture offer much more than an "explanation of last resort."

But this survey of the literature also points to substantial room for refinement of the research program. Areas for further attention include the need for a common definition of strategic culture to build theoretically progressive models, delineation of the ways that strategic culture is created, maintained, and passed on to new generations, the question of the universality of strategic culture, and refinement of models of linkages between external and internal determinants of security policy. While some scholars suggest that adoption of cultural models represents a fundamental rejection of structure, contemporary research suggests more comprehensive models of state behavior can be developed short of falsification of the realist program.[43] Contrary to neorealist critiques of ideational frameworks, few cultural scholars believe that this really is an either–or theoretical debate. Furthermore, many cultural scholars recognize the need for a defined ontology as well as falsifiable, middle-range theory. In this spirit, we offer a "to-do" list for the development of new, progressive models of strategic culture in comparative perspective.

Develop Common Definitions

Given decades of scholarship on cultural determinants, one might assume that strategic culture has become an accepted *independent* variable in causal modeling. It has not. Snyder's definition of strategic culture as "a set of semi-permanent elite beliefs, attitudes, and behavior patterns socialized into a distinctive mode of thought" set the tone for decades of investigations.[44] Today, scholars seem to agree that distinct political cultures may exist, but definitions still blur the line between preference formation, values, and state behaviors. Lucian Pye's definition of culture as "the dynamic vessel that holds and revitalizes the collective memories of a people by giving emotional life to traditions" is a case in point.[45] Here, strategic culture becomes a generator of preferences, a vehicle for the perpetuation of values and preferences, and a force of action in the revitalization and renewal of these values. Rosen's characterization of strategic culture as the "beliefs and assumptions that frame...decisions to go to war, preferences for offensive, expansionist or defensive modes of warfare, and levels of wartime casualties that would be acceptable" also blurs the line by including reference to the rules that might govern conduct in war.[46] Delineating culture as an independent variable remains challenging, and some scholarly efforts have bordered on tautology wherein domestic political structures are identified as both reflecting and shaping political culture.[47]

Constructivism has energized work on strategic culture, but it has not advanced the search for a common definition. David Elkins and Richard Simeon argued three decades ago that culture is a "shorthand expression for a mind set which has the effect of limiting attention to less than the full range of alternative behaviors, problems and solutions which are logically possible."[48] Constructivists often seem to adopt this shorthand approach to descriptions of culture as comprised of both the ideas about strategic choice and the choices themselves. Hudson's contention that culture is "an evolving system of shared meaning that governs perceptions, communications, and actions" seems intuitively correct, but offers little in the way of testable hypotheses.[49] In addition, the professed ontological agnosticism of constructivism may not provide a sufficient base for theory-building in strategic cultural studies. Scholars must recognize the difficulty of drawing linkages between political structure and state behavior but yet seek consensus on explanatory boundaries.[50]

Johnston offered one of the most promising avenues for a progressive research program on strategic culture by characterizing culture as "an ideational milieu which limits behavior choices." But in so doing, his efforts have drawn fire from both first generation culturalists and constructivists. Johnston frames strategic culture as "shared assumptions and decision rules that impose a degree of order on individual and group conceptions of their relationship to their social, organizational or political environment." While he noted that strategic subcultures may exist, "there is a generally dominant culture whose holders are interested in preserving the status quo." Johnston's conceptual approach to strategic culture was designed to be falsifiable, "or at least distinguishable from non-strategic culture variables...[that would] provide decision-makers with a uniquely ordered set of strategic choices from which we can derive predictions about behavior."[51] This work is certainly informed by progress in political psychology as well as contemporary sociological studies of the complex connections between culture and state behavior.

Participants in the Comparative Strategic Cultures project workshops of 2005–2006 developed a definition that encompassed some of the contributions, and recognized some of the pitfalls, of past scholarship. According to that group, strategic culture is a set of "shared beliefs, assumptions, and modes of behavior, derived from common experiences and accepted narratives (both oral and written), that shape collective identity and relationships to other groups, and which determine appropriate ends and means for achieving security objectives."[52] This approach recognizes strategic culture as a product of historical circumstances and national identity, but also allows it a role in shaping decisions about strategy.

Explore the Origins of Strategic Culture

History shows us that there are many sources of strategic culture, encompassing both material and ideational factors.[53] Clearly, geography, climate, and resources have been fundamental factors in strategic thinking throughout the millennia and remain important sources of strategic culture today. For many, geographical circumstance is the key to understanding why some countries adopt particular strategic policies rather than others. Proximity to great powers has been viewed as an important factor, for example, and the security policies of Norway, Finland, and even Canada reflected this throughout the Cold War.[54] Additionally, while most territorial borders are settled by negotiation, others have been forged through conflict and remain contested. Some states have multiple borders and may be confronted by different strategic factors at each point of contact with neighboring states: that is, they could have to respond to multiple security dilemmas. This has clearly shaped strategic orientations in countries like Israel, for example, which has developed a sizable nuclear arsenal for defense. Equally, ensuring access to vital resources is critical to strategy. Geographic factors in the context of a changing global territorial and resource landscape consequently continue to exert influence on strategists in the twenty-first century.

History and experience are important considerations in the birth and evolution of states, and the strategic cultural identities that comprise them. International relations theory has identified several kinds of states ranging from weak to strong, colonial to postcolonial, and premodern, modern, and postmodern. This raises the prospect that different kinds of states may confront different strategic problems and with varying material and ideational resources, apply unique responses.[55] For newly formed states the difficulties of nation building can compound insecurities and help shape strategic cultural identities. Conversely, for those states with a deep history the longevity of their existence may prompt consideration of factors that contribute to the rise and fall of great powers or civilizations and shape their policies to suit.

As illustrated in figure 3.1, another source of strategic culture is the nature of a country's political institutions and defense organizations. Some countries adopt a broadly Western liberal democratic style of government while others do not. Some are considered mature democracies while others are undergoing democratic transformation and are in various stages of consolidation. Where the latter are concerned there may be cultural variables such as tribal, religious, or ethnic allegiances that operate within and across territorial boundaries that determine the pace and depth of consolidation. Similarly, many regard defense organizations as being critical to strategic cultures but differ over the precise impact these have. Military doctrines, civil–military relations, and procurement practices also may affect strategic culture. Similarly, where civil–military relations are concerned, it is argued the debate is not so much about military doctrines, "but the preconditions for the deployment and the kind of rationality that is at stake in those deployments."[56]

Myths and symbols are considered to be part of all cultural groupings. Both can act as a stabilizing or a destabilizing factor in the evolution of strategic cultural

Physical	Political	Social/cultural
Geography	Historical experience	Myths and symbols
Climate	Political system	Defining texts
Natural resources	Elite beliefs	
Generational change	Military organizations	
Technology		
<-------------------{Transnational Normative Pressures}---------------------------->		

Figure 3.1   Potential Sources of Strategic Culture.

identities. The notion of myth can have meaning different from the traditional understanding as something unfounded or false. John Calvert writes that it can also refer to "a body of beliefs that express the fundamental, largely unconscious or assumed political values of a society—in short, as a dramatic expression of ideology."[57] Work on symbols has also suggested that these act as "socially recognized objects of more or less common understanding" and which provide a cultural community with stable points of reference for strategic thought and action.[58]

Many analysts regard key texts as important in informing actors of appropriate strategic thought and action. Traditional analyses of peace and conflict have long pointed to the influence of such texts throughout history and in different cultural settings. These may follow a historical trajectory—from Sun Tzu, who wrote the *Art of War* during the time of the warring states in ancient China, through the writings of Kautilya in ancient India, and into Western understanding as a result of Thucydides commentary on the Peloponnesian Wars and Clausewitz's observations of the Napoleonic period. At the same time, there may be competition between texts for influence on society.[59]

Generational change, technology, and transnational norms are also regarded as important sources of strategic culture.[60] Both generational change and technology, particularly information and communications technology, can have important ramifications for issues of empowerment and strategic reach. While information and communications technology has transformed societies, it has also allowed individuals or groups to communicate in novel ways and cause disruption at a distance.

Finally, Theo Farrell argues that norms can define "the purpose and possibilities of military change" in providing guidance concerning the use of force.[61] He has studied how transnational norms of military professionalism have influenced national policies and the process by which this occurs. Farrell considers that transnational norms can be transplanted into a country's cultural context either through a process involving pressure on a target community to accept the new norms (termed "political mobilization"), or by a process of voluntary adoption (termed "social learning"). Norm transplantation, as Farrell refers to it, can thus occur via a process of incremental adoption over time eventually achieving a cultural match between the transnational and national norms.[62]

Given the range of potential influences on the development of strategic culture, it is imperative for studies to accurately gauge the dynamics at work in any particular society. Material factors form only one important pillar of the milieu that can influence strategic choices. More nuanced (and well-informed) cultural studies will identify predispositions and related ideational factors that may also shape security policy.

Identify the Keepers of Strategic Culture

Identifying strategic culture as a set of shared assumptions and decision rules prompts the question of how they are maintained, and by whom. Most scholars prefer descriptions of political and strategic cultures as the "property of collectivities rather than simply of the individuals that constitute them."[63] Richard Wilson proposed:

> In the most general sense political cultures are socially constructed normative systems that are the product of both social (for example, rules that coordinate role relationships within the organizations) and psychological (for example, the preferences of individuals)

influences but are not reducible to either…A political culture is not simply the sum
of individual preferences, nor do preferences, especially those of any given individual,
necessarily correspond with normative prescriptions.[64]

Acknowledging strategic culture as an "important ideational source of national
predispositions, and thus of national security policy," suggests deep, but vague,
cultural foundations for state behavior, however.

If political culture is truly manifested in cognitive, evaluative, and expressive
dimensions, it is conceivable that actors who carry those values might be identified. In fact, various political leaders and institutions are engaged in historical
interpretation and development of the foreign policy path. This, in turn, prompts
coalition- and consensus-building efforts by specific political players. To Duffield,
"institutional sources of national predispositions are likely to reside in the central
governmental organs charged with the formulation and execution of policy." They
may shape policy by "organizational processes, routines, and standard operating procedures may constraint the types of information to which decision makers
are exposed."[65] Berger suggests that political culture can only be understood as a
combination of norms and political institutions that "exist in an interdependent
relationship."[66]

It is quite clear that elites are often the purveyors of the common historical
narrative.[67] Most scholars agree that elites are instrumental in defining foreign
policy goals and the scope and direction of policy restructuring in the face of new
challenges. Furthermore, there is a general consensus in the literature that elites
are cognitively predisposed to maintain the status quo. However, contemporary
works on policy discourse tend to argue that strategic culture is best characterized
as a "negotiated reality" among elites. Leaders clearly pay respect to deeply held
convictions such as multilateralism and historical responsibility, but the record of
past behavior for many countries also shows that leaders chose when and where
to stake claims of strategic cultural traditions; they decided when and where
to consciously move beyond previous boundaries of acceptability in foreign
policy behavior. Ultimately, contemporary scholarship contends, elite behavior
may be more consistent with the assertion that leaders are strategic "users of
culture" who "redefine the limits of the possible" in key foreign and security
policy discourses.[68] Indeed, the constructivist literature suggests that leaders can
effectively be "norm entrepreneurs" in leading a state to conceptualize a specific
strategic path.[69]

Political institutions—including military organizations, parties, and domestic
coalitions—may also have a significant impact on foreign policy behavior. The
organizational culture literature suggests that state behavior is a function of specific
institutional orientations. Whether or not military bureaucracies are the most
common keepers of strategic culture around the world, it remains the case that the
influence of organizational culture on state behavior is mediated by other institutions
and by the policymaking processes in democratic states.

Identify Scope Conditions for Strategic Culture

The events of 9/11 and the subsequent war on terrorism have prompted renewed
attention to the role of culture in shaping state (and non-state) behaviors. While
constructivism offers a fairly ambitious research agenda, I would contend that it
is important for cultural theorists to first consider the potential for middle-range

theory development. It may indeed be possible to develop scope conditions within which strategic culture could have a stronger impact on security policy. To this end, we can examine both classic perspectives and contemporary debates on strategic culture. For example, one of the most intriguing questions in the subfield actually carries over through several generations of scholarship: what types of actors are most likely to have defined strategic cultures? Snyder made a strong case for the influence of strategic culture in Soviet nuclear policy; and subsequent studies effectively framed U.S. and Soviet cultures within the larger Cold War context. But does the literature imply that authoritarian systems are more likely to have defined strategic cultures than are democratic systems? Or, are authoritarian systems simply less likely to have definable strategic subcultures? Can non-state actors have strategic cultures? Can regional organizations or meta-cultural groups have some form of strategic culture?

Sam Huntington's "civilizational thesis" certainly pushes the envelope of theoretical interpretation.[70] He contended that states are part of broader civilizations that share strong bonds of culture, societal values, religion, and ideologies. The most important of these bonds, he argued, is religion, and "the major civilizations in human history have been closely identified with the world's great religions."[71] Meta-cultural ties, taken to the broadest level of categorization, are civilizational identities that shape modern world politics and predispose identity groups toward conflict.[72] However, the civilizational thesis has drawn sharp criticism from the scholarly community. Area studies experts are critical of Huntington's willingness to propose the sweeping generalizations that were necessary to undergird the civilizational thesis. Recent investigations of Huntington's claims have concluded that there is no statistically significant causal linkage before, during, or after the Cold War.[73] In the end, Huntington's work may have undermined some of the careful, social scientific progress that had been achieved in the cultural research program.

Can the concept of strategic culture apply to non-state actors operating across territorial boundaries where identities may be formed in the realm of cyberspace? The advent of the cyber revolution has generated several issues concerning our understanding of conflict and security.[74] Technology enhances "the salience of substate extremist groups or fundamentalist groups because their ability to organize transnationally, meet virtually, and utilize terrorist tactics has been substantially enhanced by the globalization of technology and information."[75]

Finally, it may also be possible to identify scope conditions under which one is more likely to find constitutive effects of strategic culture. In a classic study, Ole Holsti lays out five "decisional settings" in which belief structures tend to have a great impact on decision-making, including: "situations that contain highly ambiguous components and are thus open to a variety of interpretations"; "non-routine situations that require more than the application of standard operating procedures and decision rules"; "responses to events that are unanticipated or contain an element of surprise"; and even "long-range policy planning...that inherently involves considerable uncertainty."[76] These hypotheses suggest that ideational foundations may be more significant in specific contexts.

More recently, Kerry Kartchner has hypothesized that a set of conditions may enable strategic culture to play a more dominant role in state behavior. They include:

> when there is a strong sense of threat to a group's existence, identity or resources, or when the group believes that it is at a critical disadvantage to other groups; when there is a pre-existing strong cultural basis for group identity; when the leadership frequently resorts

to cultural symbols in support of its national group security aspirations and programs; when there is a high degree of homogeneity within the group's strategic culture; and when historical experiences strongly predispose the group to perceive threats.[77]

Clearly, efforts to establish scope conditions within which we are more likely to identify strategic cultures that have constitutive effects represents important progress toward middle-range theory.

Develop Models of Strategic Cultural Change

The focus of most studies of strategic culture is on continuity of state behavior. Harry Eckstein suggested that the socialization of values and beliefs occurs over time. Past learning becomes sedimented in the collective consciousness and is relatively resilient to change. Lessons of the past, therefore, serve as a tight filter for any future learning that might occur.[78] Those scholars who address the potential for change (inspired by Weber, Jürgen Habermas, and Immanuel Wallerstein) face a great deal of criticism. However, an intriguing characteristic of the latest generation of cultural studies is the recognition of the possibility of change over time. If historical memory, political institutions, and multilateral commitments shape strategic culture, then, recent studies argue, it would seem logical to accept that security policies will evolve over time.[79] This contribution to the strategic culture literature is informed both by studies of foreign policy restructuring and constructivist ideas on foreign policy as discourse. Essentially, this work seeks to challenge "the distinction between behaviour and culture" by considering "culture as practice."[80] It also represents a response to the criticism of prior generations of cultural models as static and unresponsive to systemic pressures.[81]

Under what conditions can strategic culture change? When might foreign policy decisions transcend the traditional bounds of strategic culture? In my own work on the subject, I contend that at least three factors can cause "strategic cultural dilemmas" and produce changes in security policy. First, external shocks may fundamentally challenge existing beliefs and undermine past historical narratives. According to Farrell, a shock is often a "necessary condition for radical change…[shocks] undermine the legitimacy of existing norms, shift power within communities, and enable norm cultural entrepreneurs to construct a new consensus around alternative norms."[82] For German leaders in the 1990s, the scale of the humanitarian tragedies in the Balkans served as a catalyst for consideration of policy options outside the traditional bounds of German strategic culture. The recognition that groups were being systematically targeted for genocide and ethnic cleansing created a moral imperative for German action. Some experts have even suggested that ethnic cleansing in Bosnia eroded the moral legitimacy of pacifism on the German political left and led to an atmosphere more permissive of the use of force to stop such violence.[83]

However, most scholars rightly assert that any process of change would not be easy. Potential catalysts for change, Berger argued, might be "dramatic events or traumatic experiences [such as revolutions, wars, and economic catastrophes]," which would "discredit thoroughly core beliefs and values."[84] Such change would be accompanied by extreme psychological stress and would require a resocialization process, involving participation by various groups in the crafting of a compromise on a new political cultural orientation.[85]

Second, foreign policy behavior may break the traditional bounds of strategic cultural orientations when primary tenets of strategic thought come into direct conflict with one another. In other words, a country with interpretive codes of support for democracy and an aversion to the use of military force faces a strategic cultural dilemma when confronted by a challenge to democracy that necessitates a military response. The Japanese government confronted this question in relation to the struggle for self-determination in East Timor. The same type of dilemma may arise from a conflict between commitments to multilateralism and unilateral convictions that norms are being violated. Thompson, Ellis, and Wildavsky said that cultures remain vital only if their core principles continue to generate solutions that satisfy human needs and make sense of the world.[86] Products of this strategic cultural *dissonance* include occasional state defections from multilateral arrangements, the development of alternative diplomatic initiatives, or stipulations for policy cooperation.

Thus, strategic cultural dilemmas define new directions for foreign policy and demand the reconstruction of historical narratives. Changes—including abrupt and fairly dramatic reorientations of security policy behavior—appear to be possible, and strategic cultural models must be more reflective of the conditions that draw out such changes. Indeed, Swidler recognized that the relationship between state behavior and strategic culture becomes especially apparent "in unsettled cultural periods...when explicit ideologies govern action [and] structural opportunities for action determine which among competing ideologies survive in the long run."[87] As NATO leaders implement a new strategic concept, China pursues liberalized trade, and the United States leads a global war on terrorism in the twenty-first century, strategic cultural models must themselves adapt for long-term relevance.

Third, elites play a special role in strategic cultural continuity and change. Perhaps Berger is correct that strategic culture is best understood as a "negotiated reality" among foreign policy elites. While leaders clearly pay respect to deeply held convictions associated with strategic culture, the story of foreign policy development may be best understood as the pursuit of legitimation for preferred policy courses that may, or may not, conform to traditional cultural boundaries. Indeed, leaders often adopt their own specific conceptions of national identity from among a competitive marketplace of ideas.[88] Both the constructivist and culturalist literature agree on the possibility for norm entrepreneurs to approach events, frame the discourse, and begin constructing a new discursive path toward objectives.

In many ways, the U.S. response to the terrorist attacks of 9/11 is illustrative of these agents of strategic cultural change. The Bush administration's declaration of a war on terrorism represented a fundamental conversion in strategic culture prompted by an external shock. President Bush and top advisors embraced a new direction in U.S. security policy based on their reinterpretation of the threat matrix. New strategic cultural orientations included a positive affirmation of American dominance in international security affairs, priority consideration of homeland security, a new doctrine of preemption that includes a willingness to use military force to achieve security objectives, and a preference for unilateral action to reduce external constraints on U.S. behavior.[89] However, these changes have been extremely difficult and even traumatic for the American polity, prompting deep divisions.[90]

Consider Policy Implications: Strategic Culture and Coercive Diplomacy

The theory of strategic culture offers tremendous opportunity for progressive study of strategic choice in the twenty-first century, but it clearly contains a few pitfalls as well. There is a great deal of potential utility in strategic cultural studies if scholars truly pursue the goal of cumulation. Progressive models of strategic culture operating from similar sets of assumptions about the sources, influences, and implications of identity have the potential to be highly valuable policy tools. Strategic cultural models speak to concerns in key policy arenas as well, including responses to countries seeking WMD. If one accepts that there are truly different strategic cultural profiles, and that they shape security policy choices around the world, then major powers should tailor their policies to accommodate these cultural differences to the extent possible. Regarding threat assessment, for example, there are significant questions about the applicability of Western and traditional models to non-Western countries. Studies of Iranian and North Korean decision-making systems, for example, that focus on the dysfunction of the process may ignore significant cultural differences that allow those systems to focus on specific ends and means without traditionally Western orientations. A multifaceted cultural approach allows us to recognize the nuance of competing systems and may further energize our potential for accurate threat assessment.

These arguments are supported in the limited scholarship on identity and strategic choice. For example, Alexander George argues "the effectiveness of deterrence and coercive diplomacy is highly context dependent."[91] Drawing on theories from political psychology, Jacques Hymans contends that the decision to develop a nuclear arsenal is "extraordinary," and can be found to be rooted in the national identity conceptions that leaders carry with them.[92] Understanding different national identity conceptions, Hymans contends, can help us to predict whether leaders will ultimately decide to take that significant step.

Recent U.S. efforts to deal with nuclear programs in rival states such as North Korea and Iran are illustrative of the complexity of the challenges. Efforts to dissuade and deter potential enemies from developing nuclear weapons have largely been unsuccessful to date. This is not to say, of course, that U.S. diplomacy has been unsophisticated in identifying the challenges and recognizing nuances in cross-cultural communication. But one could argue that progressive models of strategic culture can only help to inform selection of policies targeted toward specific strategic cultures. Assuming that concepts such as coercion, risk, and deterrence are highly culturally specific, the development of more reflexive models becomes essential for both international cooperation and security policy success.

CONCLUSION

While constructivism may represent a paradigmatic challenge to structural realism in the discipline today, most supporters of strategic culture have adopted the more modest goal of "bringing culture back in" to the study of national security policy. In fact, these research traditions are more similar than some would believe. Scholars must work to overcome barriers to integration of these two approaches into a more comprehensive model of strategic culture formation, implementation, and change. Some argue that one of these barriers is a certain defensiveness on the part of neorealists, who contend that culturalists (and constructivists) simply seek to supplant neorealism. But ultimately, even Desch allows that cultural theories might supplement neorealism by helping to explain time lags between structural change and alterations in state behavior, by accounting for seemingly "irrational" state behavior, and in helping to explain state actions in "structurally indeterminate situations."[93] The cases of the evolution of German and Japanese security policies are better understood as a product of domestic political adjustments (rooted in culture, traditions, and common historical narratives) to changing international circumstances. Far from an exclusive interpretation, progressive models that explore external–internal linkages and their impact on discrete, strategic choices represent an important avenue for theoretical advancement.

Culture is clearly a factor in contemporary international security, but research still needs to be done on its depth and scope of influence. Considering strategic culture as "a dynamic interplay between discourse and practice" offers a means for accommodating the issue of the mutable nature of strategic culture. Similarly, it may illuminate both how strategic culture evolves from generation to generation and is transformed by competing groups through negotiation and debate.[94]

NOTES

1. Karl von Clausewitz, *On War*, ed. and trans. Michael Howard and Peter Paret (New York: Alfred A. Knopf, 1993), p. 26.
2. Two of the most prominent scholars of national character were Ruth Benedict (*The Chrysanthemum and the Sword* [Boston: Houghton Mifflin, 1946]), and Geoffrey Gorer (*The American People* [New York: W.W. Norton, 1948]).
3. David J. Elkins and Richard E.B. Simeon, "A Cause in Search of Its Effect, or What Does Political Culture Explain?" *Comparative Politics*, Vol. 11, No. 2 (January 1979), pp. 127–28.
4. For popular exceptions to this argument, see Nathan Leites, *The Operational Code of the Politburo* (New York: McGraw-Hill, 1951); and Adda B. Bozeman, *Politics and Culture in International History* (Princeton, NJ: Princeton University Press, 1960).
5. Clifford Geertz, *The Interpretation of Cultures* (New York: Basic Books, 1973). See also Sherry B. Ortner, ed., *The Fate of Culture: Geertz and Beyond* (Berkeley: University of California Press, 1997).
6. Gabriel Almond and Sidney Verba, *The Civic Culture: Political Attitudes and Democracy in Five Nations* (Boston: Little, Brown, 1965), pp. 11–14.
7. John S. Duffield, *World Power Forsaken: Political Culture, International Institutions, and German Security Policy after Unification* (Stanford: Stanford University Press, 1999), p. 23. See also Robert D. Putnam, *The Beliefs of Politicians: Ideology, Conflict, and Democracy in Britain and Italy* (New Haven: Yale University Press, 1973); Putnam, "Studying Elite Political Culture: the Case of 'Ideology,'" *American Political Science Review*, Vol. 65, No. 3 (September 1971), pp. 651–81; Bert A. Rockman, *Studying Elite Political Culture: Problems in Design and Interpretation* (Pittsburgh: University of Pittsburgh Press, 1976).
8. See Talcott Parsons, *The Social System* (Glencoe, IL.: Free Press, 1951).
9. Mary Douglas and Aaron Wildavsky, *Risk and Culture: An Essay on the Selection of Technical and Environmental Dangers* (Berkeley: University of California Press, 1982).
10. Ann Swidler, "Culture in Action: Symbols and Strategies," *American Sociological Review*, Vol. 51, No. 2 (April 1986), pp. 273.
11. Max Weber, *The Sociology of Religion* (Boston: Beacon Press, 1946a [1922–23]), p. 220. See also Weber, *The Protestant Ethic and the Spirit of Capitalism* (New York: Charles Scribner and Sons, 1958 [1904]). Related works describing the growing interest in connections between culture and political developments include: Ronald Inglehart, "The Renaissance of Political Culture," *American Political Science Review*, Vol. 82, No. 4 (1988), pp. 1203–230; Harry C. Triandis, *Culture and Social Behavior* (New York: McGraw-Hill, 1994); Aaron Wildavsky, "Choosing Preferences by Constructing Institutions: A Cultural Theory of Preference Formation," *American Political Science Review*, Vol. 81, No. 1 (1987), pp. 3–21.

12. See Charles Lockhart, "Cultural Contributions to Explaining Institutional Form, Political Change, and Rational Decisions," *Comparative Political Studies,* Vol. 32, No. 7 (October 1999), pp. 862–93; Lowell Dittmer, "Political Culture and Political Symbolism: Toward a Theoretical Syntheses," *World Politics,* Vol. 29 (1977), pp. 552–88; Ruth Lane, "Political Culture: Residual Category or General Theory?" *Comparative Political Studies,* Vol. 25, No. 4 (1992), pp. 362–87.

13. Jack Snyder, *The Soviet Strategic Culture: Implications for Nuclear Options,* R-2154-AF (Santa Monica: Rand Corporation, 1977), p. 8; See also Ken Booth, *Strategy and Ethnocentrism* (New York: Holmes and Meier, 1981).

14. Colin Gray, "National Style in Strategy: The American Example," *International Security* Vol. 6, No. 2 (Fall 1981), pp. 35–37.

15. Colin Gray, *The Geopolitics of Superpower* (Lexington: University Press of Kentucky, 1988): 42–43.

16. Yitzhak Klein, "A Theory of Strategic Culture," *Comparative Strategy,* Vol. 10, No. 1 (1991): 3. See also Richard W. Wilson, *Compliance Ideologies: Rethinking Political Culture* (New York: Cambridge University Press, 1992); Charles A. Kupchan, *The Vulnerability of Empire* (Ithaca, NY: Cornell University Press, 1994).

17. Some of the most influential works in this area for security studies are: Peter J. Katzenstein, ed., *The Culture of National Security: Norms and Identity in World Politics* (New York: Columbia University Press, 1996); Alastair Iain Johnston, "Thinking about Strategic Culture," *International Security* Vol. 19, No. 4 (Spring 1995), pp. 32–64; Stephen Peter Rosen, "Military Effectiveness: Why Society Matters," *International Security,* Vol. 19, No. 4 (Spring 1995), pp. 5–31; Elizabeth Kier, "Culture and Military Doctrine: France between the Wars," *International Security,* Vol. 19, No. 4 (Spring 1995), pp. 65–93; Richard J. Ellis and Michael Thompson, eds., *Culture Matters: Essays in Honor of Aaron Wildavsky* (Boulder: Westview Press, 1997); Yosef Lapid, "Culture's Shop: Returns and Departures in International Relations Theory," in Yosef Lapid and Friedrich Kratochwil, eds., *The Return of Culture and Identity in IR Theory* (Boulder: Lynne Rienner, 1996).

18. Alexander Wendt, "Anarchy Is What States Make of It: The Social Construction of Power Politics," *International Organization,* Vol. 46, No. 2 (Spring 1992), PP. 392.

19. Peter J. Katzenstein, Robert O. Keohane, and Stephen Krasner, "International Organization and the Study of World Politics," *International Organization,* Vol. 52, No. 4 (1998), p. 679.

20. Jacques E.C. Hymans, *The Psychology of Nuclear Proliferation* (Cambridge: Cambridge University Press, 2006), p. 17; See also Stephen Saideman, "Thinking Theoretically about Identity and Foreign Policy," in Shibley Telhami and Michael Barnett, eds., *Identity and Foreign Policy in the Middle East* (Ithaca, NY: Cornell University Press, 2002), pp. 169–70.

21. This, in spite of its proclaimed ontological agnosticism. See Ted Hopf, "The Promise of Constructivism in International Relations," *International Security,* Vol. 23, No. 1 (Summer 1998), pp. 914; See also Jeffrey W. Legro, "Culture and Preferences in the International Cooperation Two-Step," *American Political Science Review,* Vol. 90, No. 1 (March 1996), pp. 118–37.

22. Valerie M. Hudson, ed., *Culture and Foreign Policy* (Boulder, CO: Lynne Rienner, 1997), pp. 28–29.

23. For more detailed studies of norms in world politics, see Alexander Wendt, "Collective Identity Formation and the International State System," *American Political Science Review,* Vol. 88, No. 2 (1994), pp. 384–96; Martha Finnemore and Kathryn Sikkink, "International Norm Dynamics and Political Change," *International Organization,* Vol. 52, No. 4 (1998), pp. 887–917; Jeffrey Checkel, "Norms, Institutions and National Identity in Contemporary Europe," Arena Working Paper 98/16 (Oslo: Advanced Research on the Europeanisation of the Nation-State, University of Oslo, 1998).

24. Alexander Wendt, "Constructing International Politics," *International Security,* Vol. 20, No. 1 (1995), pp. 73–74.

25. Nina Tannenwald, "Stigmatizing the Bomb: Origins of the Nuclear Taboo," *International Security*, Vol. 29, No. 4 (Spring 2005), pp. 5–49; Tannenwald, "The Nuclear Taboo: The United States and the Normative Basis of Nuclear Non-Use," *International Organization*, Vol. 53, No. 3 (Fall 1999), pp. 83–114.

26. Alastair Iain Johnston, *Cultural Realism: Strategic Culture and Grand Strategy in Chinese History* (Princeton, J: Princeton University Press, 1995), p. 1.

27. Ibid., p. x.

28. Kenneth N. Waltz, "The Emerging Structure of International Politics," *International Security*, Vol. 18, No. 2 (Fall 1993), pp. 71. See also Christopher Layne, "The Unipolar Illusion: Why New Great Powers will Rise," *International Security*, Vol. 17, No. 2 (Spring 1993), pp. 5–51.

29. Thomas U. Berger, *Cultures of Antimilitarism: National Security in Germany and Japan* (Baltimore: Johns Hopkins University Press, 1998), p. 1; See also Berger, "From Sword to Chrysanthemum: Japan's Culture of Anti-Militarism," *International Security*, Vol. 17, No. 4 (Spring 1993), pp. 119–50.

30. Berger, *Cultures of Antimilitarism*, p. 9.

31. Thomas Banchoff, *The German Problem Transformed: Institutions, Politics, and Foreign Policy, 1945–1995* (Ann Arbor: University of Michigan Press, 1999), p. 2.

32. Duffield, *World Power Forsaken*, p. 4. See also Duffield, "Political Culture and State Behavior: Why Germany Confounds Neorealism," *International Organization*, Vol. 53, No. 4 (Autumn 1999), pp. 765–803.

33. Duffield, "Political Culture and State Behavior," 771.

34. Akan Malici, "Germans as Venutians: The Culture of German Foreign Policy Behavior," *Foreign Policy Analysis*, Vol. 2 (2006), pp. 37–62.

35. Kier, "Culture and Military Doctrine."

36. Rosen, *Societies and Military Power: India and Its Armies* (Ithaca, NY: Cornell University Press, 1996), p. 12.

37. Ronald L. Jepperson, Alexander Wendt, and Peter J. Katzenstein, "Norms, Identity, and Culture in National Security," in Peter J. Katzenstein, ed., *The Culture of National Security: Norms and Identity in World Politics* (New York: Columbia University Press, 1996), p. 54; Farrell and Terriff add that norms are "intersubjective beliefs [that are] rooted in, and reproduced through, social practice." Theo Farrell and Terry Terriff, *The Sources of Military Change: Culture, Politics, and Technology* (Boulder, CO: Lynne Rienner, 2002), p. 7.

38. T.V. Paul, "Nuclear Taboo and War Initiation in Regional Conflicts," *Journal of Conflict Resolution*, Vol. 39, No. 4 (December 1995), pp. 696–717; Alexander Wendt, "Constructing International Politics," *International Security*, Vol. 20, No. 1 (1995), pp. 73–74; Wendt, "Collective Identity Formation and the International State System," *American Political Science Review* Vol. 88, No. 2 (1994), pp. 384–96; Martha Finnemore and Kathryn Sikkink, "International Norm Dynamics and Political Change," *International Organization* Vol. 52, No. 4 (1998), pp. 887–917; Jeffrey Checkel, "Norms, Institutions and National Identity in Contemporary Europe," Arena Working Paper 98/16 (Oslo: Advanced Research on the Europeanisation of the Nation-State, University of Oslo, 1998); Jepperson, Wendt, and Katzenstein, "Norms, Identity and Culture," pp. 33–75; and, of course, Tannenwald's own work: "Stigmatizing the Bomb," pp. 5–49; and "The Nuclear Taboo," pp. 83–114.

39. Thomas C. Schelling, *The Strategy of Conflict*, 2nd edition (Cambridge, MA: Harvard University Press, 1980), p. 260.

40. Tannenwald, "Stigmatizing the Bomb," p. 8; see also Franz Steiner, *Taboo* (London: Cohen and West, 1956), p. 21; Mary Douglas, *Purity and Danger: An Analysis of the Concepts of Pollution and Taboo* (London: Routledge, 1966).

41. Tannenwald, "Stigmatizing the Bomb," p. 5.

42. These ideas relate to recent work on the relationship between "national identity conceptions" and decisions to acquire or develop nuclear weapons; Hymans, *The Psychology of Nuclear Proliferation*.

43. Colin S. Gray, "Strategic Culture as Context: The First Generation of Theory Strikes Back," *Review of International Studies,* Vol. 25 (1999), pp. 49–69; Keith Krause and Michael C. Williams, "Broadening the Agenda of Security Studies: Politics and Methods," *Mershon International Studies Review,* Vol. 40, No. 2 (October 1996), pp. 229–54.

44. Snyder, *The Soviet Strategic Culture,* p. 8.

45. Lucian W. Pye, *Asian Power and Politics: The Cultural Dimension of Authority* (Cambridge, MA: Harvard University Press, 1985), pp. 20–22.

46. Rosen, *Societies and Military Power,* p. 12.

47. Pye, as quoted in Lowell Dittmer, "Political Culture and Political Symbolism, toward a Theoretical Synthesis," *World Politics,* Vol. 29, No. 4 (July 1977), pp. 555.

48. David Elkins and Richard Simeon, "A Cause in Search of Its Effects, or What Does Political Culture Explain?" *Comparative Politics* Vol. 11 (1979), pp. 132.

49. Hudson, *Culture and Foreign Policy,* pp. 28–29.

50. See Wilson, *Compliance Ideologies,* pp. 246–73.

51. Ibid., p. 246.

52. Kerry M. Kartchner, Summary Report of the "Comparative Strategic Culture: Phase II Kickoff Workshop," Defense Threat Reduction Agency Advanced Systems and Concepts Office (Washington, DC: February 13, 2006).

53. These ideas are drawn from Jeffrey S. Lantis and Darryl Howlett, "Culture and National Security Policy," in John Baylis, James Wirtz, Eliot Cohen, and Colin S. Gray, eds., *Strategy in the Contemporary World* (Oxford: Oxford University Press, 2007), pp. 83–100.

54. Nina Graeger and Halvard Leira, "Norwegian Strategic Culture after World War II. From a Local to a Global Perspective," *Cooperation and Conflict,* Vol. 40, No. 1 (2005), pp. 45–66; Henrikki Heikka, "Republican Realism. Finnish Strategic Culture in Historical Perspective," *Cooperation and Conflict,* Vol. 40, No. 1 (2005), pp. 91–119.

55. Colin Gray comments that "different political and strategic cultures confront distinctive geostrategic problems through the prisms of their individual historical circumstances, and with unique sets of assets and liabilities, will make somewhat individual choices." Colin S. Gray, "The American Revolution in Military Affairs: An Interim Assessment," *The Occasional* (Wiltshire, UK: Strategic and Combat Studies Institute, 1997), p. 28.

56. Neumann and Heikka, "Grand Strategy," *Conflict and Cooperation,* Vol. 40, No. 1 (2005), pp. 16.

57. John Calvert, "The Mythic Foundations of Radical Islam," *Orbis,* Vol. 48, No. 1 (Winter 2004), pp. 29–41.

58. Charles Elder and Roger Cobb, quoted in Stuart Poore, "Strategic Culture," in John Glenn, Darryl Howlett, and Stuart Poore, eds., *Neorealism versus Strategic Culture* (Aldershot, UK: Ashgate, 2004), p. 63.

59. Nikolaos Ladis, "Assessing Greek Strategic Thought and Practice: Insights from the Strategic Culture Approach," Unpublished Doctoral Dissertation, University of Southampton, UK, 2003.

60. Theo Farrell, "Transnational Norms and Military Development: Constructing Ireland's Professional Army," *European Journal of International Relations,* Vol. 7, No. 1 (2001), pp. 63–102.

61. Farrell and Terriff, *The Sources of Military Change,* p. 7.

62. Farrell, "Transnational Norms and Military Development," pp. 63–102.

63. Duffield, *World Power Forsaken,* p. 23.

64. Wilson, *Compliance Ideologies,* p. 12.

65. Duffield, *World Power Forsaken,* p. 29.

66. Berger, *Cultures of Antimilitarism,* pp. 11–12.

67. See, e.g., Sanjoy Banerjee, "The Cultural Logic of National Identity Formation: Contending Discourses in Late Colonial India," in *Culture and Foreign Policy,* pp. 27–44.

68. Cruz, "Identity and Persuasion," p. 278. For more on the strategic "use of culture," see Ann Swidler, "Culture in Action: Symbols and Strategies," *American Sociological Review,* Vol. 51 (April 1986), pp. 273–86.

69. For more on this, see Matthew Evangelista, *Unarmed Forces* (Ithaca NY: Cornell University Press, 1999); Barry R. Posen, *The Sources of Military Doctrine* (Ithaca NY: Cornell University Press, 1984); Stephen Peter Rosen, *Winning the Next War* (Ithaca NY: Cornell University Press, 1991); Kimberly Martin Zisk, *Engaging the Enemy* (Princeton, NY: Princeton University Press, 1993); and Richard Price, "Reversing the Gun Sights: Trannational Civil Society Targets Land Mines," *International Organization*, Vol. 53, No. 3 (1998), pp. 613–44.

70. Samuel P. Huntington, "The Clash of Civilizations?" *Foreign Affairs*, Vol. 72, No. 3 (1993), pp. 22–49; Huntington, "If Not Civilizations, What? Paradigms of the Post–Cold War World," *Foreign Affairs*, Vol. 72, No. 5 (1993), pp. 186–94; Huntington, *The Clash of Civilizations and the Remaking of World Order* (New York: Simon and Schuster, 1996).

71. Huntington, *The Clash of Civilizations*, p. 47.

72. Ibid., p. 318.

73. Errol A. Henderson and Richard Tucker, "Clear and Present Strangers: The Clash of Civilizations and International Conflict," *International Studies Quarterly*, Vol. 45 (2001), pp. 317–38. See also Errol A. Henderson, "The Democratic Peace Through the Lens of Culture, 1820–1989," *International Studies Quarterly*, Vol. 42 (September 1998), pp. 461–84.

74. Gregory J. Rattray, "The Cyberterrorism Threat," in Russell D. Howard and Reid L. Sawyer, eds., *Terrorism and Counterterrorism. Understanding the New Security Environment*, (Guilford: McGraw-Hill, 2002), pp. 221–45; Stuart J.D. Schwartzstein, ed., *The Information Revolution and National Security. Dimensions and Directions* (Washington, DC: Center for Strategic and International Studies, 1996).

75. V.D. Cha, "Globalization and the Study of International Security," *Journal of Peace Research*, Vol. 37, No. 3 (2000), p. 392. See also, Audrey Kurth Cronin, "Behind the Curve. Globalization and International Terrorism," *International Security*, Vol. 27, No. 3 (Winter 2002/03), pp. 30–58.

76. Ole Holsti, "Foreign Policy Formation Viewed Cognitively," in Robert Axelrod, ed., *Structure of Decision* (Princeton: Princeton University Press, 1976), pp. 18–54. See also Alexander L. George, "The Causal Nexus between Cognitive Beliefs and Decision-Making Behavior: The 'Operational Code' Belief System," in Lawrence S. Falkowski, ed., *Psychological Models in International Politics* (Boulder, CO: Westview Press, 1979), pp. 95–124.

77. Kartchner, Summary Report of the "Comparative Strategic Culture: Phase II Kickoff Workshop."

78. Harry Eckstein, "A Culturalist Theory of Political Change," *American Political Science Review*, Vol. 82 (1998), pp. 796.

79. Banchoff, *The German Problem Transformed*, p. 2.

80. Rassmussen, " 'What's the Use of It?' Danish Strategic Culture and the Utility of Armed Force," *Conflict and Cooperation*, Vol. 40, No. 1 (2005), pp. 71.

81. See, e.g., Charles Lockhart, "Cultural Contributions to Explaining Institutional Form, Political Change, and Rational Decisions," *Comparative Political Studies*, Vol. 32, No. 7 (October 1999), pp. 862–93.

82. Farrell, "Transnational Norms and Military Development," p. 82.

83. Jeffrey S. Lantis, *Strategic Dilemmas and the Evolution of German Foreign Policy Since Unification* (Westport: Praeger, 2002).

84. Duffield, *World Power Forsaken*, p. 23.

85. Ibid., p. 14.

86. Michael Thompson, Richard Ellis, and Aaron Wildavsky, *Cultural Theory* (Boulder, CO.: Westview Press, 1990), pp. 69–70.

87. Swidler, "Culture in Action: Symbols and Strategies," p. 273.

88. Hymans, *The Psychology of Nuclear Proliferation*, p. 19. See also Jane Mansbridge and Aldon Morris, eds., *Oppositional Consciousness: The Subjective Roots of Social Protest* (Chicago: University of Chicago Press, 2001).

89. Theo Farrell, "Strategic Culture and American Empire," *SAIS Review,* Vol. 25, No. 2 (2005), pp. 3–18

90. Jeffrey S. Lantis, "American Strategic Culture and Transatlantic Security Ties," in Kerry Longhurst and Marcin Zaborowski, eds., *Old Europe, New Europe and the Transatlantic Security Agenda* (London: Routledge, 2005), pp. 175–94.

91. Alexander L. George, "The Need for Influence Theory and Actor-Specific Behavioral Models of Adversaries," in Barry R. Schneider and Jerrold M. Post, eds., "Know Thy Enemy: Profiles of Adversary Leaders and Their Strategic Cultures," U.S. Air Force Counterproliferation Center (July 2003), pp. 271–310; www.au.af.mil/au/awc/awcgate/cpc-pubs/know_thy_enemy/index.htm.

92. Hymans, *The Psychology of Nuclear Proliferation,* p. 18.

93. Ibid., p. 166.

94. Darryl Howlett and John Glenn, "Epilogue: Nordic Strategic Culture," *Cooperation and Conflict,* Vol. 40, No. 1 (2005), p. 129.

PART II

STRATEGIC CULTURE IN ACTION: EXPLAINING WMD DECISION MAKING

4

Strategic Culture and WMD Decision Making

Kerry M. Kartchner

> It is more important to understand motivation, intent, method, and culture than to have a few more meters of precision, knots of speed, or bits of bandwidth.
> —Maj. Gen. Robert H. Scales, Jr., U.S. Army (ret.),
> "Culture Centric Warfare," *Proceedings,* September 2004

The concept of "strategic culture" is undergoing a revival because it has become essential to better understand the reasons, incentives, and rationales for acquiring, proliferating, and employing weapons of mass destruction (WMD) by diverse actors under circumstances that differ significantly from those for which previous analytical constructs now seem inadequate or irrelevant. If the United States and its allies are to assure prospective friends and partners in the common battle against WMD proliferation that their respective guarantees of extended security are credible, if they are to effectively dissuade potential proliferators from engaging in counterproductive acquisition of WMD, and if they are to deter and, if necessary, defeat those actors who rebuff these assurances and dissuasions, they need to understand the strategic cultural context for these objectives.

This chapter lays out a framework for an analytic approach to the intersection of WMD and strategic culture, and sets forth some initial hypotheses regarding the role of strategic culture in the thinking, decision making, and behavior of states (and non-state actors) as they contemplate pursuing, possessing, or employing this class of weapons.

This essay is a preliminary assessment of how decisions, actions, behavior, and policies related to WMD may be affected or influenced by a nation's or group's strategic culture. In the context of the question of how strategic culture impacts WMD decisions, we are interested in identifying shared beliefs and assumptions regarding the acquisition of WMD, its proliferation, its use, and international WMD norm compliance. Strategic culture can manifest itself on many different levels, from the tribal or group level, to the organizational level, the national level, even at the civilizational level. Given the focus of this essay on issues related to WMD, the emphasis will be primarily on the national level. This is not to discount, however, the important insights and explanations that can be found through examining other levels; it is only to set out boundaries for this particular assessment.[1]

The term "WMD" has come to mean many different things, and is used in a number of different ways. However, for the purposes of this project, and as defined by Paul Bernstein, weapons of mass destruction are "nuclear chemical, biological and radiological weapons, and their associated means of delivery, primarily but not limited to ballistic missiles."[2]

When a nation state or a group considers what its actions and policies are going to be regarding WMD, it faces a range of choices. It can renounce pursuing the acquisition of WMD, and submit to international standards and regimes of nonproliferation. Or, it can choose to pursue acquiring the technology to lay the basis for a future decision to develop nuclear, chemical, or biological weapons without actually proceeding to the manufacture of such weapons, but only to give it the option of doing so if circumstances change in the future. For the purpose of setting forth a framework for assessing the possible impact of strategic culture on these types of decisions, there are four key "decision matrices"[3] that one must consider:

1. Strategic culture and compliance or noncompliance with international nonproliferation regimes and norms—does strategic culture strengthen or undermine international or domestic norm-adherence policies and behavior?
2. Strategic culture and the acquisition of WMD—does strategic culture inform or determine incentives for acquiring WMD?
3. Strategic culture and the proliferation of WMD—does strategic culture promote or inhibit tendencies to proliferate WMD?
4. Strategic culture and the use of WMD—does strategic culture influence decisions to use WMD, either in the sense of wielding WMD for deterrence and coercive purposes, or in the sense of actually conducting attacks with WMD?

It is now widely accepted that understanding the regional and cultural context for U.S. foreign and defense policy, especially with respect to combating the proliferation of WMD, and preventing their use against the United States or its allies and friends abroad, is required to effectively promote U.S. nonproliferation objectives. This is in part due to the transition from a world dominated by a simple bipolar conflict with clear ideological underpinnings and motivations, to a vastly more complex world of numerous actors (both state and non-state) whose motivations are unclear, and whose objectives may not always be explicit, or are not conveyed in terms we understand. Traditional analytical frameworks may not apply in these cases. It seems apparent that deeper forces are at play behind the events that are unfolding in the present era, forces that trace their roots back, in some cases, hundreds of years in history, stretching far back beyond the relatively short period we knew as the Cold War. These forces have been shaped by religious and cultural factors that we do not readily understand, or that fall outside the conventional analytical frameworks we have previously employed. When traditional ways of understanding no longer seem adequate, it is natural that we should look for new ways to make sense of the world.

A FRAMEWORK FOR ANALYZING STRATEGIC CULTURE AND WMD

Strategic culture offers the promise of providing insight into motivations and intentions that are not readily explained by other frameworks, and that may help make sense of forces we might otherwise overlook, misunderstand, or misinterpret.

There are several reasons why it is especially important to apply strategic culture analysis to issues related to WMD.

First, there is increasing recognition that understanding strategic culture is vital to effectively implementing and safeguarding U.S. national security and foreign policy, and combating the proliferation of WMD is among these policies' highest priorities. According to the Defense Science Board's 2004 Study on Strategic Communications, among others, hostility to U.S. national security goals and policies is undermining U.S. power, influence, and strategic alliances, and much of this hostility is driven by a lack of understanding of the cultural and regional context for U.S. policy.[4]

Cultural scripts can determine what is considered "rational." According to Valerie Hudson, "rationality itself may mean different things in different cultures." Hudson cites other studies showing that "differences in moral reasoning based on culture may skew traditional assumptions of rational-choice theory."[5] This has important implications for deterrence, and for understanding different motivations that various cultures may have for adhering to or rejecting international WMD norms, or for acquiring, proliferating, or employing WMD. For example, if one's deterrence threats are considered "irrational" by the targeted society, they may not be considered credible, or they may be misconstrued. They may not even be considered threats, or they may be considered challenges to be confronted, thus having the exact opposite effect of that desired.

Second, it is important to "know one's enemy" of course, to better assess new and emerging threats. Strategic cultural analysis can provide insights into identifying and evaluating emerging threats. But, it is also important to know one's friends and allies, to know what assures them, what inspires their confidence in American security guarantees, or conversely, what undermines such confidence, and what the basis of their own threat assessments are.[6]

Third, those groups and states at present most interested in acquiring, proliferating, or using WMD often justify their policies and actions in cultural terms. Rather than dismissing such language as mere propaganda, strategic cultural perspectives underscore the importance of such language for understanding the motivations and intentions of these actors.

A framework for further exploring the relationship between WMD and strategic culture assumes that there are three aspects of strategic culture that affect WMD-related decisions and behavior:[7]

1. Strategic culture can be considered a "shared system of meaning," with language and terms that are understood and agreed within a given culture, and identifying and defining what is considered rational within a society. It is a way of interpreting the world, a way of relating to the community, its members, and the relationship of the community to other communities. It is based on "evolving meanings conditioned by historical precedent and contemporary experience." In this sense, strategic culture helps define the "means" of a group or nation's national security policy.
2. Strategic culture may be seen as a "collection of value preferences," specifying what a group's, state's, or society's appropriate security objectives and desires are. That is, strategic culture contributes to defining the "ends" of a group or nation's national security policy.
3. Strategic culture is a source of determining what constitutes allowable or optimal behavior, or a "template for human action," relating ends and means in an appropriate, and culturally sanctioned manner. Cultural influences can be considered

a "template for human strategy" and those strategies can in turn be reflected in behavior. In other words, this aspect of culture relates the meaning of the first aspect of culture (a system of shared meaning), with the objectives representing the collective value preferences, and helps determine appropriate means for achieving those ends. Hudson explains:

> What culture provides its members is a repertoire or palette of adaptive responses from which members build off-the-shelf strategies of action. What matters is not the whole of culture, but rather "chunks" of "prefabricated" cultural response. We may not be able to predict choice and construction of a particular response by a particular member of the culture, but we can know what is on the shelf ready and available to be used or not.[8]

Strategic Culture and International Norm Adherence

Different cultures respond in different ways to the question of accepting and adhering to international law and generally accepted international norms. By international norms is meant both the explicit values recorded in the full range of international nonproliferation regimes, but also the implicit assumptions, values, and rules underlying international attitudes toward WMD, such as the "nuclear taboo," or the assumption that nuclear weapons will only be used as instruments of last resort.

A culture's predisposition to adhere and conform to international norms related to WMD, or that culture's preference for rejecting, ignoring, or flouting such norms, is an important strategic cultural indicator of how it will approach the other three decisional factors related to WMD. Since decisions related to acquiring, proliferating, or employing WMD are captured in one form of international legal constraint or another, whether a nation chooses to act against international norms is an important indicator of whether that nation can be assured, dissuaded, or deterred from acquiring, using, or employing WMD, or whether it must be confronted and ultimately defeated in a military sense in order to prevent its acquisition, proliferation, or use of WMD. Norm adherence, then, is the first and foundational factor before proceeding to examine the cultural bases for acquiring, proliferating, or employing WMD.

According to the model, rejection or denial of international WMD regimes and norms is most likely to occur when:

1. Such rejection or adherence is deemed rational within the system of shared meaning defined by the prevailing strategic culture, as sanctioned or endorsed by the keepers or holders of the strategic culture. For example, members of the culture may not view international norms as "valid" or "legitimate" especially if those norms were established by groups considered hostile to the given culture. They may not view them as relevant or enforceable, or they may even view them as tools of the adversary. These perspectives will often be conditioned by past historical experiences, shared narratives, or as precepts based on the culture's scriptural or written records.
2. Such rejection or adherence is perceived by the holders or keepers of the strategic culture as enabling the group, organization, or state to achieve culturally endorsed outcomes, or outcomes deemed appropriate by the prevailing strategic culture (whether at the organizational, societal, or systemic levels).
3. The ends and means for achieving the culturally endorsed outcome (rejecting or adhering to international WMD norm adherence) are consistent with, or enabled

by, the "repertoire or palette of adaptive responses" deemed appropriate by the keepers or holders of that strategic culture.

In a study that explicitly addressed the cultural basis for compliance with the international nuclear nonproliferation regime, authors Glenn Chafetz, Hillel Abramson, and Suzette Grillot compared Ukrainian and Belarussian attitudes toward acceding to the Nuclear Nonproliferation Treaty (NPT) immediately following the collapse of the Soviet Union, and the emergence of these states as independent nations.[9] They found that differing Ukrainian and Belarussian role conceptions followed in part from cultural differences between the two states. Ukraine's greater perceived distinctiveness from Russia, as well as its Cossak tradition, versus Belarus' greater willingness to accommodate international desires, determined how these two countries approached the question of whether they should accede to the NPT as nuclear weapon states or as nonnuclear weapon states. Both had tactical and strategic nuclear assets on their territories at the time of the breakup of the Soviet Union, and both faced the decision of whether to give up these assets, or to embrace them as new nuclear powers. The international community, including the United States, was keen to have both nations forego their nuclear status, transfer the weapons on their territories to Russia, and accede to the NPT as nonnuclear weapon states, thus preserving the core international value of nonproliferation. Allowing Ukraine and Belarus (and Kazakhstan) to retain nuclear weapons would have meant expanding the nuclear club.

Chafetz, Abramson, and Grillot concluded that

> Belarus was consistently and overwhelmingly culturally disposed to accommodative roles and thus destined to meet international expectations. For Ukraine, however, decisions were more problematic because certain physical attributes and cultural features impelled it to see itself as a great power modeled after France and Russia. This national role conception in turn justified nuclear status.[10]

Hence, Ukraine was reluctant to relinquish its nuclear weapon assets, while Belarus was more easily convinced to do so. The authors show that cultural factors, as reflected in how culture shaped national role conceptions, was an important determinant of how these two nations approached a specific international norm adherence issue.

Negative experiences with the international community can also affect a state's confidence in the ability of international norms and regimes to protect its interests, or defend it against violators, thus predisposing it to reject adherence to such regimes or norms. This was the case with Iran's experience during its eight-year-long war with Iraq, when the international community seemed aloof and unresponsive to Iran's complaints about Iraq's use of chemical weapons. Consequently, Iranian leaders have lost confidence in international collective security mechanisms. Not only can such experiences lead to lack of confidence in international regimes, it can serve as a pretext for pursuing the acquisition of an independent deterrent. According to Anthony Cain, "The conspicuous failure of the international community to act against Iraq's overt use of chemical weapons in the [Iran–Iraq] war served as a catalyst for the Iranian chemical and biological weapons program."[11]

Even in cases where strategic culture exerts powerful sway over a nation's policies and behaviors, that influence can sometimes be overturned or rationalized, or the culture itself can change and evolve. Painful national experiences can exert strong pressure on a country to deviate from or even reject strategic cultural preferences, leading to the emergence of a new strategic culture. For example, Iranian strategic culture initially predisposed the regime to forego the acquisition and employment of chemical weapons, based on Prophet Mohammed's prohibition against using poison. This was a natural reflection of its strategic culture. However, after the Iranians suffered horrific losses from Iraqi chemical attacks during the Iran–Iraq War, accompanied by the failure of the international community to effectively act against or intervene with Iraq, Ayatollah Khomeini reversed this policy. According to Cain, "the decision emerged only after the international community failed to take action to condemn or curb Iraq's use of such weapons and after intense debates within Iran between Khomeini, the military, and the clerics."[12]

Unfortunately, this decision created the conditions for a revised strategic cultural acquiescence, or even justification, for the future acquisition of nuclear and biological, as well as chemical weapons. Cain observes: "Thus, a fundamentally secular decision based upon military effectiveness calculations had to pass through the filter of Islamic law to acquire the mantle of legitimacy. With the debate settled, however, the republic's leaders relied upon the new religious precedent to justify future nuclear, chemical, and biological weapons proliferation."[13]

Different schools of thought that define the relationship between Islamic and non-Islamic international law exist with Islamic cultures.[14] In some cases, these traditions reject the legitimacy of international legal structures created outside the Islamic world, or in cases where international law has not served the interests of the Islamic community or its members. The current Iranian regime may feel less constrained by its legal obligations under the NPT because this obligation had been undertaken by the Shah's regime in 1970, prior to the Iranian revolution, and is probably seen, therefore, as not necessarily binding on the new government, as having been undertaken by an illegitimate regime, or as having been superseded by a superior (sharia) law.

Strategic Culture and the Acquisition of WMD

There are many reasons why states may seek to acquire WMD, but from a strategic culture point of view, the question focuses on the domestic sources of such motivations, the strategic cultural filters through which recent experiences are processed, and the unique language used to justify such acquisition. According to the model, the following propositions seek to shed light on the nexus between WMD acquisition and strategic culture. Again, these propositions are offered in the spirit of prospective guidelines for further research, rather than as fully developed theses.

WMD acquisition is more likely to occur when:

1. Acquiring WMD is deemed rational within the system of shared meaning defined by the prevailing strategic culture, as sanctioned or endorsed by the keepers or holders of the strategic culture. That is, adopting a decision to acquire chemical, biological, or nuclear weapons can be deemed a rational course in terms understood, accepted, and endorsed by members of the strategic culture, and the costs and benefits of such a policy are deemed acceptable and bearable, where both "costs" and "benefits," as well as trade-offs between them, are perceived and calculated in culturally endowed ways.
2. Acquiring WMD is perceived by the holders or keepers of the strategic culture as enabling the group, organization, or state to achieve culturally endorsed outcomes, or results deemed appropriate by the prevailing strategic culture (whether at the organizational, societal, or systemic levels), such as granting it the means to defend

against its perceived enemies, or bestowing the prestige considered necessary to underwrite the strategic culture's established self-appointed regional, global, or systemic role conceptions.

3. The ends and means for achieving the culturally endorsed outcome (acquiring WMD) are consistent with, or enabled by, the "repertoire or palette of adaptive responses" deemed appropriate by the keepers or holders of that strategic culture. For example, a strategic culture may provide the rationale for leaders to pursue acquiring WMD through imposing enormous deprivations on the given society.

There are some other considerations with respect to strategic culture and the acquisition of WMD. First, except for the so-called P-5 nations whose status as nuclear weapon states is codified in the NPT, any other state's efforts to acquire nuclear weapons must be considered contrary to international law and international normative prohibitions against nuclear proliferation. For chemical and biological weapons, there are no equivalents to the P-5, since international agreements completely ban such weapons, while making no exceptions for states already possessing stockpiles of chemical and/or biological weapons. This means that acquiring WMD necessarily requires either violating (in the case of erstwhile adherents to the NPT, Chemical Weapons Convention, or Biological Weapons Convention), or rebuffing (in the case of those states who are technically not signatories or adherents to these treaties and conventions) international norms against WMD proliferation.[15]

Second, nearly every state that has initiated efforts to acquire a nuclear weapons capability (while outside the NPT regime) has made the decision to do so in the immediate aftermath of some national defeat, humiliation, or other crisis. For example, it seems Israel did so in the aftermath of the 1967 war. Pakistan apparently made its decision soon after the 1971 civil war that resulted in splitting the country, partly in response to India's threat to "go nuclear." Note the context of this decision as described by George Perkovich:

> It is difficult to say precisely when Pakistan's nuclear quest began. We do know that the first Indian nuclear test in 1974 did not start Pakistan on its quest, as Pakistani propagandists used to insist. A seminal episode was the January 1972 meeting in the Chief Minister of Punjab's home in Multan, where Prime Minister Zulfikar Ali Bhutto reportedly exhorted a gathering of Pakistan's nuclear technology establishment to produce a fission bomb in three years, as the Americans had with the Manhattan Project.[16]

Of course, these decisions are clearly driven by considerations of realpolitik, and involve the classic realist mechanisms of balancing either externally or internally against a systemic threat. But from a strategic culture point of view, the threats were perceived in uniquely cultural and historic terms, and interpreted in ways understood throughout the community or society involved, and the terms used to justify the state's subsequent course of action were couched in its own unique strategic cultural language. For example, Iranian public statements have sometimes cited Iranian "culture" as one reason its leaders continue to publicly reject the pursuit of nuclear weapons as a national objective. The commander of the Iranian Revolutionary Guard Corps rejected the pursuit of nuclear weapons in a 1994 interview saying, "Political logic, morality, our own culture and above all the situation in today's world does not allow us to have such deadly weapons."[17]

Third, a nation or society must be predisposed to resort to technological solutions to security dilemmas, even when faced with serious threats. That is, it must value science and technology, and have a cadre of personnel trained and educated in the engineering and physics of WMD. The decision to acquire WMD must be made in the context of having the technological wherewithal to pursue that option. Sometimes this means establishing a long-term plan to achieve access to the WMD materials, technology, or required expertise. Sometimes it means exploiting existing national capabilities and resources, other times it means acquiring it through theft or extortion. But from a strategic culture point of view, not all countries are capable of or willing to mount a WMD acquisition program.

Fourth, intervening international political developments may be interpreted as enhancing the symbolic appeal of nuclear weapons acquisition. Anthony Cain notes: "As for nuclear and radiological weapons, the respect India and Pakistan gained after demonstrating their nuclear capabilities is unlikely to have escaped notice in Tehran."[18] "Respect" is a culturally loaded concept, and is likely to be interpreted through a cultural lens, rather than a realpolitik lens.

Strategic Culture and WMD Transfer/Proliferation

Once a state or group has acquired WMD, they may face powerful incentives to sell the technology or expertise to other states or groups, possibly to recoup the investment in acquiring it, or possibly to accrue allies in a common cause, or for the personal gain of its leaders. How might strategic culture influence a state or non-state actor's motivations regarding proliferating WMD? According to the model developed earlier, proliferation of acquired WMD is more likely to occur when:

1. Proliferating WMD is deemed rational within the system of shared meaning defined by the prevailing strategic culture, as sanctioned or endorsed by the keepers or holders of the strategic culture. That is, proliferation is seen as acceptable, or at least not proscribed, by the strategic culture.
2. Proliferating WMD is perceived by the holders or keepers of the strategic culture as enabling the group, organization, or state to achieve culturally endorsed outcomes, or outcomes deemed appropriate by the prevailing strategic culture (whether at the organizational, societal, or systemic levels).
3. The ends and means for achieving the culturally endorsed outcome (proliferating WMD) are consistent with, or enabled by, the "repertoire or palette of adaptive responses" deemed appropriate by the keepers or holders of that strategic culture.

There are several reasons why a state or non-state actor may choose to proliferate WMD. If a given strategic culture defies international norms and predisposes a state to seek counterbalancing allies, that state may believe that selling or transferring WMD technology or expertise is in its interests (e.g., North Korea). Alternatively, if a state has a culture that fosters independent actions or permits rogue players within its ranks, it may be predisposed to allow or overlook private efforts to sell or transfer WMD technology (e.g., the AQ Khan network). Another reason a state may choose to sell its WMD technology or expertise to raise funds as compensation for international isolation. Finally, a group or state may choose to sell or transfer WMD in order to destabilize or distract regional adversaries. Each of these reasons represents a strong realist calculation. However, each may also reflect a cultural perspective in terms of how the decision to transfer or proliferate WMD is justified within its own culture, and how that decision is represented to outside groups.

Strategic Culture and the Use of WMD

The decision to acquire WMD does not necessarily equate with a decision to employ it.[19] There are many reasons to acquire and possess WMD, just as there are many ways to "use" them. Therefore, even if a given strategic culture provides the rationale for acquiring or proliferating WMD, it may at the same time present strong inhibitions against the use of such WMD. Throughout the Cold War, WMD were developed, produced, and stockpiled mainly to serve as instruments of deterrence, but that may not necessarily be the case for new and emerging strategic cultures. Among traditional powers, there is a strong practice of assuming that WMD will only be used as weapons of "last resort," reinforced by international law and practice, as well as long-standing international norms. This is the basis of what is sometimes called "the presumption of non-use," or in the case of nuclear weapons, the "nuclear taboo."

Strategic culture may shape or influence the circumstances under which a state or group considers WMD use acceptable, appropriate, justified, or permissible. According to the model, employment of a group or state's WMD is more likely to occur when:

1. Employment of WMD is deemed rational within the system of shared meaning defined by the prevailing strategic culture, as sanctioned or endorsed by the keepers or holders of the strategic culture.
2. Employment of WMD is perceived by the holders or keepers of the strategic culture as enabling the group, organization, or state to achieve culturally endorsed outcomes, or outcomes deemed appropriate by the prevailing strategic culture (whether at the organizational, societal, or systemic levels).
3. The ends and means for achieving the culturally endorsed outcome (employment of WMD) are consistent with, or enabled by, the "repertoire or palette of adaptive responses" deemed appropriate by the keepers or holders of that strategic culture.

There are few examples of the actual use of WMD in attacks. Chemical weapons, which have been used on several occasions, may be an exception, as are the small number of instances where biological agents have been employed. Therefore, with respect to evaluating the interaction of strategic culture and WMD use, it may be necessary to distinguish between chemical and biological weapons on the one hand, and nuclear weapons on the other.

To understand the potential relationship between strategic culture and the use of WMD, it is useful to lay out possible reasons or strategies for conducting attacks with WMD. Barry Schneider has identified five possible strategies for using WMD[20]:

1. To fracture an allied coalition, by threatening one or more members of that coalition in a way that forces them to stand down or withdraw from the coalition. This was Iraq's strategy in the first Gulf War, for example, in attacking Israel with ballistic missiles.
2. To attack or defeat the United States at home. Threatening the United States with high casualties could undermine the credibility of U.S. extended deterrence guarantees, or erode public support of a war effort.
3. Defeat or decimate a U.S. expeditionary force that threatened to occupy or overwhelm a local or regional defense.

4. "Secure the endgame." Use as bargaining leverage to allow a leader to remain in power despite impending military defeat, for example, or to secure some other post-conflict arrangement.
5. To avenge the defeat of a regime, or to inflict punishment on the aggressor.

Anthony Cain describes two scenarios under which the Iranian government would consider resorting to chemical or biological weapons attack as "appropriate," and thus falling within the model's assumptions regarding what the culture deems as rational and "justified." One scenario would be as a defensive response to an external threat, or retaliation for an attack. The second scenario would involve an offensive operation, possibly carried out through terrorist proxies, with the objective "to energize a global or, at least, a regional Islamist bid for power."[21] In either case, Iranian strategic culture would provide the rationale or justification for such a decision in ways that have special meaning for internal audiences that shared the cultural vocabulary, even if external audiences did not understand or accept these explanations.

Recommendations for Further Study

Strategic culture captures the domestic sources of foreign and defense policy behavior in ways that other theories of behavior cannot. Nevertheless, an approach based on strategic culture analysis should not be seen as competing with other well-established analytical models for explaining group or national behavior, such as neorealism, or constructivism. Rather, these respective approaches should each be seen as contributing insights and explanatory value in different ways to different issues, and at different times.

This conceptual model has further explained strategic culture as consisting of three different aspects: (1) strategic culture as "shared system of meaning"; (2) strategic culture as "collection of value preferences"; and (3) strategic culture as "template for human action."

The preceding analysis, as preliminary as it may be, suggests three main considerations for further research and analysis.

First, the model presented in this essay should be elaborated and expanded with respect to historical case studies related to WMD. Strategic culture as a "system of shared meaning" should be explored. The idea that strategic culture represents a "collection of value preferences" needs to be developed. The culturally endorsed options that comprise strategic culture as a template for human action could be elucidated. To do this, more in-depth case studies and analytical efforts will need to be devised to focus on WMD specific decisions. This would include, for example, exploring the motivations and intentions behind the decisions of different countries to acquire WMD (Israel, India, Pakistan, and North Korea present especially intriguing examples). A series of case studies could be developed to examine strategic culture as manifested within and among non-state actors.

Second, more study is needed to explore the relationship between strategic culture and the specific national security missions of assure, dissuade, deter, and defeat. The preceding essay has endeavored to set forth some preliminary hypotheses, but these need further empirical and analytical examination. Further research and analysis into the linkages between strategic culture and other national security issues should be undertaken. For example, using a strategic cultural framework can almost certainly provide useful insights into:

- Threat assessment and threat anticipation. Strategic culture may help sort out which societies pose long-term threats.
- Understanding and confronting terrorism. The sources and motivations for terrorism are a subject of critical debate. Strategic culture may provide some understanding of the basis for terrorism.
- Democracy, negotiating style, predisposition to conform to international norms, laws, and regimes.
- Surprise attack.

Third, there is a case to be made for breaking out "nuclear weapons" into a special strategic cultural category. While this essay has generally treated "weapons of mass destruction" as a single category, drawing insights from instances related to chemical, biological, and nuclear weapons, there are some reasonable arguments for distinguishing between chemical, biological, and nuclear weapons with regard to strategic culture. Not all strategic cultures lump these three types of weapons together into the same category. In some cases, strategic cultures make a distinction between chemical and biological weapons on the one hand, and consider nuclear weapons to be an altogether different issue on the other. Chemical and biological weapons use may be justified under some circumstances when nuclear weapons use cannot be condoned. Iranian strategic culture, for example, came to justify chemical weapons acquisition and use because these weapons had been used against Iranian citizens and soldiers. The same cannot be said of nuclear weapons.

Moreover, some states have had battlefield experiences with chemical and biological weapons, while only one state has been the subject of a nuclear weapon attack.

Finally, chemical weapons, and to some extent, biological weapons, have been around much longer than nuclear weapons, and states and non-state actors have had more history with these weapons. Chemical and biological weapons are cheaper and easier to acquire, need much less infrastructure, and exploit dual-use materials to a greater extent than nuclear weapons. They represent a lower technological threshold for acquisition.

Conclusion

This chapter presented a conceptual model for organizing further research and analysis into strategic culture, especially with respect to WMD-related decisions, behaviors, and policies. This model consists of three sets of propositions within each of the four WMD decision matrices: rejecting or adhering to international norms regarding the acquisition, proliferation, or use of WMD; acquiring WMD; proliferating WMD; and actually using WMD in an attack.

Strategic culture can be a powerful tool for understanding the reasons, incentives, rationales, and motivations of different cultures to acquire, proliferate, or employ WMD. Strategic culture analysis should be considered a supplement, and not a substitute, for traditional analyses based on realism. There are specific types of circumstances where realism is an inadequate explanation, or a poor predictor of behavior, and this is especially true with regard to understanding motivation and intent. However, as the model presented earlier makes clear, further work is needed to explore the explanatory value of strategic culture analysis, and the areas of intersection and divergence between strategic culture and other models of social and political behavior.

NOTES

1. For a recent exploration of U.S. strategic culture and nuclear weapons with an explicit focus on the organizational level, see Lynn Eden, *Whole World on Fire: Organizations, Knowledge, & Nuclear Weapons Devastation* (Ithaca, NY: Cornell University Press, 2004).
2. Paul Bernstein, "Primer on WMD," prepared for the DTRA/ASCO project on Comparative Strategic Culture. See also W. Seth Carus, *Defining "Weapons of Mass Destruction,"* National Defense University Center for the Study of Weapons of Mass Destruction Occasional Paper 4, January 2006.
3. I use the term "decision matrices" because, of course, in any given case, it may not be a question of a single decision, but a series of decisions that eventually lead to a significant policy direction. Even the term "decision" may not be accurate in all cases, especially where there is little or no evidence of a specific decision, but where this analysis may be more concerned with general behaviors, certain actions, or stated or implicit policies that are reflected in how a nation or group acts toward or thinks about WMD, or may be expected to act, based on the hypotheses developed in this essay.
4. This report can be found at http://www.acq.osd.mil/dsb/reports/2004–09-Strategic_Communication.pdf, accessed October 7, 2006.
5. Hudson cites two books by Amartya Sen, *Choice, Welfare, and Measurement* (Cambridge, MA: MIT Press, 1982); and *On Ethics and Economics* (New York: Basil Blackwell, 1987).
6. For a discussion of how and why U.S. culture inherently causes friction with other cultures, including with those we consider our friends and allies, see Andrew W. Stewart, "Friction in U.S. Foreign Policy: Cultural Difficulties with the World," Carlisle: U.S. Army Strategic Studies Institute, June 2006. This report can be found at: http://www.strategicstudiesinstitute.army.mil/pdffiles/PUB706.pdf, accessed October 7, 2006.
7. Drawn from Valerie M. Hudson, "Culture and Foreign Policy: Developing a Research Agenda," in Valerie M. Hudson, ed., *Culture and Foreign Policy* (Boulder Co: Lynne Rienner, 1997), pp. 1–24.
8. Ibid., p. 9.
9. Glenn Chafetz, Hillel Abramson, and Suzette Grillot, "Culture and National Role Conceptions: Belarussian and Ukrainian Compliance with the Nuclear Nonproliferation Regime," in Hudson, ed., *Culture and Foreign Policy*, p. 183.
10. Ibid., p. 181.
11. Anthony C. Cain, "Iran's Strategic Culture and Weapons of Mass Destruction," *Maxwell Paper No. 26*, Air War College, Maxwell Air Force Base, Alabama, April 2002, p. 14.
12. Ibid.
13. Ibid., p. 5. See also Julian Perry Robinson and Jozef Goldblat, *Chemical Warfare in the Iraq–Iran War* (Stockholm International Peace Research Institute, 1984). This report can be found at: http://www.iranchamber.com/history/articles/chemical_warfare_iran_iraq_war.php, accessed October 9, 2006.
14. See the various traditions surveyed in Majid Khadduri, *The Islamic Law of Nations* (Baltimore: Johns Hopkins University Press, 1966).
15. In a survey of those states who are known to have undertaken nuclear weapon development programs, and either abandoned them at some point prior to actually producing a weapon, or later rolled back their nuclear programs, authors Chafetz, Abramson, and Grillot label several states as "violators" of international nonproliferation regimes, such as Israel. This is not technically correct except in those cases where the state in question had previously signed and acceded to the NPT (For example, Israel has never joined the NPT, and thus has

never assumed the legal obligations of an NPT member-state, but is labeled a "violater" of the NPT by Chafetz, Abramson, and Grillot.) A state that has neither signed nor ratified an agreement cannot be said later to have "violated" that agreement. Nevertheless, even those states that have not acceded to NPT membership while pursuing nuclear weapons acquisition can be said to rebuff the international nonproliferation regime because there is an established international "norm" against proliferation. See Chafetz, Abramson, and Grillot, "Culture and National Role Conceptions," especially pp. 170–72.

16. George Perkovich, "Could Anything Be Done to Stop Them?: Lessons from Pakistan," A Paper for the Nonproliferation Policy Education Center, found at http://www.npec-web.org/Essays/20060726-Perkovich-CouldAnythingBeDone.pdf, accessed October 7, 2006.

17. Cited in Paula A. DeSutter, *Denial and Jeopardy: Deterring Iranian Use of NBC Weapons* (Washington, D .C.: National Defense University Press, 1997), p. 45.

18. Cain, "Iran's Strategic Culture," p. 17.

19. This issue is addressed with respect to terrorist acquisition of nuclear weapons in Lewis A. Dunn, "Can Al Queda be Deterred from Using Nuclear Weapons?" *Occasional Paper* 3, Center for the Study of Weapons of Mass Destruction, Washington, D. C., National Defense University Press, July 2005.

20. Barry R. Schneider, "Strategies for Coping with Enemy Weapons of Mass Destruction," *Airpower Journal* (Special Edition 1996), pp. 36–47, cited in Craig Black, "Deterring Libya: The Strategic Culture of Muammar Qaddafi," *The Counterproliferation Papers*, Future Warfare Series No. 8 (USAF Counterproliferation Center: Maxwell Air Force Base, Alabama), October 2000, pp. 14–15. This monograph is based on a chapter in the following: Barry R. Schneider and Jerold M. Post, *Know Thy Enemy: Profiles of Adversary Leaders and Their Strategic Culture* (Maxwell Air Force Base, Alabama: USAF Counterproliferation Center, November 2002), pp. 247–70.

21. Cain, "Iran's Strategic Culture," p. 11.

5

U. S. Strategic and Organizational Subcultures

Thomas G. Mahnken

The notion that there is a connection between a society and its strategic culture has a long and distinguished pedigree. In his history of the Peloponnesian War, Thucydides records that the Spartan king Archidamus and the Athenian *strategos* Pericles each linked the capabilities of their military to the constitution of their state.[1] Writing more than 2,400 years later, Julian Corbett drew a distinction between the German or "continental" and British or "maritime" schools of strategic thought, with the former focusing on war between land powers and the latter on a conflict between a sea power and a land power.[2] Basil H. Liddell-Hart refined Corbett's argument, noting that Britain had historically followed a distinctive approach to war by avoiding large commitments on land and using sea power to bring economic pressure to bear against its adversaries.[3]

A nation's strategic culture flows from its geography and resources, history and experience, and society and political structure.[4] It represents an approach that a given state has found successful in the past. Although not immutable, it tends to evolve slowly. It is no coincidence, for example, that Britain has historically favored sea power and indirect strategies, or that it has traditionally eschewed the maintenance of a large army. Israel's lack of geographic depth, its small but educated population, and technological skill have produced a strategic culture that emphasizes strategic preemption, offensive operations, initiative, and—increasingly—advanced technology.[5] Australia's liminal geopolitical status, its continental rather than maritime identity, and its formative military experiences have shaped its way of war.[6]

This case study examines the strategic culture of the United States. For obvious reasons, the strategic culture of the United States has received considerable attention. The United States is the world's most powerful nation, and will be for the foreseeable future. How the United States behaves affects not only its citizens, but also those across the globe. Understanding the strategic culture of the United States is important for friends, enemies, and neutrals.

What follows is an examination of American strategic culture on the level of the nation, the military, and the armed services. As a nation, American strategic culture was shaped by free security and imbued with exceptionalism. American strategic culture emphasizes liberal idealism and views war as a discontinuation of policy.

American military culture, the so-called American way of war, emphasizes direct strategies, an industrial approach to war, and firepower- and technology-intensive approaches to combat. The U.S. armed services, in turn, vary in their structure, dominant groups, and attitudes toward technology.

Strategic Culture Defined

This case study adopts the definition of strategic culture that was formulated for the 2006 Defense Threat Reduction Agency strategic culture project: "Strategic culture is that set of shared beliefs, assumptions, and modes of behavior, derived from common experiences and accepted narratives (both oral and written), that shape collective identity and relationships to other groups, and which determine appropriate ends and means for achieving security objectives."

This is a chapter specifically about American strategic culture. It is, in the words of Colin S. Gray, "That culture referring to modes of thought and action with respect to force, derived from perception of the national historical experience, aspiration for self-characterization . . . and from all of the many distinctively American experiences (of geography, political philosophy, of civic culture, and 'way of life') that characterize an American citizen."[7]

One of the central challenges facing the scholar of any state's strategic culture lies in determining which institutions serve as the keeper and transmitter of strategic culture. Is it the state? The military as a whole? Or some subset of the military? Another lies in identifying the content of strategic culture: the most salient beliefs and attitudes that comprise culture. Last but not least is the problem of determining the extent to which strategic culture, rather than power considerations, actually determines attitudes and behavior.[8]

This case study considers strategic culture on three levels: those of the nation, the military, and the military service. At the national level, strategic culture reflects a society's values regarding the use of force. At the military level, strategic culture (or a nation's "way of war") is an expression of how the nation's military *wants* to fight wars. Although practice does not have to conform to this desire, success in waging wars that run counter to national ways of war may come only after a period of painful adaptation. Finally, strategic culture at the service level represents the organizational culture of the particular service—those values, missions, and technologies that the institution holds dear.[9]

There are two reasons why it is worthwhile to examine culture on different levels explicitly. First, although military institutions generally reflect the societies that they defend, it cannot be assumed that they will mirror one another at all times. During the 1990s, for example, a number of scholars argued that the U.S. military was becoming less representative of American society in terms of its attitudes.[10] Second, as Clausewitz noted, there is often a tension (and generally a healthy one) between the military, the government, and the society as a whole. In his view, the military generally operates in the realm of probability and chance, whereas rationality and the people generally characterize the political leadership by passion.[11]

U.S. Strategic Culture

National Strategic Culture

Both geography and history have shaped American national strategic culture. Throughout most of America's history, the United States' insular position and weak neighbors to the north and south combined to provide free security. Shielded by the Atlantic and Pacific Oceans, and the Royal Navy, the United States grew to maturity in a benign environment. The fact that the United States did not have to exhaust itself by preparing for and waging wars against its neighbors separated it from other countries, particularly the European great powers. American insularity and the existence of free security bred the view that war is a deviation from the norm of peace. American strategic culture was shaped by long periods of peace punctuated by intermittent conflicts—the War of 1812, the Civil War, World War I, and World War II—each defined as a crusade of good versus evil.

Free security, in turn, affected the American outlook on the world. As C. Vann Woodward wrote more than four decades ago, "Anxieties about security have kept the growth of optimism within bounds among other peoples…the relative absence of such anxieties in the past has helped, along with other factors, to make optimism a national philosophy in America."[12]

American strategic culture explicitly rejects the European tradition of power politics. Rather, from its founding Americans have seen themselves as exceptional. This exceptionalism has influenced the way the United States deals with others. As Walter Lippmann observed, American strategic culture "does not recognize that America is one nation among many other nations with whom it must deal as rivals, as allies, as partners." Rather, "an aggression is an armed rebellion against the universal and eternal principles of the world society. No war can end rightly, therefore, except by the unconditional surrender of the aggressor nation and by the overthrow and transformation of its political regime."[13]

The impulse to transform the international system in the service of liberal democratic ideals forms a strand that runs throughout American history. The Clinton administration's national security strategy of engagement and enlargement and the George W. Bush administration's commitment to spreading democracy, expressed most eloquently in his second inaugural address, have more in common with one another than either administration's supporters would care to admit.[14]

Much of America's Cold War foreign policy elite, steeped in the history of European power politics and schooled in the realist tradition, saw America's exceptionalism and idealism as dangerous. George Kennan, in his lectures on American diplomacy delivered in 1950, argued that the American approach to international relations was characterized by excessive "moralism and legalism" that led to the tendency to launch crusades against evil. As Kennan put it, "A war fought in the name of high moral principle finds no early end short of some form of total domination."[15]

Americans have often conceived of interstate war not as a continuation of policy, in Clausewitz's famous formulation, but as a symptom of its breakdown. J.C. Wylie was reflecting a widely held American view when he wrote:

> Is war in fact a continuation of policy? For us, I think not. War for a nonaggressor nation is actually a nearly complete collapse of policy. Once war comes, then nearly all prewar policy is utterly invalid because the setting in which it was designed to function no longer corresponds with the facts of reality. When war comes, we at once move into a radically different world.[16]

Similarly, the U.S. Army's 1936 textbook on strategy held that "Politics and strategy are radically and fundamentally things apart. Strategy begins where politics end. All that soldiers ask is that once the policy is settled, strategy and command shall be regarded as being in a sphere apart from politics."[17] Americans have, in other words, tended to think astrategically.[18]

The combination of the rejection of power politics and discontinuity between policy and strategy has yielded a dichotomy in American strategic culture: although Americans are basically peace loving, when aroused they mobilize the nation's human and material resources behind in the service of high-intensity operations. Samuel Huntington saw America's ferocity in war as the flip side of liberal pacifism outside of war. As he put it:

> The American tends to be an extremist on the subject of war: he either embraces war wholeheartedly or rejects it completely. This extremism is required by the nature of the liberal ideology. Since liberalism deprecates the moral validity of the interests of the state in security, war must be either condemned as incompatible with liberal goals or justified as an ideological movement in support of those goals. American thought has not viewed war in the conservative–military sense as an instrument of national policy.[19]

The United States has thus displayed a strong and long-standing predilection for waging war for unlimited political aims.[20] During the Civil War, President Abraham Lincoln and General Ulysses S. Grant fought to utterly defeat the Confederacy. During World War I, General John J. Pershing, the commander of the American Expeditionary Force, favored a policy of unconditional surrender toward Imperial Germany even as President Woodrow Wilson sought a negotiated end to the conflict.[21] During World War II Franklin D. Roosevelt and his commanders were of one mind that the war must lead to the overthrow of the German, Japanese, and Italian governments that had started the war. In the current war against jihadist extremists there is no sentiment for anything approaching a negotiated settlement.

Just as Americans have preferred a fight to the finish, so too have they been uncomfortable with wars for limited political aims. In both the Korean and Vietnam wars, American military leaders were cool to the idea of fighting merely to restore or maintain the status quo. Indeed, Douglas MacArthur likened anything short of total victory over communist forces on the Korean peninsula to "appeasement."[22] Similarly, the standard explanation of American failure in Vietnam—and the one most popular among U.S. military officers—is that the U.S. military would have won the war were it not for civilian interference.[23]

Americans have tended to cast their wars as crusades against evil. As Samuel Huntington put it, "For the American a war is not a war unless it is a crusade."[24] Of course, such an attitude has strong historical roots: during the twentieth century the United States fought a series of despotic regimes, from Hitler's Germany and Kim Il-Sung's North Korea to Saddam Hussein's Iraq and Slobodan Milosevic's Serbia. However, there has always been a clear tension between the need to rally the public in support of the use of force and the need to pursue limited aims. Political leaders who demonized America's adversaries often faced a backlash when the United States did not continue the war to the finish. Advisors to President George H.W. Bush, for example, bristled at his comparisons of Saddam Hussein to Adolf Hitler, fearing that it would complicate the conduct of the 1991 Gulf War.[25]

The United States has similarly encountered difficulty when it has fought adversaries who at least appear less than demonic. Although Ho Chi Minh presided over a brutal communist government, North Vietnamese propaganda and American opponents of the war in Vietnam were able to portray him as a kindly "Uncle Ho," or even a latter-day George Washington. The United States is thus fortunate to have in its war on terror an adversary such as Osama bin Laden, an individual who viscerally hates the United States and all it stands for.

Military Strategic Culture

Just as Americans as a whole exhibit certain preferences when the United States goes to war, so too does the U.S. military. And like the features of American strategic culture, those of American military culture have been marked more by continuity than change.

The notion of a distinct American military culture, a definitive "American way of war," is inextricably linked to Russell Weigley's book of the same name.[26] In it, Weigley argued that since the American Civil War the U.S. armed forces have pursued a unique approach to combat, one favoring wars of annihilation through the lavish use of firepower. In his formulation, the main characteristics of the American way of war include aggressiveness at all levels of warfare, a quest for decisive battles, and a desire to employ maximum effort. The U.S. military has viewed "the complete overthrow of the enemy, the destruction of his military power, [as] the object of war."[27] By contrast, the American military has been uncomfortable waging war with constrained means for limited or ambiguous objectives. Weigley argued that "Americans, especially American soldiers" held a narrow definition of strategy that tended to "give little regard to the non-military consequences of what they were doing."[28]

Weigley's formulation, though influential, represents a narrow interpretation of American military history. As Brian M. Linn has noted, the U.S. armed forces have in fact favored strategies of attrition over annihilation. In addition, the United States has throughout its history pursued a much wider range of strategies than Weigley's formulation indicates, including deterrence and wars for limited aims.[29] Linn and others have noted that the U.S. military has a rich tradition of fighting small wars and insurgencies. Indeed, Max Boot went so far as to propose this tradition as an alternative American way of war.[30]

Linn and Boot both offer valid critiques of Weigley's interpretation of American military history. Weigley's formulation nonetheless stands up remarkably well as a portrayal of American military strategic culture and thus the *aspirations* of the U.S. military.

Another historical tendency has been a preference for the direct approach to strategy over the indirect. The U.S. military has throughout its history sought to close with and destroy the enemy at the earliest opportunity. As Colin S. Gray has put it, "Americans have favored the quest for swift victory through the hazards of decisive battle rather than the slower approach of maritime encirclement."[31] There is perhaps no better illustration of this tendency than the debate over strategy between the American and British governments during World War II. The U.S. military, led by Army Chief of Staff George C. Marshall, sought to concentrate forces for a cross-channel invasion at the earliest possible time. The British, by contrast, sought to encircle Axis-controlled Europe, allowing the Soviets to attrit German forces while the allies carried out a strategic bombing campaign and unconventional warfare in occupied Europe, postponing the invasion until it would be little more than a *coup de grace*.[32]

Coupled with a preference for direct strategies has been an industrial approach to war. During World War II, for example, the United States provided almost two-thirds of all Allied military equipment, building some 297,000 aircraft, 193,000 artillery pieces, 86,000 tanks, 2 million trucks, 8,800 naval vessels, and 87,000 landing craft. In its first year in the war, the United States out-produced the entire Axis in aircraft, tanks, and heavy guns.[33] During the Gulf War, U.S. strategic airlift assets alone moved 500,000 people and 540,000 tons of cargo—and only 5 percent of the materiel the United States employed in the war moved by air.[34] Over the past decade and a half, the United States has demonstrated the ability to organize and deploy large forces worldwide on short notice. Even peacekeeping operations such as Bosnia and Kosovo have involved considerable logistical support.

One characteristic that flows from the industrial approach is the lavish use of firepower. Contemporary accounts of the Battle of Mogadishu focused upon the fact that eighteen American servicemen lost their lives and eighty-three were wounded. Less remarked upon was the fact that at least 500 Somalis were killed and 1000 wounded in the same engagement.[35] During the major combat phase of the campaign against the Taliban and al Qaeda in Afghanistan, U.S. air forces delivered some 22,000 bombs—including some 12,500 precision-guided munitions (PGMs)—in support of U.S. Special Forces and the Northern Alliance.[36]

A firepower-intensive approach to war makes sense, at least from a certain point of view. The United States can certainly afford the expenditure of resources to conduct such an approach. Moreover, firepower often saves American lives. However, the Vietnam War showed how a reliance on firepower could prove dysfunctional in a counterinsurgency campaign. The lavish use of artillery and air power was irrelevant to the main problem of the war: how to cut the communist insurgency off from its base of popular support. If anything, the destruction caused by the strategy increased support for the communists.[37] Similarly, the profligate use of American firepower in Afghanistan threatens to weaken support for the United States—support that is vital to ensure the viability of the government of Afghanistan and reduce support for the Taliban.

Another characteristic of the American way of war is its emphasis on technology. No nation in recent history has valued the role of technology in planning and waging war more highly than the United States. World War II witnessed the wholesale mobilization of American science and technology, culminating in the detonation of the atomic bomb. Technology played an important role in America's conduct of the Cold War as well, as the United States sought to use its qualitative advantage to counterbalance the numerical superiority of the Soviet Union and its allies. America's post–Cold War conflicts in Iraq, the former Yugoslavia, and Afghanistan highlighted its technological edge over friend and foe alike.

Empirical research into the attitudes of U.S. officers shows them to be technological optimists by and large. A survey of some 1,900 officers attending U.S. professional military education institutions conducted in 2000 by this author and James R. FitzSimonds found that most officers believed new technology, doctrine, and organizations would make it easier for the United States to use force and achieve decisive battlefield victories. They also felt that advanced technology would allow the United States to engage in high-intensity operations with substantially reduced risk of casualties and that it would substantially reduce the duration of future conflicts.[38]

As Colin Gray has observed, strategic culture is neither good nor bad. Rather, it represents the context for strategic action. As he has written:

> The machine-mindedness that is so prominent in the dominant American "way of war" is inherently neither functional nor dysfunctional. When it inclines Americans to seek what amounts to a technological, rather than a political, peace, and when it is permitted to dictate tactics regardless of the political context, then on balance it is dysfunctional. Having said that, however, prudent and innovative exploitation of the technological dimension to strategy and war can be a vital asset.[39]

America's traditional reliance upon technology in war is certainly no recipe for success. Indeed, it is a poor substitute for strategic thinking. The United States lost in Vietnam despite enjoying a considerable technological edge—at least in most areas—over its adversaries because it failed to develop an adequate strategy to achieve its political objectives. During the 1990s, the U.S. government increasingly looked to technology, in the form of standoff air- and sea-launched PGMs, to solve problems—such as terrorism and ethnic violence—that were at their root political. Washington's penchant for advanced technology also fostered the illusion among some that the United States could use force without killing American soldiers and innocent civilians, and among America's enemies the impression that the United States was averse to sustaining casualties. Saddam Hussein, for one, saw high-technology warfare as a sign of American weakness rather than strength.[40]

A more recent, and more ambiguous, tendency has been a seeming American reluctance to incur casualties. The conventional wisdom is that the American public is very sensitive to losses. Many further argue that the willingness of the American public to sustain casualties has declined significantly since the end of the Cold War.[41]

In fact, the phenomenon of casualty aversion defies such a neat formulation. In many ways, a reluctance to put American troops in harm's way was a logical response to the circumstances of the 1990s. Throughout that decade the United States fought wars for interests that were secondary, even tertiary. The low stakes involved in Somalia made it perfectly rational to withdraw after the death of eighteen American servicemen during the Battle of Mogadishu. Moreover, the U.S. advantage in air power has allowed it to use force effectively without putting a large number of American lives at risk. NATO's air campaign over Kosovo was, after all, able to achieve the alliance's political objectives short of the introduction of ground forces. In such circumstances it made little sense to put American lives at risk unnecessarily.

But there is clearly more to it than that. Recent research appears to show that the military leadership and civilian decision makers are more casualty averse than the American public.[42] Indeed, the U.S. military has consistently sought to reduce casualties. The so-called Powell Doctrine emphasizes the use of overwhelming force against U.S. adversaries not due to political or strategic imperatives, but because of the belief that it will bring victory sooner while producing fewer U.S. casualties. Similarly, the military leadership has been one of the primary advocates of "force protection" measures to reduce the risk to U.S. forces. It is notable, for example, that two of the three metrics General Wesley Clark established to measure the effectiveness of Operation *Allied Force*, NATO's air war over Serbia, involved protecting allied forces rather than compelling Milosevic to quit Kosovo.[43]

Ironically, the military's concern over casualties appears to be stronger and more persistent than that of its civilian masters. For example, there is no evidence that the U.S. political leadership established the level of U.S. casualties as a criterion for the success of the campaign against al Qaeda and the Taliban in Afghanistan. However, it appears that the military's concern over casualties played a major role in shaping the campaign's conduct. Indeed, at least one observer has attributed the seeming unwillingness of U.S. Central Command to commit large numbers of U.S. ground forces to the Battle of Tora Bora to the military leadership's concern over casualties.[44]

Real or not, the notion that the United States is casualty averse has become fixed in the mind of both allies and adversaries. U.S. allies have expressed concern that U.S. sensitivity to fatalities will constrain future military operations. As a senior British officer wrote, "in future conflicts, the United Kingdom will have to work within, or possibly around, the constraints imposed by this American aversion to casualties."[45] Chinese defense analysts see American casualty sensitivity as a weakness that can be exploited.[46] However, this may prove to be a dangerous misperception. Indeed, the idea that the United States has a glass jaw is hardly new. Allies and adversaries should remind themselves of the United States' demonstrated ability to endure hardship and suffer punishment. They should recall not only the U.S. government's response to the Beirut barracks bombing and the Battle of Mogadishu, but also its reaction to the attacks on Pearl Harbor in 1941 and the World Trade Center and Pentagon in 2001.

Service Strategic Culture

Although American military strategic culture has well-defined features, each service also has its own unique culture, one shaped by its past and that, in turn, shapes its current and future behavior.[47] Service cultures are hard to change because they are the product of the acculturation of millions of service members over decades and are supported by a network of social and professional incentives. People join the Army, Navy, Air Force, and Marine Corps, not "the military" in the abstract. Service training and education strengthen that identity. They join because they identify—or want to identify—with a service's values and its culture. It is therefore not surprising that two decades after the passage of the Goldwater–Nichols Act, which sought to promote jointness, an officer's service affiliation remains the most important determinant of his views, more than rank, age, or combat experience.[48]

In many cases, service identity is more important to officers than branch identity. All aviators, for example, are not alike: Air Force pilots have cultural attitudes that differ significantly from those of their Navy counterparts.[49] Army infantrymen similarly have views that differ significantly from their Marine Corps counterparts.[50]

One example of the way in which service culture manifests itself is in attitudes toward technology. Not all elements of the U.S. military are equally reliant on technology. Because war at sea and in the air is by definition technology-intensive, the Navy and Air Force have tended to emphasize the role of technology in war. The Army and Marine Corps, by contrast, have tended to emphasize the human element. As the old saw goes, the Air Force and Navy talk about manning equipment, whereas the Army and Marine Corps talk about equipping the man. Not surprisingly, therefore, Army and Marine Corps officers tend to be somewhat more skeptical than their Air Force and Navy counterparts regarding the impact of technology on the character and conduct of war.[51]

The services also vary in terms of their structure and dominant groups. The Marine Corps and Air Force are "monarchical," with powerful service chiefs drawn from a single dominant subgroup, whereas the Army and Navy are "feudal," with less powerful chiefs drawn from a variety of subgroups.[52] Each also has its own "altars of worship"—those things that the institution values.[53] These characteristics, in turn, affect how the services approach technology and how technology affects the service.

The U.S. Marine Corps is a unitary, monarchical organization. The smallest of the services, it is also the most cohesive.[54] Its ethos is based on the notion that all Marines are the same and that every Marine is a rifleman. Despite the fact that the Marine Corps contains all combat arms—infantry, artillery, and armor—as well as an aviation component, only one of the last ten commandants of the Marine Corps has been a non-infantryman.[55]

Of the U.S. armed forces, the Marine Corps has the strongest commitment to tradition and the status quo, one reinforced by the deliberate, self-conscious study of history. It is, for example, the only service that teaches officers history as part of Officer Candidate School.

The Marine Corps' emphasis on tradition and conformity is manifest in the Marine uniform. Not surprisingly, it has changed the least since World War II of any service's uniform. It also reflects the service's ethic of conformity; with the exception of aviators, who wear gold flight wings on their chest, it is impossible to determine a Marine's specialty from his uniform.

Marines value technology the least of any service. In part, this is the result of a culture that puts the individual warrior at the center of warfare. It is also the result of the fact that as the smallest service, the Marine Corps has had the least money to devote to technology. Until very recently, the Marines let the Army and Navy develop the majority of their equipment, adopting and adapting it as necessary.

In contrast to the Marine Corps' monarchical structure, power in the Army is shared among the traditional combat arms: infantry, cavalry (today's armor), and artillery. Not surprisingly, the position of Army chief of staff tends to rotate among these combat arms. General Peter Schoomaker was the first Special Forces branch officer to head the Army; his most recent ten predecessors included four from the infantry, three from armor, and three from the artillery.[56]

Whereas service identity is paramount to the Marine, his Army counterpart attaches great importance to branch identity. The Army is, in Carl Builder's words:

> A mutually supportive brotherhood of guilds. Both words, *brotherhood* and *guilds*, are significant here. The combat arms or branches of the Army are guilds—associations of craftsmen who take the greatest pride in their skills, as opposed to their possessions or positions. The guilds are joined in a brotherhood because, like brothers, they have a common family bond (the Army) and a recognition of their dependency upon each other in combat.[57] (Emphasis in original)

Unlike the Marine uniform, an officer's branch identity is visible on the Army uniform.

The Army has tended to assimilate technology into its existing branch structure. The widespread adoption of the helicopter, for example, did not spawn a new branch, but rather led to a redefinition of cavalry to include rotary-wing aircraft.

Army officers, like their Marine counterparts, frequently profess that technology plays a subordinate role in warfare. In fact, however, the U.S. Army has traditionally valued advanced technology. Indeed, Army leaders have consistently seen advanced technology as a comparative advantage over potential foes. Whereas the Marine Corps sought to adapt itself to the advent of nuclear weapons, for example, the Army wholeheartedly embraced the weapons.

Technology is inherently more important to naval forces than to ground forces. Navies operate in an environment that is intrinsically hostile, and sailors from time immemorial have depended on naval technology to protect them from the elements. This has produced an attitude that recognizes the importance of technology but also prizes the tried-and-true over the novel.

The twentieth century witnessed the Navy's evolution from a monarchical to a feudal organization. At the dawn of the twentieth century, navies were synonymous with surface fleets. During the twentieth century, however, the development of naval aviation and submarine forces changed the structure of the Navy fundamentally. Whereas the Army has tended to assimilate new ways of war into existing branches, the Navy responded to the advent of aircraft and submarines by adding new branches and career paths. As a result, the dominant communities in the Navy are surface, submarine, and aviation. These three branches collectively control the Navy: of the last ten chiefs of naval operations, four have been aviators, three surface warfare officers, and three submariners.[58]

The Air Force had its origins in, and continues to be defined by, the technology of manned flight. The Air Force is divided into pilots and non-pilots and between different communities of pilots. Even though combat pilots make up less than one-fifth of the Air Force, they are the ones who have dominated the service since its inception.[59] From 1947 to 1982, the Air Force chief of staff was always a bomber pilot; since 1982, the Air Force chief of staff has always been a fighter pilot.

STRATEGIC CULTURE IN ACTION

National, military, and service strategic culture has affected the way the United States has approached WMD, and nuclear weapons in particular.

National Strategic Culture

Nuclear weapons have reinforced the long-standing view in the United States that there is a sharp dichotomy between peace and war. Since early in the Cold War, the dominant view expressed by both civilian strategists and military officers has been that nuclear weapons are first and foremost weapons of deterrence. As George Kennan put it in 1961:

> The atom has simply served to make unavoidably clear what has been true all along since the day of the introduction of the machine gun and the internal combustion engine into the techniques of warfare . . . that modern warfare in the grand manner, pursued by all available means and aimed at the total destruction of the enemy's capability to resist, is . . . of such general destructiveness that it ceases to be useful as an instrument for the achievement of any coherent political purpose.[60]

In other words, the use of nuclear weapons cannot serve as a continuation of policy.

Beyond the basic view of nuclear weapons as deterrents has been the development and growth of a strong American taboo against their use. As Nina Tannenwald has observed, "Nuclear weapons have come to be defined as abhorrent and unacceptable weapons of mass destruction, with a taboo on their use."[61]

Thomas Schelling attributes the nuclear taboo to "a belief, or a feeling—a feeling somewhat beyond reach by analysis—that nuclear weapons were simply different." Reinforcing this was the belief that "nuclear weapons, once introduced into combat, could not, or probably would not, be contained, confined, or limited."[62] In his view, the nuclear taboo has affected not only nuclear weapons, but also other "peaceful nuclear explosives" and nuclear power.

American leaders regarded nuclear weapons as different militarily, politically, and psychologically from other weapons almost from the beginning. Even before the Soviets acquired nuclear weapons, let alone achieved parity, American leaders believed that U.S. use of nuclear weapons would have severe long-term political consequences for the United States.[63]

The nuclear taboo was first identified during the early Eisenhower administration. At the time, it was seen as something that the U.S. government needed to counter.[64] Over time, however, the plausible range of uses for nuclear weapons has narrowed considerably. The actual practice of nonuse of nuclear weapons in crisis and war throughout the Cold War both reflected and bolstered the taboo,[65] as did nuclear nonuse during the Vietnam War.[66] As a result, uses of nuclear weapons that were once plausible, such as the use of tactical nuclear weapons on the battlefield or direct threats to employ nuclear weapons in order to deter conventional conflict, no longer appear legitimate.

During the 1990s, opposition to nuclear weapons grew into a movement to abolish them altogether. At the forefront of the movement were senior American officers and civil servants. For example, in a speech to the National Press Club in December 1996 General Lee Butler, the former commander in chief of U.S. Strategic Command, argued that

> nuclear weapons are inherently dangerous, hugely expensive, and militarily inefficient; that implacable hostility and alienation will almost certainly over time lead to a nuclear crisis; that the failure of nuclear deterrence would imperil not just the survival of the antagonists, but of every society; and that nuclear war is a raging, insatiable beast whose instincts and appetite we pretend to understand but cannot possibly control.[67]

For him, nuclear deterrence represented not a force for stability, but rather a catalyst for conflict. In his view, deterrence was "a formula for unmitigated catastrophe...premised on a litany of unwarranted assumptions, unprovable assertions and logical contradictions." In his eyes, "the threat to use nuclear weapons is indefensible."[68] He was dubious of the ability of nuclear weapons to deter the use of chemical or biological weapons by rogue states. He claimed, in short, that a world free from the threat of nuclear war had to be devoid of nuclear weapons.[69]

Although the 1990s witnessed repeated elite calls for nuclear abolition, public surveys portray a more complex picture. The results of several surveys of the American public show considerable skepticism regarding the feasibility of completely eliminating nuclear weapons. Rather, they demonstrate that the public sees continuing value in a smaller nuclear arsenal, little optimism about the effectiveness of nuclear deterrence in a more proliferated world, and a willingness to see nuclear weapons used to deter not only nuclear, but also chemical and biological use.[70]

American attitudes toward nuclear weapons also bear the mark of the U.S. tradition of liberal idealism. As announced by President Ronald Reagan on March 23, 1983, the Strategic Defense Initiative marked a fundamental shift in thinking from deterrence to defense:

> Let me share with you a vision of the future which offers hope. It is that we embark on a program to counter the awesome Soviet missile threat with measures that are defensive. Let us turn to the very strengths in technology that spawned our great industrial base and that have given us the quality of life we enjoy today.
>
> What if free people could live secure in the knowledge that their security did not rest upon the threat of instant U.S. retaliation to deter a Soviet attack, that we could intercept and destroy strategic ballistic missiles before they reached our own soil or that of our allies?
>
> I call upon the scientific community in our country, those who gave us nuclear weapons, to turn their great talents now to the cause of mankind and world peace, to give us the means of rendering these nuclear weapons impotent and obsolete.[71]

For Reagan, at least, strategic defense offered the prospect of absolute security in the liberal idealist tradition.

Military Strategic Culture

The way the U.S. military has dealt with nuclear weapons reflects its strategic culture as well. For example, nuclear weapons comport with the emphasis the American military has traditionally placed on advanced technology. Throughout the Cold War, the U.S. military viewed its technological edge, including its lead in nuclear technology, as a competitive advantage over the Soviet Union. Nuclear weapons were seen as a counterweight to Soviet quantitative conventional superiority. During the Carter and Reagan administrations, technology came to be seen as a key arena of superpower rivalry. The Strategic Defense Initiative, for example, represented an effort to use advanced U.S. technology to render obsolete the Soviet heavy missile force.

American planning for nuclear war also reflected the tendency of the U.S. military to think in terms of war for unlimited aims with total means. As both James Schlesinger and Albert Wohlstetter argued at different times, U.S. military planning was biased toward the massive use of nuclear weapons, rather than exploring the possibility of the discriminate use of such weapons.[72]

Service Strategic Culture

Although U.S. defense policy emphasized nuclear weapons throughout the Cold War, the attitudes of individual armed services toward the weapons was mixed. The Army, Navy, and Air Force all embraced nuclear weapons during the early Cold War, but their interest in them waned thereafter.

During the early Cold War, the U.S. Army in particular embraced nuclear weapons. Indeed, in many ways the Army was predisposed to them. There was a good fit between nuclear weapons and the Army's tradition of substituting technology for manpower and its reliance on firepower. It fielded a family of nuclear weapons that ranged from the *Davy Crockett* nuclear bazooka to the massive 280-mm nuclear cannon and the *Redstone* and *Jupiter* intermediate-range ballistic missiles. The Army viewed tactical nuclear weapons not so much as small strategic bombs, but as very powerful artillery.[73]

The Navy adopted not only nuclear weapons—first bombs for carrier-based aircraft, then cruise and ballistic missiles—but also nuclear propulsion for both submarines and surface ships. The Navy readily accepted nuclear propulsion for submarines because it fit comfortably within the identity of the submarine community. Indeed, Owen Coté has termed the nuclear submarine a "true submarine," "one that needed no umbilical cord to the surface and could remain completely submerged."[74]

Not surprisingly, the Air Force wholeheartedly embraced strategic nuclear bombing as its core mission. Bomber pilots dominated the Air Force as they had the Army Air Corps, and Strategic Air Command became the most powerful organization in the service. To many air power advocates, the advent of nuclear weapons seemed to validate the concept of strategic bombing that had animated aviators since the 1920s. The Air Force's embrace of strategic nuclear bombing yielded substantial dividends. During the 1950s, the U.S. Air Force garnered the lion's share of the defense budget. Nuclear-armed bombers, then nuclear-tipped missiles, became the coin of the realm.

During the late Cold War, however, the enthusiasm of each of the services for nuclear weapons diminished. The shift was most dramatic in the case of the Army. The service that had reorganized in the mid-1950s around the possibility of nuclear warfare had by the early 1960s gone back to an organizational structure that bore more than a passing resemblance to its World War II structure.[75] Although a portion of the Army's artillery branch drew its identity from nuclear weapons, atomic arms were peripheral to the identity of the other combat arms—armor and infantry. Moreover, nuclear weapons played no role in Vietnam War and became a less prominent feature of the Army's major planning contingency, a NATO–Warsaw Pact conflict in Central Europe.

Although nuclear weapons (and nuclear power) remained central to the identity of the Navy's submarine service, both became increasingly marginal to the identity of the surface navy and naval aviation. The last nuclear missile system to be deployed on surface ships, the BGM-109A *Tomahawk* Land Attack Missile-Nuclear (TLAM-N), was a program developed and advocated by Pentagon civilians. The missile the Navy really wanted was the BGM-109B *Tomahawk* Anti-Ship Missile.[76] Even the Air Force's interest in nuclear weapons began to wane as fighter pilots displaced bomber pilots at the head of the service's hierarchy.

Conclusion

The enduring features of American strategic culture, military culture, and the organizational culture of the U.S. armed services have influenced how the United States has approached nuclear weapons. As a result, American strategic culture has been dominated by continuity rather than change. Six decades after the advent of the nuclear age, what is notable is the limited enduring impact of nuclear weapons on the way the U.S. military conceives of war.

Notes

1. Robert B. Strassler, ed., *The Landmark Thucydides: A Comprehensive Guide to the Peloponnesian War* (New York: Free Press, 1996), pp. 45–46, 81–82.
2. Julian S. Corbett, *Some Principles of Maritime Strategy* (London: Longmans Green, 1911), p. 38.
3. Basil H. Liddell-Hart, *The British Way in Warfare* (New York: MacMillan, 1933).
4. Colin S. Gray, *Modern Strategy* (Oxford: Oxford University Press, 1999), chapter 5.
5. Michael I. Handel, "The Evolution of Israeli Strategy: The Psychology of Insecurity and the Quest for Absolute Security," in Williamson Murray, MacGregor Knox, and Alvin Bernstein, eds., *The Making of Strategy: Rulers, States, and War* (Cambridge: Cambridge University Press, 1994), pp. 534–78.
6. Michael Evans, *The Tyranny of Dissonance: Australia's Strategic Culture and Way of War, 1901–2005* (Canberra: Land Warfare Studies Center, 2005).
7. Colin S. Gray, "National Style in Strategy: The American Example," *International Security*, 6, no. 2 (Fall 1981), 22.
8. Alan Macmillan, Ken Booth, and Russell Trood, "Strategic Culture," in Ken Booth and Russell Trood, eds., *Strategic Cultures in the Asia-Pacific Region* (New York: St. Martin's, 1999), pp. 8–12.
9. As Edgar Schein puts it, organizational culture is "The pattern of basic assumptions that a given group has invented, discovered, or developed in learning to cope with its problems of external adaptation and internal integration, and that have worked well enough to be considered valid, and, therefore, to be taught to new members as the correct way to perceive, think, and feel in relation to those problems." Schein, "Coming to a New Awareness of Organizational Culture," *Sloan Management Review*, Vol. 25, No. 2 (Winter 1984), pp. 3.
10. See, e.g., Ole Holsti, "A Widening Gap Between the Military and Society? Some Evidence, 1976–1996," *International Security*, Vol. 23, No. 2 (Winter 1998–99), pp. 5–42; and

Peter D. Feaver and Richard H. Kohn, *Soldiers and Civilians: The Civil–Military Gap and American National Security* (Cambridge, MA: MIT Press, 2001).

11. Carl von Clausewitz, *On War*, ed. and trans. Michael Howard and Peter Paret (Princeton NJ: Princeton University Press, 1976), p. 89.

12. C. Vann Woodward, "The Age of Reinterpretation," *American Historical Review*, Vol. 66 (October 1960), pp. 6.

13. Walter Lippmann, *Public Opinion and Foreign Policy in the United States* (London: Allen and Unwin, 1952), pp. 25–26.

14. William J. Clinton, National Security Strategy of Engagement and Enlargement (Washington, D. C: White House, 1995) at http://www.dtic.mil/doctrine/jel/research_pubs/nss.pdf. "President Bush Sworn-In to Second Term" at http://www.whitehouse.gov/inaugural/ (accessed July 16, 2006).

15. George F. Kennan, *American Diplomacy: Expanded Edition* (Chicago: University of Chicago Press, 1984), p. 100.

16. J.C. Wylie, *Military Strategy: A General Theory of Power Control* (New Brunswick, NJ: Rutgers University Press, 1967), p. 80.

17. *The Principles of Strategy for an Independent Corps or Army in a Theater of Operations* (Ft. Leavenworth, KS: Command and General Staff School Press, 1936).

18. Colin S. Gray, "National Style in Strategy: The American Example," *International Security* Vol. 6, No. 2 (Fall 1981), p. 33.

19. Samuel P. Huntington, *The Soldier and the State: The Theory and Practice of Civil–Military Relations* (Cambridge, MA: Belknap Press, 1957), p. 151.

20. As Clausewitz wrote, "War can be of two kinds, in the sense that either the objective is to *overthrow the enemy*—to render him politically helpless or militarily impotent, thus forcing him to sign whatever peace we please; or *merely to occupy some of his frontier districts* so that we can annex them or use them for bargaining at the peace negotiations. Transitions from one type to the other will of course recur in my treatment; but the fact that the aims of the two types are quite different must be clear at all times, and their points of irreconcilability brought out" (emphasis in original). Von Clausewitz, *On War*, p. 69.

21. David R. Woodward, *Trial by Friendship: Anglo-American Relations, 1917–1918* (Lexington: University Press of Kentucky, 1993), pp. 213–14.

22. See the testimony of General Douglas MacArthur in Allen Guttmann, ed., *Korea: Cold War and Limited War*, 2nd ed. (New York: D.C. Heath, 1972).

23. For alternative views, see Eliot A. Cohen, *Supreme Command: Soldiers, Statesmen, and Leadership in Wartime* (New York: Free Press, 2002), pp. 175–84; Andrew Krepinevich, *The Army and Vietnam* (Baltimore: Johns Hopkins University Press, 1986).

24. Huntington, *The Soldier and the State*, p. 152.

25. George Bush and Brent Scowcroft, *A World Transformed* (New York: Knopf, 1998), p. 389.

26. Russell F. Weigley, *The American Way of War: A History of United States Military Strategy and Policy* (Bloomington: Indiana University Press, 1973). For a more critical appraisal of the "American way of war," see Colin S. Gray, "Strategy in the Nuclear Age: The United States, 1945–1991," in *The Making of Strategy*, pp. 579–613.

27. Weigley, *American Way of War*, xxi.

28. Ibid., xviii–xix.

29. Brian M. Linn, "*The American Way of War* Revisited," *Journal of Military History*, Vol. 66 No. 2 (April 2002), p. 501–33.

30. Max Boot, *The Savage Wars of Peace: Small Wars and the Rise of American Power* (New York: Basic Books, 2002).

31. Gray, "Strategy in the Nuclear Age," pp. 594–95.

32. Kent Roberts Greenfield, *American Strategy in World War II: A Reconsideration* (Malabar, FL: Krieger, 1982), Chapter two.

33. Richard Overy, *Why the Allies Won* (New York: W.W. Norton, 1995), p. 192.

34. *Gulf War Air Power Survey*, vol. 3, *Logistics and Support* (Washington, D. C: Government Printing Office, 1993), p. 9.

35. Mark Bowden, *Black Hawk Down: A Story of Modern War* (New York: Atlantic Monthly Press, 1999), p. 333.

36. Michael E. O'Hanlon, "A Flawed Masterpiece," *Foreign Affairs*, Vol. 81, No. 3 (May/ June 2002), p. 52.

37. Krepinevich, *The Army and Vietnam*, pp. 196–205.

38. Thomas G. Mahnken and James R. FitzSimonds, *The Limits of Transformation: Officer Attitudes toward the Revolution in Military Affairs*, Newport Paper 17 (Newport, RI: Naval War College Press, 2003), Chapter six.

39. Gray, *Modern Strategy*, 147.

40. Kevin M. Woods, Michael R. Pease, Mark E. Stout, Williamson Murray, and James G. Lacey, *Iraqi Perspectives Project: A View of Operation Iraqi Freedom from Saddam's Senior Leadership* (Norfok, VA: U.S. Joint Forces Command, 2006), p. 15.

41. See, e.g., Edward N. Luttwak, "Where Are the Great Powers?" *Foreign Affairs*, Vol. 73, No. 4 (July/August 1994), pp. 23–29; Luttwak, "From Vietnam to Desert Fox: Civil–Military Relations in Modern Democracies," *Survival* Vol. 41, No. 1 (Spring 1999), pp. 99–112; Charles Moskos, "Grave Decision: When Americans Accept Casualties," *Chicago Tribune*, December 12, 1998, p. 25; and Harvey M. Sapolsky and Jeremy Shapiro, "Casualties, Technology, and America's Future Wars," *Parameters* (September 1996), pp. 119–27.

42. Peter D. Feaver and Christopher Gelpi, "How Many Deaths are Acceptable? A Surprising Answer," *The Washington Post*, November 7, 1999, p. B3.

43. The three "measures of merit" were (1) not to lose allied aircraft (2) to affect Yugoslav military and police activities on the ground in Kosovo as quickly and effectively as possible, and (3) to protect allied ground forces from retaliation. See General Wesley K. Clark, *Waging Modern War* (New York: Public Affairs, 2001), pp. 183–84.

44. See, e.g., O'Hanlon, "A Flawed Masterpiece," 57.

45. Wing Commander K.S. Balshaw, RAF, "Spending Treasure Today but Spilling Blood Tomorrow: What Are the Implications for Britain of America's Apparent Aversion to Casualties?" *Defence Studies*, Vol. 1, No. 1 (Spring 2001), p. 101.

46. See, e.g., the essays in Michael Pillsbury ed., *Chinese Views of Future Warfare* (Washington, DC : National Defense University Press, 1997).

47. Carl H. Builder, *The Masks of War: American Military Styles in Strategy and Analysis* (Baltimore: Johns Hopkins University Press, 1989), p. 7.

48. Mahnken and FitzSimonds, *Limits of Transformation*, p. 108.

49. For example, when surveyed in 2002, 41 percent of Air Force pilots but only 21 percent of Navy aviators agreed with the statement "The ability to strike an adversary with precision weapons from a distance will diminish the need for the U.S. to field ground forces."

50. For example, when surveyed in 2002, 57 percent of Army infantry officers but only 30 percent of Marine infantry officers agreed with the statement "The U.S. armed forces must radically change their approach to warfare to compete effectively with future adversaries." Sixty-five percent of Army infantry officers but only 14 percent of Marine infantry officers agreed with the statement "Modern conditions require significant changes to traditional Service roles and missions."

51. Mahnken and FitzSimonds, *Limits of Transformation:* p. 60.

52. Thomas P. Ehrhard, "Unmanned Aerial Vehicles in the United States Armed Services: A Comparative Study of Weapon System Innovation," Ph.D. dissertation (Johns Hopkins University, 2000), p. 75.

53. Builder, *Masks of War*, p. 18.

54. See, e.g., Terry Terriff, "'Innovate or Die'?: Organizational Culture and the Origins of Maneuver Warfare in the United States Marine Corps," *Journal of Strategic Studies* Vol. 29, No. 3 (June 2006), pp. 475–503.

55. General Leonard F. Chapman, Jr., who served as Commandant between 1968 and 1971, was an artilleryman.

56. Generals Fred C. Weyand, Bernard W. Rogers, Edward C. Meyer, and John A. Wickham, Jr. were infantrymen; Creighton W. Abrams, Gordon R. Sullivan, and Eric K. Shinseki

were tankers; and William C. Westmoreland, Carl E. Vuono, and Dennis J. Reimer were artillerymen.

57. Builder, *Masks of War*, p. 33.

58. Admirals Thomas H. Moorer, James L. Holloway III, Thomas B. Hayward, and Jay L. Johnson were aviators; Elmo R. Zumwalt, Jr., Jeremy R. Boorda, and Vern Clark were surface warriors; and James D. Watkins, Carlisle A.H. Trost, and Frank B. Kelso II were submariners.

59. Ehrhard, "Unmanned Aerial Vehicles," p. 89.

60. Quoted in Chris Hables Gray, *Postmodern War: The New Politics of Conflict* (London: Routledge, 1997), p. 138.

61. Nina Tannenwald, "Stigmatizing the Bomb: Origins of the Nuclear Taboo," *International Security*, Vol. 29, No. 4 (Spring 2005), p. 5.

62. Thomas C. Schelling, "An Astonishing 60 Years: The Legacy of Hiroshima," *Perspectives of the National Academy of Science*, Vol. 103, No. 16 (April 18, 2006) p. 6090.

63. Timothy J. Botti, *Ace in the Hole: Why the United States Did Not Use Nuclear Weapons in the Cold War, 1945 to 1965* (Westport, CT: Greenwood Press, 1996), Chapter 22.

64. McGeorge Bundy, *Danger and Survival: Choices about the Bomb in the First Fifty Years* (New York: Random House, 1988), pp. 241, 249.

65. Tannenwald, "Stigmatizing the Bomb," 33.

66. Nina Tannenwald, "Nuclear Weapons and the Vietnam War," *Journal of Strategic Studies*, Vol. 29, No. 4 (August 2006), pp. 675–722.

67. General Lee Butler, Abolition of Nuclear Weapons Speech, National Press Club, Washington, DC, December 4, 1996, at http://www.wagingpeace.org/butlerspeech.html.

68. General Lee Butler, "The Risks of Nuclear Deterrence: From Superpowers to Rogue Leaders," National Press Club, February 2, 1998.

69. Butler, Abolition of Nuclear Weapons Speech.

70. Dennis M. Gormley and Thomas G. Mahnken, "Facing Nuclear and Conventional Reality," *Orbis*, Vol. 44, No. 1 (Winter 2000), pp. 109–125.

71. Ronald Reagan, "Announcement of Strategic Defense Initiative," March 23, 1983, at http://www.missilethreat.com/resources/speeches/reagansdi.html (accessed August 16, 2005).

72. Desmond Ball, "The Development of the SIOP, 1960–1983," in Desmond Ball and Jeffrey Richelson, eds., *Strategic Nuclear Targeting* (Ithaca, NY: Cornell University Press, 1986), p. 63; "Policy for Planning the Employment of Nuclear Weapons," National Security Council, NSDM-242, January 17, 1974, Washington, DC; and Fred Ikle and Albert Wohlstetter, *Discriminate Deterrence: Report of The Commission on Integrated Long-Term Strategy* (Washington, DC: GPO, January 1988), p. 8.

73. A. J. Bacevich, *The Pentomic Era: the U.S. Army between Korea and Vietnam* (Washington, DC: National Defense University Press, 1986), p. 65.

74. Ibid., p. 21.

75. Major Robert A. Doughty, *The Evolution of U.S. Army Tactical Doctrine, 1946–76* (Ft. Leavenworth, KS: Combat Studies Institute, U.S. Army Command and General Staff College, 1981), p. 23.

76. Robert J. Art and Stephen E. Ockenden, "The Domestic Politics of Cruise Missile Development, 1970–1980," in Richard K. Betts, ed., *Cruise Missiles: Technology, Strategy, Politics* (Washington, DC: Brookings, 1981), pp. 359–411.

6

Russian Strategic Culture in Flux: Back to the Future?

Fritz W. Ermarth

Traditional Russian strategic culture—that of Imperial Russia from its emergence as a state in the middle of the last millennium through most of the existence of the Soviet Union into the late 1980s—has been one of the most martial and militarized such cultures in history, rivaling, if not exceeding, those of Prussia, Imperial and Nazi Germany, and Imperial Japan in this respect. Starting sometime in the 1970s, accelerating in the 1980s, dramatically so in the years after the collapse of the USSR, conditions have arisen that open the possibility of changing this nature—significantly "demilitarizing" Russian strategic culture—while also leaving open the possibility of a revival or reassertion of traditional, highly militarized, Russian strategic culture.

The purpose of this tutorial essay is to summarize the origins, contents, and implications of traditional Russian strategic culture, and then, in conclusion, to explore the possibilities for change or reassertion arising from post-Soviet conditions.

Strategic Culture Defined for the Russian Case

It is that body of broadly shared, powerfully influential, and especially enduring attitudes, perceptions, dispositions, and reflexes about national security in its broadest sense, both internal and external, that shape behavior and policy. For all its high degree of militarization, Russian strategic culture is not simply coterminous with its military culture, that is, deep attitudes about how military power should be shaped, maintained, and used. Strategic culture in the Russian case is very much influenced by political culture, how political power is defined, acquired, legitimized, and used; by foreign policy culture, how the outside world is regarded and addressed; and by economic culture—although the latter is, in the Russian case, more a product of the other influences than itself a source of influence. But that may be changing. In other words, strategic culture arises from the intersection of political, foreign policy, military, and economic cultures—and influences can flow in both directions.

Continuity and Change

In the Imperial and Soviet eras, Russia experienced changing structure of statehood, imperial expansion, the appearance of firearm weapons, the industrial revolution, a massive political revolution, several hugely destructive wars with foreign enemies, very destructive civil war, and the appearance of nuclear weapons in the tens of thousands. The continuity of Russian strategic culture through all these changes, strategic in their character, is truly striking. Fully explaining this continuity is beyond the scope of this essay. But it certainly arises in the main from a political culture and psychology shaped by geography, by a long history of "tribal" conflicts under the Mongols, in the expansion and rule of a multiethnic empire, and by deep authoritarianism. Any argument for change in strategic culture must keep this remarkable continuity in mind.

Core Elements of Russian Strategic Culture in the Imperial and Soviet Periods

The Russian state and empire emerged and expanded in conditions of almost constant warfare, initially defensive, then increasingly offensive as the empire expanded. Moscow (Muscovy) became the unifying center of the Russian state because it was most effective in "managing" the Mongol Yoke (overlordship), especially in raising taxes for tribute, and then in assembling military resources for defeating the Mongols and bringing other Russian principalities under Muscovite rule.

Physical and ethnographic geography gave Muscovy and the Russian state no readily established and defensible borders. This condition invited attack. More important, it inspired a combination of fear about vulnerability and an appetite for achieving security and status by expansion. This contributed greatly to the militarization of Russian strategic culture.

As a consequence, by early modern times (1600–1700) military power became the chief institutional foundation of Russian statehood. The monarchy was a kind of royal head on a muscular military body. Historian Richard Pipes cites a telling symbolic illustration of this: When Tsar Nicholas II abdicated the throne in 1917, he sent his letter of abdication, not to the Duma (parliament), which had demanded it, but to the chief of the Russian general staff.[1]

A seemingly contradictory point, however, is very important to understanding the intersection of Russian political and military cultures: Despite the enormous importance of the military as an institutional base and legitimizing symbol of Russian statehood and power, there is little tradition of direct or active military intervention in Russian politics. That thousands of Soviet military officers went to the camps or to execution at the hands of Stalin's secret police without the serious threat of a military coup is a striking manifestation of this. There have been some exceptions and deviations, but they almost prove the rule. The revolt of the Decembrist officers of 1825 was a significant military intervention in politics; it was not the Russian corporate military in action, however, but a clan of liberal officers. In the 1950s, Marshal Zhukov gave Khrushchev critical but very limited military support against his enemies, first Beria (1953), then the "anti-party group" (1957).

In the late Soviet and post-Soviet periods, this tradition of "nonintervention" by the military has been tested in various ways. In the late 1980s, the Soviet military was involved in suppression of local unrest in Georgia and the Baltics; but they resented this and blamed Gorbachev for sullying their corporate reputation. In August 1991, some senior military leaders supported the "putsch" intended to preserve the USSR. But those commanders most in the chain of command required for military support to the coup refused it outright or by evasion, thereby guaranteeing its failure. Some units around the parliament went over to the crowd supporting Yeltsin. The most dramatic military intervention occurred in 1993 when the Russian military went into action against the rebellious Duma on behalf of Yeltsin. But, again, this was on behalf of the superior authority of the state, such as it was then. During the 1990s, individual military leaders, such as Rutskoi, Gromov, and Lebed, turned politicians, and numerous officers were elected to the Duma. It remains to be seen whether these phenomena will lead to change in this aspect of Russian political and military culture: nonintervention by the military in politics.

Russian strategic and military cultures have from earliest times prized and exploited a resource in which Russia was rich: masses of military manpower. Russian strategy, generalship, and operational art relied heavily on this resource through World War II and the Cold War. Industrial age weapons were regarded as "mass multipliers," not as means of fighting better with fewer numbers. Ability to rely on seemingly limitless manpower encouraged a relative indifference to casualties, vividly displayed in both World Wars. It also encouraged relative indifference to the living conditions of most troops. Exploiting this ability required not only very large standing forces, but maintenance of a huge, conscripted, but only rudimentarily trained mobilization base, and a huge military industrial base to arm it. This prizing of mass has bedeviled Russian efforts to accomplish military reform to this day.

INFLUENCE OF POLITICAL CULTURE

Russian political culture has been a major contributor to strategic culture, especially to its militarization. The political culture is itself very "martial" or harmonious with military values in that it is grounded on the principle of kto-kovo (literally "who–whom"), that is, who dominates over whom by virtue of coercive power or status imparted by higher authority, for example, by God to the Tsar, the Tsar to the boyars, or by history to the communist leadership and in turn to bureaucrats and political satraps. Political conflicts are resolved by struggle and intrigue, occasionally by force, but not by negotiations, bargaining, voting, or legal adjudication.

Marxism, especially as interpreted and applied by Lenin and his colleagues, fit rather naturally with Russian political culture, despite its materialism in contrast to Russians' notions about the "spirituality" of their culture. This is because Marxism is as much a martial doctrine, that is, a summons to combat, as a political and social philosophy.

After the turbulence of the first post-Soviet decade, it is clear that elements of traditional Russian political culture strongly reasserted themselves under Vladimir Putin. The essence of this reassertion is not just in moves toward more authoritarian rule, which have been relatively mild by Russian and Soviet standards. Rather it is the clear tendency of those who wield or strive for political power in Russia to regard the features of normal democratic life—parties, parliament, a meaningful press, election campaigns—not as the enabling conditions of a legitimate polity, but as instruments to be manipulated, controlled, or combated for the benefit of the central authority.

Foreign Policy Culture

Russian foreign policy culture is a reflection of political culture to a significant degree. Russian leaders have generally been capable of artful and accommodating diplomacy when the situation demanded it, as displayed by the statecraft of Goncharov in the nineteenth century, and Soviet pursuit of various flavors of détente in the twentieth.

But there has always been an underlying attitude that views foreign states or actors as either enemies, or subjects, or transient allies, or useful fools to be manipulated, that is, the attitude of "kto-kovo."

Russian political and foreign policy cultures have always had some element of messianism, that is, a sense of national and international mission beyond security and prosperity for the country. In the Imperial period, this messianism—the idea of Moscow as the Third Rome, the heir of a legendary religious and imperial tradition—helped to legitimize not only national expansion, but also a sense of national and cultural superiority. In the Soviet period, this mission was to spread "world revolution," an ideological label for Soviet national power, but also a pretense to supra-national, pseudo-religious, values of justice and progress. Military power has long been seen as a means for pursuing messianic goals or as a protective base from which to pursue them by other means, such as diplomacy, political action (overt or covert), and foreign assistance.

In rhetoric and action, Russian foreign policy culture has often expressed a puzzling combination of contradictory attitudes: defensiveness bordering on paranoia, on one hand, combined with assertiveness bordering on pugnacity, on the other. In the Russian mentality, both an inferiority complex and a superiority complex can be simultaneously on display. The traumatic effects of the break up of the USSR and decline of Russia's role as a great power have intensified these complexes, especially among Russia's national security elites. The partial recovery of Russia's international standing under Putin's more disciplined and, as the result of energy revenues, better-funded regime, has produced another amplification of these complexes in the pronouncements of leaders and pundits.

Perhaps despite, or perhaps because of, the balance among these conflicting complexes, Russian strategic leadership has on the whole been notably risk averse at the level of action and operations. It has not been given to daring, high-risk, high-payoff initiatives such as characterized the strategic leadership of Napoleon and Hitler. This was certainly the case throughout the Soviet period. Khrushchev's deployment of nuclear missiles to Cuba in 1962 may be seen as a dramatic exception. At the same time, the record shows that (i) because the United States was accelerating its strategic build up and had recently discovered how the Soviets actually lagged, Khrushchev had good reason to believe bold action was less risky than doing nothing, and (ii) he saw U.S. actions leading up to his move as indications he would get away with it. It was as much a miscalculation as a daring initiative that failed, despite accusations of "adventurism" Khrushchev subsequently faced. The invasion of Afghanistan was clearly such a miscalculation by a very risk-averse Brezhnev leadership.

THE CHALLENGE OF NUCLEAR WEAPONS FOR SOVIET AND RUSSIAN STRATEGIC CULTURE

The appearance of nuclear weapons and their deployment by the USSR and its NATO, and then Chinese, adversaries in large numbers presented a paradoxical challenge for strategic and military culture at a very fundamental level of thinking and policy action. On one hand, they vastly amplified the destructive power available to the Soviet military. But, as probable enemies had them in large numbers as well, they called into serious question the very feasibility of mass warfare, a challenge to a core value of the strategic culture, and to the survivability of the Soviet state, a challenge to the core of the ruling ideology.

Stalin and his successors, at least up to Gorbachev, never seemed to have entertained any serious doubts about the necessity to build and maintain vast nuclear forces, although Khrushchev expressed some ambivalence in his memoirs.[2] The problem was how to think about and manage this power in the strategic context, that is, in relation to the pursuit of offensive and defensive state goals.

Initially, even as he recognized the great destructive power of nuclear weapons and maximized efforts to get them, Stalin sought to minimize their doctrinal impact, or the strategic discontinuity they represented. This found expression in his doctrine of the "permanently operating factors" that brought victory in World War II and supposedly still obtained despite nuclear weapons: size of forces, industrial base, ideology and morale, and so on.

After Stalin's death, Soviet military and political leaders had to develop a more robust and sophisticated way of thinking, which they did over the course of the 1950s and early 1960s. The implications of this thinking for statecraft and military posture unfolded over the next two decades.

Managing the Nuclear Paradox

The Soviets managed the nuclear paradox by constructing different doctrines and policies for different aspects of it, somewhat in tension, but basically in harmony.

At the level of foreign policy and strategic diplomacy, the Soviets recognized the enormous danger and destructive consequences of nuclear war and embraced doctrines of peaceful coexistence, détente, arms control, and crisis management to contain this danger and avoid its destructive consequences. These doctrines sprang from both moral and practical appreciations of an apocalyptic predicament. In that sense, they were certainly sincere. At the same time, the Soviets saw the diplomatic, political, and other interactions involved as means to continue the "international class struggle," the "struggle against imperialism," the "struggle for peace," in other words, as means to achieve fundamental shifts in the global power balance in their favor. Thus, arms control negotiations and the surrounding politics and propaganda were seen as means to constrain the United States and its allies from exploiting their superior technology and economic power to achieve strategic superiority over the USSR. This led them in the mid-1960s to accept the idea of limits on ballistic missile defense, an idea at variance with Russian strategic culture. The combative—competitive elements of strategic culture were by no means laid to rest at this level of doctrine, for all its pacific pretensions.

At the level of military doctrine, especially with respect to building and exercising forces, the combative—competitive element was more vividly displayed. Although embracing deterrence as the first objective of strategy, the Soviets also embraced the notion that there was a plausible theory of victory in nuclear war. Both to make deterrence and the peacetime influence of their military posture as robust as possible and to keep open the possibility of victory, they sought to build comprehensive war-fighting forces for all levels of potential conflict. This involved:

- Diverse survivable counterforce capabilities in intercontinental and theater nuclear strike forces.
- Active and passive (civil) defense of the homeland.
- Very massive theater land-combat combined arms forces, especially for the conquest of Europe in nuclear conditions.

Like U.S. strategic planners, Soviet planners considered and made some provisions for limited nuclear conflict that could see the effective use of nuclear weapons while avoiding escalation to all out nuclear exchanges. Also like U.S. planners, the Soviets did not have high confidence that such limits would actually work.

Despite embracing and effecting in their force building a plausible theory of victory in nuclear war, Soviet leaders recognized that large-scale use of nuclear weapons could probably sweep away the battlefield for mass warfare and destroy their homeland. This appreciation certainly reinforced their aversion to risk of confrontation.

It is important to note that there was a kind of double think going on here. Despite deep doubts about the workability of their strategic theories of victory and superiority, the Soviets believed that as strategists, Russians, and Soviet communists, they should strive as much as possible to make them work; that they should not give up on traditional strategic and military thinking because of the destructiveness of nuclear weapons. This doctrinally animated striving had much to do with the hypermilitarization of the Soviet economy and its ultimate failure. It is also important to note that much of the pressure for this came not from the Soviet military, but from the military industrial complex, which had acquired enormous political weight in the years after World War II. (There was a U.S. counterpart to this strategic double think. Sorting out the similarities and differences, with the benefit of hindsight, would be a really interesting exercise in comparative strategic culture.)

THE APOTHEOSIS OF SOVIET STRATEGIC CULTURE . . . AND THEN DECLINE

Soviet strategic culture, in its expression in military power and foreign policy behavior, reached a kind of peak or apotheosis in the mid-to-late 1970s. Soviet political and military leaders came to believe that they had achieved or were on the way to achieving a kind of strategic superiority over the West based on robust strategic nuclear forces, theater force superiority both conventional and nuclear, and the beginnings of capabilities to project force beyond the Eurasian continent. Equally important, they came to believe, especially after America's withdrawal from Vietnam, that "historic trends in the global correlation of forces"—military, political, and ideological—were running in their favor.

This new level of strategic confidence never approached such heights that Soviet political and military leaders believed they could safely initiate or court confrontations with the United States and its allies that might escalate to military conflict. Rather, they viewed their strategic status as a platform from which they could conduct more assertive and ambitious foreign policies in the Third World to win new allies and dependencies, and in Europe to detach traditional allies from the United States. Moreover, they believed that because of its power and "in the interest of peace" Western leaders would have to acquiesce in the expansion of Soviet influence.

Then began what in historical terms was a rather sudden phase of crisis and collapse, running from the late 1970s into the 1990s, important elements of which continue to this day. The institutional, material, and human embodiments of Soviet strategic culture fell apart. The spiritual, intellectual, and attitudinal contents of that culture came under severe and, potentially, transforming stress.

Soviet military spending began to flatten out in the mid-1970s. It had been growing in absolute terms every year since U.S. intelligence had sought to measure it and had come to represent about 15 percent of GNP, according to U.S. estimates, and perhaps as much as 20 percent according to later Russian assessments. Despite the flush of oil and gas revenues, the military burden was becoming too much for the economy (something it appears Putin-era Russian leaders remember).

The United States and its NATO allies launched new advances in conventional war-fighting technology, especially for precision strike, that made Soviet deficiencies in these areas worrisome to senior military officers, such as Marshal Nikolai Ogarkov, who voiced their worries to political ears. It then became increasingly apparent to both political and military leaders that the military competition was entering a technology era in which the Soviet Union would be unable to compete. This brought the issue of systemic, especially economic, reform out of the precincts of a few dissident economists into the center of strategic concern.

The United States stepped up its challenge to Soviet power and influence expansion in a number of ways: supporting Soviet enemies in the unconventional conflicts in Afghanistan, Africa, and Central America; with its NATO allies, countering Soviet deployment of intermediate range nuclear strike systems with similar deployments in NATO; and the Reagan administration displaying an unexpected willingness to confront Moscow rhetorically and ideologically. These developments were not just troubling or threatening, they were "strategically demoralizing" because they negated Moscow's confidence that "historic trends in the correlation of forces" were running in its favor. This perilous state of affairs was the fundamental reason why Gorbachev came to power. The party leadership sought someone to "get the country moving again."

From the mid-1980s to the end of the decade, Gorbachev initiated a series of reform moves and processes that rapidly escalated. Initially with military support, Gorbachev cut the military budget and proclaimed a much less demanding defensive military doctrine. He escalated pursuit of détente and arms control with the United States. He began to reduce Soviet forces in East Europe.

A chance incident during this period, the landing of a small foreign plane on Red Square after passing through hundreds of miles of warning and air defenses, was a severe blow to military prestige in the eyes of the political leadership. This prestige had already suffered greatly from failures in Afghanistan, abysmal living conditions for most soldiers, and the debunking of the military's record in World War II when glasnost permitted more objective history.

Then came the collapse of the Warsaw Pact, that is, Soviet control of East Europe, and then the collapse of the USSR and communist rule, and more than a decade of decay and deep crisis within the Russian military.

The details and chronology of this history, especially its impact on the Soviet military, are adequately related in Odom's *The Collapse of the Soviet Military*.[3] But it is important to try to draw some implications about the meaning of this history of crisis and collapse for Russian strategic culture in the future before turning to the recent past in which a recovery of sorts is in progress.

LESSONS FROM RECENT HISTORY

Although crucial developments happened quickly, this era of crisis and collapse has been going on now for nearly thirty years. This is long enough for even deeply ingrained attitudes and beliefs to possibly be changed by protracted discrediting.

Despite its enormous size and power, the Soviet military could not or would not save the Soviet bloc, the USSR, or communist rule. This was in part owing to Gorbachev's distaste for bloodshed. But the military had no taste for quelling domestic disorders either. The bottom line for culture, however, is that in the midst of revolutionary developments concerning the locus, extent, and nature of state power, in a state where military power has long been the foundation of the state, military power was simply irrelevant. In the Russian–Soviet strategic culture tradition, this was quite different from the record of 1916–1922 when the Russian military, while failing to save the Tsar, was transformed into the Red Army that saved the Bolshevik regime in its infancy.

This period of strategic irrelevance has also been a period of institutional rot in that corruption, mismanagement, high rates of crime, accident, and suicide have beset the Russian military. This has hurt its internal morale and external respect.

Over hundreds of years, the Russian–Soviet strategic cultural tradition said that military power was useful, successful, and greatly deserving of respect. The legacy of the past quarter century has been one of enormous and destructive burden on the state, strategic irrelevance, and rot. One needs to ask what the impact of that legacy will be on Russian strategic culture.

Russian Strategic Culture—Resurgence…Or Transformation?

The early Yeltsin years, 1992–1996, saw the attitudinal and certainly the behavioral elements of traditional strategic culture go into a deep—but not comatose—hibernation. Most of the Russian public and most of the elites signed up for propositions quite antithetical to traditional strategic culture:

- Russia must become a "normal" country, that is, a law-governed democracy with a genuine market economy.
- Russia must integrate with the West.
- The West, especially the United States, is not a threat, but a source of help.
- The Russian military is largely not needed to deal with the surrounding world, but may be needed to keep Russia from disintegrating.

Russian defense spending plunged further from already unprecedented low levels of Gorbachev's last years. The most pressing problem was to find housing for troops pulled out of East Europe and the former Soviet republics. The U.S. government pitched in with billions of dollars in aid to safeguard Russian nuclear and other dangerous materials.

The events of these years and their impacts are well described in Odom, Blank, and Golts.[4] Their titles capture the essence of developments.

At the attitudinal level, however, elements of the old strategic culture remained alive, if terribly unwell, among the military and security services and the nationalists in the political elites. They harbored:

- a deep resentment about the break-up of the USSR and loss of international standing for Russia, and toward the leaders held responsible for this;
- still strong perceptions of threat from the West and also from China and the Islamic world;
- a strong desire to reestablish Russian international standing, and some semblance of Muscovite influence in the former empire;
- a belief that military power had to be a significant part of this recovery process.

At the same time, there emerged a fairly broad consensus, at least in principle, on the need for fundamental military reform and modernization. This meant raising the human, material, and operational quality of the Russian military on the basis of smaller but better forces and a smaller but better military industrial complex. It meant shifting from conscription to a largely volunteer (contracted) force.

As described by Odom, Blank, and Golts, however, agreement in principle did not in any way mean progress in practice. Little agreement emerged on how to reform and modernize. More important, reform and modernization require money and the Russian state was broke because of economic collapse and "bandit capitalism's" appropriation of state assets.

Resurgence of Traditional Russian Strategic Culture

Toward the end of Yeltsin's presidency, 1996–1999, attitudinal elements of the old strategic culture began a strong recovery among elites and publics, especially hostility to and perceptions of threat from the West, and resentment about loss of Russian status. This occurred in part because of specific U.S. and NATO actions: NATO enlargement, and intervention against Russia's historic friend in the Balkans, Serbia. More broadly, it was stimulated by a fantasy-based disappointment that the United States and the West had not rescued Russia, especially from its economic crisis; and also by a reality-based perception that Western leaders, advisors, and greedy businesses were significantly responsible for the "bandit privatization and capitalism" that impoverished most Russians and created a hated class of wealthy, politically powerful "oligarchs."

Under Putin the political and foreign policy elements of strategic culture—combativeness and competitiveness, perceptions of foreign threat (especially from the United States and the West), and political assertiveness bordering on pugnacity—became increasingly prominent, so much so that "Russia's return" as a demanding and pushy power in the world was a dominant theme of commentary among pundits and politicians prior to the July 2006 summit of the G8, chaired by Putin in Russia.

The "ideology" on which this reassertion is riding is essentially nationalism, replacing at least to a modest degree the role of communist ideology in Soviet times. This nationalism, centered on Russia's interests, security, and influence as an international actor, is accompanied by assertions of a supra-national Russian mission to advance a multi-polar world that contains U.S. power, to establish a Eurasian geopolitical identity distinct from the West, and to combat perceived threats from Western culture.

This new assertiveness is definitely fueled by the dramatic economic recovery of recent years that oil and gas revenues have stimulated. The Putin regime declared its intent to use Russia's energy resources, and the tight supply situation prevailing in the global energy market, to make Russia a "great energy power," even an energy superpower. A complete strategy for doing this was not publicly articulated, but it clearly involves (i) state domination of extraction; (ii) state monopoly of transport (pipelines); and (iii) efforts to push Russian business (ever more dominated by the state) downstream into the processing, distribution, and marketing environments of consumer markets. Alarming to many is a continuing readiness on the part of the Kremlin to use its energy clout on behalf of political–strategic interests, on display when Russia cut gas supplies to Ukraine, and hence to Europe, in a pricing dispute in early 2006. This was perceived not merely as a commercial dispute, but an effort to punish Ukraine for the pro-Western turn of its internal politics.

The Russian Military and the Resurgence of Russian Strategic Culture

At the same time, energy revenues have fueled a significant increase of resources to the Russian military, whose budgets, purchase of new equipment, and exercise activity are up by significant percentages compared to levels of the past decade. Moreover, Putin personally, and the regime more generally, paid laudatory public attention to the military in the form of visits to facilities and rhetorical promotion of military modernization. Pride of place on this front has clearly gone to the goal of sustaining and modernizing Russia's strategic nuclear deterrent against the United States (and also but much less explicitly against China), mainly through deployments of the Topol-M intercontinental ballistic missile and the Bulava submarine-launched ballistic missile. Also highlighted, by Putin personally, is a hypersonic maneuvering reentry vehicle that can defeat any ballistic missile defense. The United States is clearly the potential "main enemy" in this posturing, partly for reasons of deterrence, partly for political show.

Military reform and modernization objectives debated for over a decade are now asserted, at least rhetorically, more consistently. Russia must have, according to its current leaders, a modernized military that can wage "global war" (but this seems in context to mean strategic nuclear retaliation for deterrence but not a massive global war on the scale of World War II or what World War III might look like); several large scale regional conflicts; and local conflicts against insurgents, terrorists, and the like. Overall Russian military spending rose rapidly in percentage terms under Putin, but from a very low base, remaining far below historic levels of spending seen in Soviet times, and far too low to accomplish real reform and modernization of the general purpose forces, according to many military and expert civilian voices. Moreover, we know from Russian audit authorities that much Russian military spending is siphoned off for "unintended purposes."[5]

Nuclear weapons play, if anything, a more prominent role in current Russian strategy than they did in Soviet times, at least in a qualitative sense. This is avowedly to make up for deficiencies in Russian general purpose land combat forces. This force multiplying role of nuclear weapons was widely discussed in Soviet military writings during the 1990s. Then this discussion went silent, suggesting that something serious was going on. From past public discussion and more recent comments by informed defense experts, the aim is not only to preserve a robust strategic nuclear deterrent, but to develop highly accurate long-range nuclear strike options for selective, strategic operations; and to develop new tactical or battlefield nuclear options suitable (presumably because of low yield) near Russian forces and even on Russian territory. This seems to include options for very limited, non-damaging demonstration firings aimed at stopping and "deescalating" a conflict. Possible conflict with NATO and the US (implicitly also China) is the contemplated setting for these capabilities.

IS TRADITIONAL RUSSIAN STRATEGIC CULTURE COMING BACK?

This question cannot be convincingly answered at present because the story is still unfolding. It leads to further questions pertinent to tracking that process.

Is the Russian military coming back, finally? The rhetoric and budget increases would suggest so. But it remains unclear. Although large in percentage terms, budget increases still leave Russian military spending relatively modest, certainly by historical (Soviet) standards. Russia now spends about 2.7 percent of its GDP on defense, akin to that of advanced European countries, as its leaders point out. Military leaders protest that this is far too little to accomplish professed goals, while civilian leaders, including the minister of defense, proclaim that Russia is not going to "militarize" its federal budget or economy as in Soviet times. The priority goal of sustaining the strategic nuclear deterrent can be accomplished relatively cheaply, compared to reforming and modernizing the general purpose forces.

For all the rhetoric and increased defense spending, it would appear that, at least for now, Russia's political leaders either care less about military power than their predecessors over decades and centuries, or they have a plan for gradually reforming and modernizing the military according to professed goals with the benefit of energy wealth coming in over many years.

Why might they care less about military power today than in the past? Despite articulated threat perceptions and professed goals, Russian leaders actually perceive an historically mild threat environment. The United States and NATO present no real military threat to Russia for the foreseeable future. Russo-Chinese relations are the best in decades; underlying political and strategic interests bode for them to remain so for the foreseeable future. The prospect of a real military threat from the Islamic south, perhaps from some new Caliphate, is distant at best. In short, military power—except for the strategic nuclear deterrent, the remaining military basis for Russia's claims to be a great power—is not terribly relevant to Russia's current environment. This condition could bode for either the enduring subsidence of the military element of Russian strategic culture or its gradual, carefully planned return as resources permit and threat environments encourage or demand.

What about Russia as an energy power? An old aphorism held that Russia had only two reliable allies, its army and navy. Today pundits rephrase this to proclaim that oil and gas are now Russia's reliable allies. Does this mean that Russia's leaders view energy resources as promising to the kind of power to coerce, intimidate, and control for which they once relied on military power? Their rhetoric and actions like that against Ukraine suggest that they do. Might the enduring tightness of the energy supply regime in the global market actually permit fulfillment of such ambitions? This is not at all clear. Energy is, after all, a form of economic power and leverage. But that leverage, ultimately, must be exercised in a marketplace of competing, but also cooperating, political and economic interests, where the actors must respect each others' interests and well-being. Acting only on competitive or combative instincts risks breaking down the market and loss of both the wealth and influence that economic leverage promises. This suggests the possibility that, over time, the quest to make Russia an energy power could exercise an educational, dare one say "civilizing," influence on Russian strategic culture, especially as new generations come into the elite. Were this the effect, the result could be a less combative–competitive political element in strategic culture, and its more lasting demilitarization.

But we must remember, as noted earlier: The combative and militaristic qualities of Russian strategic culture have survived revolutionary change before. They may do so again, but not inevitably.

CONCLUSION

Concluding Note 1: The Bearers of Russian Strategic Culture

In Imperial times, the bearers of Russia's strategic culture—perhaps steward would be a better term—were the military leadership, the monarchy, and the nobility. In Soviet times, they were the party leadership, especially in its strong symbiosis with the leaders of the Soviet military industrial complex, and the military leadership.

In post-Soviet times, the picture is more confused. The military leadership is clearly the embattled bearer of the traditional culture of mass forces based on conscription and mobilization. The political combative element is sustained by a host of actors and influences, from the governing regime and its allies in the security services to a range of experts, journalists, academics, and ideologues of nationalist persuasion. Broad publics and elites clearly believe in a strong Russia, and that military power has to be a part of that strength. But there is also broad consensus that the military excesses of the Soviet period should not be repeated.

Concluding Note 2: The Role of WMD

During Soviet times, nuclear weapons became central to strategy and posture, but certainly did not displace general purpose forces. The Soviets also invested lavishly in biological and chemical weapons, the noxious legacy of which lingers today.

Post-Soviet Russia seeks nuclear weapons, not merely as very important, but as a godsend to protect Russia during a time of internal weakness against foreign intrusion or attack such as Russia suffered during similar times in the past. It sees nuclear proliferation as a danger for Russia, but as a more serious challenge to the United States in the near to middle term.

There are some indications that Russia continues a biological weapons program of some scale, probably as a hedge against what others might do in an era of revolutionary developments in biotechnology. The main concern with respect to chemical weapons is probably to eliminate the huge stocks that remain, while maintaining some research on exotic new possibilities.

NOTES

1. Richard Pipes, *The Russian Revolution* (New York: Alfred A. Knopf, Inc, 1990), p. 316.
2. See Strobe Talbott, ed., *Khrushchev Remembers* (Boston, Toronto: Little, Brown and Company, 1970), and Strobe Talbott, ed., *Krushchev Remembers: The Last Testament* (Boston, Toronto: Little, Brown and Company, 1974).
3. William E. Odom, *The Collapse of the Soviet Military* (New Haven, CT: Yale University Press, 1998).
4. Ibid.; also Stephen J. Blank, *Potemkin's Treadmill: Russian Military Modernization* (National Bureau of Asian Research, 2005), and Aleksandr Golts, *Eleven Lost Years* (Moscow: I.V. Zakharov, 2004) [In Russian; the only English translation of this book known to the author is from the U.S. Government's Open Source Center, formerly FBIS].
5. For more details on Russian military spending, see www.warfare.ru posted by Julian Cooper of the University of Birmingham.

7

Continuity and Change in Israel's Strategic Culture

Gregory F. Giles

The definition of strategic culture selected for this volume is well-suited to consideration of the Israeli case: "Shared beliefs, assumptions, and modes of behavior derived from common experiences and accepted narratives (both oral and written), that shape collective identity and relationships to other groups, and which determine appropriate ends and means for achieving security objectives." As explained later, Israel has cultivated—some would say imposed—a set of beliefs and assumptions on its citizenry as a means of simultaneously building and defending the fledgling Jewish state in the face of deep Islamic hostility. This belief system is rooted, in part, in such ancient texts as the Bible but is under considerable pressure from contemporary demographic, ideological, and religious changes in Israeli society. As a result, there is both continuity and change in what passes for "appropriate" ends and means of achieving security in Israeli terms. Indeed, the strategic culture framework could provide a useful tool for anticipating how the Jewish state might come to grips with its ongoing internal, as well as external, security challenges.

Israeli Strategic Culture

Israel's is a strategic culture in transition. The Jewish people have been subject to exile and persecution since antiquity, as manifested in various pogroms, particularly in the late-19th century and the Nazi Holocaust, which claimed the lives of some six million Jews. In order to preserve their religious, ideological, political, cultural and physical existence as a people, Jews require a national homeland. That homeland is their ancestral Israel.

With conflicting claims over this land from Palestinians who are backed politically, militarily, and economically by the larger Arab world (and, increasingly Iran), the state of Israel is under constant threat of annihilation. Thus, Israel must be actively defended by all the resources the state can bring to bear, particularly its citizenry and technological base, which must be organized into qualitatively superior military forces. Because its resources are limited and it lacks strategic depth, Israel must rely on deterrence, backed by a rapid mobilization capability, and be prepared to act preemptively should deterrence seem to be eroding. In any event, Israel must immediately "carry the fight" to the enemy's territory to achieve a quick victory and spare the Israeli home front.

To hedge against conventional military defeat, international isolation, and attack with weapons of mass destruction (WMD), Israel must have its own WMD options, particularly a nuclear weapons capability. To avoid alienating Israel's international supporters and further enflaming Arab enmity, that capability should remain officially unacknowledged for as long as possible. Finally, Israel must further reinforce a perception of national inviolability by minimizing the impact of terrorism on Israeli society, while simultaneously preserving Jewish norms of ethical conduct in war.

A variety of factors, such as disillusionment with the performance of the Israeli Defense Forces (IDF), particularly since 1973, and the changing complexion of Israeli society have given rise to competing subcultures, as detailed later. With areas of overlap as well as divergence, these subgroupings add complexity and dynamism to Israeli strategic culture.

Origins of the "Shared Narrative"

A full recounting of the Jewish saga is beyond the scope of this chapter. Nonetheless, it is necessary to highlight the major events and circumstances that have given rise to Israel's distinctive strategic culture. To begin, it bears recalling the ancient roots of Judaism.

According to Hebrew mythology, around 1200 BC, the Israelite tribes under the leadership of Joshua conquered part of the land of Canaan. This nascent, monotheistic Jewish civilization was built up under the reign of King David. Legend has it that God had promised this land, which later became known as Palestine, to the Jewish people. Under David, bitter battles were fought over the so-called promised land, resulting in the annihilation of the Philistines residing there. In 587 BC, King Nebuchadnezzar conquered Judea and deported much of its population to Babylon. Judea was later reestablished, only to be destroyed again, this time by the Romans, in AD 70. It was during this era that a group of Jewish zealots took refuge in Masada. Legend holds that rather than submit to Roman slavery, these Jews committed mass suicide—a heroic, "freedom fighter" myth that is propagated to this day, for example, in the indoctrination of IDF soldiers.[1] Forced exile, the Diaspora, resulted in four-fifths of the Jewish world population residing in Eastern Europe by the beginning of the nineteenth century, although a "culture of return" to the Holy Land had long since taken root.

Anti-Semitic persecutions, or pogroms, swept through the Russian empire in 1881–1882, triggering Jewish immigration to America and, to a lesser extent, to "Zion," the biblical name of Jerusalem and the Holy Land. The so-called Zionist movement, led by these Ashkenazi or Occidental Jews, gathered momentum in the late-1890s, raising funds, purchasing land in Palestine, and then settling it. Socialist and communist ideas combined with nationalist goals, resulting in a Zionist strategy to establish an exclusively Jewish communal society that would later become the basis for a state. To further this goal, underground Zionist militias were set up to protect Jewish settlements from the growing frictions with the local Palestinian community. These activities set the stage for a culture of secrecy and militarism in the eventual Israeli state.[2]

With the end of British colonial rule on May 14, 1948, the Jewish community in Palestine declared its national independence. The following day, troops from several Arab states launched an invasion. Born of war, Israel prevailed and nearly quadrupled its territory from the 5,000 square kilometers proposed under the 1937

British partition plan, to 21,000 square kilometers following an armistice with the Arabs in 1949. Israel's strategic culture has been shaped by subsequent waves of Jewish immigration and violent struggle over land—a country comparable in size to the state of New Jersey—and national existence ever since.

Characteristics of Israel's Strategic Culture

Keepers of Strategic Culture

Israel's strategic culture has been carefully crafted over the past six decades. The primary vehicles for doing so have been state institutions. Among these, the IDF is paramount. The IDF has various means at its disposal to indoctrinate Israeli Jews, particularly recent immigrants, into the dominant security culture. Mainly, this is accomplished through universal conscription. Israeli men in the age range of eighteen to twenty-one must serve in the IDF for three years while women must serve for two years, with certain exceptions and caveats. In addition, following conscription, Israelis must remain in the IDF reserves with annual call-up for training, up to age fifty-four in some cases. This is a powerful means by which the IDF penetrates civil society and inculcates it with a sense of constant threat and need to sacrifice in the name of "security." Because IDF service is a prerequisite for state welfare benefits, and helps open doors to well-paying civilian jobs, the Israeli state uses economic leverage to further solidify this indoctrination. Those prohibited from IDF service, namely Israeli Arabs, are condemned to the margins of Israeli society and are not intended to participate in the state's strategic culture and related benefits. The IDF further propagates its image and reach into civil society by engaging in various nonmilitary activities, such as popular entertainment (e.g., via Army Radio).

The IDF also makes tremendous demands on the Israeli economy and industry, amounting to some 16–20 percent of national government expenditures. This is a decrease from previous levels that reached as high as 40 percent in the mid-1980s but still represents one of the heaviest national defense burdens globally. In short, the Israeli military–industrial complex plays a major role in reinforcing Israel's self-image as a "nation in arms" and one that must permanently maintain military superiority in the region.

The state has further inculcated strategic culture by various forms of military commemoration. This includes national holidays of war remembrance, sanctification of military cemeteries, parades and other military displays. Israeli artists and the media have traditionally supported this effort by using stories, poems, movies, and newspaper supplements to honor the heroism of Israeli soldiers. The state has consciously used other symbols to reinforce its strategic culture, such as the choice of the Star of David for the national flag, as a link between the State of Israel and its ancestry in the Holy Land. Other state institutions reinforcing the sense that Israel is under current threat and that all national and personal goals should be subordinate to national security are the educational system, which helps serve as a preparatory school for the IDF, and the court system.

These efforts over the years have built considerable public support for, and trust in, Israel's national security ethos. Despite its occasional misfortunes (see later), the IDF remains one of the most highly respected institutions in Israel, as measured in public opinion polls, second only to the corruption-battling State comptroller, and far ahead of Israeli politicians and Knesset members.[3] Also telling is the willingness of Israeli youth to serve in the IDF, even if it should become an all-volunteer force.

Strategic Subcultures

Baruch Kimmerling, a scholar representing the "third wave" of Israeli sociologists, has identified three "orientations" within Israeli society, essentially strategic cultures that have some commonality in strategic beliefs, as well as important differences. These are the "security orientation," the "conflict orientation," and the "settlement" or "peace orientation." Each is briefly summarized here (see also figure 7.1).[4]

The security orientation believes that Israel is locked in a battle for survival with its Arab neighbors, and that a major Israeli military defeat would mean annihilation of Israeli Jews. The primary means to prevent this is absolute and permanent Israeli military superiority in the region. It is the supreme duty of every member of Israeli society to do his or her utmost in military service to the state. The authority of the state to determine the nature of that military service is absolute. However, it is not unconditional, as the state is expected to not abuse this readiness for self-sacrifice and to use the military only for what are believed to be matters of survival.

The security orientation is said to be highly heterogeneous and the political culture of most mainstream social groups. Politically, this orientation channels its votes to the two largest parties, Likud and Labor.

The conflict orientation assumes that the Jewish–Arab conflict is just another incarnation of historic anti-Semitism. Given the current geopolitical situation, no peaceful settlement with Israel's neighbors is possible in the foreseeable future. Apparently influenced by realist thought, this group believes that power and military strength are the only factors that matter in relations between different national, ethnic, or religious groups. Periodic wars are inevitable and must be won. All other collective or private goals are subordinate to this.

The conflict orientation has a very strong, indeed moral and sacred, connection to the Land of Israel and insists that the state must hold to as much of this territory

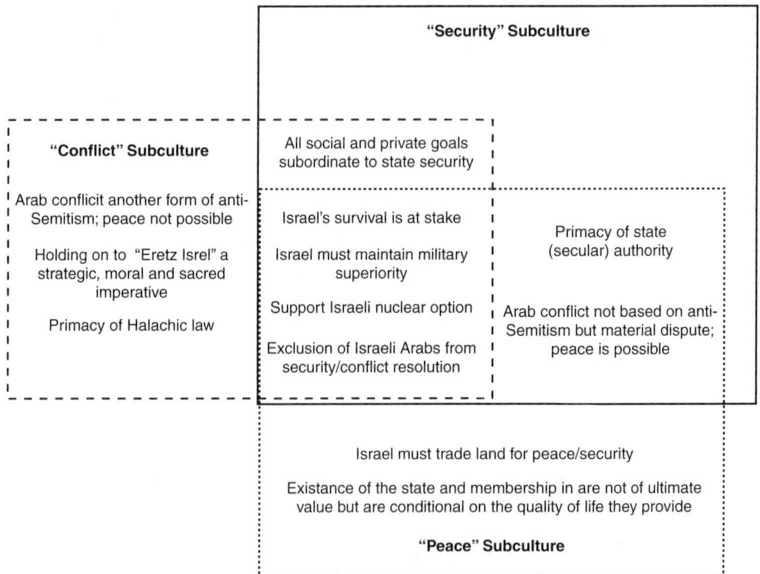

Figure 7.1   Notional Mapping of Strategic Culture in Israel.

as possible. This grouping is highly ethnocentric in nature and gives priority to Hebrew or Halachic law over democratic and legal institutions and practices. Settlers in the occupied territories of the West Bank form the nucleus of this orientation.

The peace orientation is diametrically opposed to the conflict orientation. The former sees the Jewish–Arab conflict as no different from any other negotiable dispute and is unconnected to the persecution of Jews in the past. This grouping frames the conflict mainly in terms of material interests, such as land, markets, boundaries, and water. According to this view, peace is the road to further Israeli development of democracy, economic growth, and cultural progress. It is defined as Israel's acceptance in the region as a legitimate state and society and is equated with security. To achieve peace and security will require compromise.

In this orientation, state and society have a universal civilian basis, without discrimination according to religion, ethnicity, or race. There is mutual reciprocation in state–citizen relations. The state must provide security, well-being, and human rights, while citizens are obligated to obey the state's laws, perform military service (if needed), and pay reasonable taxes.

The institutional expression of this orientation is the peace protest movement and the large output from journalists and artists. The peace orientation is reflected mainly in the upper middle class Ashkenazi strata of Israeli society, which is politically identified with the Meretz party. The national daily newspaper, Ha'aretz, is identified as a major outlet of the peace orientation.

Despite the differences among these three cultures, there are important similarities. They all perceive a real threat to the survival of Israel as a Jewish settler society. They also acknowledge that Israeli military might is central to that survival. Indeed, peace-oriented advocates of returning the occupied territories are ardent supporters of Israel's nuclear capability as the ultimate protector of a smaller Israeli state. This support for Israel's nuclear capability is not universal, however. A small minority of right-wingers, who believe that territorial depth is the key to Israeli security, are suspicious of the nuclear program precisely because it undermines the rationale for holding on to the occupied territories. Finally, all three orientations believe that Israeli Arabs have virtually no role in the state security apparatus or in conflict resolution.

Kimmerling contends that these three orientations cut across most of the cultures comprising Israeli society writ large, such as the Ashkenazi, traditional Mizrahim (Oriental Jews), "national religious" (a euphemism for religious fundamentalists), Orthodox religious, and new Russian immigrants.

Strategic Culture in Transition

Of these three groupings, the security orientation has effectively provided the basis of Israeli strategic culture since the inception of the Jewish state. The dominance of this culture has been eroded, however, since 1973 as a result of IDF wartime and training mishaps, demographic and generational changes, shifts in the role of the media and academia, the rise of individualism, and the emergence of religious nationalism. Indeed, such changes are responsible for the very emergence of the "conflict" and "peace" strategic subcultures.

The early stages of the 1973 Yom Kippur War went very poorly for the IDF, raising the prospect that Israel might be overrun by the combined armies of Egypt and Syria. While the IDF fought brilliantly to avert this catastrophe, irreparable harm was done to the institution as the linchpin of Israeli security and strategic culture.

Further doubt was cast upon the professional competency of the IDF in the wake of the ill-fated 1982 war in Lebanon, which, as current events underscore, failed to secure Israel's border with Lebanon. The inability of the IDF to suppress militarily the 1987 Intifada by the Palestinians cast further doubt on the institution's ability to "get the job done."

In contrast to all prior wars, the 1982 invasion of Lebanon was deemed to be a "war by choice," and consequently at odds with traditional Jewish definitions of a just and legal war (see later). This triggered a national debate that deepened the questioning of fundamental beliefs and assumptions at the core of Israeli strategic culture. Influential in this regard was the shifting role of Israeli media and academia. Previously, these institutions were full subscribers to the infallibility of the IDF, that is, critical examination had been subsumed in the name of national security. From 1973 onward, however, Israeli media, academia, and even artists increasingly became vocal critics of the national security ethos. For example, instead of the customary articles run on Rosh Hashanah (New Year's) and Independence Day praising Israeli military heroism, the media began to run exposés on the IDF's operational failures, the harsh fate of prisoners of war, and victims of battle fatigue.[5] There remains one important bastion of press deference, however: Israel's nuclear capability (as described later).

For its part, academia spawned a so-called third wave of sociologists more inclined to critically assess the relationship between the Israeli military and civil society than its predecessors. Second-wave sociologists defend their work, in part, by acknowledging that over time, they have too have increasingly questioned many of the assumptions behind Israel's national security ethos.[6]

Other changes in Israeli society have challenged the traditional consensus on strategic culture. The influx of 800,000 Russian immigrants following the demise of the Soviet Union posed a major challenge of absorption, assimilation, and preservation of national identity. Here again, the IDF has served as the nation's melting pot, helping to make self-evident to the new immigrants the sense of constant threat and need for military sacrifice on behalf of the Israeli state. Yet, because this pool of manpower has become so large, the IDF cannot absorb it. This has led to modifications in IDF conscription and reserve duty policy and has diluted the concept that all Israelis must make sacrifices in the name of national security.

This influx of Russian immigrants has coincided with changing values, particularly amongst the previously dominant ethnic and cultural community, the Ashkenazi. Whereas military service was highly valued by this group, a broader trend now casts the high technology entrepreneur, lawyer, or media celebrity as the "ideal Israeli."[7] This is reflected in a growing trend of evasion of reserve duty. According to a 1997 estimate, for every eleven IDF reservists, only two actually serve.[8] The deterioration of reservist morale forced the IDF senior command to exclude reservists from service in Lebanon during the controversial 1982 war and from security service in the occupied territories beginning in 1997. While this policy underscored the IDF's adaptability, it also introduced new constraints on the military's operations that would have been inconceivable during the first half of Israel's existence. Indeed, one Israeli analyst contends that it was this decline in reservists' willingness to serve that finally convinced Prime Minister Yitzhak Rabin to reach a political settlement with the Palestinian Liberation Organization at Oslo.[9]

While some segments of Israeli society have become alienated from Israel's military ethos in recent years, other communities have stepped forward to fill the breach. In particular, the so-called national religious groups have previously been on the margins of Israeli society. Yet, since the late 1980s they have made a focused and sustained effort to utilize the IDF as a vehicle to gain greater influence and access. Particularly noteworthy is the growing representation of national religious youth in the IDF's elite military units. By the end of 1996, for example, this community comprised 15 percent of the IDF's overall manpower but 30 percent of its voluntary elite units, which have been the traditional path to advancement in and beyond the IDF. National religious students have comprised 40 percent of the members in certain officers' courses. What makes this shift worrisome from the perspective of Israeli analysts is that, whereas other groups were motivated to serve in the IDF mainly because they accepted the dominant ethos of sacrifice in the name of national security, religious soldiers appear to be largely motivated by hatred of Arabs and a desire for revenge on them. This could produce a radical change in the value system of the IDF's senior officer ranks in the next few years.[10] Already by 1998, the first national religious officer was promoted to the rank of lieutenant-general, with a seat on the IDF general staff.[11]

Thus, while Israel succeeded in rapidly creating a national identity as an immigrant settler society and promoted the Israeli soldier as the natural inheritor of that heroism, within the span of roughly two generations, various internal and external pressures have significantly diluted the original conception of that ethos. This is evident in the emergence of alternative strategic sub-cultures and other trends reflective of the growing pluralism within Israeli society, such as the rise of the national religious generally, and within the IDF officer corps in particular.

Indeed, the 2005 implementation of the Israeli government's decision to withdraw unilaterally and permanently from the Gaza strip and from four settlements in the West Bank put to the test whether the IDF's religious soldiers would obey rabbinical or secular authority. Following the Knesset vote to implement the withdrawal plan, the Judea and Samaria Council of Rabbis declared that no government had the right to give away "God's land" and that it was "God's will" that soldiers not obey the orders to remove Israeli settlers. In the end, only about 30 officers and soldiers out of the 11,000 involved in the disengagement refused to carry out the eviction orders. Punishment for the soldiers came swiftly in the form of jail time, while officers were mustered out of the IDF. This very small rate of insubordination belied earlier concerns voiced by Israeli analysts and scholars over the potential for a large-scale IDF mutiny or even military coup over the issue of withdrawal.

The flare-up between Israel and Hamas/Hezbollah in the summer of 2006 provided a timely window into the impact these various societal trends are having on the redefinition of Israeli strategic culture. For example, to the extent that the kidnapping and killing of Israeli soldiers by these extremists in July 2006 were commonly viewed by Israeli Jews as clear provocations—and the IDF succeeded in suppressing if not eliminating these threats—there could be restored faith in the armed forces. Such developments would tend to reinforce the dominant, "securitist" culture. Similarly, if the preceding withdrawal of the IDF from Gaza and south Lebanon were seen as having invited these attacks, support for the peace subculture could be significantly reduced, to the benefit of the securitist and conflict orientations. Moreover, achievement in battle during this latest conflict could further the careers of religious soldiers, thereby advancing within the IDF officer corps and perhaps the broader national security establishment the conflict subculture's influence over national policy. By the fall of 2006, many Israelis had indeed concluded that the policy of withdrawal from occupied territory had been a mistake, and the movement to expand Jewish settlements in the West Bank was experiencing a revival.[12]

As for the performance of the IDF, it was clear to Israelis that their military strategy and force posture, which relied heavily upon high-tech stand-off attacks by the air force to reduce the exposure of Israeli ground forces, failed the test of battle against an enemy like Hezbollah.[13] Further soul-searching on fundamental Israeli security issues can be expected in the wake of the 2006 conflict with Hezbollah.

Threat Perception

At the heart of Israeli strategic culture is an immutable threat perception, the huge demographic disparity vis-à-vis the Arab (and increasingly pan-Muslim) world. Israeli political and military thought subdivides this macro-threat into a series of concentric circles that are roughly geographic in nature (see figure 7.2).[14] The most proximate threat is the "Palestinian circle," which includes Palestinian citizens of Israel, as well as Palestinians living in the occupied territories and in exile elsewhere. This circle corresponds to "internal security threats" in Israeli parlance, that is, insurgent activities and guerrilla-type attacks against Israeli civilian and military targets emanating from within the state's borders, the Gaza strip, or the West Bank.

In the next ring are the immediate Arab states, comprising Lebanon, Syria, Jordan, and Egypt. Here the threat is perceived largely in terms of cross-border incursions. This threat has fluctuated between raids by marauders operating from neighboring states (e.g., Palestinians and Lebanese Hezbollah) to large-scale attacks by massed Arab armies.

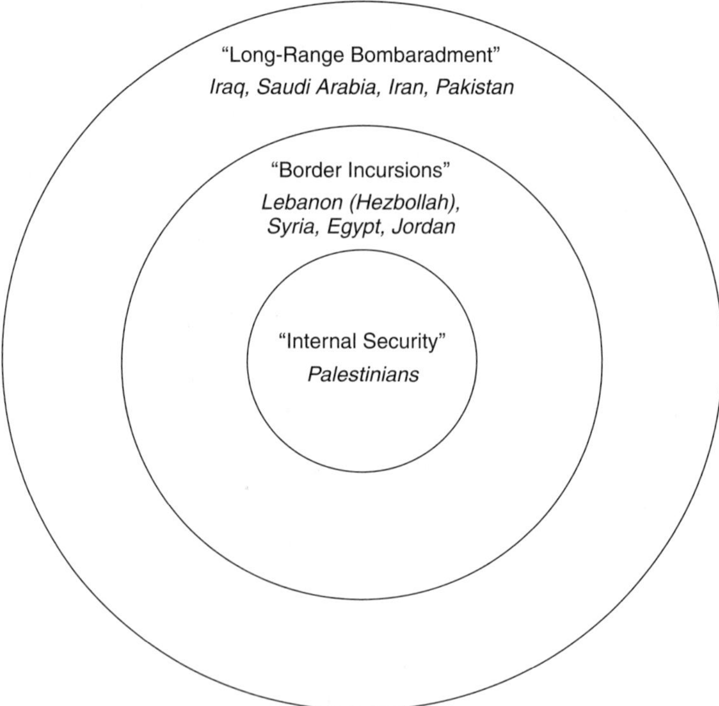

Figure 7.2   Israel's Threat Perception Framework.

Beyond this ring lies the broader Arab (e.g., Iraq, Saudi Arabia, etc.) and Muslim (e.g., Iran, Pakistan) world. Traditionally, this has been viewed in Israel as a remote threat, but Saddam Hussein's use of long-range missiles against Israel in the 1991 Gulf War and Iran's suspected instigation of the July 2006 attacks by Hamas and Hezbollah underscore the ability of "peripheral" states to inflict damage on the Jewish state, directly or indirectly. For a time, the Soviet Union was considered by some also to lie within this outermost ring, in light of its military support to the Arab confrontation states. Direct Soviet intervention would likely have transformed the Arab–Israeli conflict into a superpower showdown, however, as suggested by the 1973 war. In any event, the "threat" from contemporary Russia lies more in its missile and nuclear trade with Iran.

The Necessity of Violence and Laws of War

As noted earlier, the state, acting through the IDF system of universal conscription and reserve duty, has socially constructed a sense of imminent threat of attack bordering on fatalism. Indeed, former IDF chief of staff Rafeal Eitan recalled in his memoirs how he was once called home from abroad to participate in a military action: "I know that I am back home…there is war. I do not complain: each people with its destiny."[15] Eitan's comments capture the widespread belief in Israel in the inevitability of war, consonant with Judaism's historic struggle for survival in a hostile environment.[16]

While war may seem inevitable to Israelis, it is by no means desired or, to use the Clausewitzian formulation, simply a continuation of politics by other means. Indeed, Clausewitz is widely renounced in the Israeli military ethos. In a speech to IDF senior officers, Prime Minister Menachem Begin declared: "Clausewitz['s] famous quote that war is the continuation of policy by other means has no place in today's reality. War does not continue anything. It is a break from everything; it is a world in itself, primarily because it is associated with killings; politically it is also an entirely different issue."[17]

Because war is a strictly negative phenomenon in Judaism, the Israelis have developed a prism that transfers responsibility for war to the party that initiates it. In essence, Israeli Jews have embraced as part of their strategic culture the biblical distinction between wars that are forced upon the state (i.e., "obligatory") and those that are undertaken at the discretion of the ruler (i.e., "optional"). Ethically, the former are considered "just" wars that require full public support, while the latter lack consensus and, by extension, moral clarity.[18] In secular terms, this duality is expressed as "no choice war" versus "war by choice." Generally, Israelis regard all of their wars to date as being "no choice," with the exception of the 1982 and 2006 wars in Lebanon.

Israeli scholars draw a more nuanced distinction, encompassing "defensive" wars, where the enemy "fires the first shot"; "preventive" wars, which are launched to destroy the potential threat of the enemy; and "preemptive" wars, where strikes are initiated in anticipation of immediate enemy aggression. Accordingly, they characterize the wars of 1948, 1969–1970, and 1973 as purely defensive; the 1956 war as preventive; and the 1967 war as preemptive.[19]

The 1982 invasion of Lebanon sparked a far-reaching national debate in Israel. Political and military leaders at the time tried unsuccessfully to justify the conflict as a no-choice war. Their subsequent efforts to change the well-understood national political terminology of conflict (by introducing the phrase "war by choice") likewise failed, and as the goals of the operation expanded, and Israeli casualties mounted, initial public support for the war dissipated.[20]

Other biblical teachings are said to set the parameters for Israeli conduct in war. Among these is the stipulation to seek peace before resorting to war. This is typically equated with the ten-day "waiting period" between Israel's mobilization in 1967, in response to the massing of Egyptian troops, and the launching of Israel's devastating preemptive attack. Indeed, this waiting period is seen in Israel as reinforcing the "justness" of that war. Israel's efforts to warn Saddam Hussein off the path to nuclear weapons prior to launching its preemptive attack against the Osiraq reactor in 1981—and similar efforts in recent years to dissuade Iran—are consistent with this self-image.

Efforts to imbue Israeli soldiers with high ethical standards are institutionalized through the IDF chief education officer, a brigadier general, the military rabbinate, and various military training programs. As noted on the IDF website: "IDF soldiers will operate according to the IDF values and orders, while adhering to the laws of the state and norms of human dignity, and honoring the values of the State of Israel as a Jewish and democratic state."[21]

Among these values is the concept of "purity of arms," which traces back to the origins of the IDF. According to this "value":

> The IDF servicemen and women will use their weapons and force only for the purpose of their mission, only to the necessary extent and will maintain their humanity even during combat. IDF soldiers will not use their weapons and force to harm human beings who are not combatants or prisoners of war, and will do all in their power to avoid causing harm to their lives, bodies, dignity and property.[22]

The reported refusal of some Israeli Air Force pilots to drop their bombs during the 1982 war in Lebanon because of the risk to civilians is consistent with this value.[23]

Not all IDF chief education officers have embraced the purity of arms concept, however.[24] Rather, there is an acknowledgment, if not expectation, that because IDF soldiers operate in an emotionally charged atmosphere, some will engage in unethical behavior. The aim is to contain such incidents. This expectation is rooted, no doubt, in past atrocities by some of the extremist pre-independence Jewish militias, as well as the IDF proper. Among these:

- In April 1948, the Jewish right wing National Military Organization (IZL) retaliated against an Arab attack by massacring and then mutilating the bodies of 200 Arab men, women, and children.[25]
- Another retaliatory raid, this time by the IDF commando "Unit 101," under the command of then-major Ariel Sharon, against the Jordanian village of Kibbiya in 1953 left sixty-nine civilians, including women and children, dead. Under international pressure, the IDF disbanded this unit.
- In 1967, IDF soldiers killed nearly fifty unarmed Egyptian prisoners. With the discovery of the prisoners' remains in 1995, the Israeli government offered compensation to the families of the victims and asserted that Israeli prisoners had also been killed by Egyptian soldiers.[26]

By the late-1980s, Israeli civil society had become less deferential to the military. This greater scrutiny of the armed forces led to a wave of civil court cases in Israel for "deviant acts" committed by IDF officers and soldiers, particularly those of the elite "Mistarvim" (special hit units), during the Intifada.[27]

More recently, a team of Israeli professors, commanders, and former judges developed a code of conduct to address the specific challenges of low-intensity warfare. Regular and reserve IDF units are taught the following eleven rules of conduct, which supplement the military's "spirit" and "values":

- Military action can only be taken against military targets.
- The use of force must be proportional.
- Soldiers may only use weaponry they were issued by the IDF.
- Anyone who surrenders cannot be attacked.
- Only those who are properly trained can interrogate prisoners.
- Soldiers must accord dignity and respect to the Palestinian population and those arrested.
- Soldiers must give appropriate medical care, when conditions allow, to oneself and one's enemy.
- Pillaging is absolutely and totally illegal.
- Soldiers must show proper respect for religious and cultural sites and artifacts.
- Soldiers must protect international aid workers, including their property and vehicles.
- Soldiers must report all violations of this code.[28]

As another indicator of Israel's desire to adhere to humane standards of war, by 1994, the Jewish state joined the international moratorium on the sale of antipersonnel mines. The following year, it signed two of the three protocols of the international treaty banning the use of inhumane conventional weapons. These protocols limit the use of landmines, as well as antipersonnel weapons that rely on fragments that are too small to be detected by X-ray, thus impeding medical treatment.[29]

ROLE OF STRATEGIC CULTURE IN SHAPING ISRAEL'S SECURITY ORGANIZATION AND DECISION-MAKING STYLE

Organization

In many respects, Israel's strategic culture is indistinguishable from its national identity. Case in point is the organizing principle of its armed forces. The 1948 War of Independence was fought by various militias cobbled together into the nascent IDF. That force structure was heavily depleted as a result of casualties, demobilization, and purges designed to remove extremists from its ranks. The IDF then faced a choice of moving to a model based on small elite units or a "people's army." Facing an influx of immigrants, Israel opted for the latter with the intent of using military service as the chief means of molding the immigrants into ideal Israeli citizens committed to self-sacrifice on behalf of the state.[30] As noted, this has been accomplished through the policy of universal conscription and reserve duty.

By design, the IDF thus relies upon a small cadre of professional officers (historically, less than 10 percent of the total force), a conscript base (105,000 troops in 2006), and a larger manpower reserve (exceeding 500,000). The standing conscript force is intended to defend Israel against a major attack for twenty-four to thirty-six hours, by which point, the reserves will be fully mobilized, enabling the IDF to conduct strategic counterattacks into enemy territory.

In the 1980s, the IDF senior command under Chief of Staff Rafael Eitan made a far-reaching decision to organize Israeli settlers in the occupied territories into special reservist units under the "area defense" system. In so doing, he intentionally institutionalized a close link between the religiously inspired settlers, who believe in the sanctity of Israeli land, and the IDF in the hopes of thwarting any future efforts to relinquish the occupied territories.[31] This politicization of the IDF has produced a legacy of embarrassment, including the use of an army-issued sub-machine gun by Baruch Goldstein in a 1994 attack that killed 29 Muslims and wounded another 125 in Hebron.[32]

Decision Making

Unable to bridge the gap between its secular and religious constituencies, the fledging Jewish state had to forego the adoption of a written constitution. Instead, Israel has relied on so-called Basic Laws passed by the Knesset over the decades to define governmental authority. In the national security field, a Basic Law governing the relationship between civilian authority and the military was not put in place until 1976, and even then only as a result of the 1973 near-disaster. This delay and the inherent ambiguity in the law underscore the degree of informality and fluidity that lies at the heart of Israeli national security decision making.

Ben-Gurion established the principle that the IDF is unconditionally subordinate to the civilian government in 1949.[33] In essence, the elected government—embodied in the Knesset members who comprise the cabinet and prime minister—is the commander-in-chief of the armed forces. However, because Ben-Gurion (and a number of his successors) simultaneously held the posts of prime minister and defense minister, the relationship between those positions and the IDF chief of staff has been in constant flux. This has, for example, resulted in defense ministers who, like Ariel Sharon in the 1980s, wielded enormous influence over military affairs—effectively operating as a "super Chief of Staff."

Despite the give-and-take nature of this triumvirate, by monopolizing military expertise and related staff resources, as well as exploiting the permeable boundaries between it and civil society, the IDF has enjoyed significant advantages in advancing its corporate interests over the years. For example, the IDF Intelligence Branch alone prepares the national intelligence estimate for Israel's top political leaders. Efforts to create a National Security Council, alternatively in the defense minister's and the prime minister's office, as a counterweight to the IDF general staff have amounted to little since the late 1970s. By contrast, the mandated early retirement of IDF officers (usually by age forty-five) ensures that a significant number of higher ranking officers enter the civilian sector annually. In many cases, these officers "parachute" into Israeli politics with very explicit agendas. For example, when Maj. Gen. (Res.) Ori Orr became chairman of the Knesset's Foreign Affairs and Defense Committee, he made it clear that his mission was to protect and advance the interests of the IDF.[34]

By the same token, the IDF has learned the hard way that getting too close to policy formulation can carry a stiff price. Prime Minister Yitzhak Rabin's utilization of IDF generals to help negotiate the implementation of the Oslo compromise with the PLO (to better exercise his control over the process and co-opt military opposition) carried with it an ideologically driven backlash against the IDF command by the successor Netanyahu government.[35]

ROLE OF STRATEGIC CULTURE IN SHAPING ISRAELI DOCTRINE AND OPERATIONS

The development of Israeli military doctrine and its execution in war, including limitations thereon, provide numerous examples of how strategic culture helps to determine the appropriate means and ends of achieving security. For example, Israel's lack of strategic depth and limited resources has historically precluded the adoption of defensive war-fighting strategies. Indeed, the very high social and economic cost of full mobilization, which puts virtually the entire male population under arms, signifies that war is all but inevitable. Such was Israel's dilemma in 1967. It had perceived Egypt's troop mobilization and closure of the Straits of Tiran as clear signs that deterrence was eroding and that another Arab–Israeli war would be needed to reestablish it.[36] The government decided that it could not sustain the IDF's mobilization beyond ten days, and so the decision was made to launch a preemptive attack. Israel's inability to remain mobilized for extended periods without suffering major economic damage likewise compelled the Jewish state to escalate its strikes against Egypt in 1970 in order to break Cairo's year-long attempt to ensnare Israel in a war of attrition.

The stunning military success of the 1967 war was seen by many Israelis as divine intervention that reinforced their self-identity as "God's chosen people."[37] However, it was not matched by political foresight that could secure the peace, since the newly acquired territory carried with it an enormous and hostile Arab population. Given the collective's own experience with genocide, Jewish leaders could not bring themselves to conduct an ethnic cleansing of that magnitude.[38] Nor could they accept a bi-national state, which would deprive the Jewish state of its raison d'etre. Hence, core ethical beliefs and identities that transcend partisan politics have prevented Israel from de jure annexation of the occupied territories.

The Jewish military ethos is also evident in Israel's response to the 1972 massacre in Munich, Germany, of its Olympic athletes at the hands of the "Black September" Palestinian terrorist group. In essence, Prime Minister Golda Meir formed a secret committee that authorized the Israeli intelligence service, Mossad, to hunt down and kill Black September members involved directly or indirectly in the massacre. General Aharon Yariv, who oversaw what became known as "Operation Wrath of God," echoed the "no-choice" theme and other biblical sources of Israeli strategic culture when he explained the rationale behind the decision: "We had no choice. We had to make them stop, and there was no other way...we are not very proud about it. But it was a question of sheer necessity. We went back to the old biblical rule of an eye for an eye..."[39]

Other interpretations of what constitutes appropriate means of achieving security can be found in the IDF's handling of the 1987 Intifada. As noted earlier, the IDF decided that rather than risk a broader break-down in its mobilization capability—the key to Israel's overall military power and national integrity—it would accept constraints on its operations and exempt reservists from operations to suppress the Intifada. Eventually, the IDF command publicly acknowledged that it could not engage in the types of operations needed to eliminate the Intifada without violating societal norms. In essence, IDF chief of staff Dan Shomron declared that there was no acceptable military solution to the uprising and that it had to be resolved politically. While principled, this stand proved to be highly unpopular with Israeli political leaders and some sections of Israeli society.[40]

IMPACT OF STRATEGIC CULTURE ON ISRAEL'S WMD POSTURE

The Legacy of the Holocaust

As a small state in a hostile environment, Israel very much fits into the realist model—needing to amass power to ward off attack. As the realist framework lays out, Israel had two basic options, to develop its internal sources of power or to seek strong allies. During the critical early period of statehood, Israel actually pursued both paths. Under the highly charismatic leadership of Ben-Gurion, Israel sought an alliance with one or more Western powers that would guarantee it security. It also embarked on a program to develop weapons of mass destruction (WMD).[41] Arguably, the latter path has proven more fruitful. Still, realism alone is insufficient in explaining Israeli behavior with respect to WMD, for Israel has staked out a unique posture—one in which it is widely perceived as possessing nuclear weapons without any official acknowledgment of that being the case. Strategic culture has helped shape this and other aspects of Israel's attitudes and policies governing WMD.

The historical legacy of the Holocaust and Arab refusal to accept the Jewish state despite its victory in 1948 weighed heavily on Ben-Gurion's mind. Utmost was his fear that a future unified Arab attack—the *inevitable* "next round"—would lead to the destruction of Israel. Ben-Gurion and a very small circle of advisors immediately grasped that the only way to avert another Holocaust would be to attain the capability to inflict one. This "never again" and no choice mentality is evident in a private letter of Ernst Bergmann who, as the first director of Israel's Atomic Energy Commission, played a key role in helping Israel achieve its nuclear goals:

> There is no person in this country who does not fear nuclear war and there is no man in this country who does not hope that, despite it all, logic will rule in the world of tomorrow. But we are not permitted to exchange precise knowledge and realistic evaluations for hopes and illusions. I cannot forget that the Holocaust came on the Jewish people by surprise. The Jewish people cannot allow themselves such an illusion for the second time.[42]

It is the perceived lessons of the Holocaust that give full meaning to Ben-Gurion's pursuit of not just nuclear weapons but also chemical weapons. With not just the Israeli state hanging in the balance but also the fate of the Jewish people, the moral ironies of pursuing WMD, including "poison gas,"[43] were subsumed by the no choice rationale.

Other facets of Israel's strategic culture influenced the path by which the Jewish state pursued nuclear weapons. As Israel's preeminent "founding father," Ben-Gurion established decision-making patterns that endure to this day. Chief among them is the informality and secrecy that govern military decision making in general, and nuclear decision making in particular. Because of the highly sensitive nature of the nuclear project, Ben-Gurion kept the number of personnel "in the loop" to an absolute minimum. To underscore, he did not:

- bring the decision to construct the Dimona reactor before the Cabinet;
- formally consult with IDF leaders besides Chief of Staff Moshe Dayan;

- specifically mention or leave a written record of the nuclear project by name;
- identify the project in the national budget, or rely solely on state funds to pay for it.

The nature of that sensitivity stemmed from a variety of factors including: debate amongst Israel's scientific cadre that it could build such a reactor on its own; France's own reluctance to make known its unprecedented negotiations and subsequent agreement with Israel to help build the reactor and a plutonium reprocessing facility; and, concern that if Dimona was discovered prematurely, the Arabs would launch a preventive war. This issue became even more sensitive when U.S. intelligence uncovered the project between 1958 and 1960, and particularly the Kennedy administration made known to Ben-Gurion and his successors that the United States—a potentially major benefactor—was opposed to Israeli nuclear proliferation.

Israeli politicians and the public at large helped solidify this culture of informality and secrecy governing nuclear affairs.[44] Both communities accepted the notion that Israeli national security would be compromised by a public discourse on the subject. Alternative but limited consultative arrangements were devised for select lawmakers, and the combination of self- and military-censorship helped ensure that only a sterile and inconsequential public debate took place. Indeed, while Israeli media, academics, and the public at large have become more critical of the national security establishment over the years, the nuclear issue remains perhaps the last area of tacit agreement on the need to maintain public silence.[45]

Behind the scenes in 1962, the real debate was taking place between two schools of military thought as to the posture Israel should adopt now that Dimona was nearing completion, namely, should Israel shift its defense posture from conventional to nuclear forces.[46] A small group of protagonists from each school met with Ben-Gurion to make their respective cases. According to accounts from the participants, their debate reflected many of the functional issues faced by Western powers at the time. Among these was the argument that nuclear weapons could not substitute for conventional forces, and if the former were funded at the expense of the latter, a weakened conventional defense might actually invite (Arab) attack. Notably, this "conventionalist" school asserted that Israeli deployment of nuclear weapons would only precipitate Arab nuclearization, to Israel's overall detriment. By the same token, conventional force proponents did not rule out the need for a nuclear "bomb in the basement" that could be quickly brought to bear if needed. In the end, Ben-Gurion appears to have concluded it would be unwise to put all of the IDF's "eggs in the nuclear basket." In the realist paradigm, Israel's pioneering and far-reaching decision not to acknowledge openly its possession of nuclear weapons represented a rare case of a state constraining its military capability in explicit recognition of the so-called security dilemma—wherein increasing one's own security can bring about greater instability as the opponent builds up its own arms in response.

"Nuclear Opacity" and Deterrence

Still, for Israel to derive any hoped-for deterrent effect from the possession of a bomb in the basement, it had to strike a balance between alluding to this capability without provoking a counterproductive Arab response. Here, Israel has managed to achieve what has been described as "nuclear opacity"—the ability to influence other nation's perceptions in the absence of official acknowledgment of nuclear weapons possession and with only circumstantial evidence that such weapons exist.[47] It has done so using a skillfully devising declaratory policy that "Israel will not be the first to introduce nuclear weapons into the Middle East"—a construct Shimon Peres apparently improvised during an impromptu private talk with the President Kennedy in early 1963, but which has become Israel's nuclear mantra ever since.[48] The cause of nuclear opacity was likewise served, intentionally or not, by the 1986 revelations of Mordecai Vanunu, a technician at Dimona who had been laid off for his pro-Palestinian views. Vanunu asserted that Israel had some 200 nuclear weapons in its "basement." The information and photographs Vanunu provided to the London *Sunday Times*—before he was kidnapped by Mossad and jailed for revealing state secrets—suggested that Israel's nuclear arsenal included sophisticated boosted-fission and thermonuclear designs.[49]

The growing concern that Saddam Hussein might use chemical and biological weapons against Israel in an effort to widen the 1991 Gulf War brought the following exchange between reporter Chris Wallace and General Avihu Ben-Nun, then-commander of the Israeli Air Force, during a broadcast of ABC's *World News Tonight*[50]:

> *Ben-Nun*: "Would they really decide to send a non-conventional missile on the population of Israel? My own opinion is that that's very unlikely."
> *Wallace*: "Because?"
> *Ben-Nun*: "Even if Saddam Hussein is crazy, he's still not going to commit suicide."
> *Wallace*: "And would it be suicide if he were to use chemical weapons against Israel?"
> *Ben-Nun*: "He should think that he's going to commit suicide, I believe."
> *Wallace*: "There has been talk that if he uses chemical weapons he might face nuclear counter-response."
> *Ben-Nun*: "Maybe."
> *Wallace*: "Maybe?"
> *Ben-Nun*: "Maybe that's what he should think about."

While Ben-Nun's comments are a rare exception to the IDF's customary silence about Israeli nuclear capabilities, they underscore how deterrence is waged under conditions of nuclear opacity. While Saddam did fire some forty missiles into Israel during conflict, none of them were armed with WMD.

Under the constraints of nuclear opacity, it cannot be known with any degree of certainty what doctrine would guide the actual use of Israel's nuclear weapons. Consistent with Israel's strategic culture, however, we might expect the Jewish state to employ nuclear weapons:

- *Only after it had made major diplomatic and political efforts to warn off an aggressor.* In a severe crisis, this might entail the erosion or complete abandonment of the official Israeli policy of nuclear opacity.
- *When the political leadership perceives that it has "no alternative."* Such a perception might arise from a strategic defeat of Israeli conventional forces that left the home front open to attack—along with a sense of abandonment by Israel's erstwhile allies in the West. It could also arise from indicators that the enemy was about to use WMD against Israel. This suggests the possibility of last-resort escalation to shock the enemy into a cease-fire and nuclear preemption, respectively.
- *In retaliation for WMD use against Israel.* Given Israel's small size and the concentration of its population, it has been characterized by some analysts, and ominously by Iran,[51] as a "one-bomb state"—able to be destroyed with a single nuclear explosion. In such an event, Israeli behavior might once again be driven by biblical notions of vengeance. Metaphorically, this has been expressed as the "Samson Option,"[52] and translates into a determination by Israelis to "take down"

with them as many Muslims as possible. Such a desire would likely entail measures to ensure that Israeli nuclear forces could survive a nuclear attack in such numbers, and with adequate command and control arrangements, as to strike the major population centers of the Arab states and the "outer-rim" of Iran and Pakistan, if necessary.

Nonproliferation and Counter-Proliferation

Concerns about the acquisition of WMD, particularly nuclear weapons, by its enemies have compelled the Jewish state to devise strategies to forestall that event. Essentially, the choices lay in two areas: efforts to build norms against acquisition of WMD (i.e., nonproliferation), and active measures to disrupt physically such acquisition (i.e., counter-proliferation). Of these, Israel has clearly favored the latter.

With the advent of the Nuclear Non-Proliferation Treaty (NPT) in 1968, Israel, under heavy pressure from the United States, initially indicated its willingness to sign the NPT—even voting for a nonbinding resolution in the UN General Assembly endorsing the treaty. However, this posturing only temporarily concealed Israel's steadfast unwillingness to surrender its bomb in the basement, particularly in the absence of a meaningful security guarantee from the United States. Concern that Israel's failure to sign the NPT could stimulate further nuclear proliferation in the Middle East appears not to have weighed heavily, if at all, in the leadership's calculations at the time. To the contrary, Israel asserted privately to U.S. officials that continuing ambiguity about its nuclear status served to deter Egyptian aggression. In short, Israel saw a greater threat from the Arab conventional military threat and contended that until general disarmament could be achieved, nuclear disarmament was meaningless to the Jewish state.[53]

With little trust in multilateral nonproliferation, Israel preferred direct action to disrupt enemy efforts to acquire WMD and long-range delivery systems. For example, in the early 1960s, Egyptian president Gamal Abdel Nasser recruited German rocket scientists to help him build missiles capable of striking deep into Israel. The involvement of Germans in a project designed to kill Jews triggered obvious connections to the Holocaust. Israel's response was "Operation Damocles," a covert action plan using letter-bombs and other tactics to intimidate the German scientists from providing further technical assistance to Nasser.[54] In time, the Germans ceased their cooperation and the rocket program collapsed.

Two decades later, Israel launched a daring air strike against the Iraqi nuclear reactor nearing completion at Osiraq, just outside Baghdad. Publicly defending the operation, Prime Minister Begin touched on a central tenet of Israeli strategic culture: "If the nuclear reactor had not been destroyed, another Holocaust would have happened in the history of the Jewish people. There will never be another Holocaust...Never again! Never again!"[55]

This strike, which is widely acknowledged as pushing back Saddam Hussein's nuclear weapons timetable by a decade—before the Iraqi program was eventually ended by US and UN actions—laid the basis for the so-called Begin Doctrine, which asserted that, "under no circumstances would we allow the enemy to develop weapons of mass destruction against our nation; we will defend Israel's citizens, in time, with all the means at our disposal."[56] In reality, Israeli considerations of preemptive counter-proliferation are more nuanced and include such criteria as the magnitude and severity of the threat, the feasibility of a military strike, and the domestic and international costs of the action.[57]

Nonetheless, these issues have taken on greater saliency with the convergence of a number of troubling developments that touch on fundamental tenets of Israel's strategic culture, namely, the sudden emergence of an extremist Iranian president in 2005, Mahmoud Ahmadinejad, who has publicly denied that the Holocaust ever happened and has called for Israel to be "removed from the page of history;" Iran's enrichment of uranium in 2006, in defiance of the UN Security Council and International Atomic Energy Agency; and the continuing lack of an international consensus over how to thwart Iran's nuclear weapons ambitions. Israel's response to these provocations encapsulates the preceding analysis of the Jewish state's strategic culture. Speaking in December 2005, Raanan Gissin, a spokesman for the then-prime minister Ariel Sharon noted, "Just to remind Mr. Ahmadinejad, we've been here long before his ancestors were here. Therefore, we have a birthright to be here in the land of our forefathers and to live here. Thank God we have the capability to deter and prevent such a statement from becoming a reality."[58]

While certainly not the only methodology available, further refinement and use of strategic culture may provide a useful framework for helping scholars, analysts, and decision-makers anticipate how the Jewish state might respond to the growing threat of regional nuclear proliferation and, if necessary, cope with the loss of its decades-old nuclear weapons monopoly in the Middle East. Indeed, by the fall of 2006, Israeli scholars and strategists were turning to this issue in earnest.[59] A year later, the Israeli government tipped its hand by reportedly conducting an air strike against a Syrian facility.[60] The continuing secrecy surrounding the raid, and public speculation that the facility had a nuclear connection, suggest that Israel's leadership continues to prefer active measures to prolong its nuclear monopoly as the ultimate guarantor of state survival. Whether the September 2007 air strike will help to deter Syrian and Iranian acquisition of nuclear weapons capability or merely serve as a "warm up" for more far-reaching applications of the Begin Doctrine remains to be seen.

NOTES

 1. Recent Israeli scholarship casts doubt on this heroic account. See Baruch Kimmerling, *The Invention and Decline of Israeliness: State, Society, and the Military* (Berkeley: University of California Press, 2001), p. 18, n. 2.
 2. Ibid., p. 27.
 3. Luis Roniger, "Organizational Complexity, Trust, and Deceit in the Israeli Air Force," in Daniel Maman et al., eds., *Military, State and Society in Israel* (New Brunswick, NJ: Transaction, 2001), pp. 371–72.
 4. Kimmerling, *The Invention and Decline of Israeliness*, pp. 208–28.
 5. Yoram Peri, "Civil–Military Relations in Israel in Crisis," in *Military, State and Society*, p. 110. See also, Uri Ben-Eliezer, "From Military Role Expansion to Difficulties in Peace-Making: The Israel Defense Forces 50 Years On," in *Military, State and Society*, pp. 153–54.
 6. See "Preface," in *Military, State and Society*, pp. i–v.
 7. Peri, "Civil–Military Relations in Israel," p. 109.
 8. Ibid., 126.
 9. Ibid., 128.
10. Information in this paragraph is taken from ibid., pp. 130–31.
11. Stuart Cohen, "The Scroll or the Sword? Tensions between Judaism and Military Service in Israel," in Stuart Cohen, ed., *Democratic Societies and Their Armed Forces: Israel in Comparative Context* (London: Frank Cass, 2000), p. 271, n. 13.
12. Scott Wilson, "War Turns the Tide For Israeli Settlers," *Washington Post,* September 25, 2006, A1, http://www.washingtonpost.com/wp-dyn/content/article/2006/09/24/AR2006092400757.html.

13. Molly Moore, "Israelis Face 'New Kind of War'; High-Tech Tactics Fail to Halt Rocket Fire," *Washington Post*, August 9, 2006, A11, http://www.washingtonpost.com/wp-dyn/content/article/2006/08/08/AR2006080801229.html.
14. Baruch Kimmerling, "The Social Construction of Israel's 'National Security,'" in *Democratic Societies and Their Armed Forces*, pp. 221–22. See also Rueven Gal, "The Israeli Defense Forces (IDF): A Conservative or Adaptive Organization?" in *Military, State and Society*, p. 364.
15. Quoted in Efraim Inbar, "The 'No Choice War' Debate in Israel," *Journal of Strategic Studies*, March 1989, 23.
16. Ibid., 23–24.
17. Quoted in ibid., p. 33. Clausewitzian thought was further discredited in Israel due to its association with extreme rightist politicians.
18. Charles Ben-Dor, "War & Peace: Jewish Tradition and the Conduct of War," *Israeli Defense Forces Journal*, Vol. 3, No. 4 (Fall 1986), pp. 47–50.
19. Inbar, "The 'No Choice War,'" p. 23. Ben-Dor, "War & Peace," pp. 47–49.
20. Inbar, "The 'No Choice War.'"
21. Official IDF website: http://www1.idf.il/DOVER/site/mainpage.asp?sl=EN&id=32.
22. Ibid.
23. Anthony H. Cordesman and Abraham R. Wager, *The Lessons of Modern War, Volume I: The Arab-Israeli Conflicts, 1973–1989* (Boulder, CO: Westview Press, 1990), pp. 113–14.
24. See "An Interview with Brig. Gen. Nehemia Dagan, Chief Education Officer, IDF," *IDF Journal*, Vol. 3, No. 4 (Fall 1986), pp. 51–52.
25. James Burk, "From Wars of Independence to Democratic Peace, Comparing the Cases of Israel and the United States," in *Military, State and Society*, p. 96.
26. Youssef Ibrahim, "Egypt Says Israeli's Killed P.O.W.'s in '67 War," *New York Times*, September 21, 1995, A1. See also "Rabin: POW Question Could Open 'Pandora's Box,'" Foreign Broadcast Information Service, FBIS-NES-95–165, August 22, 1995, pp. 47–48.
27. Peri, "Civil–Military Relations in Israel," pp. 112–14.
28. See "Code of Conduct Against Terrorists," Wikipedia, http://en.wikipedia.org/wiki/Israel_Defense_Forces.
29. "Government Signs Treaty Banning 'Inhumane' Arms," Foreign Broadcast Information Service, FBIS-NES-95–106, June 2, 1995, p. 39. Israel did not sign the protocol banning the use of incendiary weapons, such as napalm.
30. Kimmerling, "The Social Construction of Israel's 'National Security,'" p. 224.
31. Ben-Eliezer, "From Military Role Expansion to Difficulties," pp. 156–57.
32. Ibid., p. 157.
33. Amir Bar-Or, "The Link between the Government and IDF During Israel's First 50 Years: The Shifting Role of the Defense Minister," in *Military, State and Society*, p. 323.
34. Ben-Eliezer, "From Military Role Expansion to Difficulties," p. 149.
35. Bar-Or, "The Link between the Government," pp. 330–33.
36. Kimmerling, "The Social Construction of Israel's 'National Security,'" p. 229.
37. Ibid., p. 231.
38. Kimmerling contends that Israel, in effect, conducted an ethnic cleansing of the territory it conquered during the 1948 war, turning some 700,000–900,000 Palestinians into refugees. *The Invention and Decline of Israeliness*, p. 40.
39. See "Munich Massacre," Wikipedia, http://en.wikipedia.org/wiki/Munich_Massacre. See also Dan Raviv and Yossi Melman, *Every Spy a Prince* (Boston: Houghton Miffilin Company, 1990), pp. 184–92.
40. Peri, "Civil–Military Relations in Israel," p. 111.
41. Avner Cohen, *Israel and the Bomb* (New York: Columbia University Press, 1998), p. 66.
42. Ibid., p. 16.
43. Ibid., pp. 48–49.
44. Cohen, *Israel and the Bomb*, pp. 143–46, 147.
45. Kimmerling, "The Social Construction of Israel's 'National Security,'" p. 242.
46. Cohen, *Israel and the Bomb*, pp. 148–51.

47. The phrase "opaque proliferation" was coined by Benjamin Frankel in 1987 and jointly elaborated with Avner Cohen in 1991.

48. Cohen, *Israel and the Bomb*, pp. 118–19, 380, n. 21.

49. Seymour M. Hersh, *The Samson Option* (New York: Random House, 1991), pp. 196–207.

50. John Pike, "Nuclear Threats during the Gulf War," Federation of American Scientists website, February 19, 1998, http://www.fas.org/irp/eprint/ds-threats.htm.

51. In December 2001, Hashemi Rafsanjani, head of Iran's influential Expediency Council, said: "If one day…the world of Islam comes to possess the weapons currently in Israel's possession [i.e., nuclear weapons]—on that day this method of global arrogance would come to a dead end. This…is because the use of a nuclear bomb in Israel will leave nothing on the ground, whereas it will only damage the world of Islam." "Former Iranian President Rafsanjani on Using a Nuclear Bomb against Israel," Middle East Media Research Institute, *Special Dispatch*, No. 325, January 3, 2002, http://www.memri.org/bin/articles.cgi?Area=iran&ID=SP32502.

52. This phrase was coined by Norman Podhoretz in 1976 and popularized by Seymour Hersh in 1991. See Hersh, *The Samson Option*, p. 137 n.

53. Cohen, *Israel and the Bomb*, pp. 293–338.

54. Raviv and Melman, *Every Spy a Prince*, pp. 122–25.

55. Quoted in Hersh, *The Samson Option*, p. 10.

56. Israeli government statement quoted in Shlomo Brom, "Is the Begin Doctrine Still A Viable Option for Israel?" in Henry Sokolski and Patrick Clawson, eds., *Getting Ready for A Nuclear-Ready Iran*, US Army Strategic Studies Institute, October 2005, http://www.strategicstudiesinstitute.army.mil/pdffiles/pub629.pdf.

57. Ibid., pp. 140–45.

58. Paul Hughes, "Iran's Ahmadinejad Casts Doubt on Holocaust," *Reuters*, December 9, 2005. Available at http://in.news.yahoo.com/051208/137/61g2k.html.

59. Dan Williams, "Israel Seen Lifting Nuclear Veil In Iran Stand-Off," *Reuters*, September 2, 2006. Available at http://www.mg.co.za/articlePage.aspx?articleid=284838&area=/breaking_news/breaking_news__international_news/#.

60. David E. Sanger and Mark Mazzetti, "Israel Struck Syrian Nuclear Project, Analysts Say," *New York Times*, October 14, 2007, at http://www.nytimes.com/2007/10/14/washington/14weapons.html?adxnnl=1&adxnnlx=1199559600 NyTltMUEqEMr7hML1FLZjA.

8

India's Strategic Culture and the Origins of Omniscient Paternalism

Rodney W. Jones

India's Strategic Culture Defined

India's strategic culture is not monolithic, rather it is mosaic-like, but as a composite is more distinct and coherent than that of most contemporary nation-states. This is due to its substantial continuity with the symbolism of premodern Indian state systems and threads of Hindu or Vedic civilization dating back several millennia. Embedded in educated social elites, the consciousness of Hindu values has been resident in essentially the same territorial space, namely, the Indian subcontinent. This continuity of values was battered and overlaid but never severed or completely submerged, whether by Muslim invasions and Mughal rule, the seaborne arrival of French and Portuguese adventurers and missionaries, or the encroachment of the British Empire—with its implantation of representative political institutions and modern law. Indian culture is assimilative, and during the rise of nationalism under British rule, India's strategic culture assimilated much of what we think of as twentieth-century "modernity." This composite culture informed India's behavior after 1947 as an independent nation.

On the surface, India's strategic culture today operates through, and affirms, a parliamentary-style republic, a secular constitution, popularly elected national and state governments, and modern diplomatic channels that are cognizant of international law and globalizing trade practices. Most of India's top leaders and civil servants are well educated, use English (and other foreign languages) in external relations, and are sophisticated in the ways of the modern world. Internally, Indian society is highly diverse, and generalizations invariably have exceptions. But there are common threads of attachment to India as India, even among the educated layers of India's religious minorities.

Discerning the underlying traits of India's strategic culture, its distinctiveness, and its resonance in India's contemporary actions may take some effort. But it can be done. There are core traits of Indian strategic culture that have persisted since independence despite shifts in India's strategic foreign and security policies during and after the Cold War, and notwithstanding the gathering momentum of the forces of globalization. However, it is foreseeable that some of the core traits may be subject to modification in the coming decades due to generational changes in Indian leadership who are less steeped in tradition, the rise of new business entrepreneurs in high-technology spheres who operate with a less parochial and more globally oriented paradigm, and the impetus of regional political leaders and upward mobility of lower strata of society who are less easily socialized in a standard strategic outlook.[1]

The provisional definition of strategic culture that was adopted in the earlier workshops[2] is serviceable enough in the Indian case, with one caveat. Before one arrives at security ends and means, the *content* of what is strategic and what is to be secured under the rubric of Indian "security objectives" must be recognized as based on metaphors of "Indian-ness" (or *Bharatvarsha* and *Hindutva*),[3] an outlook that transcends the Republic of India—the divided nation and territory—that emerged after partition from British colonial rule in 1947.

INDIA'S STRATEGIC CULTURE PROFILE: TRAITS

We begin here with propositions on the traits of Indian strategic culture—listed in figure 8.1—in two sections, the first related to the conceptual origins of the traits, and the second to their instrumental or behavioral implications. These are discussed and illustrated later, in terms of specific actions and events. Encompassing these traits, and as a provisional simplification, Indian strategic culture can be labeled as an *omniscient patrician* type[4]: A description of each element of the philosophical and mythological factors that form the foundation of this culture follows.

Sacred Permeates Indian Identity

Indian strategic culture has a collective consciousness of the sacred origins of Indianness that give mythological and metaphysical significance to the subcontinent as a territorial expression. Great rivers symbolize life-giving and cleansing properties in the material world and connect mortals to the gods and to the underlying cosmic

---

A. Philosophical and mythological foundation:

- Sacred permeates Indian identity
- Goals are timeless, not time bound
- India's status is a given, not earned
- Knowledge of truth is the key to action and power
- World order is hierarchical, not egalitarian

B. Instrumental implications:

- India's external visage is enigmatic
- Self-interest expressed externally is impersonal and absolute
- Contradictions in the real world are natural and affirmed
- Force has its place, but guile may trump force
- Actions have consequences, good intent does not absolve injury
- Entitlement inhibits ordinary compromise (hard to split differences, truth is not at ease with quid pro quo)
- Compromise easily viewed as internal defeat (ephemeral, bends truth, dents sovereignty)
- Trust is in right knowledge and action, is impersonal, and hard to build or replenish
- Security is sedentary (encompasses a geographic setting and way of life)
- Strategy is assimilative (appearance changes, reality is constant)

Figure 8.1 Traits of India's *Omniscient Patrician* Strategic Culture.

forces they manifest. Enlarged by tributaries, the Ganges River (after, Ganga, goddess of purification) is dotted with places of pilgrimage and temples from its source in the Himalayas through the plains before flowing into the Bay of Bengal.[5] India's natural (and spiritual) frontier begins in the Himalayas where the great rivers rise and follows to where they join the sea.[6] Modern concepts of security would protect this way of life and the territorial domain in which it exists. Affinity for the sacred in this society should not be confused with religious fundamentalism or literalist acceptance of religious texts. The shared outlook is not personal, not specifically faith-based or historically grounded, as in the Judaeo-Christian or Islamic belief systems, and not necessarily doctrinal or doctrinaire. It is rather a cosmic consciousness, timeless and also pervasive. It is the heritage of the Pundits (sages, priests, and teachers).

Goals Are Timeless, Not Time Bound

The collective reference points of Indian strategic culture are timeless. The thought process is ahistorical,[7] and generally resists being event-driven or trapped by deadlines, which tend to be regarded as ephemeral. Underlying forces matter (e.g., demographic trends, rates of economic growth) but their effects are seldom sudden or overwhelming. Official goals may be framed as five-year plans, but if they are not accomplished within that time frame, they are reset as future targets without excessive rancor or disappointment. Painstakingly decided official goals are rarely discredited or set aside entirely. Strategic objectives are embedded in a long haul outlook. Patience and persistence are rewarded over time. This public style is quite the opposite of a postindustrial business or entrepreneurial outlook, in which "time is money" and opportunity costs are high. Business traits may operate in the private sector and in individual careers but are not dominant in the public domain.

India's Status Is a Given, Not Earned

This widely held premise is rooted in collective consciousness of India's ageless and rich civilization—a natural claim to greatness. It appears to be reinforced by traditional norms of status in India's society based on ascriptive criteria (caste, family, and upbringing), not only performance-driven mechanisms. In India, caste structure still assigns status and tilts opportunity. Those who have a natural affinity for knowledge, Brahmins particularly but some other high castes as well, have been disproportionately successful in rising educationally and competing for the elected and salaried positions of government, public enterprise, and the professions that have given modern content to India's strategic culture. Those who have risen in these channels in the nationalist era have been inducted into an outlook of cultural superiority versus the outside world. This outlook holds India's importance to be singular and self-evident, an entitlement that does not need to be earned, proved, or demonstrated.[8] This trait is reflected in the doggedness of India's negotiations with the outside world. India's external affairs leadership prizes being respected. Merely being liked by officials in other countries, though welcomed in interpersonal relationships, is not regarded as necessarily additive to India's prestige or critical to India's achievement of key objectives. India's strategic culture sees status as an objective reality, a matter for other state to recognize and act in accordance with, not a favor for other states to confer.

Knowledge of Truth Is the Key to Action and Power

In the abstract, this proposition about knowledge of "truth" as key to action and power could be applied to participants in a theocratic as well as in a scientifically endowed or secular strategic culture. In this case, the reference is to the truth inherited from Indian civilization. During the colonial era, India's assimilative strategic culture came to prize modern scientific and instrumental knowledge. This trait drove India's investment in modern science and engineering across the board, its acquisition of modern military technology and large standing military forces, its development of nuclear and missile capabilities—against international opposition— and its secret development of chemical weapons. In India's case, however, its top political leaders, the carriers of strategic culture, were versed not only in modern knowledge but in a cultural frame of reference that had metaphysical and spiritual properties. Ageless cultural and cosmic metaphors set their modern knowledge in a context that placed a premium on deep thinking, instilled a penchant for under-standing the interplay of underlying forces over the long term, and inculcated values that reward patience, persistence, and devotion to the national interest. This outlook aimed for deeper knowledge, a secular approximation of omniscience.

In India this trait is most pronounced among those reared in Brahmin and high-caste families, whose heritage often is pedagogical, as transmitters of learning, including the legendary epics, philosophies, and cultural mores. This outlook was propagated internally in a way that structures a unique sense of obligation among peers and that is particularly instrumental to the achievement of India's strategic goals. This trait is conducive to Indian practitioners in strategic decision making and negotiations being better informed and more analytically focused than most of their external interlocutors, and also much less concerned about immediate gratification or the passage of time.

World Order Is Hierarchical, Not Egalitarian

India's strategic culture is elite-driven and patrician-like rather than democratic in inspiration or style. It sees the outside world hierarchically both in measures of material power and in attributes of intellectual and ideological competence. It recognizes and adapts to but is not intimidated by a foreign power's temporal perfor-mance. It adheres to a long-term perspective in which today's impressions may prove evanescent or unreliable. This hierarchical view of the world is informed by the basket of distinctive Hindu mythologies and symbols, which emphasize both what is worthy morally and of durable practical importance. It also draws on Chanakya's (Kautilya's) secular treatise, the *Arthashastra*, which closely parallels Niccolo Machiavelli's *The Prince*, as an exposition of monarchical statecraft, realpolitik in interstate balances of power, and the practices of war and peace.

This is not to say that Indian strategic decision makers and diplomats reject contemporary principles of international law that subscribe to equality among sov-ereign nations and that give weaker countries leverage against the more powerful. On the contrary, whenever they work in India's favor, international legal norms are exploited to the hilt. Independent India has been a strong proponent of the United Nations and active participant in the elaboration of international law. Jawaharlal Nehru, India's first prime minister and a giant on the international scene, adhered to some principles and policies that arguably were idealistic in their inspiration. But India's strategic culture—omniscient and patrician—is hard-nosed. It harbors no illusions about the ultimate importance of international norms in comparison with the importance of objective realities, and the role of accumulated prestige and power in fortifying sovereignty and self-determination.

India's Strategic Culture in Action

The profile of India's strategic culture presented earlier focuses on distinctive traits rooted in India's ancient cultural and religious heritage, as they were manifested after independence. These traits may be considered the core or skeleton of India's strategic culture. They have not changed essentially since independence. Our analysis now shifts to how these traits of India's strategic culture have been reflected in or reinforced by international interaction. Necessarily brief and selective, the analysis brings out the implementation of India's strategic culture in the face of external challenges and live security threats, including threats to internal security. This fleshes out the skeleton of India's strategic culture. It may also portray India in a way that most strategic observers can more easily relate to—in terms of geopolitics and national interest.

East–West competition during the Cold War and challenges in the immediate region—particularly India's partition and subsequent wars with Pakistan, and the 1962 military skirmish with China—enlivened and added texture to India's strategic culture but arguably did not fundamentally alter it. India suffered from a variety of security problems after independence, but, apart from partition in 1947, it did not undergo any severe nationwide traumas of violent revolution, civil war, or military defeat and protracted occupation by a major external power. Had any such trauma occurred, it might have forced changes in India's strategic culture. The emerging relationship of strategic cooperation with the United States and the effects of globalization within India could, conceivably, have certain transforming effects, but this remains to be seen. India's homegrown strategic culture has been carved in the minds of elites and its dominant parameters have been very resilient since 1947.

Partition of India and Residues of Communal Conflict

India's prospective geopolitical options and threat environment were profoundly altered by the rise of Muslim nationalism, and by the partition of India and creation of Pakistan as the last acts of British colonial power. The state of Jammu and Kashmir, formerly a princely state, with territory bordering on China, was divided de facto but left unresolved and became a lasting bone of contention. Partition truncated India as a holistic geographical expression, and therefore constrained a full assertion of the underlying strategic culture in terms that the rest of the world could have viewed as self-explanatory.

Geopolitically, this partition had three profound effects. One was to limit India's natural influence on Iran, Afghanistan, and formerly Soviet Central Asia—since the newly independent state of Pakistan now existed squarely between India and these former neighbors. (East Pakistan as an enclave in the Muslim-majority districts of Bengal also complicated India's reach to the east, and thus limited its natural influence on Burma and defense-preparedness against China, illustrated by the Chinese incursion of October 1962.) Second, the fact that this partition of India was based on the Hindu–Muslim communal divide meant that the Muslim minorities dispersed in the rest of India could, potentially, rise in agitation and jeopardize India's internal solidarity. This domestic factor inhibited India's full assertion externally of what its subcontinental strategic culture implied. Third, the struggle over Kashmir hobbled India even as it threatened Pakistan, leading to recurring limited wars between India and Pakistan, and stoked Pakistan's determination to follow India down the nuclear path.

India's possessiveness of Kashmir is a natural expression, however, of the territorial premises of its strategic culture. Eastern Kashmir is part of the Himalayan chain and is thus linked to ancient Hindu holy places of pilgrimage and legendary as well as historical Indian empires in the same region. Tenets of India's strategic culture hold that religious differences can be absorbed and do not contradict Indianness as a unifying feature of those reared together in the subcontinent. This tenet that is at odds with Pakistan's emergence as a homeland for Muslims of the subcontinent implicitly calls the basis for Pakistan into question. The timelessness of Indian goals provides a perspective on Kashmir that frustrates negotiations and suggests to bystanders as well as those involved that India cannot help but prevail in the long run.

The consensual understanding in Indian strategic culture of the virtue of the long view, exercising patience as temporal trends shift, has enabled India's top leadership to build Indian strength internally to mitigate Pakistan's initial curtailment of Indian power. India's greatest strategic feat in the first three decades of independence was to head off further potential fragmentation of its territory both from Muslim disquiet after partition and from language-based subnational movements in southern and western India. The Congress Party-led system defused a grassroots movement of Tamil-speakers whose demands once verged on independence. It also overcame agitations by Gujarati- and Marathi-speakers by giving them separate linguistically based states in India's federal system.

It is difficult to overstate the importance of this successful internal political integration of India in the early years. India's internal diversity made it uncertain at the outset whether unity could be preserved. But the political victories of integration were cumulative and underwrote India's success with representative and electoral institutions and economic stability. They gradually strengthened India's capacity to cope not only with the challenges from Pakistan but to overcome or manage a series of other secessionist threats, such as the Sikh Khalistani movement in Punjab in the 1980s and the Naga, Mizo, and other tribal independence movements on the periphery of Assam in eastern India. Achieving internal unity was also instrumental in recruiting and modernizing India's military services, expanding the scientific, industrial, and manufacturing sectors of the economy, and in projecting India's image abroad of a rising regional power, if not prospective great power.

Pakistan's capacity to challenge India politically and militarily was curtailed by India's first strategic military operation in the 1971 War, in which Indian forces invaded and forced the surrender of Pakistan's military forces in East Pakistan, and enabled the Bengali nationalist movement there to set up the newly independent state of Bangladesh. This action reflected the realpolitik strands of India's strategic culture, dismembering Pakistan as a sovereign entity after preparing and using offensive force decisively. India limited its risks in this venture by concluding the Indo-Soviet Friendship Treaty with Moscow, although this impaired its much touted doctrine of nonalignment.

Pakistan's loss of the eastern province and acceptance of the 1972 Simla Accord set back residual hopes to win its claims to all of Kashmir by military means. Thereafter, Pakistani military leaders tacitly recognized the fact of India's conventional military superiority over Pakistan. Pakistan's nuclear weapons program was started secretly in 1972, but this was not known until some years later. Pakistan's military challenge over Kashmir went silent for the next eighteen years. Pakistan's relatively compliant posture after the 1971 War tended to confirm India's view of its strategic culture tenets, especially its sense of superiority, hierarchical view of world order, and conception that truth and power go hand in hand over the long haul. India also managed internal communal problems relatively well in the 1970s and 1980s, reinforcing an organic sense of national unity no longer vitally challenged by linguistic or regional differences, with minor exceptions in India's northeastern tribal areas.

Cold War, the Superpowers, and China

Modern India's independence coincided with the Truman Doctrine and the onset of the postwar U.S.–Soviet rivalry in Europe and the Near East, but predated the communist revolution in China and the Korean War. India's foreign policy doctrine of nonalignment reflected its distinct worldview and sense of status as well as its political fragility after partition. Just as the newly formed United States feared "entangling alliances," India's leaders consciously avoided explicit alignment with the West or the Soviet bloc, fearing this would lead to dependency and that foreign quarrels might exacerbate divisions within Indian society. Thus, despite affection for British parliamentary institutions, law, and literature—in which two generations of India's nationalist leaders had been steeped—India's strategic culture urged political distance from the West, to seal out European or American neo-imperialist influence. In India's nationalist narratives, the British had, after all, employed "divide and rule" strategies to control the subcontinent and had, ultimately, caved in to Muslim agitation to partition India. Nonalignment was a secular rationale for an anti-imperialist or hands-off posture.

Sealing out Western and Soviet political and military influence had to be done in such a way, however, as to leave open the flow of modern scientific knowledge and high technology. Here there were tradeoffs. India's strategic elite believed, correctly, in its own intrinsic capacity to absorb and master modern scientific knowledge and technology, provided it had open access. This elite held a nearly ideological determination, however, that India be self-sufficient in modern science, technology, and means of national power. By endorsing an autarchic approach to defense production and high technology development, and by demanding technology flows as a matter of entitlement, the Indian establishment initially retarded national progress in those same sectors.

Nonalignment was conducive to the aims of domestic autarky, but externally, in the context of the Cold War, it was a tool for geopolitical leverage. It was a means of playing the Soviet Union off against the West, and vice versa. Although this approach required patience and a long-term perspective, it also enabled India to squeeze high technology offers and military equipment supplies from both sides in the Cold War, more often than not at lower than market prices. While this approach failed to open a flood of technology transfers for India, its steady benefits seemed sufficient in the minds of the strategic culture elite at the time to validate their premises.

Only later did it become obvious that with India's heavy reliance on public sector industries for defense, atomic energy, electronics, and space technologies, the practice of squeezing of technology and arms from both sides during the Cold War also had negative effects on its capacity to achieve self-reliance in the most sophisticated areas of technology. India's indigenous development of high technology was much slower, more painful, and less successful than public rhetoric implied. India's shared strategic culture inhibited open criticism and remedies for these shortcomings, until the Cold War had passed, and, indeed, have operated that way until very recently.

India's nonalignment was replete with contradictions that illustrate the strategic culture's capacity to absorb inconsistencies. Nonalignment was never a scrupulous policy of neutrality. Over time, Indian foreign policy tilted toward the Soviet Union and the Communist Bloc, even when the Soviet Union intervened militarily abroad, as in Afghanistan. Although touted today to cement U.S.–Indian strategic partnership, India's professed "democratic values" failed to align it with the West during the Cold War.

Several pragmatic reasons for India's pro-Soviet leanings can be adduced. First, U.S. containment policy favored Pakistan, along with Turkey, Iran, and the northern tier Arab states as allies against Soviet expansion. Indian leaders viewed Western military assistance to Pakistan as threatening to Indian interests. The Soviet Union, for its part, routinely supported India's position on Kashmir against Pakistan in the United Nations. Second, but less widely understood, India and the Soviet Union had a tacit common interest in managing Muslim populations peacefully within their respective borders. India's early proclivity for socialism, more Laskiite than Leninist in inspiration, had the same secular objective as Moscow's nationalities policies, of denying space for "political Islam." Third, India's pro-Soviet tilt gave India leverage in Moscow to forestall Comintern temptation to stoke subversion of India through external financing of India's communist parties. India's international support for Soviet positions was also instrumental in negotiating Soviet arms supply at bargain basement rates.

India's relationship with China was not so easily managed, despite initially solicitous Indian policies. India attempted to cultivate a friendly relationship with Communist China, assuming that it would, as a less developed Third World nation with anticolonial reflexes, sympathize with India's leadership of the nonaligned movement. This appeared to work for a time. But in a humiliating blow to India's omniscient patrician stance in October 1962, China sent troops through Himalayan passes into poorly defended eastern India. This was apparently meant to convey to India that its inflexibility on negotiations over disputed Himalayan borders (based on British colonial era claims) must change. Having made its political point, China unilaterally withdrew behind its own border several weeks later. India's sense of entitlement to those northern regions made it inflexible in its territorial dispute with China, setting up a contest of wills between governments that remains, like the Kashmir dispute with Pakistan, unresolved till today.

China's 1962 military incursion into India humiliated India and stimulated the construction of access roads and fortifications in the Himalayas as well as a sustained Indian conventional arms buildup. By the early 1970s, the Indian military was well prepared to block another such incursion by China. Meanwhile, China became a source of military assistance and arms transfers to Pakistan and, until recently, a supporter of Pakistan's side in the Kashmir dispute. India's strategic culture helps explain its resistance to settling what it considers entitlement issues by pragmatic compromise and its determination to wait the opponent out. China's patience likewise appears to be a match for India's.

The 1962 Chinese incursion temporarily brought India closer to the United States, although Washington was preoccupied at the time by the Cuban Missile Crisis. President Kennedy offered India military assistance to improve its defenses against China, and some assistance was delivered. India briefly considered longer term offers but finally walked away because of real or supposed strings attached. The same trait of resistance to pragmatic compromise—India's inability to deal with quid pro quos in a two-way relationship—operated on one side with China as an adversary, and on the other side with the United States when it was eager to help. These outcomes can also be attributed in India's strategic culture to the traits of superiority, presumed deeper knowledge, and a profound sense of entitlement. Admittedly, the unilateral Chinese withdrawal removed the immediate pressure on India. A different test would have applied had China extended and fortified its occupation of that Indian real estate in 1962.

U.S. overtures to India in the 1960s bore other less well-known fruit, for instance, technical intelligence cooperation in monitoring China's development and testing of nuclear weapons. China's first nuclear detonation was achieved in October 1964. Obtaining technical data on that first test and subsequent Chinese nuclear tests was facilitated by U.S. instrumentation, placed with Indian permission in the Himalayas. Those programs were kept out of public view and are not well known even today. India's strategic culture may have reinforced a deep suspicion of U.S. intelligence, particularly of the CIA, with allegations frequently surfacing in India's Parliament. India generally held U.S. overtures for military cooperation at bay. The strategic culture favored a self-imposed Indian demand for self-sufficiency long before this was technically realistic. India also disparaged the U.S. involvement in the Vietnam War, a troubling undercurrent in relations from the Kennedy to the Nixon administration.

Protagonists of India's strategic culture shaped and propagated a strategic myth that further poisoned U.S.–India relations at the time of Pakistan's dismemberment at Indian hands in December 1971. Indian leaders claimed, and the Indian press amplified, reports that a U.S. carrier task force had entered the Bay of Bengal to relieve pressure on, or perhaps rescue, Pakistani military forces in East Pakistan. The media campaign suggested that the task force was nuclear-equipped and posed a direct U.S. nuclear threat to India as a crude act of coercive diplomacy, aiming to compel India's disengagement from the conflict with Pakistan. This rendition of the event instilled a shared memory in the Indian elite that the United States might go to extreme lengths, even threatening India with the use of nuclear weapons, to protect Pakistan.[9] This theme was replayed from time to time later as a justification for India's steps toward nuclear weapons.[10]

Covert Nuclear Proliferation and Declared Nuclear Weapons

The "knowledge-as-power," "goals-are-timeless," and mystical features of India's strategic culture have been epitomized in Indian nuclear programs and policies, both in how India presented these to the world, and in how it evaluated Pakistan's nuclear weapons progress in later years. The U.S. use of nuclear weapons on Hiroshima and Nagasaki in 1945 was a defining moment for elites around the world, and certainly in India. The dualism of creative and destructive potentials in splitting the atom resonated with India's strategic culture's reflection of mythology and the Hindu pantheon—especially with Brahma "the creator" and Siva "the destroyer." Among Indian scientists, the challenge of divining the timeless mysteries of particle physics and quantum mechanics evoked traditional consciousness of cosmic forces, fusing the realm of the sacred with action in the real world. India's scientific community moved actively into this area even as the new nation gained independence and formed new political institutions.

India's top political leadership sensed the importance of mastering the laws of nature for the development of the nation and the opportunity to lift its huge population out of poverty to a respectable standard of living. India's scientific community viewed this as an entitlement that they would take charge of, dedicating themselves to India's transformation and elevation to a status on par with the great powers of the world. Nuclear energy and technology was by no means the only area of modern scientific endeavor that Indian leadership aimed to master, but it was a uniquely potent one that could be expected to have a galvanizing effect on the rest.

India's policy of ambiguity on nuclear weapons is so well known today that there is a tendency to assume that India's posture was intentionally ambiguous from the start. This overstates the case. India's leaders, political and technocratic, naturally sought to master this technology. A few among them, but certainly all the atomic energy commission scientists, knew that full mastery of nuclear technology would bring nuclear weapons capability as a matter of course. The construction of plutonium production and chemical separation facilities began early, in the mid-1950s, and plutonium separation was demonstrated in 1965, just seventeen years after independence.

The top political leadership under Jawaharlal Nehru believed India's moral and political stature would gain from emphasizing the peaceful aspects of nuclear energy and assuring the world India opposed nuclear weapons. This was consistent with the strategic culture tenets of India's deeper, moral knowledge and desire to enhance its world stature by setting an example that might encourage the nuclear weapon states to change course and begin disarmament.

After China went nuclear in 1964, the rationale for India setting an example of weapons abstinence was less compelling, but not given up entirely. India had been one of the primary advocates of a nuclear nonproliferation treaty at the outset, yet declined to join the NPT when the negotiations were completed in 1968. India's third prime minister, Indira Gandhi, authorized the scientists to complete the technical preparations for the so-called peaceful nuclear explosion (PNE) around 1969. Her motivations may have been partly to remove doubts about her own political leadership, and partly to show the world—in those years India's international image had been slipping—that India had the requisite will and capability, and its status should not be discounted.

That nearly four and a half years elapsed before the actual nuclear test is surprising. There may have been a precursor test device that failed. The policy of ambiguity, however, was firmly established by the May 1974 nuclear explosive test. The test program broke the news to the leadership in Delhi telephonically with the code words: "the Buddha smiles." India's overt declaration of nuclear weapons came with the nuclear tests of 1998, after another twenty-four years, illustrating the timeless goals and patience of India's strategic culture.

The strategic culture traits of knowledge as power and long haul endurance were reflected in the determination to avoid international controls over the nuclear program, even at the cost of being denied open nuclear commerce and technology transfer. India's indigenous construction of nuclear power plants for urban electricity supply proceeded, but at a painfully slow rate, and with plants of small size and dubious safety. Forty years after construction began on the first two power reactors at Tarapur, India's nuclear power plants today still make up barely 2.6 percent of its electric power supply.

The elements of intellectual superiority and status as an entitlement in India's strategic culture have been reflected in the Indian leadership's disdain toward Pakistan's nuclear weapons program. Admittedly, starting later and with far smaller resources, Pakistan's nuclear research and power program was almost miniscule in comparison with India's. Pakistan's options for obtaining nuclear technology through normal channels were even more constrained than India's after the 1974 test, since that test precipitated a steady tightening of Western nuclear export controls on sensitive and dual-use technologies. Focused on developing nuclear weapons after the 1971 War, Pakistan's major breakthrough was in production of highly enriched uranium (HEU), beginning about 1979, using covertly imported materials and indigenously assembled gas-centrifuge equipment. Pakistan developed a plutonium production reactor and chemical separation plant much later, coming on line in the late 1990s.

India's success between July 2005 and March 2006 in winning Bush administration's acceptance of an Indian civil–military nuclear separation plan (with limited IAEA safeguards on the civilian segment) as a basis both for terminating U.S. nuclear sanctions imposed on India in 1974 and for reopening U.S. civil nuclear cooperation with India in the future is an extraordinary example of India's negotiating steadfastness, and diplomatic vindication of the omniscience and entitlement traits of its strategic culture. This case further illustrates how that strategic culture resists ordinary compromise and quid pro quos on matters of strategic value, enabling its practitioners to hold out indefinitely if necessary.[11]

Economic Factors and Decision Making

India's strategic culture was well reflected in its autarkic economic decision making until 1991, when a shift in policy toward foreign trade liberalization occurred that might be considered adaptive. India's centralized economic policies after independence were heavily influenced by the socialist teachings of Harold Laski at the London School of Economics and the Soviet Union's central planning and command economy model. India's Western trained economists were first rate and optimistic about macroeconomic management. Nehru and his socialist-leaning Congress party associates imparted to the Planning Commission a view that India's poverty and pre-sumably weak industrial trade competitiveness could best be overcome by allocating resources in accordance with five-year plans and closely managed import restrictions and controls on international currency. This perspective was deeply suspicious of "capitalism," "profit," foreign investment, and market principles.

This suspicion of profit and openness to international capital flows was not only a Marxist fashion but fit the omniscient patrician strategic culture like a glove. The science management culture from abroad reinforced the domestic strategic culture that accorded deeper knowledge to the nationalist elite on how to make the economy grow, and a paternalistic responsibility for distributing the benefits equitably to the masses for overall welfare. This meant relying on public sector industries for key sectors, especially in infrastructure and defense—railroads, ship-building, electric power generation, coal mining, steel production, heavy machinery manufacturing, telecommunications, and essentially all defense production. India's economic performance in the agricultural sector was incrementally improved by using geneti-cally improved seeds and expanded irrigation—leading to the "green revolution" in Punjab and Gujarat. But India's centrally planned industrial performance was so tepid through the first three decades that critics dubbed it the "Hindu rate of growth."

India's reliance on public sector management went hand in hand with tight restrictions on foreign capital and high tariffs on imported goods. The approach slowed the growth of indigenous private firms in the domestic economy, and the absence of external competition meant poor quality control in modern Indian manufacturing (e.g., automobiles, capital equipment), typically making products uncompetitive abroad. It was the view at the top that the political leadership knew what was good for India and that it would excel in an autarchic environment that prevailed until the 1980s, and retarded India's economic development. In this respect, the strategic culture was a severe handicap to Indian performance. It was only the dramatic export-led economic expansion of the Asian tigers (South Korea, Malaysia, Singapore, Thailand, and Indonesia) and the extraordinary trade performance of "communist" China throughout the 1980s that finally sank into Indian consciousness and made the government willing to adopt a change in course.

While Indian policymakers began a series of small economic and trade reform steps in the late 1980s, the 1990–1991 financial crisis over hemorrhaging foreign exchange and the adverse effects on Indian workers overseas from the first Gulf War against Iraq forced a shift in economic and trade policy that became cumulatively important in the 1990s. This shift began essentially as a technocratic policy of liberalization of India's business tax and trading license environment. India opened the doors to its own entrepreneurs importing and exporting more freely, even when it required use of foreign exchange. The government also moved in steps toward the convertibility of the rupee and the dollar, and began, in phases, to open up various sectors of the economy to foreign investment—though foreigners were not permitted to take majority control or buy out Indian firms. This liberalization was fortunate to occur when it did, because it enabled the Silicon Valley developments in the computer and information technology industry in the United States to flow to Asia and take root in India quickly—where education had provided a large labor pool of English-speaking engineers and other technically able workers, and enabled India to capture big chunks of the offshoring of software development and database service activities of many Western and multinational corporations.

One of the ironies of India's excellent performance in the computer software and information technology industries is the vindication of the Indian strategic culture tenets that emphasize deep knowledge, knowledge as power, and the enhancement of status this gives India in international circles. Yet these market-driven economic developments would seem to be at odds with the basic emphasis in the strategic culture on traditional mythology, symbolism, and timeless values. Nothing could be more driven by time and money than the production schedules of the information technology businesses. Yet there is a link with cosmic and timeless values metaphorically in the infinite potential for invention and elaboration of information technology applications. That said, the very success of Indian entrepreneurs abroad and at home in these booming business areas also has a burnishing effect on India's sense of status and those traits of Indian strategic culture that suggest India is rightfully superior in what it brings to the modern world. Thus these dynamic new developments tend, in the final analysis, to reinforce certain aspects of the strategic culture, even as they challenge others, for example, the autarchic impulses. But just as ironically, the challenges—which may be reflected as real world contradictions—are easily reconciled by an outlook that is comfortable in its essence with contradictions.

War and Peace Themes in India's Strategic Culture

India's strategic culture has drawn selectively from various threads of its past civilization values and larger political culture. The dominant war and peace elements of India's strategic culture lean more to the realpolitik side of the mythological and religious spectrum, and away from the pacifist themes that had gained prominence, temporarily, as a result of publicity about Mahatma Gandhi's influence on the nationalist movement. But both sources of inspiration, a readiness for war and pacifist inclinations, have validity in the strategic culture. The emphasis may shift in facing different challenges over time. The guardians of strategic culture are comfortable with contradictions. The nature of this dualism and occasional tension is worth discussing further, especially inasmuch as Nehru's leadership on foreign policy and India's role in the NAM evoked moral sympathy in the West for the Gandhian image of India.

Popular Indian mythology draws heavily on the great epics, the Ramayana (life story of godlike prince Rama) and the Mahabharata (literally, the story of "greater India" as epic struggles between good kings and demonic adversaries—their ancestries usually connected with the gods). These epics are recorded in ancient Sanskrit, but are disseminated to ordinary persons (including illiterates) through local theatrical and dance presentations (in regional languages), seasonal festivals, certain temple rituals and, contemporaneously, in Bollywood movies. What the epics teach, implicitly, is that good and evil forces collide, and that the good usually prevails—albeit often after long suffering and many losses. The "good" is demonstrated both in exemplary acts of personal morality (including heroism and romantic fidelity) and also in accounts of good governance withstanding evil forces. The epics are set in the context of kings, courts, and rivalries that lead to wars, epic in scale and duration. Resort to force in these rivalries is treated as natural. Some of the stories involve god-kings employing extraordinary weapons—thunderbolts, for example—that raise connotations of weapons of mass destruction (WMD). War is not necessarily celebrated as such, but deadly combat certainly is approved as acceptable when good fights evil. These popular images are shared by the Hindu elite and population as a whole—either as beliefs or as metaphors—and are important unifying features of a diverse society.

Kautilya's *Arthashastra*, an ancient treatise on principles of statecraft, was written by an actual court advisor who served Maurya dynasty monarchs. The writing is down-to-earth—not connected with the epic legends. But it is embedded in the same composite civilization and reflects a period of the Indian subcontinent when rival Hindu kingdoms were the norm. Its advice to rulers addresses the use of force, poisons (or toxins and chemical weapons), and tools of espionage, in detail. It presupposes that wars will occur and therefore provides guidance on how to construct military alliances with other states in the Indian state system, for the survival or safety of the home state.

Gandhi shunned the use of physical force and opposed violence in politics. It should be added that his philosophy and technique of nonviolent resistance to the British was, nevertheless, politically steely and unyielding. His concept of resistance was *Satyagraha*, or "force of truth." Gandhi's approach was philosophical and reflected "reform" variants of Hinduism (more in touch with devotional books, such as the Bhagavad Gita, or "Song of the Lord," and the philosophical Upanishads, as well as Jain religious teachings) more than the popular and mainstream Hindu tradition. His philosophy emphasized reverence for human life (Jainism venerates all life forms, human, animal, and vegetable) and a sense of horror in killing or shedding blood (*ahimsa*). This perspective is based on the belief of the continuity of all life, or the great chain of being, and interprets all life forms as incarnations. While it would be going too far to say today's guardians of India's strategic culture hold these Gandhian precepts dear, his espousal of Satyagraha, or unyielding "truth-based resistance," has an appeal. Gandhi's reverence for life would also be acknowledged as the preferred high ground, but Gandhi's doctrinal opposition to violence and the shedding of blood would not be considered as an absolute value, only a preferred norm when peace prevails and nothing vital is at stake.

Perceptions of Adversaries

How does Indian strategic culture conceptualize "the enemy"? The enemy is an alien (organized) force whose aims or actions would deprive India of its sacred territory or subvert its society by undermining its civilized values. While the strategic culture is ahistorical in its conscious roots, proponents of Indian strategic culture have ample historical reference points for enemies over the last millennium.[12] Chinese empires as such did not figure prominently in this South Asian history. Rather, the subcontinent was invaded over land by successive waves of Muslim armies, typically from the northwest—through what we know today as Afghanistan. Muslim rulers overthrew numerous preexisting Hindu monarchies in north and south India, and established their own hegemony by force, conversion, and institutions of government.

The Muslim invader is a particularly potent example of an enemy in India's concept. British leaders probably had an advantage in gaining Indian allegiance for the British Empire in India because the British unseated the Moghul emperors and contained other less powerful Muslim kingdoms (e.g., the state of Hyderabad) that had established themselves in the subcontinent. In theory, Indian society had long absorbed alien intruders by their assimilation of its superior teachings, traditions, and civilized values. Muslim beliefs and practices were less permeable and could not be absorbed and transformed. Rather, monotheistic Islam challenged Hindu society and belief by its efforts to stigmatize and purge polytheism and idolatry, and by its egalitarian inspiration (status is earned, not given) that set it against the caste system and therefore the underlying Indian social order. The Muslim impulse to convert unbelievers also challenged Hinduism directly. Over time, Muslim governments adapted to Indian society by restraining forcible conversion, and by recruiting Hindus from urban and upper castes to help run government and from middle and lower castes to fill out military ranks, thereby avoiding incessant internal warfare and rebellion. But Muslim hegemony was imposed, and this mutual accommodation was inherently unstable.

The European invaders came by sea, not over land, combined superior means of waging war with commercial and missionary interests, and carried the early forms of modern scientific and industrial knowledge. The British did better than the Portuguese and French in making territorial inroads in the subcontinent. British encroachments initially were efforts to protect their trade through commercial enclaves. Modern and English-language education came with missionaries, and over time Indian graduates from affluent Indian families continued their educations in the United Kingdom and occasionally elsewhere in Western Europe. As the British colonial system expanded, it introduced modern law and courts, civil and police services, and eventually elective representative institutions. British rulers and colonialists were also "enemies" but mainstream Indian coexistence with the British was not quite so unstable because it displaced or eroded former Muslim power and brought advantages of mechanized transport, industry, science, and modern education. Culturally predisposed to the concept of "knowledge brings power," Indian upper classes took to the new educational system, and eventually used their knowledge and political organization to gain experience in self-rule and then agitated for independence. The Western colonialist enemy was still alien but softer and more tractable, particularly when his own means of superiority were mastered and turned against him. Inasmuch as the nationalist movement ultimately forced the British to grant India independence, this principle of mastering new knowledge was a particularly potent source of inspiration for modern Indian strategic culture.

Chinese Rivalry

China did not figure prominently as a classical enemy, but a sense of Indian rivalry with China has emerged. In antiquity, the Himalayan wall stood in the way of invasions from the northeast. Buddhism that emerged in India as a reform of Hinduism migrated east by osmosis, not conquest, into Tibet, China, Japan, and most of Southeast Asia. Classical Chinese empires were oriented to the great rivers and agricultural resources of central and eastern China, and simply did not have reasons or energy to invade India and never threatened to colonize India. Tibet was a forbidding high-altitude province, lightly populated, and of no special resource significance. The British did press frontiers outward and concerned themselves with boundary issues, including with Tibet. Since Himalayan boundaries were never settled by formal British agreements with imperial China, however, this legacy for India was a source of potential disputes. While India has been concerned with the sources of the great sacred rivers, as discussed earlier, it did not challenge Chinese interests in controlling Tibet, but did claim territory along the Himalayan watershed that would encompass the sources of most of these rivers (the Brahmaputra where it rises and flows east in Tibet being an important exception). Given partition and the creation of Pakistan, and the dispute over Kashmir, India's concern about defining and defending these frontiers was easily understandable. But it did provoke a Chinese military incursion into eastern India in 1962, a political act inasmuch as China just as quickly withdrew rather than fight any prolonged war.

Insofar as China figures in Indian strategic culture as an "enemy," it has several components. First, India is sensitive to China's appeal as an alternative ancient civilization, with a large modern population, that is almost bound to collide with India in seeking influence for security and commercial purposes in adjacent regions. Second, China managed to go nuclear relatively quickly, presenting a possible threat of nuclear blackmail. Third, China has been a major source of military and nuclear assistance to Pakistan, giving China an ally or partner on the Arabian Sea. This concern about China as a potential enemy is easily explained both in Kautilyan and modern balance of power terms. China's nuclear and missile assistance to Pakistan have been serious sore points. Nevertheless, concerns about China are not indigenous in Indian strategic culture. Rather, India's sense of civilization and antiquity is seen as at least equal (if not superior) to China's, and modern India has been prudent in seeking a nonconfrontational relationship with China in which trade channels and other forms of exchange are growing and are being used to limit China's reliance on Pakistan.

Revolutionaries and Terrorists

In the postindependence world, India has faced another enemy (actually a series of enemies) that wages guerrilla war against India, including in contemporary parlance by "terrorist" means. In most cases, these threats are from non-Hindu tribal societies seeking independence or autonomy from India. There are also Maoist (Naxalite) revolutionary groups within India dating back to the 1960s that have fomented insurrection in efforts to establish local bastions of power in Bengal, near Nepal, in Andhra Pradesh, and most recently among aboriginal tribes in Chhattisgarh in central India. The newer variant of terrorism is that of Islamic extremist organizations operating from Afghanistan, Pakistan, and Bangladesh, or within Indian-held Kashmir, with occasional operations deep in the Indian interior. India has had to cope with terrorist enemies long before the post-9/11 War on Terrorism, and has a great deal of experience with them. The components of India's strategic culture that are particularly relevant to countering terrorism are timeless goals (patience) and knowledge of truth as power (a superior understanding of the correlation of forces). India's increasingly wholesale public identification of Islamic extremist groups and terrorist attacks with Pakistan since 9/11 is a major inflammatory factor in that relationship, given nuclear arms on both sides.

Note that Indian leaders do not single out "Islam" or "the Muslim world" as categorically the enemy. To do so would stigmatize and alienate the 13 percent, or some 140 million, of India's own population that are Muslim. India's relationship with the Arab countries and the larger Muslim world, however, has been complicated and uneasy. India's strategic culture has no soft corner of admiration for Islam. India long withheld diplomatic recognition from Israel because it was expedient to have close relations with the more powerful Arab countries, particularly Egypt and Iraq. Iraq has been important to India as a source of imported energy. Similarly, India has worked hard to foster closer relations with Iran, partly, as with Iraq, for secure maritime energy supply. This Indian policy of preemptive diplomacy with Arab and Muslim countries in the Middle East naturally weakened Pakistan's natural influence over the same countries.

Only in 1992, with Saddam Hussein under international constraints, the Cold War over, and the importance of the NAM diminished, and in need of better relations with key Western countries, did India establish formal diplomatic relations with Israel. The Indian–Israeli relationship has since become very close. Even so, India has worked hard to maintain positive relations with Arab and Muslim countries. These particular shifts are not foreordained by, but are consistent with, India's omniscient patrician strategic culture, which puts a premium on the long view and on cultivating counteralliances with Pakistan's neighbors, and with external powers that can arrest extremist infiltration into India, whenever possible.

Strategic Culture and WMD

India's strategic culture is not enthusiastic about the acquisition and prospective use of nuclear weapons and other weapons of mass destruction, but is fatalistic about their proliferation and potential use. This allows for a view of WMD as a regrettable evil, but one among many cosmic evils that cannot be wished away by political fiat and that can be adjusted to, as necessary. It is noteworthy that India secretly developed and stockpiled chemical weapons, denying their existence until the Chemical Weapons Convention was concluded, leading to a sudden turnabout. In all likelihood, India has done intensive research on biological weapons, especially on virulent diseases such as smallpox and pathogens such as anthrax, as a hedge against unforeseen contingencies. India's strategic culture affirms mastering each of these scientific thresholds, however unpleasant their wartime consequences may be.

The project of developing nuclear weapons despite policy level ambivalence in the early years and against intense international pressure was shepherded by a strategic enclave that reflected India's strategic culture.[13] After India went nuclear openly in 1998, the policy declarations that some observers confuse with nuclear doctrine were often enigmatic, conveying the impression that India was reluctant to embark on nuclear weapons but was forced into the arena by circumstances. India's declarations of a posture of "minimum credible deterrence" and a nuclear "no first use" policy in 1998, coupled with a policy of not physically deploying combat-ready nuclear forces were conveyed to the world as India's conscious decisions not to repeat the alleged mistakes of the Cold War superpowers: vastly excessive arsenals, destabilizing arms races, and war-fighting doctrines. The omniscient patrician strategic culture thus reached one of its more distilled and refined high points in justifying both to the Indian public and the rest of the world why India had to acquire and demonstrate nuclear weapons. India would continue to teach the world, but have its cake too.

Embracing contradictions, a selection of India's strategists serving on an official advisory board produced in August 1999 a so-called draft nuclear doctrine (DND) paper that was released to the public. This DND paper provided a rationale for credible nuclear deterrence based on the features of a full-fledged triad, with postulated requirements for massive retaliation against nuclear attack and the survivability of the force and its surveillance and command and control components under attack. It omitted only strategic antimissile defenses.

While this DND paper was not then adopted as official policy, in January 2003 a press release "on operationalizing India's nuclear doctrine" announced that a civilian National Command Authority (NCA) and triservice Strategic Forces Command (SFC) had been established. The press release said that a review had been conducted of India's nuclear "command and control structures, the state of readiness, the targeting strategy for a retaliatory attack, and operating procedures for various stages of alert and launch." It did not stipulate that nuclear forces had been deployed nor did it describe force characteristics, service assignments, the adversaries targeted, or the nature of alert procedures. The release did, however, undermine the NFU policy with two loopholes. It indicated first that India would not bar the use of nuclear weapons in retaliation against a *chemical or biological* attack on India or on Indian forces. Second, it promised Indian nuclear retaliation not only against a nuclear attack on Indian territory *but on Indian forces anywhere.*

India's strategic culture proponents of nuclear weapons were comfortable castigating the nuclear arsenals and policies of the Western powers and the Soviet Union and differentiating India's posture as a minimum deterrent leashed by a no first use policy, on one hand, and in emulating a superpower-like, expansive nuclear triad with built-in capacity for absorbing strikes without fatal compromise of survivability on the other. The 2003 release emulated recent U.S. and former Soviet postures of prospective nuclear retaliation for any WMD attack on national territory or on forward deployed forces.

India's enigmatic approach to strategic nuclear forces suits, on the side of minimalist rhetoric, the nation's still limited economic resources and the long lead times it faces for deployment of credible long-range nuclear forces vis-à-vis China. On the side of its long-term ambitions, the DND template is a guiding framework for long-range air-, sea-, and land-based nuclear strike forces. If India proceeds to accomplish these maximalist options, the cryptic language it employs today will be described in retrospect as visionary and prophetic, the natural expression of an omniscient patrician. If it falls short of those objectives or the world changes so fundamentally that they are no longer believed needed or are overtaken by events, shifting course is just as easily explained by reverting to the minimum deterrence language and the usual rhetorical bows to postulated nuclear disarmament objectives.

CONCLUSIONS

India's omniscient patrician type of strategic culture is a complex mosaic of sacred myths and legends and memories of ancient states and civilizations, with the subcontinent as a geographical frame of reference, and with a modern overlay of nationalism supporting a vision of Indian greatness and expectations that India be treated with unmitigated respect. With leadership strata that traditionally prized knowledge as a source both of natural understanding and practical power, the elite carriers of strategic culture adapted modern science and technology to their own purposes in building and fortifying an independent nation. The carriers of that outlook retain a sense of intellectual and moral superiority, however, that is sensitive and reactive to external disapproval or other challenges. The *shapers* of India's strategic culture are primarily nationally recognized political party leaders, senior bureaucratic officials, and notables in the leading universities, think tanks, and the press. With few exceptions, senior military officers have not been shapers of Indian strategic culture, although they are naturally involved in the implementation of government policies that reflect strategic culture. The *carriers* of India's strategic culture include politically oriented professionals at large, in the legal and educational systems, and in public sector industries.

While Indian strategic culture supports ethical views that accord respect for human life, good governance, just administration of law, and social morality in ways that dovetail naturally with contemporary international norms of human rights, that strategic culture is flexible rather than doctrinally prescriptive on specific issues of war and peace, foreign or defense policy, and possession and use of nuclear and other WMD. The strategic frame of reference provides a matrix in which leaders can more readily chart out more explicit national policies and postures, and that enables a complex society to develop forms of consensus to support those initiatives, or, alternately, that permits forces of opposition that gain popular support to resist or reshape those initiatives.

India's strategic culture posits the defense of India as a geographical expression and Indian values as a society. It does not stipulate a general basis for Indian imperial ambitions (e.g., beyond specific territories in dispute in the Himalayan and Kashmir regions), although it contains a certain ambivalence about the finality of independence in Pakistan and Bangladesh. It posits no absolute friends or enemies, although real conflicts with Pakistan and China tend to put both in the inimical category as a practical matter. Apart from the defence of India as such, the most predictable effects of Indian strategic culture are in international policy areas that are perceived to enhance or detract from India's international status and aspirations for recognition as a great power, and in India's unforgiving negotiating style in the same status-related arenas.

India's strategic culture did not, for instance, specifically foreordain that India should acquire a large conventional arsenal or nuclear weapons. But that strategic culture certainly provided a matrix of intellectual and emotional bases for India's major conventional and nuclear weapons acquisitions, once these became affordable or available, and once they were connected by decision makers to India's standing and credibility with the other major powers. By the same token, India's strategic culture does not foreordain specifically whether, or exactly how, India will actually use nuclear weapons if it suffers a nuclear or other WMD attack, or believes it faces an imminent threat of this nature. Nothing in the strategic culture would, however, prohibit nuclear response. Elements of the strategic culture could be invoked for moderation, but moderation could also be subject to debate, based on other strands of strategic culture.

Notes

1. Stephen P. Cohen's book *India: Emerging Power* (Washington, DC: Brookings Institution, 2001), particularly chapter two, thoughtfully examines the shifts in strategic orientation and in the foreign and defense policies of India under Congress Party leaders from Nehru through his daughter, Indira Gandhi, and grandson Rajiv Gandhi, to the rise of the more explicit promotion of Hindu culture under the Bharatiya Janata Party (BJP), led by Atal Behari Vajpayee. What is remarkable notwithstanding these *policy* shifts is the resilience of core values and premises of strategic culture.

2. For the purposes of this text, strategic culture is defined as "that set of shared beliefs, assumptions, and modes of behavior, derived from common experiences and accepted narratives (both oral and written), that shape collective identity and relationships to other groups, and which determine appropriate ends and means for achieving security objectives." Note: (1) This general definition seems to be a satisfactory working definition for strategic culture in the Indian case. However, it does not seem to cover rationales for acquisitive or imperialist behavior, that is, for "objectives" beyond security in the status quo sense, that may be present in other strategic cultures. (2) My understanding of Indian strategic culture is that it forms "loose" drivers (organic predispositions) that differentiate Indian approaches to the outside world—but not tight predictors of behavior, specific policies, or outcomes of Indian diplomatic-, military-, or security-related activities.

3. *Hindutva* usually applies to Hindu revivalism in specifically religious and cultural forms, but the term is also used politically to connote traditional Indian civilization and cultural consciousness in a broader sense. Many proponents regard their promotion of *hindutva* as inoffensive because Hinduism is multifaceted, rooted in natural forces and mythologies, does not require personal adherence to any narrow doctrine, has no centralized hierarchy of priesthood or catechism, and is by its polytheist nature diverse in rituals and forms of worship, is not oriented to proselytization, and is tolerant of many paths to the understanding of the divine.

4. The Indian flavor of the *omniscient patrician* type is neatly suggested by the Sanskrit phrase, *bharat jagat guru,* or "India: the World's Teacher." A sampling of other strategic culture types, for contrast, might be: theocratic, mercantilist, frontier expansionist, imperial bureaucratic, revolutionary technocratic, and marauding or predatory.

5. "The Ganga, especially, is the river of India, beloved of her people, round which are intertwined her memories, her hopes and fears, her songs of triumph, her victories and her defeats. She has been a symbol of India's age-long culture and civilization, ever changing, ever flowing, and yet ever the same Ganga." Words of Jawaharlal Nehru, first prime minister of India, born in Allahabad on the Ganges.

6. The other great rivers of the subcontinent that rise in the Himalayas are the Indus (rising north of Himachal Pradesh before flowing north and then southwest through the Indus valley of Pakistan to the Arabian Sea) and the Brahmaputra (literally, "God's son"), which rises in Tibet and flows east before turning south into India's easternmost extremity, and then southwest to the Bay of Bengal. The Saraswati, another great river rising from the Himalayan watershed, symbolically the most important during the Vedic period, is believed to have flowed south and west through present day Haryana–Punjab, Rajasthan, and southern Pakistan to exit through what is now the Rann of Kutch marshland. The Saraswati River has long since disappeared, probably due to geological changes. In mythology, Saraswati was a daughter of Brahma, the creator, and as a goddess is associated with speech, learning, wisdom, and the arts.

7. History as a subject of chronological study was not indigenous (with some exceptions under Muslim rulers) but rather was imported into India and developed as an intellectual discipline only in the nationalist period.

8. World-class proficiencies demonstrated in other quarters, as in the graduates of India's excellent engineering schools—the publicly funded and highly competitive Indian Institutes of Technology—tend to reinforce this sense of cultural superiority in the private sector, as well as in the public sector. This is true, notwithstanding the fact that these graduates are, as individuals, exemplary high performers whose future status in most cases

could be described as being earned rather than being a result of birth into families of high social status.

9. A U.S. carrier task force did transit through the region at that time, from the Pacific Ocean and around the subcontinent to the Arabian Sea. But its mission was not to threaten India, nor to intervene in the India–Pakistan War, nor to rescue the Pakistani military in East Pakistan. Its course did not change to go north into the Bay of Bengal as such. Rather, the U.S. task force had been assigned to follow and monitor a Soviet naval flotilla that had sailed south from Vladivostok in the Pacific Ocean and then headed west into the Indian Ocean, and finally north toward the Arabian Sea. If the U.S. naval movement had a political–military message, it was to the Soviet Union, cautioning it not to intervene in the South Asian conflict.

10. Although the Indian political decision secretly to prepare for the 1974 nuclear explosive test probably was made as early as 1969, and not as a reaction to the events of 1971, some commentary after 1974 implied that the test was a delayed reaction to the type of threat India faced in the so-called intervention of the U.S. naval task force.

11. In order to secure a breakthrough with India on broader strategic cooperation, the Bush administration gave up a series of ongoing positions and essentially accepted Indian demands that two fast-breeder reactors and eight conventional power reactors, as well as all nuclear research and development facilities, be available to the Indian "military program" and exempt from IAEA safeguards. India also rejected the ongoing U.S. proposal that it accept a moratorium on further production of fissile material. India agreed only to retain its *voluntary* moratorium on nuclear testing, to *participate* in international negotiations on a fissile material cutoff treaty (if such negotiations resume), and to place eight unsafe-guarded power reactors and future power reactors under *limited* IAEA safeguards. India accepted the principle of perpetuity of these safeguards only on condition that foreign fuel supply agreements for these and six other already safeguarded reactors are also maintained for perpetuity. This will require major changes in long-standing U.S. nuclear export legislation. Against the background of the history of U.S. positions on nuclear nonprolif-eration and on India's past proliferation record, India's success in pushing through such an unyielding position is remarkable.

12. Alexander the Great, the Macedonian–Greek invader from the northwest, left important archaeological traces two millennia ago in the subcontinent, but apparently no deep sociocultural imprints that manifest themselves in Indian society and culture today.

13. For a somewhat romanticized but entertaining account of the movers and shakers in India's bomb and missile programs, with operational glimpses into Indian strategic culture, see Raj Chengappa, *Weapons of Peace: The Secret Story of India's Quest to Be a Nuclear Power* (New Delhi: HarperCollins, 2000).

9

Iranian Strategic Culture and Its Persian Origins

Willis Stanley

Strategic Culture Defined

Iranian history is, at first glance, fertile ground for a discussion of strategic culture. It is tempting to begin the discussion of strategic culture with the emergence of Iranian culture itself. However, there is a continuity of human history in and around the Iranian plateau that extends from the emergence of Neolithic society and agriculture around 8000 BCE through to the present day. There are certainly trends within this arc of history that warrant analysis from the perspective of strategic culture; for example, the parallels between the old Iranian belief in absolute kingship and the modern concept of *Velayat-e Faqih* (rule of the jurisprudent) developed by Ayatollah Ruhullah Khomeini wherein clerical authority was institutionalized in the person of a supreme leader.[1] However, addressing this sort of issue raises some questions of methodology that ought to be made explicit.

As an approach to applied strategic culture, this chapter is focused on fleshing out more traditional political–military analysis to construct a comprehensive theory of Iranian strategic culture. In so doing, I will try to demonstrate how some of the concepts that would play in a discussion of Iran's strategic culture have direct import for explaining a current political–military problem faced by U.S. policymakers, and provide resources to help those policymakers weigh their options for responding to the problem.

This analysis will identify those elements of strategic culture that appear to be influential in shaping the decision-making of the current leadership of the Islamic Republic of Iran (IRI), particularly with reference to decision-making on issues related to weapons of mass destruction (WMD). Inherent in that bounded mission is the caution that this essay is not seeking a general theory of Iranian behavior that is as applicable to Cyrus the Great (around 559–530 BCE) as it is to the ruling clerics in modern Tehran. After all, while the modern Iranian may still celebrate the "new year" festival of Nawrooz that dates back to Cyrus and his Acheamenid Empire, it would be folly to believe that modern Iranians have not learned from and been shaped by the intervening historical experience.

Similarly, it is important that any study of Iran's strategic culture avoid the trap of mistaking broad cultural observations for a measured assessment of what Iranians believe and why they believe it. For example, one mid-nineteenth-century French diplomat's description of the behavior of Iranian merchants and craftsmen includes the following:

> The habits of frenzied usury, of constant debts, of expedients, of lack of good faith, and of prodigies of skill provide much fun to Persians but do not contribute to raising their moral level. The life of all this world is spent in a movement of perpetual intrigue. Everyone has only one idea: not to do what he ought…From top to bottom of the social hierarchy, there is measureless and unlimited knavery—I would add an irremediable knavery.[2]

Are we to draw from this that Iranians have some inherent predisposition toward "knavery"? It may, after all, be interesting to note that the IRI's leadership has engaged in fiscal irregularities that would impress even our nineteenth-century French diplomat. However, this is a slippery slope that does not advance our understanding of why the Iranians make certain decisions or how they see the world. At best, it notes a point of continuity in how Western observers have documented Iranian conduct. At worst it is a casual exercise in stereotyping that undermines the credibility of strategic culture as a useful tool.

Those cautions in mind, this chapter will continue by taking the modern IRI as a point of departure. The focus on WMD decision-making bounds the discussion in an important way—those parts of the regime that directly take or influence WMD decisions are the main concern. How Iran decides its agricultural policies or its views on censoring films are not particularly relevant to this subset of security decisions. The following will offer a summary "profile" of Iranian strategic culture in this narrow context, followed by a more detailed discussion of the component elements within the Iranian narrative that appear to be of particular influence. This includes an understanding of how Iranians perceive: Iran's history and shared identity; geography; other groups, the broader world and their place in it; threats; assets in play (e.g., resources, economic vulnerabilities); and ideology and religion. Based on these, I will continue by offering a discussion of how this strategic culture appears to operate; identifying its characteristics with regard to the broader context of Iranian society (e.g, are there competing strategic cultures, who are the custodians of this particular culture, are there other factors that might shape how effectively this strategic culture can operate?). We will conclude with an assessment of the strategic culture "in action." More specifically, the concluding section will demonstrate how WMD decision-making appears to have been influenced by the strategic culture, what caveats should be in place when applying this profile, and what this profile suggests with respect to future IRI decision-making on WMD.

THE IRANIAN "PROBLEM"

The trajectory begun with Ayatollah[3] Khomeini's revolution to depose the Shah in 1979 has placed Tehran in direct conflict with U.S. interests. In summary description, the Iranian regime has a constitutional government designed to give the clerical elite (personified by the supreme leader) extraordinary power to control internal politics and affect policy decisions that it deems critical to regime survival.[4] While there is an elected president and legislature, clerical bodies exist to assure the "Islamic" character of policy decisions and laws passed and vet candidates who would stand for election. Parallel to the government's formal organization of ministries there is a "shadow" set of offices under the supreme leader who often exercise the real decision-making authority on important issues. Parallel to the country's regular military establishment, the Islamic Revolutionary Guard Corps (IRGC) provides the regime with a separate, ideologically reliable military force under the authority of the supreme leader. The Basij, a paramilitary organization within the IRGC, is often used to put down civilian unrest, for example during university-based protests. Even in the economic realm, a significant portion of the country's productive capability is tied to large parastatal organizations called Bonyads. Theoretically organizations that serve charitable and social functions, Bonyads have become large holding companies (with leaders appointed by and answerable to the supreme leader) that have served to divide up the "spoils" of the revolution among the clerical elite, empower the IRGC, and guarantee the regime's ability to direct the domestic economy toward its preferred ends (which presumably includes forestalling the rise of economically based competitors for power).

Although this picture suggests that the supreme leader has fairly comprehensive powers within the system, it is important to recognize that the office was crafted for and defined by the immense personal authority wielded by Ayatollah Khomeini; his successor is neither as highly regarded nor as practically powerful. Khamenei is at the center of a small, collective leadership. Given his need to negotiate consensus and compromise among a range of influential power centers and individuals, Khamenei's web of patronage and personal ties is extensive.

The more public face of the IRI is its current president Mahmud Ahmadinejad. While much is made of Ahmadinejad's strident rhetoric regarding Israel's right to exist and his anti-Americanism, there is little about the Iranian populist that appears particularly original. As summarized by Jahangir Amuzegar:

> Ahmadinejad's agenda has been neither distinctly original nor particularly sound. His Islamic orthodoxy, enmity towards the United States and even his infamous call for wiping Israel off the world map all echo the goals, wishes and words of Ayatollah Khomeini himself in the 1970s and 1980s. His embrace of the Palestinian cause and support of the Lebanese Hezbollah and Shia factions in Iraq are both part and parcel of the position taken by all the Islamic Republic's leaders since 1979. His populist blandishments echo the writings of Ali Shariati—a rabblerousing advocate of Islamic egalitarianism prior to the 1979 revolution. His anti-banker and anti-rich-economic posture—and particularly his latest mind-boggling pro-natal "large-family" advocacy—are copied from Mir Hossein Mussavi, a leftist wartime prime minister and a Khomeini protege. His advocacy of infrastructure build-up, and even his much drummed-up "justice shares" are echoes of ex-president Rafsanjani's positions and campaign promises. His emphasis on peace, love and happiness is a page taken from Khatami's book. His messianic vision of the impending return of the Twelfth Imam reflects the teaching of his guru, Ayatollah Mesbah Yazdi—with perhaps a subtle theological undertone regarding Iran's current theocratic oligarchy. His ardent defense of Iran's nuclear program reflects a nationalistic pride reminiscent of Premier Mossadeq's 1951 oil nationalization. And even the tedious oratory style of his speeches resembles that of the traditional house-calling preachers (rozeh khans).[5]

With a background in the IRGC and connections to the most hardline elements of the clerical elite (e.g., Mesbah Yazdi), Ahmadinejad is something of a wild card. It is unclear if Ahmadinejad represents the leading edge of a more politically vocal IRGC, a popular rejection of government corruption, inefficiency, and haphazard repression, or a compromise by the supreme leader within the ebb and flow of intra-elite squabbling for political power—most likely, he is a mix of all of these. From the U.S. perspective, Ahmadinejad's embrace of the nuclear program is perhaps the most vexing aspect of his presidency.

Iran's nuclear program has prompted stark warnings from the United States. In October 2007, President George W. Bush said that because Iran has threatened Israel's existence, "if you're interested in avoiding World War III, it seems like you ought to be interested in preventing [Iran] from having the knowledge necessary to make a nuclear weapon."[6] The Iranian nuclear program, if it is not intended to provide the regime with ready access to a weapons development effort, is difficult to understand. As summarized by *The Economist*:

> Iran has poured an estimated $10 billion into building a complete, home-grown nuclear industry, yet it has just one nuclear power plant, the Russian-built Bushehr reactor, due to come on stream next year. The same money could have built ten conventional plants of the same capacity, fired solely by the natural gas that Iran currently flares off into the sky, because it has not invested in the technology to recover it. Russia has pledged a ten-year supply of fuel for the Bushehr reactor, meaning that there should be no use, any time soon, for the output of Iran's costly nuclear-enrichment plant at Natanz. The purpose of its heavy-water facility at Arak is even more obscure.[7]

In addition to its nuclear potential, Iran's proliferation-related activities extend to other WMD and long-range delivery systems, principally ballistic missiles.[8] Iran regularly claims to have made significant advances in conventional military capabilities; for example, in April 2006, Iran demonstrated what it called a "Hoot" torpedo capable of speeds of 223 mph (and resembling the Russian Shkval torpedo).[9] Although Iran claims the Hoot as a domestic achievement, it more likely required significant Russian (or other former Soviet states) or Chinese assistance. If Iran's demonstration reflects a credible capability, it is clearly aimed at the U.S. naval presence in the Persian Gulf. Iran's arsenal of less sophisticated military hardware, including small patrol boats and anti-ship missiles, remains a significant threat to civilian shipping that must transit the narrow Strait of Hormuz (i.e., oil tankers).

While there are reasons to doubt Iranian conventional military bluster, there is ample evidence that Iran is willing and able to use terrorism to strike at its adversaries in the region and globally. According to U.S. military officials, Iran is aiding both Shia and Sunni insurgents in Iraq.[10] Iran also supports Lebanese Hezbollah and the Palestinian rejectionist groups responsible for much of the terrorism against Israel. Evidence of Iran's global reach, Argentina has pressed for the arrest of several senior Iranian political figures in association with the 1994 bombing of a Jewish community center in Buenos Aires.[11]

In diplomatic terms, Iran is being no less problematic from a U.S. perspective. Regionally, Iran is pursuing a close relationship with dictator Bashar al-Assad's Syria. Syria provides Iran with a vehicle for aiding and rearming its Lebanese client Hezbollah in the wake of the summer 2006 war with Israel; prestige in the region for supporting a "frontline" state in the ongoing Arab–Israeli dispute; and an Arab ally that can aid Tehran on issues ranging from support for the Iraqi insurgency to relations with Iran's other Arab neighbors. Looking toward Central Asia, Iran is lobbying both Russia and China to allow it full member status in the Shanghai Cooperative Organization (SCO). The SCO is ostensibly an organization devoted to opposing terrorism, separatism, and extremism. In fact, it increasingly functions as a vehicle for opposing U.S. influence in Central Asia. Given the oil and gas reserves controlled by the members, an expanded SCO would, in the words of one expert, be an "OPEC with bombs."[12] Even more broadly, Iran is seeking to acquire allies such as Venezuela—a country that has supported Iran within the International Atomic Energy Agency (IAEA) and has a leader in Hugo Chavez that shares Tehran's antipathy toward the United States.[13]

Finally, Iran, as one of the world's top three holders of proven oil and natural gas reserves, will continue to have an important role in the global economy.[14] Its status as a supplier of an essential raw material is definitely a double-edged sword; three-fourths of the country's income is generated by oil and gas exports while the overall economy remains weak, characterized by corruption, dependence on the government, and high unemployment with per capita income still below pre-Revolution levels.[15] Iran is acutely aware of both its need for foreign investment and technology in the energy sector and the importance of its exports to customers such as China, Japan, Italy, and France. Iran has secured investment from China (deals worth over $100 billion) and proposed a new price-fixing cartel to Russia (itself one of the world's main oil and gas powers). Iran has also tried to discourage payment for oil transactions in dollars, presuming other currencies such as the Euro to be less vulnerable to pressure from Washington.

Given this broad and quickly drawn picture of the current Iranian regime, an analyst interested in mining Iranian "strategic culture" for insights can use that picture as a lens to focus analysis. In effect, a pass through the history of Iranian "culture" will hopefully illustrate some of the origins of current Iranian strategic behavior.

HISTORICAL CONTEXT FOR IRAN'S EMERGING STRATEGIC CULTURE

Iran's modern strategic culture has emerged over the course of many centuries, and finds its roots deep in the Persian civilization. This section provides a brief synopsis of this history, highlighting key points that may have resonance for a later discussion of the IRI's behavior.

Iranian History

As noted earlier, it is productive to begin around 559 BCE with Cyrus's uniting the tribes that had settled on the Iranian plateau (after migration from the Asian steppes) and forging the Achaemenid Empire that would rule from Egypt in the west to Pakistan and the Indus River in the east. Like many of the successful empires to follow, Cyrus and his Achaemenid successors governed by co-opting the local elites of conquered territory and utilizing the inevitable product of civilization and empire: bureaucracy. Cyrus was also the first in what was to become a tradition of absolute kingship, the ruler exercising godlike and god-granted authority.

Coincident with the birth of Cyrus's empire was the rise of Zoroastrianism in Iran. The prophet Zoroaster developed a theology in which the god of all good, Ahura Mazda, was balanced by the equally powerful god of all evil and death, Ahriman. Under the commandment to do good works, have good thoughts, and do good deeds, Zoroaster's followers saw themselves as in service to Ahura Mazda in the eternal struggle against the powers of his evil counterpart. Like the monotheisms that were to follow (Judaism, Christianity, and Islam), each immortal soul would be granted its place in Heaven or Hell depending on the person's conduct in the continual struggle between good and evil. This is the "duality" of Zoroastrianism so often mentioned when scholars seek to assess the influence of this ancient religion (Zoroastrians remain a recognized religion, along with Judaism and Christianity, even in the Islamic Republic).

Long after the Achaemenids, conquerors both foreign (Arab, Mongol) and Iranian would avail themselves of administrative networks and individuals with skill sets developed and handed down over generations of imperial service. By 331 BCE Alexander the Great conquered the aging remnants of the Achaemenids. Alexander's passing ushered in a competition leading to more than 150 years of lesser regional powers followed by consolidation of the Parthian Empire in 163 BCE. The Parthian rulers claimed for themselves the divine right of rule, checked the eastward expansion of Rome, and lead a rejection of the Hellenic influence brought by Alexander and his immediate successors. The uniquely Iranian germ of a national identity had survived its first foreign invasion and occupation.

Yet the Parthians lasted only 400 years and in their place rose the first Sassanian "King of Kings," Ardeshir, who himself laid claim to God's mandate to rule. The Sassanian dynasty saw a new flowering of Iranian science, art, architecture, and culture that rivaled only their Achaemenid predecessors. More importantly, the Sassanian rulers used the institutionalization of Zoroastrianism to legitimate their rule as ordained by Ahura Mazda and to solidify a caste system that served to minimize discord among the elites who might otherwise fracture the empire that stretched once again from Syria to India. By the sixth and seventh century CE, the pressure of fighting off Byzantines and maintaining internal stability was too much even for the evolved administrative tools of Iranian bureaucracy. As the regime crumbled, the heretofore ignored Arab tribes swept out of the deserts, united under the new religion of Islam.

In the mid-seventh century CE, the weakened Iranian empire fell to the advancing armies of Islam and underwent a transformation more profound than any wrought by Alexander. Islam had just undergone the painful process of Mohammad's successors (the new leader was called caliph or deputy of the Prophet) consolidating rule over Arab tribes wont to go their own way in the wake of the Prophet's death. The wars of "reconversion" over, the faithful were ready to extend their dominion in all directions. The coming victories and conquests would confirm in the Arab mind the truth of Mohammed's prophecy and their right to impose it in the lands once ruled by Cyrus and Ardeshir.

Islam, a potent fusing of political ideology and theology, posited itself as the last and complete revelation of the word of God as communicated through his Prophet Mohammad. As such, the Muslim caliph's duty to God was to extend Islam's dominion, giving all a chance to accept the true faith. While Judaism and Christianity, Islam's monotheistic and acknowledged predecessors in revelation, would be acceptable within the lands of Islam, adherents to those faiths would have to endure second-class status, pay exorbitant taxes, and so forth. Polytheism was less well tolerated by the new rulers although it is a measure of Iran's cultural distinction that Zoroastrianism (passably close to monotheism itself) continued to survive under the Arab conquest. In fact, there remains a small Zoroastrian community in modern Iran acknowledged in the Islamic Republic's constitution.

During these early years of Islamic conquest, a development in the Arab leadership of the expanding empire would emerge that would have profound impact on the direction of Iranian Islam. A split in the leadership over who should be rightfully chosen caliph developed between Mohammad's closest companions and his cousin (also his son-in-law) Ali. Intrigue, regicide, and finally civil war followed as competitors jockeyed to be acknowledged as rightful caliph with Ali finally achieving the position after the murder of the third caliph, Uthman, in 656 CE. Ali himself only survived until his murder in 661 CE and the beginning of the Umayyad dynasty's rule over the new Arab empire. Even in this period, the partisans of Ali, known as the Shi'ites, sought to restore their vision of the rightful succession extending from Mohammad through his family.[16]

In 680, Ali's son Hussein led an impossibly small group of family and followers into battle at Karbala against the Umayyad army and were all slaughtered. This sacrifice in the name of rightful succession is a central event in the development of Shi'ism as a distinct branch of Islam. The Shia reverence for martyrdom comes from reference to Hussein's death and the desire of the faithful to atone for the failure of the faithful (Shia who were not with the party at Karbala) to stand with Hussein and die.

It is important to remember that Shi'ism arose as a political dispute, not an issue of theology, and as an intra-Arab matter—Shi'ism is not native to Iran or Iranians. In fact, the consolidation of Iran as the physical heartland of Shi'ism was not to occur until the sixteenth century. As a defeated political movement, the Shia gradually retreated from politics, their leader, the Imam, a descendent of Ali.

The development of Shi'ism as a distinct legal tradition from the dominant Sunni version of Islam began with the sixth Imam, Jafar as-Sadiq, and formalized the ways in which the Shia faithful would conduct their affairs given that their leader was often not the recognized political authority. The Imams, deported to Iraq and sometimes imprisoned by the Caliphs, are themselves considered infallible and martyrs by the Shia. In 874 CE, the young twelfth imam, according to Shia tradition, went into hiding to avoid death at the hands of the current caliph. For sixty-seven years, the imam is said to have communicated with his followers through letters sent via messenger. In 941, the Imam ended his contact with his followers entering the period called the "great occultation." The Shia community believes that this twelfth imam, called the Mahdi, remains in hiding even today and will at some point return as a messianic figure to usher in legitimate Islamic (Shia) government.[17]

The problem the Shia have faced since 941 is how to conduct themselves in the absence of a legitimate, infallible ruler—generally while living in lands controlled by Arab monarchs they view as illegitimate. These rulers are governed by reference to the Kuran, Islam's holy book, the conduct and recorded sayings of Mohammad, and the conduct of Mohammad's closest followers, his Companions. To oversimplify a bit, Sunni Islam uses only these references to govern, issue legal rulings, and enforce the holy law (for Muslims, the only legitimate law) Sharia. The Sunnis believe that God would not allow the community of Muslims to go astray so a consensus would provide guidance on questions fundamental to the faith—an approach decidedly unappealing to the minority Shi'ite faction. In contrast, the Shia reference to the conduct and the rulings of the infallible imams. After the great occultation, and hence no guidance from a rightful Imam, the Shia developed the process of allowing qualified scholars to make "legal rulings based on rational considerations,"[18] an interpretive legal technique called *ijtihad* developed first by the scholar al-Allama al-Hilli who died in 1325. It is not difficult to see why this minority version of Islam, chafing under the control of rulers it did not accept, would find traction among Iranians chafing under the domination of Arabs to whom they felt culturally superior.

From the beginning of the Islamic conquests, the Arab tribes were well equipped to conquer and plunder, less so to rule and govern a far-flung empire. The Iranian legacy of administrative and bureaucratic innovation would play a crucial role in giving the Arab empire the tools necessary to govern, for example, the skill of bookkeeping and the organization of administrative departments within governments. As Arab rulers came and fell, much as traditional monarchs rather than as religious leaders, many of Iran's learned court families adapted to serve new masters, in this context becoming quite powerful. The move of the capital of the Caliphate to Baghdad in 762 would increase the influence of Iran in the Islamic world significantly.[19] From Baghdad, the Abbasid dynasty was to dominate the empire for the next 500 years. According to one Abbasid Caliph: "The Persians ruled for a thousand years and did not need us even for a day; we [Arabs] have been ruling for one or two centuries and cannot do without them for an hour."[20]

The Mongol Conquest

The Abbasid Caliphate ended, crushed under the hooves of Mongol war ponies. In 1218 the Ruler of much of Iran at the time, Khwarizm-Shah Muhammad II (who was at odds with the Caliph in Baghdad), decided to execute a party of Mongol ambassadors as spies. This bit of reflexive cruelty (with perhaps a bit of larceny thrown in as some sources suggest robbery was the true motive) earned the wrath of the Mongol leader Genghis Khan, the "World Conqueror." Mongol retribution, as witnessed by the historian Ibn al-Athir, was catastrophic and comprehensive on a scale that changed the region:

> If anyone were to say that at no time since the creation of man by the great God had the world experienced anything like it he would only be telling the truth. In fact, nothing comparable is reported in past chronicles...[The Mongols] killed women, men and children, ripped open the bodies of the pregnant and slaughtered the unborn...[T]he evil spread everywhere. It moved across the lands like a cloud before the wind.[21]

While al-Athir's account is likely exaggerated, Genghis Khan brooked no opposition and respected no title or position, effectively decapitating the existing social hierarchies throughout Central Asia and eliminating cities that resisted, or worse, mistook instances of Mongol leniency for weakness.[22] By all indications, the Mongol propaganda effort actually encouraged the most lurid and extreme accounts of their victories, the better to undermine the likelihood of future resistance.[23] In any event, the 400,000 troops of Khwarizm-Shah Muhammad II were bested by Genghis and his 150,000-man army.

The Mongols returned under Genghis's grandson and established the Ilkhanid dynasty of local Mongol rulers that governed, again, with the aid of native Iranian administration and advice. The Ilkhanids converted to Islam in 1295, but the dynasty fairly quickly fractured into an array of local and regional rulers.[24] That disarray was briefly reversed by Tamerlane, a nomad in the fourteenth century who repeated some of the Mongols successful tactics (including dependence on Iranian bureaucrats). The next significant period in Iranian history would be marked by extremism and the fateful fusion of Shi'ia Islam with Iranian national identity.

Iranian National Identity

The political chaos of the late fifteenth century laid the groundwork for Iran to assert its national identity for the first time in Shia form. In 1501, Ismail, a young Shia sheikh, using converted Turkomen tribesmen as soldiers, conquered the city of Tabriz and soon claimed for Shia Islam the whole territory once governed by Iran's Sassanids. Ismail, who may have considered himself a living god,[25] was regarded by many of his followers as a direct descendent of Ali. Ismail made Shi'ism the official religion of the new Safavid dynasty, his troops marching forward under blood-red turbans with the slogan: "We are Hussein's men, and this is our epoch. In devotion we are the slaves of the Imam; Our name is 'zealot' and our title 'martyr.' "[26]

Mass conversion to the Shia faith became the rule in Safavid Iran—a rule that was unhealthy to resist. Iran's national identity, always distinct from its Arab conquerors, gained new dimensions of difference as a Shia power reaching from India in the east to the Persian Gulf, northward to the Black Sea (its boundaries east of the Tigris and not including Baghdad) and the eastern coast of the Caspian Sea. To the west lay the Sunni Ottoman Empire. Further, Ismail's self-appointed role as the Islamically legitimate absolute ruler resonated with an Iranian culture that was historically conditioned to accept the divine right of kingship and remembered the greatness of those like Cyrus who had embodied it. The Iranian national identity was articulated in terms of the Shia's historical passion play of martyrdom and suffering; the deliverance once preached about by Zoroaster now offered up to Iranians in the form of the Shia expectation that the messianic figure of the Mahdi would return to set everything right. Although Ismail's path of conquest was ultimately checked by the Ottomans and he died in 1524, the Dynasty lived on for another 200 years. However it took through the eighteenth century for the slowly shrinking Safavid territory to become predominantly Shia.[27]

It was during this period also that the learned scholars of Shi'ism began to coalesce into a definable clerical caste with a loose hierarchy of authority. The clerics, particularly in those areas most remote from officialdom were the ones who collected the faithful's obligatory taxes (a religious duty, not a remittance to the state), administered mosques and schools, and settled legal disputes.

Despite the official Shi'ite character of the regime, the tension between the emerging religious caste, the ulama, and the king, or Shah, were apparent and never fully resolved. Some of the leading clerics, in keeping with Shia rejection of political authority not vested in the rightful Imam Mahdi, opposed the monarchy. Thus as the ulama consolidated, it also became a potential rival source of legitimacy, the core of any real opposition to a particular Shah—a circumstance first evident in the Safavid period and equally true in the 1979 Islamic Revolution. However, many were willing to accommodate the secular aspects of the monarchy and the ulama often enjoyed close relations with the Shah until the Qajar dynasty united Iran in the late eighteenth and nineteenth centuries.

Ottoman Empire and Modernization

The Qajar Shahs ruled Iran from 1796 to 1925 and were Turkomen. Without any credible claim to the linage of Ali and the Prophet, the division between a secular monarchy (nominally a foreign one at that) and the Shia ulama was more pronounced than ever. This did not, however, mean open conflict. Instead, a tacit accommodation emerged in which the Shahs physically protected the state while the ulama did not challenge their authority. Physical threats to Iran were not an idle consideration. Iran stood facing the Ottomans to the west and the Indian Islamic Mughal Empire to the east and the Russians to the north. On the Arabian Peninsula itself, the puritan Wahhabi sect entered into an accord with the Saud clan and laid the foundation for modern Saudi Arabia and a version of Islam that drew even broader distinctions between the two major divisions of the religion. Perhaps most notably, European presence in terms of warships and trade became unavoidable. Modern concepts of the nation-state, with its fixed borders, foreign policy, and sovereignty issues came to the Iranian world. The railroad and telegraph were only two of the inventions that challenged an Iranian elite that had evolved over centuries and was conditioned to accept the Iranian Islamic world as the pinnacle of intellectual and technological development. The shock was profound for the whole Muslim world and continues to reverberate into the twenty-first century.

Western powers, Russia and Britain chiefly, pressed home their advantages negotiating painfully lopsided trade concessions from the Iranians and diving Iran into respective "spheres of influence." The ulama in general retreated from active alliance with the state, becoming quiescent. This apolitical trend reflects the mainstream of Shia clerical attitudes toward secular authority through today. However, the ulama did on occasion "stand up" to the secular authority as in the 1891–1892 "tobacco revolt." In exchange for personal financial compensation, the Shah conceded to the British monopoly on the marketing of Iranian tobacco. Boycotts, riots, and a united and vocal position taken by the ulama, in conjunction with the Iranian merchant class (the Bazaaris), forced the Shah to ultimately rescind the concession.[28] This was also some of the first modern "flexing" of Iranian nationalist muscle in response to the Western colonial presence (which, although burdensome, was, after all, not the equivalent of Mongol predations).

This uneasy tension, the economic predations of the colonial powers and the unsettling reformist intent of the Shah led to Constitutionalist Revolution of the early twentieth century in which the Shah, just before his death, was forced to accept a parliament, or Majlis, that represented Iran's merchant, landowning, and clerical elite. The new Shah was intent on reversing his father's concessions to the constitutionalists and through 1907–1908 the sides jockeyed fiercely for advantage. Protests, warfare, assassination attempts, and economic ruin were the result.

In 1909, the chaos engulfed Tehran and the Shah, who was supported by Russian troops, took refuge in the Russian embassy and abdicated in favor of his twelve-year-old son. It is notable that even in this precarious climate, the Iranian constitutionalists were not in favor of abolishing the monarchy. Moreover, the constitutionalists were not above squabbling among themselves the result being that the Majlis never matured into a truly functioning organ of government. The Majlis was finally ended in 1912 when the young Shah backed by Russian troops settled the matter by forcibly dissolving the body.

In 1925, Reza Shah Pahlavi toppled the last Qajar Shah and attempted to move Iran toward becoming a "modern" state. Principally, that meant serious structural changes intended to provide the military and technological advantages so evident in the hands of acquisitive Western powers eager to exploit these advantages in dealing with the Muslims. Ataturk's Turkish model of development was the objective. As the Shah's state Westernized, the ulama's space of control grew increasingly restricted. The legal system was secularized, the educational system adopted Western-style universities, and local administration slipped from the clerics' grasp. While these moves were discomforting for the ulama, Iran made steady economic progress during the new Shah's first years in power. In addition to the ulama, other remnants of the Qajar elite suffered as well. The Bazaar merchants were dislodged from centuries-old family-based control of Iran's trade by newly empowered institutions and functionaries and state-controlled monopolies. Many of the feudal landowners were displaced as the state, in the person of the Shah, appropriated their land.

In the end, the ulama's worst fear during the constitutional period—that dissolving the monarchy would usher in secularization—was brought near fruition by the Shah himself. Recognizing the ulama as a potential rival power base, the Shah sought to tie his legitimacy to the legacy of Cyrus and the pre-Islamic empires rather than the legal reasoning of Shia scholars. That said scholars were also eager to keep tax monies, land, prestige, and authority for themselves made secularization all the more compelling for the Shah.

Continued foreign interference was also a risk, but the Shah balanced British and Russian encroachments more successfully than did his predecessor. In 1941 as the wartime British and Russian allies occupied Iran (U.S. troop presence in Iran began in 1942), the Shah abdicated rather than accommodate the Allied powers and went into exile. His son Muhammad Reza would become the next and last Pahlavi Shah.

Iran during the Cold War

In the post–World War II period, the new Iranian Shah confronted all of the tensions the Qajar Shahs and his father had faced as well as the new dynamic of the Cold War—an a new American role gently supplanting the British involvement in shoring up the Shah's regime (this time in opposition to their former Soviet allies). The Shah survived by balancing these competing pressures. From 1951 to 1953, the Shah briefly lost that balance when Prime Minister Muhammad Mossadeq ruled as de facto dictator from a position shored up by nationalizing the Anglo-Iranian Oil Company (AIOC). Dealing with communist revolutionaries, ardent national-ists, and the British who refused to reach meaningful compromise on the division of profits from AIOC, the Shah was unable to foresee the prime minister's agenda and the speed with which he would act. As Mossadeq stepped into a vacuum of author-ity, he relied on violent street demonstrations to keep his agenda moving forward through much of 1952 as his support in the Majlis eroded. He purged the military and was unable to revive the economy in the wake of a foreign boycott of Iranian oil subsequent to the nationalization. Ultimately, Mossadeq dissolved the Majlis when it refused to support him. By 1953 the Shah had found it advisable to leave the country. However, he was able to return by August of that year when an Army coup supported by anti-Mossadeq street demonstrations won the day and returned the Shah to his throne. The U.S. Central Intelligence Agency (CIA) and British intelligence role in organizing and helping the pro-Shah forces is often cited in Iran as yet another in a long history of foreign interference and an affront to Iranian sovereignty.[29]

During the Mossadeq era, the ulama were generally wary both of Mossadeq's secular, leftist agenda and the Shah's cooperation with British and American inter-ests. However, after his return to the throne, the Shah made certain to cement his absolute control of Iran and use the once-again flowing oil monies to press forward with a modernization of Iran. As dictator, the Shah left the clerics and others little room to maneuver as he began his "white revolution" to shake up almost every facet of Iranian life. For the clerics, this "revolution" was catastrophic. The Shah intruded on spheres normally reserved for the judgment of learned Shia scholars, for example, the rights of women to divorce and the banning of women's head scarves.

In the post–World War II period, select Shia scholars developed a new train of thought on the role of the clerical caste in politics; one that saw the clergy's role as active rather than passive. These scholars focused on the twin dangers of secularization and Westernization that they defined as threats that might tempt the faithful away from the truth of Islam by offering them the material bounty flaunted by the imperialist. For these clerics, the Shah's white revolution was a direct assault on Islam coupled with an abandonment of Iran to foreign occupation and domination. The Americans were no more welcome than were the Mongol hordes.

While in 1971 the Shah was hosting lavish celebrations of the 2500th anniversary of the Iranian monarchy, the activist clerics became revolutionaries.

Ruhollah Khomeini, with his title "ayatollah" denoting his status as a widely respected clerical authority, had been exiled for opposing the Shah in the early 1960s. By the 1970s, Khomeini had developed an ideological tool he called *Velayat-i Faqih* or the rule of the jurisprudent. The concept is in many ways an extension of the gradual accumulation of clerical authority begun under the Safavids. Without the Mahdi to provide a true just government, Khomeini's theory held, it fell to the learned scholars of Shia Islam to act as trustees and provide the political leadership that the Prophet and the imams had provided. Just as Shia were bound to take their guidance on matters of religious authority (and all matters were religious matters) from a learned scholar they chose to emulate in his piety, so too should an Islamic government take guidance from a learned scholar whose direction would be considered near absolute. In many ways, just as the Shah was celebrating his divine right to absolute kingship, Khomeini was asserting his own divine right to absolute authority as he would ultimately become the Islamic Republic's founding supreme leader.

The 1979 Revolution

A broad range of factors contributed to the 1979 Iranian Revolution. Among them were: large-scale population migration from rural land to cities; land reform initiatives that shook up the landed elite; increasingly repressive conduct of the feared SAVAK secret police; and an almost willful desire by the Shah to offend the sensibilities of Shia Muslims by embracing the most decadent and opulent of Western excesses. The Shah had overreached and Iran snapped. In rebelling against the Shah and removing one absolute ruler, the Iranians were quite willing to accept another absolute ruler—as had Iranian revolutionaries in the past.

The small clique of clerics and their many more devoted followers seized the balance of power within the chaos of the Revolution and used the religious legitimacy personified by Ayatollah Khomeini to claim absolute rule. A constitution was drawn up creating a modern government with an executive, a parliament, and a judiciary. However at every step in the system, there is a vehicle for clerical oversight. For example, candidates can stand for election to Parliament, but they must first be approved by a panel dominated by clerics, only a cleric can head the secret police, and the regular army is mirrored by a powerful new military force called the Iranian Revolutionary Guard Corps, which protects first and foremost the Revolution.

What follows is a summary strategic profile of the current leadership of the Islamic Republic, only removed a few years from the personal oversight (and unquestioned authority) of Ayatollah Khomeini. This profile has been informed by an array of research methods and sources including anthropology, history, political psychology, history, religion, and interviews with Iranians, Arabs, Israelis, and others who have had direct personal experience with the Iranian leadership (e.g., diplomats, businesspeople).

Iranian Strategic Culture in Action

The current Iranian leadership has a distinct worldview and perspective that is extreme in its embodiment of broader trends in Iranian society. Indeed, the regime itself is in a state of flux, not far removed from the initial fervor of the 1979 Islamic Revolution, the horrific costs of the 1980–1988 war with Iraq (known as the Imposed

War in Iran), and the consolidation of a new ruling elite drawn from the ranks of the nation's Shi'ite Muslim clerics. Where this process goes as the generation of men who made the revolution fade from view while a new generation of men and women who have borne the brunt of this transition come of age is uncertain. In many respects, the IRI is a novelty both to Iran with its long tradition of Kings and to Shi'ite Islam as religion/political ideology. We will begin with some very basic assertions that are intended as much to demonstrate what the regime is not as to illuminate what the regime is.

The IRI leadership connects ends and means in an intelligible manner. Given the biases often present in our Western perception of how Islam functions as both a religious system and a political ideology, it is important to disabuse analysts of the notion that Iran's leaders are "mad mullahs" driven to irrational or illogical behavior by devotion to existential goals.[30] The logic and experience defined by Shia Islam shapes their decision-making and there is clear historical evidence that they perceive and place observable reality within that context and act accordingly. In short, they appear to connect means and ends and act accordingly.

The IRI's leadership is a small collective group of decision-makers that is, in large part, well informed and constrained in its behavior by the competing interests of various individuals and factions within the elite. While the current supreme leader, Ayatollah Ali Khamenei, is vested with vast powers over the government, he does not have the personal authority embodied in his predecessor, the Revolution's founder, Ayatollah Khomeini. Khamenei must negotiate among the regime's economic interests,[31] ideological factions,[32] and institutions. Perhaps the most important institution in the currently emerging configuration is the previously mentioned IRGC. The IRGC was formed in the immediate post-Revolutionary period from the militias that helped Ayatollah Khomeini seize and consolidate power. Born in part from distrust of the Shah's military, the IRGC has historically emphasized ideological fervor over military professionalism.[33] President Ahmadinejad and many of those he has brought into the government are former IRGC officials.[34]

The Iranian regime's inner workings are unfortunately opaque. However, Iranian society writ large and the formal organization of the government are rather more transparent (particularly in comparison to other authoritarian regimes in the region), providing significant data on the social, economic, and political information that flows into the decision-making process.

Iranian Hostility toward the West

The IRI leadership appears to have a uniformly hostile view of the West in general and the United States in particular; unsurprising given Iran's long-term experience with outright invasion and occupation and direct experience with British and Russian colonialism. From the Iranian perspective, interaction with the modern West has not been pleasant. Nineteenth-century wars with Russia, and the annexation of much Iranian territory, gave way to twentieth-century violations of Iran's declared neutrality during World Wars I and II and the widely held belief that Iranian experiments with constitutional forms of government were undermined by the West in the Mossadeq period. After the Revolution, the West's support for Saddam Hussein's Iraq as a bulwark against the alarming radicalism of the new regime (epitomized by the seizure of the American embassy and its personnel) was viewed in Tehran as conclusive evidence that the Western powers were implacably committed to strangling the Islamic government. Additional factors shaping this perspective include: Khomeini's exposure to the anticolonial rhetoric of the 1950s and 1960s; Iranian culture's internalization of the notion of duality in ancient Zoroastrianism; and long experience of Iranian subjugation at the hands of successive waves of conquerors including the Arabs and the Mongols. While the regime is adept at receiving and interpreting U.S. messages, its fundamental hostility to the "Great Satan" colors its interpretation of U.S. actions and intentions.

Political-Religious Ideology

The current Iranian leadership appears to have recognizable goals derived from its unique political ideology. That ideology makes use of: Shia Islam's gradual consolidation of a clerical caste and historical Iran's concerns about sovereignty and acceptance of an absolute ruler. In this ideology, Iran and Shia Islam are one and the same, indivisible. Iran operates under Khomeini's unique politico-religious doctrine that stresses the survival of the regime as the ultimate service to Islam. In Khomeini's formulation, the regime is the embodiment of Shia Islam's authority on earth and to abandon it would be to abandon the will of God.[35] Thus the survival of this government and its form is an existential imperative as well as an expression of self-interest and Iranian nationalism. It must be recalled that concept is novel in Shia theology, albeit reflective of existing currents and therefore not simply created out of whole cloth. Remember too that Shi'ism has, of necessity, historically frowned upon religious figures participating in government, given that any government before the Mahdi returns would be considered illegitimate. Clerical rule in the IRI has also formalized the clerical hierarchy more completely, a process begun so long ago by the Safavids.

In sum, the regime's survival interest, honed by centuries of living under Sunni Arab domination is reflected in the IRI's identifiable "red lines": defense against foreign invasion, opposition to externally supported revolution, and resisting outside control over IRI oil exports.

Threat perceptions are an important manifestation of strategic culture. The style of IRI leadership reflects flexible, adaptive elements derived from both Iranian/Persian culture and Shia Islam. These include the cultural and religious sanction of deception and façade when necessary to preserve the faith, one's life, or, most importantly, the regime. The roots of this flexibility are not difficult to intuit: living as Shia in a sea of Sunnis, and as Iranians in a sea of Arabs required developing the survival skills of the often weak and powerless. Indeed, the degree to which Iranian elites were able to co-opt their conquerors through application of the administrative skills developed over centuries speaks to the flexibility that has kept Iran's unique cultural identity alive through the present day.

Finally, in the wake of Iran's horrific experience with the "Imposed War," the leadership has appeared reasonably cautious in terms of military adventurism. During the war, Iran demonstrated a clear willingness to accept great costs to sustain and expand the Revolution, at first embracing aims that clearly went beyond preserving Iranian territorial integrity. While this motive did not survive battlefield setbacks and an Iranian perception that the United States was perilously close to entering the war in overt support of Saddam, it remains an instructive example of the directions in which Iranian nationalism and revolutionary zeal can be channeled given the proper circumstances. In this respect, the zeal of Iran to march "first to Baghdad, then to Jerusalem" reflects a worrisome similarity to the zeal with which the Safavids spread the word of Shi'ism with the sword.

Perhaps more hopefully, it is often noted that modern Iran is refreshingly free of territorial ambitions (save for a few small but strategically located islands in the Persian Gulf); there is no appetite for reassembling the Acheamenian Empire or even a "Greater Iran."

Factors Shaping the Islamic Republic of Iran's Strategic Culture

This profile of the strategic culture of the IRI's leadership flows from a survey of the range of experience, ideology, and practical realities that modern Iranians have inherited from their ancestors.

Geography has provided an important influence on the emergence of a unique Iranian strategic culture. Within the natural boundaries of the Iranian plateau, Iranian nationalism was born and flourished alongside the development of civilization and empire. This was in marked contrast to the nomadic and therefore largely tribal system that gave birth to Islam in the forbidding climate of the Hijaz (or the steppe culture of the Mongol conquerors that would follow the Arabs centuries later). Shi'ism took hold as a reflection of Iranian alienation from their Arab conquerors, a unique trick of identity assertion within the universalist message of Islam. Iranian nationalism since 1979 has been expressed through the vehicle of Shi'ism and the Iranian Revolution was a perfect expression of that synergy.

However, there are reminders of Iran's glorious pre-Islamic past. Much of Iran's history remains current for modern Iranians and is communicated not just through the traditions of Shi'ite Islam but through cultural artifacts that even the current clerical regime does not challenge. For example, the literature of the great Iranian empires is most clearly captured in Ferdowsi's epic poem *Shahnameh* ("Book of Kings"), which lays out the evolution of the divine right through which Iranian kings rule (and how they may lose it).[36] Another literary strand is the series of "Mirrors for Princes" in which Iranian scholars and officials provided gentle instruction to their conquerors regarding how to govern. These texts of ancient Iran coupled with the Shia story of oppression comprise the shared narrative of modern Iranians, kept alive through festivals such as Nawrooz and Ashura.[37]

As implied earlier, the IRI leadership sees Iran as both oppressed (religiously and physically) and challenged by the seductive power of the West as an alternative to the righteous path of *Velayat-e Faqih*. From the Iranian perspective, the West looked on or actually aided Saddam as Iraq waged a long and costly war aimed at (once again) repressing the Shia—including the use of WMD against Iran. This experience defines both Iran's view of the outside world and its place in the world order, and its perception of threat. Published statements by the Supreme Leader and senior figures in the government make clear that this immediate history shapes their current strategic perspective and their conviction that the West, and the United States in particular, is an existential threat, a "Great Satan" standing in opposition to God and the House of Islam.

The Centrality of Oil

No discussion of Iranian strategic behavior can avoid the role oil and gas play in enabling this leadership to both remain in power and identify and pursue strategic objectives. In short, oil and gas exports are definitive for the survival of the Iranian economy. As summarized by the U.S. Department of Energy:

> Iran's economy relies heavily on oil export revenues—around 80–90 percent of total export earnings and 40–50 percent of the government budget. Strong oil prices the past few years have boosted Iran's oil export revenues and helped Iran's economic situation. For 2004, Iran's real GDP increased by around 4.8 percent. For 2005 and 2006, real GDP is expected to grow by around 5.6 percent and 4.8 percent, respectively. Inflation is running at around 15 percent per year.[38]

Despite this wealth of resources (and likely access to more as Caspian fields are developed), Iran's oil and gas infrastructure is rapidly aging and production is only now nearing pre-Revolutionary levels. Many of the factors that have heretofore limited the infusion of foreign investment and technology that would improve productivity are also those that have limited broader economic development: the prevalence of corruption and mismanagement; an arcane network of quasi-official "charities" that function as huge conglomerates and may account for as much as 40 percent of Iranian GDP; nationalist suspicion of foreign interests; and alarming levels of capital flight.

The Influence of Shi'ism

Finally, and perhaps most centrally, Shia Islam plays a defining role in shaping the worldview of Iran's decision-making elite. The Iranian constitution enshrines Khomeini's *Velayat-e Faqih* and the structure of the government guarantees that the clerical elite retain the authority to enforce its interpretation Islamic law on the populace.[39]

One way that Shi'ism conditions both thought and actions is through the concept of martyrdom. The IRI leadership uses the term to legitimate sacrifices made for the preservation of the Revolution, thus tying the practical survival of the regime to the spiritual context of Shia Islam. The "human wave" attacks during the Imposed War are often cited as an example of the extremes to which this notion of sacrifice can be taken. While raw nationalism had its role, the willingness with which Shia soldiers were willing to sacrifice themselves cannot be divorced from the Shia passion play of Hussein's martyrdom at Karbala in 680 and the Shia mandate to atone for not fighting and dying alongside Ali's grandson.

Another concept is *maslaha*, loosely defined as "in the public interest" without necessarily referring to the strict tenets of Islamic jurisprudence.[40] More familiar to Western audiences is the notion of jihad. "Holy war" can mean a range of things from actual battle against an enemy of Islam, to a person's internal struggle with Islam. However, historically it is difficult to find meaningful usage outside the martial context.[41] In the IRI it may appear that both definitions are used—the IRI is fighting a "jihad" against the infidels (e.g., Israel, United States), fighting a jihad to lead the Iranian people to become good Muslims, and so forth; however, there is sufficient room for skepticism that the leadership's intent is to embrace the more benign (and quite modern) interpretation of jihad.

Without an exhaustive reading of Islamic culture beyond the scope of this essay, it is difficult to adequately convey the degree to which Shia Islam has been fused with the Iranian national identity. Suffice it to say that the last Pahlavi Shah suffered his fate in part because important elements of the Iranian populace were offended by his heavy-handed attempts to Westernize Iran and foster a "cult of monarchy" drawing its legitimacy from the roots of Cyrus rather than from Islam and the Koran.[42]

Given this grounding, the boundaries of Iran's strategic culture are fairly well defined conceptually (e.g., as an evolution of Shia jurisprudence), in terms of material drivers (e.g., control over vast quantities of oil and gas) and experiences within the "immediate" scope of Iranians shared historical narrative (immediate to include the formative events of Shi'ism as well as the more directly experienced impact of the Imposed War). Based on this understanding of Iranian strategic culture we can begin to ask questions about specific circumstances that may (or already do) face this leadership with respect to WMD.

IRANIAN STRATEGIC CULTURE AND WMD DECISION - MAKING

Before describing how strategic culture informs an analysis of Iranian WMD decision-making, it is necessary to briefly identify what this regime hopes to gain from WMD acquisition and how it hopes to realize those objectives. Nuclear power status would be an enormous credential for Iran's clerical leaders, helping to solidify their hold on power and stall the fortunes of those would liberalize Iranian society and economy (i.e., increase Iranian's exposure to the "toxic" corruption of the West). A nuclear weapon capability also would help to fulfill the leadership's ambition to make Iran the Islamic world's preeminent power, a fulfillment of Iran's self-appointed role as regional hegemon and as a beacon for all to convert to the true Islam. It also secures the continued existence of a legitimate Islamic government until the return of the hidden twelfth Imam Mahdi, in effect preparing the way for his messianic delivery of the faithful. Finally, Iran's leaders appear to believe a nuclear capability would prevent meaningful U.S. opposition to their domestic and foreign policy agendas. The United States, in their view, would be unwilling to confront a nuclear-armed Iran much as the United States appears unwilling to confront a nuclear armed North Korea. On the nuclear issue in particular, the regime has skillfully created domestic support for an inordinately expensive civilian nuclear power program as a matter of national pride and symbol of cultural progress.

From that understanding of the stakes involved, analysts can begin to frame possible, or even likely, Iranian responses to specific questions; for example, IRI responses to U.S. deterrent or coercive threats related to Iran's nuclear program. Other potential questions might address the likelihood that inducements in the form of economic or technological incentives would either be so tempting as to undermine IRI strategic objectives, or the propensity of the regime to believe that Western offers of such assistance are genuine.

In the economic sphere, either inducements or sanctions must consider the near total role petroleum products play in Iran's calculus. A UN oil embargo would be a serious threat to IRI values. Unfortunately, the mechanics for organizing such an effort are vulnerable to exactly the tactics at which the Iranian leadership excels. For example, since 2004, IRI has been aggressively courting foreign investment in the oil sector, particularly from countries such as China and Japan, as one step in minimizing the likelihood of a credible embargo threat. Even without skilled opposition, the ability to organize such an effort in a timeframe relevant to the progress of IRI nuclear technology is highly questionable.

Militarily, Iranian caution appears conditioned on the maintenance of a comfort zone in which they do not perceive actions to be the opening phase of a regime change effort. Should the UN or some subset of major countries contemplate military action to retard the Iranian nuclear program, the potential for an effective strike has to be weighed against the possibility that Iranian leaders could miscalculate the strike's impact on the regime's chances for survival. In the event of such a strike, understanding Iranian redlines and thresholds will be critical to disciplining Iran's response via its traditional post-1988 means—terrorism.

Diplomatically, Iranian lack of trust in the international "system" makes it difficult to construct a set of positive inducements that would both preclude Iranian deception and provide reassurance to the Iranians that the deal struck will be honored by the "Great Satan" and its minions. For example, Iranian conduct of nuclear negotiations with the EU-3 (Britain, France, and Germany) and the IAEA have led a steadily progressing nuclear program in Iran and much frustration in London, Paris, and Berlin.[43] From the Iranian perspective, the negotiations appear to be a thinly veiled U.S. initiative to deprive Iran of perhaps the only capability and technology capable of deterring the United States when Washington considers overt aggression against the Islamic Republic.[44]

CONCLUSION

As is obvious, this approach to strategic culture does not produce a predictive model of behavior although it has clearly suggested that some outcomes are more likely than others—and why. But it does provide historical context and a framework upon which to hang logical and evidentiary support, both of which can be tested and subjected to revision. Moreover, the findings from this sort of approach can be challenged in the way that even culturally informed stereotypes cannot. Conclusions from this sort of review should be able to stand up to empirical scrutiny through review and assessment of formative observations about history, resources, religion, and so forth. Errors of fact and reason can be more readily identified and corrected than either the unquestioned assumptions within stereotypes or the simplifying hyperrationality common to more formalized approaches to decision modeling.

NOTES

1. The concept was invented by Ayatollah Ruhollah Khomeini to establish an absolute clerical ruler serving as the Shadow of God, until the Mahdi (the twelfth imam) returns to install a just Islamic government. The concept is novel in Shia theology and contrary to some Shia tradition by which religious figures would not participate in government, given that any government before the Mahdi is considered illegitimate. However, it is also a logical extension of the imam's presumed role in Shia society and the gradual accumulation of authority within a clerical elite that dates back to the sixteenth century. Today the supreme leader is Ayatollah Ali Khamenei; he has final say in all aspects of Iranian life, society, and government.
2. Arthur de Gobineau quoted in Charles Philip Issawi, ed., *The Economic History of Iran, 1800–1914* (Chicago: University of Chicago Press, 1971), p. 40.
3. Ayatollah or "sign of God" is a religious title given to very senior Shia scholars. Shi'ism emerged from a political dispute over succession after the death of Mohammad and has become a legal school distinct from the dominant Sunni tradition within Islam. For a discussion of the development of Shi'ism, see Heinz Halm, *Shi'a Islam: From Religion to Revolution*, trans. Allison Brown (Princeton, NJ: Markus Wiener Publishers, 1996).
4. For a discussion of the origins of the Iranian constitutional system, see Asghar Schirazi, *The Constitution of Iran: Politics and the State in the Islamic Republic* (London: I. B. Tauris, 1998).
5. Jahangir Amuzegar, "The Ahmadinejad Era: Preparing for the Apocalypse," *Journal of International Affairs,* Vol. 60, No. 2 (2007), http://www.questia.com/read/5020722886 (accessed November 28, 2007).
6. Matt Spetalnick, "Bush: Threat of World War III If Iran Goes Nuclear," *Yahoo News,* October 18, 2007, http://news.yahoo.com/s/nm/20071017/ts_nm/iran_bush_dc (accessed October 23, 2007).

7. "Iran: They think they have right on their side," *The Economist*, November 22, 2007, http://www.economist.com/world/africa/displaystory.cfm?story_id=10181134 (accessed November 26, 2007).

8. Robert Einhorn, *Robert J. Einhorn, Assistant Secretary of State for Nonproliferation, Testimony Before the Senate Foreign Relations* (Washington, DC: 2000), http://www.state.gov/www/policy_remarks/2000/001005_einhorn_sfrc.html (accessed October 23, 2007).

9. Ali Akbar Dareini, "Iran Touts Torpedo, Claims 'Superiority,'" *The Boston Globe*, April 3, 2006, http://www.boston.com/news/world/middleeast/articles/2006/04/03/iran_touts_torpedo_claims_superiority/ (accessed October 23, 2007).

10. Alissa J. Rubin, "U.S. Suspects that Iran Aids Both Sunni and Shiite Militias," *The New York Times*, April 12, 2007, http://www.nytimes.com/2007/04/12/world/middleeast/12iraq.html?_r=1&oref=login (accessed November 15, 2007).

11. Monte Reel, "Argentina Pursues Iran in '94 Blast As Neighbors Court Ahmadinejad," *Washington Post*, January 14, 2007, http://www.washingtonpost.com/wp-dyn/content/article/2007/01/13/AR2007011301253.html (accessed October 23, 2007).

12. Kin-Ming Liu, "The Most Dangerous Unknown Pact," *The New York Sun*, June 13, 2006, http://www.nysun.com/article/34366?page_no=2 (accessed October 23, 2007).

13. For example, the countries have reportedly set up a joint $2 billion fund to assist countries seeking, in Chavez's words, "to liberate themselves from the [U.S.] imperialist yoke." "Chavez And Iran Unveil Anti-Us Fund," *AlJazeera.net*, January 14, 2007, http://english.aljazeera.net/NR/exeres/FBBF5028–87F2–4FD5-A411-BF01B23FCBF9.htm (accessed October 23, 2007).

14. "Iran Energy Data, Statistics and Analysis—Oil, Gas, Electricity, Coal," http://www.eia.doe.gov/emeu/cabs/Iran/Background.html (accessed October 23, 2007).

15. Lionel Beehner, *Tehran's Oil Dysfunction* (Council on Foreign Relations, 2007), http://www.cfr.org/publication/12625/#2 (accessed October 23, 2007).

16. For a more detailed discussion of the Arab developments, see Bernard Lewis, *The Arabs in History* (New York: Oxford University Press, 1993).

17. There are other sects of Shia that end the line of infallible imams at the seventh imam. "Twelver" Shi'ite Islam, as described here, is the dominant version.

18. Halm, *Shi'a Islam*, p. 102.

19. For a book length treatment of the Abbasid period, see Hugh Kennedy, *When Baghdad Ruled the Muslim World* (Cambridge, MA: Da Capo Press, 2005).

20. Patrick Clawson and Michael Rubin, *Eternal Iran: Continuity and Chaos* (New York: Palgrave Macmillan, 2005), p. 18.

21. Bertold Spuler, *History of the Mongols* (New York: Barnes & Noble, 1968), p. 30.

22. For example, Nishapur where the residents revolted against the Mongols in 1221, in the process killing Genghis Khan's son-in-law. The Khan allowed his widowed daughter to decide the city's punishment. Widely circulated reports state that no living creature (including dogs and cats) was allowed to survive. Jack Weatherford, *Genghis Khan and the Making of the Modern World* (New York: Three Rivers Press, 2004), p. 117.

23. Both Christian and Muslim sources from the period often exaggerate the barbarity and bloodiness with which the Mongols conducted their campaigns, providing lurid accounts of battles killing millions. The Mongols were indeed merciless and brutal in the service of strategic objectives or avenging themselves (see note 6), but seldom demonstrated the recreational cruelty with which Christian and Muslim leaders sometimes treated captive Mongol soldiers. Mongol slaughter and rapine pushed at the boundaries of the norms of war and conquest at the time, but was hardly unique in its brutality; it was most distinctive in the efficiency and speed with which it was conducted.

24. One Mongol Khan was converted to Shi'ism, but his successors returned to Sunni Islam.

25. Muslim rulers after Mohammad on occasion took significant liberties with regard to their theologically defined status, sometimes announcing themselves to be the Prophet's (or God's) successor and equal.

26. Clive Irving, *Crossroads of Civilization* (New York: Barnes & Noble, 1979), p. 157.

27. Shia and Sunni both responded to oppression within the Islamic world by migrating to areas in which they were majority; the selective repression of other religious minorities

(e.g., Christians and Jews) being subject to the whims not only of religious dictate but of political expediency.

28. Another act of defiance was in 1948 when several leading clerics issued a ruling, or fatwa, declaring that women would henceforth have to wear the chador, a black garment covering head to toe.

29. See the CIA history of the 1953 Coup at http:\\www.gwu.edu/~nsarchiv/NSAEBB/NSAEBB28//index.html.

30. For perspective on this, see Karl Vick, "Misreading Tehran," *Washington Post*, June 25, 2006. p. B1.

31. Many senior clerics established extraordinary personal wealth in the process of the regime's confiscation of the Iranian monarchy's holdings. Others enriched themselves through control over the government and its functions (e.g., export licenses, subsidized farming, etc.). See Paul Klebnikov, "Millionare Mullahs," *Forbes*, July 21, 2003.

32. The regime's leadership has methodically marginalized the internal resources of those within the elite seeking to take a less strident tone in Iran's relationship with the outside world, particularly the West. That group has been personified by former president Mohammad Khatami (his allies were called the "2nd of Khordad Movement"). The emerging faction represented by current president Mahmoud Ahmadinejad appears to be much more radical, less experienced (e.g., less education abroad), and less tied to the first generation of Revolutionary political elites. See Ilan Berman, *The Iranian Nuclear Impasse: Next Steps*, Statement before the U.S. Senate Homeland Security and Governmental Affairs, Committee Subcommittee on Federal Financial Management, Government Information and International Security, July 20, 2006.

33. There is some debate on how professional the IRGC has become and how representative its members are of the prevailing attitudes in the population as a whole.

34. For an introduction to the IRGC, see Kenneth Katzman, *The Warriors of Islam: Iran's Revolutionary Guard* (Boulder, CO: Westview Press, 1993).

35. Ruhollah Khomeini, *Islamic Government* (Arlington, VA: Joint Publications Research Service, 1979).

36. Abolqasem Ferdowsi, *Shahnameh: The Persian Book of Kings* (New York: Viking Press, 2006).

37. Ashura is the festival to mourn the death of Hussein at Karbala in 680 CE. The climax of the ten-day holiday is self-flagellation by men with chains, and cutting oneself (in extreme cases), followed by chants, and chest beating. For a fuller description of the origins, see Halm, *Shi'a Islam*, pp. 41–44.

38. U.S. Department of Energy, Energy Information Administration, *Country Analysis Brief: Iran*, January 2006, http://www.eia.doe.gov/emeu/cabs/Iran/Background.html (accessed March 7, 2006).

39. For one discussion, see Asghar Schirazi, *The Constitution of Iran* (London: IB Tauris, 1997).

40. The word actually has Arabic roots, but the concept is quite consistent with Iranian Shi'ism that accepts a more interpretive approach to jurisprudence than is allowed by strict Sunni schools.

41. David Cook, *Understanding Jihad* (Berkeley, CA: University of California Press, 2005).

42. In addition, the resources that supported Iran's pre-revolutionary commercial and religious elite were threatened by the Shah's land reform and economic initiatives—thus there was a purely material reason for many influential clerics to actively oppose the Shah.

43. For example in November 2004 the EU-3 and Iran reached an agreement that included a suspension of IRI nuclear activity. Iran accelerated its nuclear work as the deadline neared, clearly indicating that contrary to European hopes, a real long-term halt to Iran's nuclear program was not on the table. For example, see Ian Traynor and Suzanne Goldenberg, "Fresh Suspicion over Iran's Nuclear Aims," *The Guardian*, November 20, 2004, p. 1.

44. And reflective of Iranian memory of the Mossadeq period.

10

The Making of Syria's Strategic Culture

Murhaf Jouejati

Syria's Strategic Culture

By virtue of its leading role in the Arab national movement, Syria's strategic culture is rooted in its view of itself as the champion of Arab rights against what it perceives to be Western penetration of the Middle East, with Israel as its bridgehead. That perception is derived from Syria's bitter experience with Western colonial powers, especially Britain, which first fragmented the Middle East, then colonized it, and later supported European Jews in the usurpation of Palestine. It is also derived from Syria's frustration with the United States, which provides Israel massive military, political, and economic support—even as Israel occupies Arab territories in violation of United Nations Security Council land-for-peace resolutions.

With the advent of the more pragmatic Hafez Assad regime in 1970, Syria limited its objectives vis-à-vis Israel: from the liberation of Palestine to the recovery of the Arab territories Israel occupied during the 1967 war (and the establishment of a Palestinian state in the West Bank and Gaza). To this end, Assad sought to enhance Syria's bargaining position by attempting to reach strategic parity with Israel through the bolstering of Syria's offensive and defensive capabilities and by using militant anti-Israel groups as instruments of Syria's power. With the collapse of Syria's former Soviet patron, its efforts to reach strategic parity with Israel came to a halt. Upon Assad's death in June 2000, all his son and successor Bashar could do to defend Syria was to rely on its aging military equipment, the deterrent threat of Syria's chemical weapons, and the ability to mobilize militant anti-Israel groups.

Factors Shaping Syria's Strategic Culture

Syria's strategic culture has been shaped by a variety of influences. Among these are its geography, by the origins and sources of its shared historical narrative, by its bitter experience with Western colonial powers, by its perceptions of threats, ideology, and religion, the desperate economics of its mainly agrarian society, and its leadership style and structure.

Geography

Syria's political geography is an important factor in shaping its strategic culture: Whereas Greater Syria once included contemporary Syria, Lebanon, Jordan, and Palestine, contemporary Syria has been hemmed in by artificial boundaries that Britain and France imposed on it following their World War I victory over the Ottoman Empire.[1] Moreover, Syria's only natural defensive barrier, the mountainous Golan Heights, was occupied by Israel during the Six-Day War in 1967.

Origins, Sources, "Shared Narrative"

History is another factor that shaped Syria's strategic culture. The origins of Syria's strategic culture are rooted in its bitter experience with Western colonial powers. According to the Syrian narrative, Britain betrayed the Arabs by failing to fulfill its World War I promise to the Syrian-backed *Emir* (Prince) Hussain, *Sharif* (governor) of Mecca, to support an independent Arab state in return for an Arab revolt against the Ottoman Empire.[2] Instead, following the defeat and demise of the Ottoman Empire, Britain took over former Ottoman territories and, together with France, Britain's wartime ally, divided them into separate political units that the two European powers then colonized: Britain took over Palestine, Transjordan, and Iraq, and France occupied Syria and Lebanon. Adding insult to injury, the British promised the Jewish people a "national home" in Palestine, until then southern Syria.[3]

Relationships to Other Groups

Syria's bitter experience with Western colonial powers is a critical component of Syria's worldview. Following the dismemberment of Greater Syria and the loss of Palestine, Syria's relationship with both state and non-state actors became a function of their relations with the newly created Jewish state. This goes a long way in explaining both Syria's anti-Western predisposition and its support for militant anti-Israel guerrilla groups.

Unlike the United States, Israel, and several Western states that consider anti-Israel groups as "terrorist organizations," Syria (along with other Arab and several Third World states) view them as legitimate national resistance movements struggling to end Israel's illegal occupation of their lands. Syria also uses these groups as leverage against independent-minded Palestinian organizations (i.e., Fatah, the mainstream Palestinian organization) to prevent the latter from adopting a separate Palestinian–Israeli deal that might, according to Syrian thinking, weaken the broader Arab front against Israel. Alternatively, Damascus uses these groups to derail diplomatic initiatives that fail to take Syrian interests (i.e., the recovery of the Golan Heights) into account.

However, Syria (under the two Assads) consistently denied militant Palestinian groups the right to use Syrian territory as a base from which to launch operations against Israel. This policy is part and parcel of Syria's broader security policy of scrupulously adhering to the terms of the disengagement of forces agreement with Israel that former U.S. Secretary of State Henry Kissinger brokered in 1974 following the 1973 war.

Threat Perception

Threat perception is yet another factor shaping Syria's strategic culture. From a Syrian perspective, Israel (which is located only forty miles southwest of the Syrian capital of Damascus) represents the greatest threat to both Syrian security and regional security.

Syria (along with other Arab states) and Israel went to war in 1948, 1956, 1967, and 1973. During the "Six-Day War" in June 1967, Israel occupied Syria's Golan Heights, Egypt's Sinai Peninsula, and the West Bank of the Jordan River (Palestinian territory that had been administered by Jordan since 1948). In 1982, Syria and Israel confronted each other in Lebanon. Although Syria and Israel engaged in peace talks during the 1990s as part of the Middle East peace process, the peace talks failed, Israel continued to occupy the Syrian Golan, and the two states continue to be locked in a state of war.

Syria's sense of threat springs from Israel's territorial aggrandizement that has been sustained by Israel's U.S.-backed superior conventional military power. That sense of threat is heightened by Israel's nuclear power. Most public estimates of Israel's nuclear capability range between 100 and 200 weapons,[4] but one analyst, Harold Hough, concludes that the Israeli nuclear arsenal contains as many as 400 deliverable nuclear and thermonuclear weapons.[5] Furthermore, Israel has an active chemical weapons program, including the production of mustard and nerve agents, and a biological warfare capability.

To make matters worse, although Syria, along with 185 other states, signed the Treaty on the Non-Proliferation of Nuclear Weapons (the Non-Proliferation Treaty or NPT) in force since 1970, Israel is the only country in the Middle East not among the signatories to that treaty.

On a broader level, Syria feels vulnerable to its U.S.-dominated regional security environment. In addition to Washington's massive military, political, and economic support to Israel, the United States extends its tentacles throughout the region. A quick glance at the map buttresses this argument: To Syria's north is Turkey—a powerful U.S. ally and NATO member—with which Syria has traditionally had a tense relationship. Syria and Turkey share 714 miles of border. Although Syrian–Turkish relations improved significantly after Bashar Assad's landmark visit to Turkey in January 2004, some of the underlying issues that divide the two states have not been entirely resolved.[6] Moreover, Turkey and Israel—Syria's archrival—are allies and, by the terms of their strategic alliance, Turkish authorities allow the Israeli air force to train in Turkish airspace, close to northern Syria.[7]

To Syria's east lies Iraq, with which Syria shares some 376 miles of border and where the United States has deployed 140,000 troops since March 2003. Although Syria views the American military presence in Iraq as a threat to its security, Syria's Iraqi challenge predates the U.S. occupation of that country. In addition to the personal animus between the late Syrian leader Hafez Assad and Iraq's ousted leader, Saddam Hussein, and to the ideological competition that pitted the two rival factions of the Ba'th Party that dominated the two states, Syria and Iraq have for a long time been locked in a classic geopolitical rivalry.[8] As a result, the two states tried to destabilize each other during the 1970s and 1980s and came close to armed conflict on several occasions. Moreover, Saddam Hussein's ability and willingness to use chemical weapons against Iraq's Kurdish minority and against Iran heightened Syria's threat perception.

To the south, Syria shares a 300-mile border with Jordan, a state with which Syria maintains an uneasy relationship in large part because the Jordanian elite is among Washington's closest Arab allies and often does its bidding.

Finally, off Syria's western coastline, the U.S. Sixth fleet is firmly anchored in the Mediterranean. In these circumstances, it is easy to understand why Syria feels the need to be strong. It is also easy to understand why Syria maintained a sizeable force inside Lebanon, Syria's western neighbor, until 2005, when the UN Security Council, at the behest of the United States and France, ordered Syria to withdraw its troops from that country.[9]

Ideology and Religion

Islam is the religion of the majority of Syrians. In its essence, Islam, like Christianity, recognizes the concept of "just war." *Jihad* (Holy war) by force of arms may be either defensive—to defend oneself from attack—or offensive—to liberate the oppressed. But Islam emphasizes the defensive aspects of jihad rather than the offensive ones. The dictates of Islamic law include such principles as advance notice, discrimination in selecting targets, and proportionality. With regard to weapons of mass destruction (WMD), Islam is highly likely to prohibit their use as these weapons do not discriminate between civilian and military targets. It is on this basis that senior Iranian officials have denied that Iran is pursuing the development of nuclear weapons.[10]

However, since there were no WMD when the Koran was written (there are no Koranic verses that deal with this issue specifically) there has been no systematic work by Muslim scholars on the ethical issues surrounding the use of nuclear, chemical, and biological weapons, despite the fact that several Muslim states possess at least some of these weapons.

Still, there is general agreement that since the enemies of Islam possess such weapons, Muslim countries are justified in acquiring them, but only for purposes of deterrence and, if used, only as a second-strike weapon.[11]

Whatever the case, Islamic doctrine does not appear to have a significant impact on the Syrian elites' strategic calculations. As we shall see, they have been more influenced by Arab nationalism's secular ideology.

Economics

Syria's economic base is too slim to support its foreign and security policies. Although the Syrian economy has enjoyed a good rate of growth, it remains transitional. Mainly agrarian, it has only a modest industrial sector.

Under the radical Ba'th Party (1966–1970), Syria embarked on a socialist course that sought to curb economic ties to the West, seen as obstacles to integrated national development and constraints on a nationalist foreign policy. A new state-dominated economy emerged, aimed at self-sufficiency but supported by the former Soviet bloc. The regime's simultaneous commitment to an ambitious development program, populist welfare, and a militant foreign policy put severe strains on its resources.[12]

Under Hafez Assad, Syria was forced to rebuild ties to the Western market and Gulf countries in a search for new resources. Unabated growth in military, investment, and consumption expenditures made Syria increasingly dependent on external economic support, chiefly from the Arab oil-producing countries and the former Soviet bloc. This support was crucial in sustaining Syria's foreign policy stance, but Syria's dependence was also a constraint on policy, diluted only by its distribution among several ideologically disparate sources. Dependence on Saudi Arabia, in particular, had a powerful moderating effect on Syrian policy.[13]

Although low oil prices in the late 1990s forced Saudi Arabia and other Arab oil-producing states to reduce their economic assistance to Syria, the recent shift toward a market economy promises to further moderate Syrian policy. Indeed, the economic reforms that Bashar Assad's administration has put in place since coming to power in July 2000 are designed to integrate Syria into the world market economy. To date, the Syrian government has given the private sector more space, including the establishment of private banks, private insurance companies, and in the near future, a stock market.[14] Despite the financial benefits and projected growth that this shift is likely to produce, there is little likelihood that Syria's economy will be able to sustain its foreign policy and security objectives, especially that Syria's oil deposits are projected to dry up in 2010.[15]

Type of Government/Leadership Structure

In its constitutional provisions, Syria's presidential system makes the president the center of power. The president is supreme commander, declares war, concludes treaties, proposes and vetoes legislation, and may rule through decree under emergency powers. He appoints vice presidents, prime ministers, and the council of ministers—the cabinet or "government"—which may issue "decisions" having the force of law. The president enjoys a vast power of patronage that makes legions of officials beholden to him and ensures the loyalty and customary deference of the state apparatus. Presidential appointees include army commanders, the heads of the security apparatus, senior civil servants, heads of autonomous agencies, governors, newspaper editors, university presidents, judges, major religious officials, and public sector managers. Through the council of ministers, over which he may directly preside, the president commands the sprawling state bureaucracy and can personally intervene at any level to achieve his objectives if the chain of command proves sluggish.

The president is chief legislator, the dominant source of major policy innovation. He can legislate by decree during "emergencies" (a condition loosely defined) and when parliament is not in session. He can also put proposals to the people in plebiscites that always give such proposals overwhelming approval. The president normally controls a docile majority in parliament, which regularly translates his proposals into law. His control of parliament stems from his ability to dismiss it at will and from his leadership of the ruling Ba'th Party that dominates it.

Finally, the president bears primary responsibility for the defense of the country and is the supreme commander of the armed forces. He presides over the National Security Council, which coordinates defense policy and planning, and assumes operational command in time of war.

That said, although policymaking in Syria appears to be a one-man show, Syria's presidential system includes a powerful subsystem in the form of the Ba'th Party.[16] The influence of the Ba'th Party is clearly spelled out in the Syrian constitution, which states that the Ba'th Arab Socialist Party is the leading party in the state. It leads a National Progressive Front (NPF) whose duty is "to mobilize the potentials of the masses and place them in the service of the Arab nation's objectives."[17] According to the Syrian Constitution, therefore, the Ba'th Party is the core institutional unit in the Syrian political system. And although in theory the Ba'th is supposed to share power with other political parties in the NPF, in reality it remains the primary institutional actor. Indeed, the charter of the NPF unequivocally states that political activity, except by the Ba'th, is prohibited in the two sensitive sectors of society, the armed forces and the educational institutions.[18]

The influence of the Ba'th Party in Syria's decision-making process furthermore relates to Assad's own perception of his role vis-à-vis the party. For example, much of the Assad regime's legitimacy rests on the system of values advocated by the Ba'th. Thus, to undermine the influence and prestige of the party could lead to the weakening of the regime itself. Consequently, the two institutions of the presidency and the party in Syria tend to be interdependent, relying on each other for ideological credibility and political survival.[19] It is very unlikely, therefore, for Assad to take an important decision unilaterally without consulting the top leadership of the party, whose members are frequently involved in high-level consultations.

Still, the individuals who make up the Syrian political elite and who participate in decision making do not have an independent power base of their own. Rather, they derive their power from their access to the president. Moreover, in recent years, the Ba'th Party has been downgraded, de-ideologized, and turned into a patronage machine with little capacity for independent action.[20] It has not made key foreign policy decisions in a long time.[21]

In sum, although Assad was somewhat constrained in the formulation of foreign policy, he was nonetheless the central figure in the decision-making process.

CHARACTERISTICS OF SYRIA'S STRATEGIC CULTURE

Syria's strategic culture is a reflection of its multiple, transient identities: On the one hand, Syrians regard themselves as Arab. On the other hand, they are fragmented along ethnic, sectarian, and urban/rural lines. Despite sixty years of independence, a purely Syrian identity is only now beginning to emerge. As we shall see, the question of identity has had a significant impact on Syria's strategic culture.

That Syrians should identify themselves as Arab is natural. Syria is part of the Arab hinterland with which it shares language, religion, and culture. In the absence of political boundaries prior to the collapse of the Ottoman empire, these shared values helped construct an imagined community, with Damascus at its center, extending far beyond Syria's actual boundaries—an imagined community that survived the fragmentation of Greater Syria. Thus, when Syria gained its independence from France in 1946, Syrians scoffed at the boundaries of their new state. After all, the new truncated Syria was but an artificial creation of Western imperialism.

From then on, however, a gradual decline in Syria's supranational and subnational identification has taken place. Simultaneously, Syria's modernization schemes gradually led to the emergence of a purely Syrian identity. Indeed, with the establishment of a network of roads linking cities, towns, and rural areas; a public education system whereby Syrians study from the same textbooks; a central legal system; and so on, the inhabitants of Syria have come to share in a new, purely Syrian experience.

Rate of Change/What Causes Change?

This gradual shift—from an Arab to a Syrian identity—has had a significant impact on Syria's strategic culture. Whereas Syria once viewed itself as the champion of Arab rights, Arabism has declined as a determinant of Syria's external action. Rather, Syria under Hafez Assad acted increasingly along statist lines, albeit never entirely: the Ba'th Party tended to act as a counterbalance to Assad's more pragmatic approach, and, as a result, policies were frequently a compromise between the party's gravitation toward ideological orthodoxy and political militancy and Assad's tendency toward pragmatic solutions. This is not to imply that the late Syrian leader lacked ideological commitment, but, enacting a different role from the party ideologue, his interpretation of ideological imperatives was balanced by an appreciation of prevalent environmental constraints, and consequently tended to be more pragmatic and flexible.

Who Maintains the Culture?

The Ba'th Party is the gate keeper of Syria's Arab nationalist culture, but it is the security apparatus and the military wing of the Ba'th Party that maintain Syria's strategic culture.

The Ba'th Party is the brainchild of two French-educated Syrian intellectuals—Michel Aflaq, a Greek Orthodox, and Salah al-Din al-Bitar, a Sunni Muslim. It was officially established in Damascus on April 7, 1947, when its first congress approved its constitution and established its executive committee.

The Ba'th Party's ideology is pan-Arab, secular nationalism. The "Unity" of Arab states is at the core of Ba'th doctrine and prevails over its second and third objectives: those of "Freedom" and "Socialism," respectively. According to Aflaq, the Arab peoples form a single nation with the aspiration of becoming a state with its own specific role in the world. Although persuaded of the importance of secularity, Aflaq recognized the impact of Islam. He also advocated socialism and, in 1953, the Ba'th Party merged with Akram Hawrani's Arab Socialist Party—a Hama-based political party that sought to promote peasant rights vis-à-vis large landowners. The merger—the Ba'th Arab Socialist Party—created a broader based movement. On March 8, 1963, the Ba'th Military Committee seized power in Syria in a military coup. One month earlier, the Ba'th Party seized power in Iraq.

Ba'thist ideology spread slowly by educating followers to its intellectual attractions. Significant expansion beyond Syria's borders took place only after the war of 1948, when lack of Arab unity was widely perceived as partly responsible for the loss of Palestine to the new state of Israel. The Iraqi branch of the Ba'th Party was established in 1954.

Ba'th Party presence in the armed forces is separate but parallel to that in the civilian apparatus. The two wings (civilian and military) of the Ba'th Party join only at the Regional Command, to which both military and civilian members belong, and where delegates from party organizations in military units meet at regional congresses. The military wing of the Ba'th Party has established branches down to the battalion level. The leader of such a branch is called a *Tawjihi* (political guide). The *Tawjihi* is a full-time party cadre with specialized training in indoctrination. He is not the commander, and the commander may not be a *Tawjihi*. Moreover, not all military officers were party members, but it was almost a prerequisite for advancement to flag rank.

According to the organizational report submitted to the ninth Regional Congress (June 2000), the number of Ba'th Party branches, sections, and divisions within the armed forces were, respectively, 27, 212, and 1,656.

What Does Syria's Strategic Culture Say about the "Enemy?"

Since the Ba'th Party, through its avowedly Arab nationalist ideology, has perceived itself as the guardian of all Arab nationalist causes, its position on Israel has always been vociferously militant. Thus, Israel is viewed as the scion of Western imperialism, a Western bridgehead of sorts into the Arab world. In this view, Israel is an aggressive, expansionist, settler–colonial state: Israel colonized Palestine, tossed out a segment of Palestine's local inhabitants from their ancestral homes, maintained a brutal occupation over another segment, and, at various times, invaded each and every one of its neighbors, occupying parts of their territory in flagrant violation of international law.[22]

What Does Syria's Strategic Culture Say about Conflict and the International System, the Utility of Violence, and the Laws of War?

Although Syria is a leading member of the nonaligned movement—Third World states that refused to be part of either of the two blocs during the Cold War—it aligned itself with the former Soviet Union in the early 1980s through a "Treaty of Friendship and Cooperation." This was not out of ideological affinity but rather in reaction to the U.S. strategic alliance with Israel. Given the zero-sum nature of Syria's perceptions vis-à-vis Israel, and given the benefits that accrue to Israel from the special U.S.–Israeli relationship, Syria prefers the bipolar international system to the current U.S.-dominated international system.

That said, even under the bipolar system, the thrust of Syrian policy was that a peaceful settlement of the Arab–Israeli conflict could be achieved only if the United States persuaded Israel to abide by UN land-for-peace resolutions, specifically UN Security Council Resolutions 242 and 338 (which require Israel to withdraw from territories it occupied during the 1967 conflict and Arab states to recognize Israel). To this end, Syria used the "carrot and stick" approach with Washington. On the one hand, Syria tried to befriend the United States, the only power that has sufficient leverage over Israel, so as to demonstrate to Washington that Syria can be a useful and stabilizing force in the Middle East. Syria's intervention in Lebanon during the Lebanese civil war of 1975–1976 on the side of right wing Lebanese forces (against the Palestinian/leftist Lebanese coalition) is one case in point; Syria's successful efforts in securing the release of American hostages in Lebanon during the 1980s is another; Syria's participation alongside the U.S.-led coalition of forces in Iraq in 1991 is yet another.

On the other hand, Syria employed violence-by-proxy to torpedo any U.S. diplomatic initiative that did not take Syrian interests (namely, the recovery of the Golan Heights) into account. The U.S.-brokered May 17, 2006, agreement between Lebanon and Israel is one case in point.

Underlying this realist strategy is Syria's conviction that a negotiated settlement of the Arab–Israeli conflict, one that fully restores Arab rights, could be had only if Arabs back their diplomacy with teeth. Within this context, while Syria generally abides by international law, it occasionally resorts to violence, albeit indirectly.

Syria's Strategic Culture in Action

Syria's strategic culture is critical in shaping its security orientation. The conflict with Israel facilitated the military establishment's hold on political power in general and on the Ba'th Party in particular.

Organization

Organizationally, the Ba'th Party is of a pyramidal structure, at the top of which lie the Regional (Syrian) and National (Arab) Commands. In addition to Assad, who acts as the Ba'th Party's secretary general, the twenty-one-man Regional Command includes influential members of the policymaking elite. Parallel to the Regional Command is the twenty-one-man National Command, whose sphere of responsibility lies in the foreign sector, particularly with the Arab world.[23]

Although the Regional Command is the highest decision-making body, and although its members represent the party's top elite, this body stands on the third level of the Syrian regime's power structure. At the first level is Assad, who concentrates all the critical threads in his hands. Immediately below him are the chiefs of the multiple intelligence and security networks, which function independently of one another, enjoy broad latitude, and keep a close watch on everything in the country that is of concern to the regime. They form in effect Assad's eyes and ears. On the same second level, and also directly answerable to Assad, are the commanders of the politically relevant, regime-shielding, coup-deterring, elite armed formations, such as the Republican Guard, the Special Forces, the Third Armored Division. It is these formations, which alone are allowed in the capital, that constitute the essential underpinning of Assad's power.[24]

Further below, on the third level, stands the Regional Command. Except for Assad, who is its secretary general, its members scarcely compare in importance to the intelligence chiefs or commanders of the elite forces. In essence, the Regional Command serves as a consultative body for Assad and at the same time watches, through the party machine, over the proper implementation of his policies by the elements on the fourth level, namely, the ministers, the higher bureaucrats, the provincial governors, the members of the executive boards of the local councils, and the leaders of the party's ancillary mass organizations and their subordinate organs.[25]

Decision Making

In his capacity as regional secretary, Assad chairs all Regional Command meetings. When he is absent, the assistant regional secretary substitutes for him. In consultation with Assad, the assistant secretary sets the agenda for the meetings.

A degree of open deliberation is allowed. The various sides to a complex issue are heard and different or opposite claims are weighed. Criticism of the way certain policies are implemented is also tolerated. This does not conflict with Assad's interests, but helps him formulate more workable or meaningful policies and to exercise his power in a smoother manner. The side to which he lends his weight prevails.

One key difference with regard to the importance of the Regional Command and that of its members has to do with the different styles of the two Assads: Whereas Hafez Assad consulted with Regional Command members and took their views into account, Bashar Assad has increasingly used this body as a rubber stamp.

Historical Events That Have Been Shaped by Syria's Strategic Culture

That Syria's strategic culture is a major determinant of Syria's external action is illustrated by the following examples: Although Syria could have stayed out of the war in 1948, the then small Syrian army rushed to the frontline in support of its Palestinian brethren in their conflict with the emerging Jewish state. In 1956, although Egypt alone was the target of the tripartite Israeli/British/French alliance, Syria joined the conflict—out of Arab solidarity—by, among other things, blowing up the British-owned Tapline pipeline that ran from Iraq to Syria's Mediterranean port of Lattakia. During the 1960s, although Israel's attempts to channel water from the Jordan River to the Negev desert did not affect Syria, the Syrian government set out to divert the Jordan River's head waters—fueling tensions between Arabs and Israelis that culminated in the Six-Day War.

Impact of Strategic Culture on WMD Conceptions, Calculations, and Policies

As noted earlier, in 1970 the more moderate faction of the Ba'th, led by Hafez Assad, limited Syria's objective to the containment of Israel to within its 1967 boundaries. Despite Syria's limited objectives vis-à-vis Israel, and given Israel's superior military power, Syria engaged in the development of chemical weapons so as to deter Israel from attacking Syria. From a Syrian perspective, should Israel attack Syria, Damascus would then be in a position to strike Israel's centers of mobilization and inflict unacceptable harm.[26]

According to the Monterey Institute of International Studies' Center for Nonproliferation Studies (CNS) and to other specialized organizations, Syria has a large and advanced chemical weapons capability. That capability is said to include chemical warheads for SCUD ballistic missiles and chemical gravity bombs for delivery by aircraft. Syria's chemical weapons stockpile is in the hundreds of tons. Agents are believed to include Sarin (a nerve agent that can be lethal to victims who inhale it or absorb it through the skin or via eye contact), VX (an even more potent nerve agent), and mustard gas with major production facilities near the cities of Damascus and Homs.[27]

Syria began developing chemical weapons in the early 1980s as part of Hafez Assad's quest to reach strategic parity with Israel. Assad sought parity with Israel to strengthen his hand in future negotiations over the terms of peace between Israel and the Arabs. For Assad, strategic parity did not necessarily mean matching Israel tank-for-tank and plane-for-plane. To do so in terms of conventional military power was, given Syria's slim resources, beyond Syria's capability. Indeed, Syria had always been militarily inferior to Israel. During the 1948 Palestine War, Syria could deploy no more than 2,000 poorly armed personnel along the old Palestine border. In June 1967, the Syrian army was decimated by Israel's invading force. In three days of combat, Israel's army seized the entire Golan Heights. It was not until the 1973 October War that Syria could claim some successes against Israel. However, when Egypt, Syria's wartime ally, announced a ceasefire just a few days into the war (enabling in the process Israeli forces to concentrate along the Syrian front), the Syrian army nearly collapsed as Israel's army broke through Syrian defenses, reaching the town of Sa'sa' twenty five miles from Damascus. Although Israel later withdrew from that portion of Syrian territory, Israel's withdrawal was only as a result of the U.S.-brokered 1974 disengagement of forces agreement. In the process, however, the disparity of power between Israel and Syria brought the message home to Assad that, in the absence of a deterrent capability, Israeli forces could easily overrun Damascus. Even as Assad later tried to bolster the conventional offensive and defensive capabilities of Syria's armed forces, the balance of power between the two foes continued to be lopsided: In 1982 Israel invaded Lebanon and its armor routed Syrian forces there. Although the retreat of Syrian ground forces was orderly, the Syrian air force did not fare as well: Syria lost eighty-two aircraft (for the loss of one Israeli combat aircraft) in one day of dogfights. Seeing that the Syrian air force is no match for the Israeli air force, Assad decided to acquire long range surface-to-surface missiles.[28] It is shortly thereafter that he decided to develop a chemical warfare capability.

Hafez Assad's decision to seek strategic parity with Israel was the stepchild of his earlier attempts to alter the balance of power—all of which failed. Assad's thinking was that the balance of power could be attained if Arab states worked together to force Israel to the negotiating table. The first attempt was, as mentioned earlier, in 1973 when Syria and Egypt launched a surprise attack against Israel. That attempt failed because Egypt later engaged in separate talks with Israel that led to the Egyptian–Israeli peace treaty. The second attempt was in 1979 when Assad sought to build an eastern Arab front in compensation for the loss of Egypt from the Arab power equation. That attempt also failed: The Arab states that made up the front (Iraq, Jordan, and the Palestine Liberation Organization) were far too divided among themselves to pursue "joint-Arab action."

Despite Assad's efforts to bring Syria's armed forces at par, however, Syria was unable to alter the balance of power. Syria had to abandon its quest for strategic parity with Israel in April 1997 when, during a visit by Assad to Moscow, Soviet General Secretary Mikhail Gorbachev indicated that the Soviet Union would no longer accommodate that quest. Gorbachev warned Assad that efforts to achieve parity would not succeed: Israel would strike preemptively long before Syria attained its goal and, with firm U.S. support, would come out ahead in any arms race.[29] Since the demise of Syria's Soviet patron, the asymmetry in conventional power between Syria and Israel steadily widened as Syria has not been able to systematically upgrade its weapons systems. What is more, Russia, the Soviet successor state, now demands payment in cash before it will supply Syria's armed forces with the spare parts needed to keep Syria's ageing equipment running—cash that Syria's shrinking economy is unable to generate.

In these circumstances, the strategic value of Syria's chemical weapons arsenal has, from a Syrian perspective, multiplied and chemical weapons continue to be the choice of weapon with which to deter and contain Israel. This raises the following questions: (1) Will Syria ever use its chemical weapons? (2) Will Damascus transfer chemical weapons to terrorist groups?

There is nothing in the historical record to suggest that Syria might actually use chemical weapons against its foes, Israel included. Unlike Saddam's Iraq, which used chemical weapons against Iraq's Kurdish minority in March 1988 and against Iran at various times during the Iran–Iraq War, Syria never resorted to the use of chemical weapons, either against its internal opponents (the Muslim Brotherhood in 1982 in Hama) or its external ones (Israeli forces during the Israeli invasion of Lebanon in 1982). Over and above that, there is no indication that Syria might willingly transfer chemical weapons to the militant anti-Israel groups it supports. According to former U.S. Undersecretary of State for Arms Control John Bolton, "there is currently no information indicating that the Syrian government has transferred WMD to terrorist organizations or would permit such groups to acquire them."[30] In this regard, the record shows that Syria has kept a very tight rein over these groups. This caution is a product of Syria's acute awareness that it would ultimately pay the price for any major terrorist incident it was believed to be behind, especially against Israel.[31]

CONCLUSION

Syria's strategic culture is exceptionally monolithic, given its derivation from the Assad family and regime, yet is also enriched by influences from its geography, economics, religion, and ideology. It also provides an important perception lens through which its perceptions of allies and threats is shaped and interpreted. Through this lens, Syria has a sense of acute military weakness relative to Israel. Yet, relying on Syria's awareness of its military weakness vis-à-vis Israel is not necessarily cause for comfort. Syria is determined to recover its Israeli-occupied Golan Heights—by hook or by crook, and this forms an important objective as well as source of strategic cultural legitimacy. As Bashar Assad himself put it to a Kuwaiti newspaper recently, "If there is no peace, naturally you should expect that war may come."[32] In other words, if Syria does not recover its Israeli-occupied Golan Heights through negotiations, it will try to do so through war, a prospect that might have horrific consequences for the entire region.

NOTES

1. British and French diplomats agreed on the division of Greater Syria (contained in the secret Sykes–Picot agreement) as early as 1916. The treaty became publicly known only in 1917 as a result of its leaking by the Bolsheviks. For further reading on this question, see Charles D. Smith, *Palestine and the Arab–Israel Conflict*, 5th ed. (Boston and New York: Bedford/St. Martin's, 2004), pp. 64–67.

2. Syrian officers backed the Sharif because of the prestige of his position (Guardian of the Holy Shrines) and the legitimacy it would confer upon their cause. For the British promise to the Arabs, see the Husayn–MacMahon correspondence in ibid., p. 91. The literature on this subject is massive, but for a concise description, see ibid., pp. 55–84.

3. On the British promise to the Jews, see the Balfour Declaration in ibid., pp. 67–69.

4. See, Amy Dockser Marcus, "Growing Dangers: U.S. Drive to Curb Doomsday Weapons in Mideast Is Faltering," *Wall Street Journal*, September 6, 1966, p. A1. For a more detailed account of Israel's nuclear capability, see Rodney W. Jones and Mark G. McDonough, *Tracking Nuclear Proliferation* (Carnegie Endowment for International Peace, 1998), chapter 7.

5. Harold Hough, "Could Israel's Nuclear Assets Survive A First Strike?" *Jane's Intelligence Review*, September 1997, p. 410.

6. One of the major issues dividing Syria and Turkey is the question of riparian rights over the Euphrates River. Another issue is the territorial dispute over the province of Alexandretta (known as "Hatai" to Turks; "Iskenderun" to Syrians). That province was ceded by France to Turkey in 1939 in order to entice Turkey to not enter into an alliance with Nazi Germany. Syria was then under the French mandate, and Syrians were not consulted. For further reading, see Murhaf Jouejati, "Water Politics As High Politics: The Case of Turkey and Syria," in Henri J. Barkey, ed. *Reluctant Neighbor: Turkey's Role in the Middle East* (Washington, DC: US Institute of Peace, 1996), pp. 131–46.

7. For further reading on the Turkey–Israel alliance, see Gregory A. Burris, "Turkey–Israel: Speed Bumps," *The Middle East Quarterly*, Vol. 10, No. 4 (Fall 2003), pp. 67–80, available at http://www.meforum.org/article/569.

8. For the best account of the Syrian–Iraqi rivalry, see Eberhard Kienle, *Ba'th versus Ba'th: The Conflict Between Syria and Iraq, 1968–1989* (St. Martin's, 1991).

9. Syria's military intervention in Lebanon in 1975–1976 to stop the Lebanese civil war was mandated by the Arab League. Syrian forces remained in Lebanon until UNSCR 1559, adopted on September 2, 2004, called for Syria's withdrawal and the disarming of Lebanese and non-Lebanese armed groups.

10. According to Mohamed Mehdi Zahedi, Iran's minister of science, research, and technology, "Islamic doctrine does not allow us to produce mass destruction weapons or nuclear ones and the Iranian state is based on that principle." *Associated Press*, "Iranian Minister: WMD Outlawed in Islam," June 27, 2006. This statement followed a similar statement made by Iran's foreign Minister Kamal Kharrazi before the Iranian Parliament on June 8, 2006.

11. "Islamic   Laws   On   War   And   Peace,"   www.federationpress.com.au/pdf/ IslamicLawsonWarPeace.pdf, p. 59.

12. Raymond A Bahgat Korany and Ali E. Hillal Dessouki, eds., Hinnebusch, "Revisionist Dreams, Realist Strategies: The Foreign Policy of Syria," in *The Foreign Policy of Arab States*, (Cairo: American University of Cairo Press, 1984), pp. 285–87.

13. Ibid.

14. "Syria Slams Private, Public Monopolies," *The Daily Star*, October 19, 2005.

15. Syria's oil production has recently dropped from 600,000 b/d to 450,000 b/d. Revenues from oil exports account for 70 percent of GNP.

16. The term "Ba'th" means "renaissance" or "rebirth" in Arabic, hence, the rebirth of the Arab Nation.

17. Antoine Guine, *The New Syria* (Damascus: SAMA, 1975), p. 103.

18. Articles 7 and 9 of the Charter, published in Damascus by the National Command of the Ba'th Arab Socialist Party, Bureau of Documentation, Information and Broadcast, March 7, 1972.

19. Adeed I. Dawisha, "Syria and the Sadat Initiative," *World Today*, Vol. 34, No. 5 (May 1978), p. 194.

20. Raymond A. Hinnebusch, "Asad's Syria and the New World Order: The Struggle for Regime Survival," *Middle East Policy*, Vol. 2, No. 1 (1993), p. 2.

21. Raymond A. Hinnebusch, "Syria: The Politics of Peace and Regime Survival," *Middle East Policy*, Vol. 3 (1995), p. 78.

22. Article II of the United Nations Charter speaks of the "inadmissibility of the acquisition of territory by force." In the context of the Arab–Israeli conflict, Israel, according to the Syrian perspective, acquired Arab territories in June 1967 purely by force.

23. The number of members of the Regional Command was reduced to fifteen following the twentieth Ba'th Party Congress in June 2005. Reports which claimed the Ba'th Congress would shut down the National Command were not confirmed.

24. Hanna Batatu, *Syria's Peasantry, The Descendents of Its Lesser Rural Notables, and Their Politics* (Princeton: Princeton University Press, 1999), pp. 206–07.

25. Ibid.

26. See Murhaf Jouejati, "Syrian Motives for Its WMD Programs and What to Do about Them," *Middle East Journal*, Vol. 59, No. 1 (Winter 2005), pp. 52–61; and Jouejati, "Syrian WMD Programs in Context," in James A. Russell, ed., *Proliferation of Weapons of Mass Destruction in the Middle East* (New York: Palgrave Macmillan, 2006), pp. 63–73.

27. See http://cns.miis.edu/research/wedme/syria.htm; and "Top US Officials Voice Concern About Syria's WMD Capability," *Arms Control Today*, May 2003, at www.armscontrol. org/act/2003_05/syria_may03.

28. Anthony H. Cordesman, *Weapons of Mass Destruction in the Middle East* (New York: Council on Foreign Relations Press, 1991), p. 165.

29. Alasdair Drysdale and Raymond A. Hinnebusch, *Syria and the Middle East Peace Process* (New York: Council on foreign Relations Press, 1991), p. 165.

30. John R. Bolton's testimony before the House International Relations Committee, September 16, 2003, "Syria's Weapons of Mass Destruction and Missile Development Programs," in http://www.state.gov/t/us/rm/24135.htm.

31. Syria has not been directly implicated in any terrorist activity since the 1986 "Hindawi affair" (the attempted bombing of an El Al flight from London).

32. *Al Anba* interview with Syrian President Bashar Assad, Sunday, October 8, 2006.

11

A Dragon on Defense: Explaining China's Strategic Culture

Huiyun Feng

China's ascension on the global stage is drawing increasing concern worldwide. Among the primary debates, two theoretical perspectives deserve particular attention. Western scholars and policymakers tend to express concerns over China's rise from either structural realist or cultural realist perspectives. Structural realists (neorealists, offensive realists, and power transition realists) believe that, like previous great powers, China will expand in order to accumulate relative power. China will challenge U.S. hegemony, resort to the use of military force in order to solve historic territorial disputes, and try to achieve systemic change through wars. Therefore, even though China does not have sufficient capability now, a rising China will be an unstable factor for the international system and should be contained.

Cultural realists emphasize the impact of Chinese strategic culture on Chinese foreign policy decisions. They point out that China has two strategic cultures—Confucian strategic culture and Parabellum strategic culture, but argue that it is the realpolitik–Parabellum strategic culture—not Confucian influence—that affects Chinese grand strategy making. This argument is made most prominently in Alastair Ian Johnston's book *Cultural Realism: Strategic Culture and Grand Strategy in Chinese History* (1995).[1] Johnston argues that Mao, and leaders after him, draw from a Parabellum strategic culture and under its impact Chinese grand strategy displays a strong aggressiveness. China has historically been an expansionist country and remains so.

Starting from different theoretical angles in analyzing China's rise and its impact, structural and cultural realists come to the same conclusion: a rising China will mean wars and should be contained.

This chapter raises the hypothesis that China's strategic culture has displayed a more defensive posture than current scholarship accounts for. Using content analysis of leaders' public speeches through the automated Verbs in Context System (VICS), the operational codes of Mao Zedong and Deng Xiaoping are analyzed here to test the variation and continuity of their propensity toward Confucian or Parabellum strategic cultures in the foreign policy domain in times of war and peace.

STRATEGIC CULTURE AND CHINA'S RISE

The strategic culture approach to analysis has done much to remedy the deficiencies of traditional realist postures. Within the strategic culture paradigm, the determinants of a state's grand strategy are not limited to material capabilities, but include the cultural and historical prisms through which state leaders regard their world. Strategic culture is reflected in the beliefs, decisions, norms, and values of key decision makers and state leaders. Simply put, culture affects individuals, and individual leaders make policy.

How culture affects people is a complicated question. This chapter applies cognitive political psychological analysis that emphasizes that leaders' belief systems are forged through cultural influence on socialization, education, and cognitive development. Therefore, grand strategies are a construct determined, in part, by a state's strategic cultural traditions.[2] Understanding these cultural processes is important for understanding regime specific crisis situations, crisis resolution and management, and confidence building measures.

Johnston picks up this theme where China is concerned and rightly argues for a strategic culture approach in understanding Beijing's security behavior. Johnston is convincing in his argument that China's strategic culture has been offensive despite its weak material capability, and other scholars have examined and applied this claim to different cases.[3]

While Johnston's contributions to advancing strategic culture theory in a positivist vein are impressive, this author takes exception to his particular conclusions on China, which are inappropriately skewed toward one side of the scale due to several types of bias. A first is source selection bias. Johnston relies on the seven military classics for his analysis. These detail how to fight a war once it has started—not grand strategy.[4] Second are mistakes emanating from Chinese translation bias. Johnston uses the phrase *Parabellum*, which comes from the realpolitician's axiom *si pacem, parabellum* ("if you want peace, then prepare for war"), as parallel to the Chinese idiom *ju an si wei, wu bei you huan* ("while residing in peace, think about dangers; without military preparations there will be calamity"). The phrases are translated into similar meanings. But in the original Chinese phrase, *ju an si wei, wu bei you huan* has two meanings: it might mean, as Johnston argues, to prepare for war and initiate war for peace as offensive means. However, prepare for war does not necessarily mean to initiate war, which Johnston ignores.[5] And finally, case selection bias. Johnston's emphasis on the Ming Dynasty is unrepresentative and problematic as Ming China was particularly belligerent and weak in control and governance.[6]

As a result, the contrasting Confucian view of China's strategic culture is underrepresented. The influence of Confucius' philosophy would produce a China that, in general, shows a reluctance to use force. Even under security threats, diplomatic means and negotiations would be preferred and proposed as the first preference. This does not mean that Beijing would be so reluctant to use force that, even facing foreign invasion, it would not fight back or try to win. If needed, the Chinese will fight fiercely to protect their territory and national pride, as demonstrated in the anti-Japanese war.[7] However, even when force is employed after all other means turn out to be unsuccessful, Confucian influence would prompt the Chinese to pursue opportunities to go back to the negotiating table for peaceful settlements, and reduce further destruction. This pattern is, in fact, what we have seen in the Civil War, the Korean War, and the Sino-Indian and Sino-Vietnam wars.[8]

Johnston himself does not dispute the existence of Confucian cultural traditions in China, he simply undervalues their influence. In order to contrast Johnston's perspective with the work being done here, this chapter will employ Johnston's description of Confucian culture. He summarizes its three basic elements: "War is inauspicious and to be avoided; the enemy is not necessarily demonized; violence is a last resort." He explains,

> When violence is used by the state to deal with external security threats, it is generally applied defensively and is limited in nature. This reflects a view that violence is not particularly efficacious in eliminating threats or producing security. Rather, the more reliable basis for state security is the moral and administrative quality of internal rulership.[9]

The main hypothesis of this chapter is that Chinese strategic culture shows a far more defensive strain of precisely the type described earlier than Johnston's work acknowledges.

To test this hypothesis, the operational codes of two Chinese leaders—Mao Zedong and Deng Xiaoping—are analyzed during the Korean and Sino-Vietnamese War periods. The research compares their beliefs and belief changes, and codes these in order to make predictive statements about the likely strategic orientations of Chinese foreign policy. Mao and Deng are useful case studies as they form the core of the first and second generations of Chinese leaders, and represent the key decision makers in war and crisis situations. In addition, both Mao and Deng are strong revolutionary leaders with a military background; thus their belief system should reflect closely the state's strategic preferences.[10]

OPERATIONAL CODE ANALYSIS

The operational code approach applied here was first systematically defined by Alexander George.[11] This section compares this operational code construct with strategic culture and shows that the two concepts share high commensurability. The following section then applies operational code analysis to measure and test the strategic cultural orientations of Mao and Deng, respectively.

Given the specific challenge to Johnston's claims about Chinese strategic culture, it would seem most appropriate to use his definition of the concept. His definition of strategic culture combines two parts:

> [T]he first consists of basic assumptions about the orderliness of the strategic environment—that is, about the role of war in human affairs (whether it is aberrant or inevitable), about the nature of the adversary and the threat it poses (zero-sum or positive sum), and about the efficacy of the use of force (the ability to control outcomes and eliminate threats and the conditions under which the use of force is useful). Together these comprise the central paradigm of a strategic culture. The second part consists of assumptions at a more operational level about what strategic options are the most efficacious for dealing with the threat environment as defined by answers to these three sets of questions. These lower-level assumptions should flow logically from the central paradigm.[12]

The operational code construct defined by George distinguishes between "philosophical" (P) and "instrumental" (I) beliefs. Philosophical beliefs refer to the assumptions and premises made by an actor regarding world politics and political

---

The Philosophical Beliefs in an Operational Code

P-1. What is the "essential" nature of political life? Is the political universe essentially one of harmony or conflict? What is the fundamental character of one's political opponents?

P-2. What are the prospects for the eventual realization of one's fundamental values and aspirations? Can one be optimistic, or must one be pessimistic on this score; and in what respects the one and/or the other?

P-3. Is the political future predictable? In what sense and to what extent?

P-4. How much "control" or "mastery" can one have over historical development? What
is one's role in "moving" and "shaping" history in the desired direction?

P-5. What is the role of "chance" in human affairs and in historical development?

The Instrumental Beliefs in an Operational Code

I-1. What is the best approach for selecting goals or objectives for political action?

I-2. How are the goals of action pursued most effectively?

I-3. How are the risks of political action calculated, controlled, and accepted?

I-4. What is the best "timing" of action to advance one's interests?

I-5. What is the utility and role of different means for advancing one's interests?

Figure 11.1   Operational Code Beliefs.

conflict. Instrumental beliefs, on the other hand, have to do with questions of correct strategy and tactics.[13] For the purposes of the proposed analysis, P-1, P-4, and I-1 are the beliefs that will be tracked out of the ten possibilities shown in figure 11.1.

In explaining why he did not apply operational code analysis in his work on China, Johnston acknowledged that the two concepts share many similarities, but argued that an essential difference between the two concepts is "strategic culture is collective: it refers to collectively held preferences" while operational code analysis studies an individual's beliefs and behavior.[14]

Johnston, however, ignores the development of operational code construct. Operational code analysis was, in fact, first developed as a cultural and aggregate concept. In the 1950s, the operational code construct was developed by Nathan Leites to study the beliefs of the Soviet Bolshevik politburo.[15] Leites discovered that the negotiation style and decision-making process of the Soviets reflected the Soviet culture and was distinctively different from the American approach.

Later, Alexander George more systematically defined operational code using the ten questions listed in figure 11.1.[16] With the development of cognitive political psychology, Ole Holsti developed a typology,[17] which was later modified by Stephen Walker to capture the motivational foundations of leaders' beliefs (the needs for power, affiliation, and achievement) (See figure 11.2).[18]

In the Holsti/Walker typology, there are four types of leaders (A, B, C, and DEF). Type A and C are Confucian leaders who see the world as peaceful and are cooperation oriented. Type C leaders believe they have "high" control over historical development and, therefore, may display more aggressiveness than Type A leaders. In general, however, these two types of leaders' strategic preference ranking places "settle" first rather than "dominate."

Types DEF and B are realist leaders with hostile worldviews, who believe conflicts are unavoidable. Type B is the more aggressive offensive realist type while Types DE and F are defensive realist types. The three master beliefs I-1, P-1, and P-4 locate a leader in the typology.

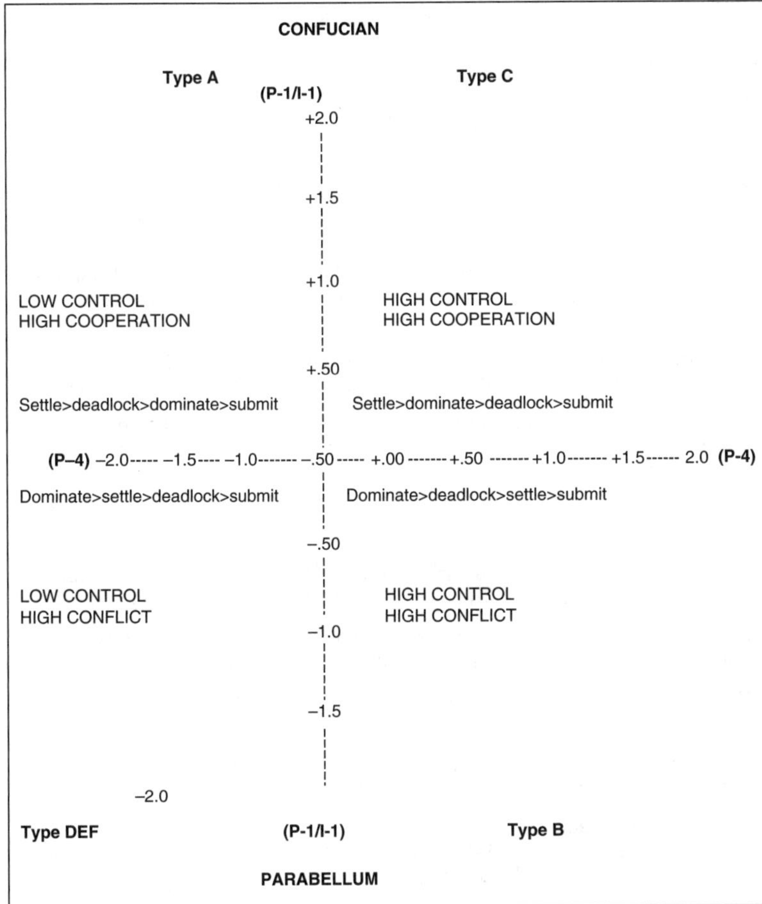

Figure 11.2   Holsti/Walker Typology and Strategic Culture.

The operational code research program has evolved to using automated computerized content analysis.[19] With the VICS, leaders' public statements can be processed for operational code analysis. Figure 11.3 shows how VICS indices are calculated.[20] Using the VICS raw scores, the operational codes of leaders are compared with a norming group of world leaders.[21]

Departing from Johnston's argument that the operational code construct is incompatible with strategic culture, this chapter applies operational code analysis as a quantitative tool in the study of strategic culture. China's two strategic cultures—Confucian and Parabellum—each have a corresponding set of operational code beliefs and strategic preferences. By coding the public statements of Mao and Deng, I infer which kind of strategic culture seems to dominate the foreign policy decisions of each. Confucian leaders are Type A or C while realist leaders should be Type B or DEF, with Type B representing the classic offensive Parabellum type leader. Confucian leaders prefer peaceful and cooperative strategies (settle first) while realist leaders prefer conflict and expansion strategies (dominate first).

PHILOSOPHICAL BELIEFS

	Elements	Index*	Interpretation
P-1.	Nature of the Political Universe (Image of Others)	%Positive minus %Negative Transitive Other Attributions	+1.0 friendly to −1.0 hostile
P-2.	Realization of Political Values (Optimism/ Pessimism)	Mean Intensity of Transitive Other Attributions divided by 3	+1.0 optimistic to −1.0 pessimistic
P-3.	Political Future (Predictability of Others Tactics)	1 minus Index of Qualitative Variation** for Other Attributions	1.0 predictable to 0.0 uncertain
P-4.	Historical Development (Locus of Control)	Self Attributions divided by [Self plus Other Attributions]	1.0 high to 0.0 low self control
P-5.	Role of Chance (Absence of Control)	1 minus [Political Future x Historical Development Index]	1.0 high role to 0.0 low role

INSTRUMENTAL BELIEFS

	Elements	Index	Interpretation
I-1.	Approach to Goals (Direction of Strategy)	%Positive minus %Negative Transitive Self Attributions	+1.0 high cooperation to −1.0 high conflict
I-2.	Pursuit of Goals (Intensity of Tactics)	Mean Intensity of Transitive Self Attributions divided by 3	+1.0 high cooperation to −1.0 high conflict
I-3.	Risk Orientation (Predictability of Tactics)	1 minus Index of Qualitative Variation for Self Attributions	1.0 risk acceptant to 0.0 riskaverse
I-4.	Timing of Action (Flexibilbility of Tactics)	1 minus Absolute Value [%X minus %Y Self Attributions]	1.0 high to 0.0 low shift propensity
	a. Coop v. Conf Tactics	Where X = Coop and Y = Conf	
	b. Word v. Deed Tactics	Where X = Word and Y = Deed	
I-5.	Utility of Means (Exercise of Power)	Percentages for Exercise of Power Categories a through f	+1.0 very frequent to 0.0 infrequent
	a. Reward	a's frequency divided by total	
	b. Promise	b's frequency divided by total	
	c. Appeal/Support	c's frequency divided by total	
	d. Oppose/Resist	d's frequency divided by total	
	e. Threaten	e's frequency divided by total	
	f. Punish	f's frequency divided by total	

Figure 11.3   Indices for Philosophical and Instrumental Beliefs.

*All indices vary between 0 and 1.0 except for P-1, P-2, I-1, and I-2, which vary between −1.0 and 1.0. P-2 and I-2 are divided by 3 to standardize the range.
**The Index of Qualitative Variation is a ratio of the number of different pairs of observations in a distribution to the maximum possible number of different pairs for a distribution with the same N (number of cases) and the same number of variable classifications.

The data sources for this analysis are public statements from Lexis Nexis Index, *Beijing Review, People's Daily,* and the Chinese Foreign Ministry and its embassies' web pages. The research comprised purposeful rather than random sampling due to the foreign policy focus of the analysis. The final sample included eighteen speeches for

Mao Zedong (1946–1953) and twenty-four for Deng Xiaoping (1977–1981), which were analyzed for two validity tests: The first is that Mao Zedong is a Parabellum (offensive) realist, as Johnston argued in his chapter "Cultural Realism and Strategy in Maoist China," appearing in Peter Katzenstein's *The Culture of National Security: Norms and Identity in World Politics* (1996).[22] The other is that Chinese leaders after Mao are also Parabellum realists, which Johnston hypothesizes in the book *Unipolar Politics: Realism and State Strategies After the Cold War* (1999) but does not test.[23]

The Operational Codes of Mao Zedong and Deng Xiaoping

Figure 11.4 shows the results produced by the content analysis method described earlier, and compares the operational codes of Mao and Deng with average world leaders. Mao's key beliefs (P-1, I-1, and P-4) differ significantly from the average world leader, and his P-1 and I-1 scores are more than 1.5 standard deviations from the mean. Thus, although Mao's view of how much control he has over historical development (P-4) remains close to the norming group, his view of the political world and his chosen means are far more hostile and conflictual than the average.

Deng's operational code scores demonstrate a significant departure from Mao's style. Deng's scores are relatively close to the average world leader's and even higher than the mean. In terms of standard deviations from the mean, Deng's scores for "other" are (P-4 = −.20, P-1 = .006) and for "self" are (P-4 = .20, I-1 = .04). His beliefs are also basically in line with Confucianism when faced with an unfriendly opponent from a position of relative strength.

Comparing the operational code beliefs of the two leaders to the norming group, we notice that Deng's view of the political universe (P-1 = .303) is almost equal to the mean (P-1 = .301) while Mao sees the political universe as significantly more conflictual than both Deng and the norming group (P-1 = −.209). Both Mao and Deng are close to the norming group's view regarding the control of historical development though Deng is higher (Mao P-4 = .232, Deng P-4 = .25, Group P-4 = .224). Regarding the strategic orientation index, Deng (I-1 = .417) again is very close to the norming group (I-1 = .401) and Mao is significantly more conflictual (I-1 = −.283).

According to their major beliefs (I-1, P-1, and P-4), Deng sees the political universe as more friendly while Mao has a propensity to diagnose the political universe as very hostile. Mao is more pessimistic about the realization of political values in contrast to Deng, who is somewhat optimistic about the realization of political values. Mao has a stronger propensity to choose a conflictual strategy and implement it with conflictual tactics. Mao will choose punishments, while Deng is more likely to use rewards, promises, and appeals. These results support Johnston's claim that Mao was not a Confucian leader but a Parabellum leader. However, Deng's statistical scores show that he is not an offensive realist. His views of "other" are Confucian in nature, as are his instrumental beliefs.

Moving to the Holsti/Walker typology, we can see that Mao's view of "other" is in Type DEF and view of "self" is Type B. He is an offensive realist while Deng is a Type C Confucian leader. The preference order of strategies for Mao's Type B self-identity is *dominate>deadlock>settle>submit*, and his strategy for other is *dominate>settle>deadlock >submit*. Mao is a Parabellum realist who perceives a very hostile world (see figure 11.5). As seen from figure 11.2, Deng's view of "other" falls in the Type A quadrant and view of self in the Type C quadrant. The preferences for

	Mao (N=18)	Norming Group (N=164)	Deng (N=24)
Philosophical Beliefs			
P-1 Nature of Political Universe (Conflict/Cooperation)	−.209*	.301	.303
P-2 Realization of Political Values (Optimism/Pessimism)	−.193*	.147	.177
P-3 Political Future (Unpredictable/Predictable)	.214**	.134	.158
P-4 Historical Development (Low Control/High Control)	.232	.224	.250*
P-5 Role of Chance (Small Role/Large Role)	.934**	.968	.961
Instrumental Beliefs			
I-1 Strategic Approach to Goals (Conflict/Cooperation)	−.283**	.401	.417
I-2 Intensity of Tactics (Conflict/Cooperation)	−.306**	.178	.184
I-3 Risk Orientation (Averse/Acceptant)	.386	.332	.329
I-4 Timing of Action			
a. Conflict/Cooperation	.521	.503	.479
b. Words/Deeds	.602***	.464	.531
I-5 Utility of Means			
Reward	.064**	.157	.167
Promise	.062	.075	.021**
Appeal	.231*	.468	.520
Oppose	.191	.154	.173
Threaten	.075	.034	.016
Punish	.375***	.112	.100

Figure 11.4   A Comparison of the Operational Codes of Mao and Deng with the Norming Group.

* Significant at P≤.001 level (two-tailed) from the norming group.
** Significant at P≤.05 level (two-tailed) from the norming group.
*** Significant at P≤.10 level (two-tailed) from the norming group.

strategies by Deng as a Type C leader are: *settle>dominate>deadlock>submit* against a perceived Type A opponent with preferences of *settle>deadlock>dominate>submit*.

Both tests yield results that corroborate Johnston's claim that Mao was a Parabellum (offensive) realist, but raise some important qualifiers. In the sample, Mao's philosophical beliefs support Johnston's result that Mao views the world in realist terms, but his belief in control over historical development (P-4) is very close to the mean for the norming group of world leaders. Therefore, to conclude that Mao is a simple Parabellum realist deserves more tests. The test on Mao's successor, Deng Xiaoping, disconfirms Johnston's conclusion about Chinese leaders after Mao. Deng turns out a Confucian leader, as cooperative as other world leaders. He prefers peaceful settlement to conflicts. These aggregate scores for the general operational codes of the two leaders are now explored further to see if they remain stable in the different contexts of peace and war.

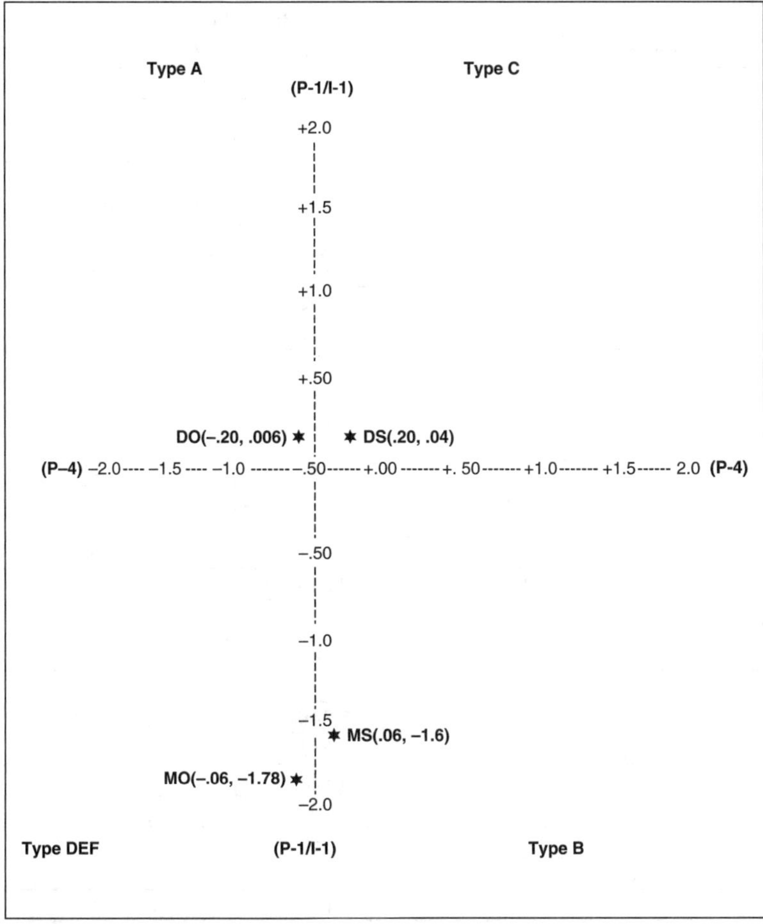

Figure 11.5   The Operational Codes of Mao Zedong and Deng Xiaoping.
*MS4 = (Mao's Self); MO4 = (Mao's Other) for the four speeches test. MS = (Mao's Self); MO = (Mao's Other); DS = (Deng's Self); DO = (Deng's Other) for the larger speech sample test are in bold.

Mao and Deng in Peace and War

To test the conditions under which leaders' beliefs change and how they change, I have conducted a multivariate analysis of variance (MANOVA) test of construct validity. The MANOVA tests summarized in figures 11.6 and 11.7 show the various effects of leader and time period, that is, under what conditions operational code beliefs differ between leaders and change for the same leader. A control variable situation (war/peace) is introduced for testing construct validity.[24] War situations are coded as C = 1 (the Korean War for Mao and Sino-Vietnamese War for Deng), and peace situations are coded NC = 2.

The results in figure 11.6 suggest that the situational context (war/peace) had a significant impact on the leaders' beliefs. These findings suggest that changes in the external environment, specifically increased threat, have a significant impact on

		Main Effects (N = 42)	
Independent Factors		**F. (1, 38)**	**P Value* (two-tailed)**
Leader			
	P-1	44.661	.000*
	P-2	43.409	.000*
	P-3	4.683	.037*
	P-4	.267	.608
	P-5	4.896	.033*
	I-1	18.106	.000*
	I-2	24.653	.000*
	I-3	.687	.412
	I-4a	.001	.970
	I-4b	.467	.498
	I-5 Reward	7.184	.916
	I-5 Promise	.932	.340
	I-5 Appeal	12.921	.001*
	I-5 Oppose	.011	.290
	I-5 Threaten	1.150	.000*
	I-5 Punish	20.648	.000*
Period			
	P-1	3.628	.057*
	P-2	2.532	.120
	P-3	6.346	.016*
	P-4	12.312	.001*
	P-5	8.775	.005*
	I-1	.067	.797
	I-2	.250	.621
	I-3	.437	.513
	I-4a	.143	.708
	I-4b	.329	.570
	I-5 Reward	3.628	.064*
	I-5 Promise	.636	.430
	I-5 Appeal	.109	.743
	I-5 Oppose	.102	.752
	I-5 Threaten	.068	.796
	I-5 Punish	.021	.886
Leader × Period			
	P-1	3.982	.053*
	P-2	3.468	.070*
	P-3	12.486	.001*
	P-4	5.909	.020*
	P-5	10.781	.002*
	I-4a	2.8899	.097*

Figure 11.6 Mao and Deng's Beliefs in a Two-Factor Multivariate Analysis of Variance Design (Leader * Period).

*P ≤ .10 level (two-tailed).

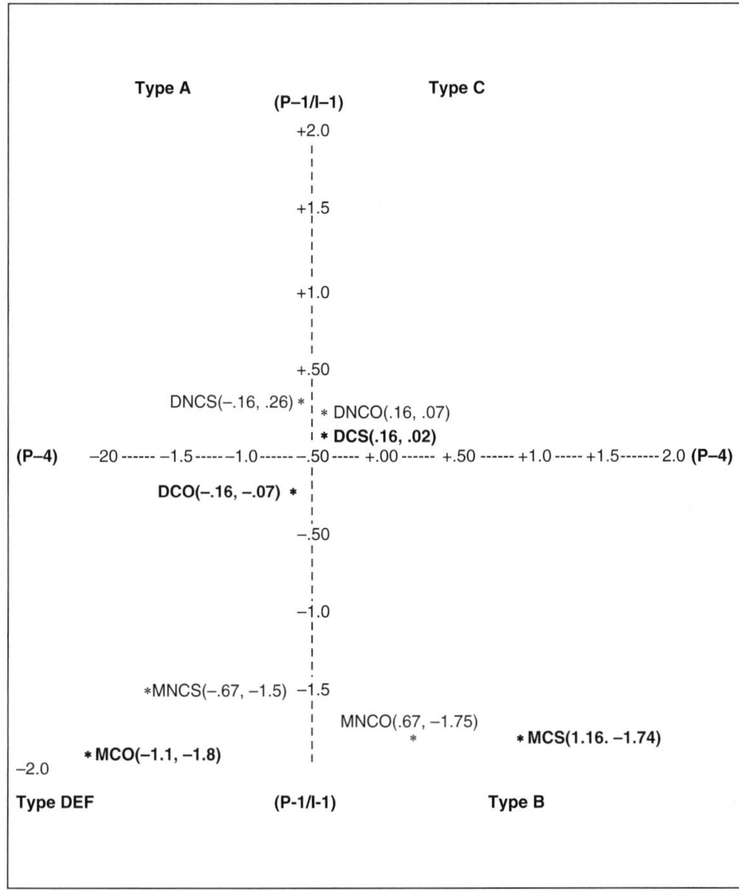

Figure 11.7   The Operational Code of Mao and Deng for Non-Crisis and Crisis Periods.

Note: Normed crisis scores as standard deviations from the average world leader are in bold and non-crisis scores are not.

MNCS = Mao Non-Crisis Self; MNCO = Mao Non-Crisis Other; MCS = Mao Crisis Self; MCO = Mao Crisis Other; DNCS = Deng Non-Crisis Self; DNCO = Deng Non-Crisis Other; DCS = Deng Crisis Self; DCO = Deng Crisis Other.

the leaders' diagnosis of the political universe. Independent of whether the leader was Mao or Deng, the peace and war environment had a significant impact on belief changes for P-1, P-3, P-4, and P-5 (see figure 11.7).

The results in figure 11.6 also show that leaders matter. Cultures may offer competing narratives and policy traditions, and the particular personality in power may be predisposed to emphasize one tradition over another. There are substantial differences between Mao and Deng independent of time (peace or war) for several philosophical and instrumental beliefs (P-1, P-2, P-3, P-5, I-1, I-2, I-5AP, I-5TH, and I-5PU). They differed significantly in their propensity to diagnose the political universe. Mao's world is much more conflictual than Deng's. They differ also in their view regarding the realization of the political values. Mao was much more pessimistic than Deng, understandably so due to their historical international situations.

In terms of instrumental beliefs, they tended to choose different strategies and tactics, as Deng tended to be much more cooperative than Mao. They also differed in their propensity to choose expressions of appeal/support, or threats and punishments.

These patterns of key philosophical and instrumental beliefs of Mao and Deng over war and peace situations can also be seen from figure 11.3. The leader and time period interaction results show that the leaders' impact on the operational code beliefs is conditioned by time periods and historical era. Mao's operational code beliefs became significantly more hostile in shifts from peace to war, while Deng's changed very little. Finally, Mao's self-beliefs (P-4, I-1) shift in figure 11.7 from Type DEF to the more bellicose Type B from peace to war time (the Korean War), and Deng's self beliefs shift in figure 11.4 from Type A to Type C from peace time to war time (the Sino-Vietnam War). He continues to prefer "settle" to any other option, but sees himself in the more assertive position of having increased control over his environment.

To sum up, both leader and situational factors affect strategic decisions, producing interaction effects. Mao is a Parabellum realist in wartime. Deng remains a Confucian leader, but his beliefs also shift to become less cooperative in crisis and war situations. Both leaders view the opponent in a crisis as a defensive realist, but Mao views others as much more hostile. The two leaders also differ significantly regarding the image of the outside world during peace periods. Here again, Mao's view is more hostile.

The earlier analysis matches with the behavioral practice exhibited by Mao and Deng during wartime. In the Korean War, the newly founded People's Republic had to confront a superpower. Mao was fully aware of the military capability disparity between China and the United States. Mao claimed that the imperialists were paper tigers, and atomic bombs were not to be feared, but after eight years of anti-Japanese war and four years of civil war, the PRC was experiencing domestic insurgencies and economic hardships. The military was in need of a rest, and Taiwan was not yet recovered. Therefore, Mao manifest great hesitation over whether to send the PLA to Korea. When General MacArthur's troops crossed the 38th parallel, however, the threat to national survival pushed Mao to make up his mind to "Fight the Americans and Assist Korea, Defend our Homeland."[25] The security threat caused Mao to change his beliefs from a defensive realist to an offensive realist in war time.

In contrast, the Sino-Vietnamese War during Deng's tenure was fought with a party that cannot be compared with the United States in terms of military capability and influence. Although Vietnam declared itself an Asian military power and formed alliance relations with the Soviet Union, the threat posed by Vietnam was far from that of the United States during Mao's administration. In the late 1970s, after the Great Cultural Revolution, China was in a phase of self-adjustment. A policy of reform and opening up had just been put into practice and remained highly dependent on a stable environment. When Vietnam invaded Kampuchea and began a steady stream of border clashes, this stable external environment for domestic economic construction was endangered. Strategically, it made sense to fight with Vietnam in order to remedy this disruptive external security issue and push back Vietnam's hegemonic ambitions in Indo-China. After achieving strategic advantage, however, the PLA did not push forward. It retreated. This strategy would seem to confirm, despite the changes in Deng's operational code beliefs, that he steered clear of parabellum expansionist tendencies, and remained a Confucian leader even in war time.

STRATEGIC CULTURAL IMPACT ON CHINA'S POLICY TOWARD WEAPONS OF MASS DESTRUCTION

An operational code analysis of Mao Zedong and Deng Xiaoping reveals a more complex reality than a structural analysis of Chinese strategic culture would have anticipated. The results also show that Johnston's cultural realism claim that Chinese strategic culture is offensive in nature is too simplistic. One could argue, in fact, that Mao's Parabellum tendencies were the exception rather than the rule and that, overall, China's grand strategy shows a strong Confucian track.[26]

Throughout history, despite the opportunities to expand when China had the capability, China seldom resorted to the use of force with its neighbors except when under minority rule in the Yuan and Qing Dynasties.[27] The three major wars that modern China has fought—the Korean War, Sino-Indian War, and Sino-Vietnamese War—all exhibit a defensive cultural underpinning. With increases in China's power capability, structural realists and Johnston's brand of cultural realists would predict aggressiveness and revisionist moves from China's elite. In contrast to these predictions, however, Chinese foreign policy since the 1990s has emphasized the importance of peaceful settlement of disputes, and extensive security dialogues and consultations.

China's evolutionary policy on weapons of mass destruction (WMD) is a good example of how the interaction between the Confucian strategic culture and the external environment is shaping China's foreign policy behavior. During the Cold War, strategic competition and security threats intensified Mao's Parabellum belief in nuclear weapons as the only security guarantee for China. However, soon after its successful nuclear test in the 1960s, China declared a no-first-use policy, the first nuclear power to announce such a policy in the world. While this posture may also be attributed to technical and strategic considerations, it represented a natural fit with China's deeply rooted defensive Confucian strategic culture.

After Deng and the new generations of leadership (Jiang and Hu[28]) came to power, China's WMD policy became more cooperative in the international community, especially with the United States. Since the 1980s, China has joined all the major international and regional regimes on nonproliferation, abiding by their norms in general practices. In 2003, China issued its first White Paper on nonproliferation, stating its policy positions and practices. Chinese leaders are well aware of the destructive forces of WMD and the possible threat to the world if these weapons were to fall into the wrong hands. China has cooperated with the United States and other countries to work on stopping the proliferation issue.

During the recent North Korean nuclear crisis, China played an active and indispensable role in encouraging North Korea to cooperate with the international community by mediating the multilateral negotiations and talks among the key powers in the region. As a result, North Korea has promised to close its nuclear program and allow international inspectors to monitor progress. Although the future of the North Korean nuclear crisis is still unclear, China's cooperative policy has been widely recognized. The record is certainly not perfect. The United States continues to criticize China's missile sales and technological transfers to Iran and Pakistan. China has defended its actions according to regional balance of power considerations but demonstrated restrictive efforts nonetheless.

Whether Beijing will conduct a cooperative policy with the United States in the future, especially during the U.S. war on terror, will largely depend on U.S. policy toward China. China can fully cooperate with the United States to prevent the proliferation of WMD if the United States does not threaten China's vital interests in Taiwan. Continuing U.S. arms sales to Taiwan in the 1990s directly encouraged independence forces there and damaged the balance of power across the Taiwan Strait. Although the Confucian strategic culture oriented the Chinese leadership to prefer more cooperative policies toward the outside world, especially with the United States, the deteriorating strategic environment (e.g. the Taiwan crisis) may push China in an offensive direction.

Given the asymmetry of military power between China and the United States, the United States enjoys an upper-hand to determine the nature of Sino-U.S. relations. If the United States chooses to cooperate with China to maintain the status quo across the Taiwan Strait, China will definitely return the favor on the WMD issue. However, if the United States pushes China in the wrong direction on Taiwan, the Confucian strategic culture will not preclude Chinese leaders from using force, including the proliferation of WMD and asymmetric warfare, to defend China's national interests.

NOTES

Part of this chapter was originally published in an earlier article in *Security Studies*. See Huiyun Feng, "The Operational Codes of Mao Zedong: Offensive or Defensive Realists?" *Security Studies* Vol. 14, No. 4 (October–December 2005): 637–62; and also Huiyun Feng, *Chinese Strategic Culture and Foreign Policy Decision-Making: Confucianism, Leadership and War* (London: Routledge 2007). The author thanks *Security Studies* and Routledge for permission to use the relevant material in this chapter.

1. Alastair Iain Johnston, *Cultural Realism: Strategic Culture and Grand Strategy in Chinese History* (Princeton: Princeton University Press, 1995).
2. Strategic culture as a concept was coined during the Cold War by Jack Snyder in his famous study of the Soviet strategic decision-making process. Jack Snyder, *The Soviet Strategic Culture: Implications for Limited Nuclear Operations* (Santa Monica, CA: RAND Corporation Report R-2154-AF, September 1977); also Snyder, "The Concept of Strategic Culture: Caveat Emptor," in Carl Jacobsen, ed., *Strategic Power: USA/USSR* (London: MacMillan, 1990): 35–49. Some recent works on Chinese strategic culture include Jonathan R. Adelman and Chih-yu Shih, *Symbolic War: The Chinese Use of Force, 1840–1980* (Taiwan: National Chengchi University, 1993); Zhang, Shu Guang, "China: Traditional and Revolutionary Heritage," in Ken Booth and Russell Trood, eds., *Strategic Cultures in the Asia-Pacific Region* (New York: St. Martin's Press, INC., 1999); Jing-dong Yuan, "Culture Matters: Chinese Approaches to Arms Control and Disarmament," in Keith R. Krause, ed., *Culture and Security: Multilateralism, Arms Control and Security Building* (London, Portland, OR: Frank Cass, 1999); Michael D. Swaine and Ashley J. Tellis, *Interpreting China's Grand Strategy: Past, Present, and Future* (Santa Monica, CA.: RAND Corporation, 2000); Andrew Scobell, "China and Strategic Culture" (Carlisle, PA: US Army War College, Strategic Studies Institute, 2002), available at http:www.strategicstudiesinstitute.army.mil/pubs/display.cfm?pubID=60; Scobell, "The Chinese Cult of Defense," *Issues and Studies,* Vol. 37, No. 5 (2001): 100–27; Yuan-kang Wang, "Culture and Foreign Policy: What Imperial China Tells Us?" Paper presented at the 2002 APSA Annual Conference, Boston 2002 (with author's permission to cite); Shu Guang Zhang, *Deterrence and Strategic Culture: Chinese–American Confrontations, 1949–1958* (Ithaca, NY: Cornell University Press, 1993); Tiejun Zhang, "Chinese Strategic Culture: Traditional and Present Features," *Comparative Strategy,* Vol. 21, No. 2 (2002): 73–90; and chapters by Lawrence C. Katzenstein, "Change, Myth, and the Reunification of China," and Rosita Dellios, "'How May the World be at Peace?': Idealism as Realism in Chinese Strategic Culture," in Valerie M. Hudson, ed., *Culture and Foreign Policy* (Boulder, CO: Lynne Rienner, 1997).

3. Although acknowledging that Chinese strategic culture is offensive, these scholars disagree about how many strategic cultures China has, i.e., if there is one or two strategic cultures. Some state that China has only one strategic culture, which is realpolitik because Confucianism does not function in actual policymaking. Others stress that China has one strategic culture, but it is the Confucian strategic culture that is influencing the beliefs and behavior of Chinese leaders. A more complex view is that there are two strategic cultures, and the Chinese apply the Confucian strategic culture when building upon their self-image while resorting to the realist Parabellum norms when encountering other countries, e.g., Thomas Kane argues for the influence of Legalism, which is the realpolitik counterpart of Confucianism. See Thomas Kane, "China's Foundations: Guiding Principles of Chinese Foreign Policy," *Comparative Strategy*, Vol. 20, No. 1 (January 1, 2001): 45–55; Alastair I. Johnston, "Cultural Realism and Strategy in Maoist China," in Peter Katzenstein, ed., *The Culture of National Security: Norms and Identity in World Politics* (New York: Columbia University Press, 1996), pp. 216–70; Johnston, "Realism(s) and Chinese Security Policy in the Post–Cold–War Period," in Ethan B. Kapstein and Michael Mastanduno, eds., *Unipolar Politics: Realism and State Strategies after the Cold War* (New York: Columbia University Press, 1999), pp. 261–318; Thomas J. Christensen, "Chinese Realpolitik: Reading Beijing's World-View," *Foreign Affairs,* Vol. 75 (September/ October 1996): 37–52; and Wang Yuan-kang, "Culture and Foreign Policy: What Imperial China Tells Us?" Zhang Tiejun, "Chinese Strategic Culture: Traditional and Present Features," *Comparative Strategy*, Vol. 21, No. 2 (April 1, 2002): 73–90; Scobell, "The Chinese Cult of Defense," pp. 100–27; Scobell, "China and Strategic Culture."
4. This criticism is also highlighted in work by Tiejun Zhang, "Chinese Strategic Culture," 73–90.
5. Johnston, "Cultural Realism and Strategy," p. 217, n. 2. See also Huiyun Feng, "The Operational Code of Mao Zedong: Defensive or Offensive Realist?" *Security Studies* Vol. 14, No. 4 (October–December 2005): 637–62. Zhang, "Chinese Strategic Culture: Traditional and Present Features," pp. 73–90.
6. For a more detailed discussion of the selection bias noted here see Huiyun Feng, "The Operational Code of Mao Zedong," 637–62.
7. As Deng Xiaoping said during his visit to the United States in 1979, "The Chinese People suffered amply from the miseries of war. We do not wish to fight a war unless it is forced upon us. We are firmly against a new world war…we want peace—a genuine peace in which the people of each country may develop and progress as they wish, free from aggression, interference, and bullying …" *Beijing Review*, February 9, 1979.
8. Neville Maxwell, *India's China War* (Garden City, NY: Anchor Books, 1972); Allen S. Whiting, *China Crosses the Yalu: The Decision to Enter the Korean War* (Palo Alto, CA: Stanford University Press, 1960); Whiting, "China's Use of Force, 1950–96, and Taiwan," *International Security*, Vol. 26, No. 2 (2001): 103–31; and Whiting, *The Chinese Calculus of Deterrence* (Ann Arbor, MI: University of Michigan Press, 1975).
9. Johnston, *Cultural Realism*, p. 66.
10. Jian Chen, *Mao's China and the Cold War* (Chapel Hill, NC: University of North Carolina Press, 2001).
11. Alexander George, "The Operational Code," *International Studies Quarterly*, Vol. 13 (1969): 190–222.
12. Johnston, *Cultural Realism*, pp. 37–38.
13. George, "The Operational Code." For the ten questions, see pp. 201–16.
14. Alastair I. Johnston, "Thinking about Strategic Culture," *International Security*, Vol. 19, No. 4 (1995): 32–64; and Johnston, *Cultural Realism*, p. 37, fn. 3.
15. Nathan C. Leites, *The Operational Code of the Politburo* (New York: McGraw-Hill Book Company, 1951); and Leites, *A Study of Bolshevism* (Glencoe, IL: Free Press, 1953). Leites defined the operational code as the conceptions of political "strategy" and behavioral rules of conduct in Bolshevik doctrine. A leader's operational code, therefore, can be examined to see if these beliefs and attitudes are consistent with the norms and beliefs of the strategic culture.

16. George, "The Operational Code." Also Stephen G. Walker, "The Motivational Foundations of Political Belief Systems," *International Studies Quarterly,* Vol. 27, No. 2 (June 1983): 179–202; and Walker, "The Evolution of Operational Code Analysis," *Political Psychology,* Vol. 11 (1990): 403–18.
17. Ole R. Holsti, "The 'Operational Code' As An Approach to the Analysis of Belief Systems," Final Report to the National Science Foundation, Grant No. SCO 75–14368 (1977).
18. Walker, "The Motivational Foundations," pp. 179–202; and Walker, "The Evolution of Operational Code Analysis," pp. 403–18.
19. The most recent development of the operational code research program is to apply operational code analysis to study the strategic interactions of states through subjective games developed by Steven Brams. Stephen G. Walker, *Forecasting the Political Behavior of Leaders with the Verbs in Context System of Operational Code Analysis* (Hilliard, OH: Social Science Automation, 2000).
20. Stephen G. Walker, Mark Schafer, and Michael Young, "Profiling the Operational Codes of Political Leaders"; Walker, Schafer, and Young, "William Jefferson Clinton: Beliefs and Integrative Complexity. Operational Code Beliefs and Object Appraisal"; and Walker, Schafer, and Young, "Saddam Hussein: Beliefs and Integrative Complexity. Operational Code Beliefs and Objective Appraisal," all in Jerrold M. Post, ed., *The Psychological Assessment of Political Leaders* (University of Michigan Press, 2003), pp. 387–390.
21. The scores are provided by Prof. Mark Schafer, Department of Political Science, Louisiana State University, Baton Rouge. The norming group now includes about 300 speeches of some 35 leaders.
22. Katzenstein, *The Culture of National Security: Norms and Identity in World Politics.*
23. In his chapter in *The Culture of National Security,* Johnston argues "China has historically exhibited a relatively consistent hard realpolitik or Parabellum strategic culture that has persisted across different structural contexts into the Maoist period (and beyond). Chinese decision makers have internalized this strategic culture such that China's strategic behavior exhibits a preference for offensive uses of force, mediated by a keen sensitivity to relative capabilities. Their preferences are often a reasonably accurate guide to strategic behavior. The persistence of an ideationally based hard realpolitik, however, suggests that structural accounts of realpolitik behavior are incomplete, precisely because this empirically observable *cultural realpolitik has persisted across vastly different interstate systems, regime types, levels of technology, and types of threat. And it persists into the post-Mao period* at a time when objectively and subjectively China's threat environment is the most benign in several decades" (emphasis added). Johnston, "Cultural Realism and Strategy in Maoist China," pp. 217–18. In his recent article in *International Security,* Johnston changed his view toward historical inference. When pointing out the problem of evidence, he stated, "the evidence is most problematic concerning the goal of establishing Chinese hegemony in the region or beyond. Most scholars, government officials, and pundits who routinely make this claim infer it from particular readings of particular parts of Chinese history...Those who use historical analogies to reason about the current Chinese leadership's intentions tend to commit one of two kinds of analytical errors. Either they are unclear about why precisely China's current leaders would have internalized some historical analogies...and not others. Or they are imprecise about why China's foreign policy preferences today are similar to those of Chinese or Europe leaders in earlier times, and apparently uncorrupted, or unaltered by obviously new and different historical conditions." It is hard to judge what Johnston will say about his own study of Chinese offensive grand strategy in history. Johnston, "Is China a Status Quo Power?" *International Security,* Vol. 27, No. 4 (March 1, 2003): 28.
24. To assess construct validity involves three distinct steps. "First, the theoretical relationship between concepts themselves must be specified. Second, the empirical relationship between the measures of the concepts must be examined. Finally, the empirical evidence must be interpreted in terms of how it clarifies the construct validity of the particular measure." Construct validity involves a theoretical framework, which requires "one be able to state several theoretically derived hypotheses involving the particular concept."

Edward G. Carmines and Richard A. Zeller, *Reliability and Validity Assessment* (Beverly Hills, CA: Sage, 1979), pp. 22–23.

25. This is a translation of a Chinese slogan publicized worldwide during the Korean War: *Kang Mei Yuan Chao, Bao Jia Wei Guo.*

26. John K. Fairbank and Frank A. Kierman, Jr. eds., *Chinese Ways in Warfare* (Cambridge, MA: Harvard University Press, 1974); King Chen, *China's War with Vietnam, 1979: Issues, Decisions and Implications* (Palo Alto, CA: Hoover Institution Press, 1987); and Andrew Scobell and Larry Wortzel, *The Lessons of History: The Chinese People's Liberation Army at 75* (Carlisle, PA: Strategic Studies Institute, U.S. Army War College, 2003).

27. Some Western scholars point out that Emperor Wu's policy toward the Xiongnu minority people reflects the aggressiveness of the Han Dynasty's court, and China exploited the Vietnamese for over 1000 years.

28. Follow-up research by the author further confirms the argument in this chapter. With increasing power capability, the operational code beliefs of two key current Chinese leaders—Jiang Zemin and Hu Jintao—show that they are even more cooperative than Mao and Deng. They are Type A Confucian leaders. When the Taiwan crises, 1999 Embassy bombing, and 2001 EP-3 incident are introduced as control variables, the belief systems of Jiang and Hu display strong stability. This shows that despite changes in the external environment, the current Chinese leaders' strategic preferences continue to show a strong Confucian cooperative orientation.

12

North Korea and the Political Uses of Strategic Culture

Joseph S. Bermudez, Jr.

North Korea's Strategic Culture Described

More than any other nation today, the strategic culture of the Democratic People's Republic of Korea (DPRK) is the product of the personal dreams and ambitions of a single individual—Kim Il-sung. Kim was the world's longest reigning leader, having assumed power in the northern portion of the Korean Peninsula during 1948 and maintaining that position until his death in 1994. This has resulted in a worldview and strategic culture built upon six central, interrelated, and overlapping principles.

- The survival of the Kim clan (i.e., "the center of the revolution") and its power and influence. This is the primal principle to which all others are subordinate.
- Elimination of all internal threats to the power of the Kim clan by the establishment and ruthless maintenance of an extremely small, privileged, and powerful military and power-holding elite—all of whom owe absolute allegiance to the Kim clan.
- Reunification of the Fatherland (i.e., the entire Korean Peninsula).
- Establishment and maintenance of overwhelming conventional military strength to facilitate the reunification of the Fatherland.
- Acquisition of weapons of mass destruction (WMD) and ballistic missiles.
- Deterrence of the United States and the Republic of Korea (ROK) by the maintenance of overwhelming conventional military strength and the acquisition of WMD and ballistic missiles.

These six principles are themselves processed through the DPRK's political ideology known as Chuche and what is termed as a "lens of self-deception" composed of four elements:[1]

- historical worldview;
- political indoctrination;
- hatred for the United States;
- authoritarian cultural rules.

The result of this lens of self-deception is that it often distorts and misrepresents the reality of a situation.

Although he is better educated and better informed about world events than his father, Kim Chong-il—who assumed absolute leadership of the DPRK following his father's death—has not significantly deviated from the worldview or strategic culture established by his father.[2] Despite minor efforts to address economic issues Kim Chong-il has vigorously emphasized the strengthening of the military and the continued development of WMD through his "military first" policies. He has proven himself ruthless and dispassionate in dealing with disloyalty of those individuals whom he perceives as a threat—including members of his own extended family.[3]

By all accounts Kim Chong-il is a workaholic, micromanager, "information junkie," technologically savvy, impatient, quick-tempered, intelligent, and ruthless. By his own admission he surfs the Internet daily, regularly watches NHK (Japan), CCTV (China), and CNN, and has foreign books and articles (especially anything written about himself) translated and summarized for him. He prefers to manage almost everything directly, down to the most minor of details. Without his personal approval, nothing of significance can be initiated or accomplished. He insists on numerous detailed reports from all organizations and then spends long hours at his office reading them. He doesn't necessarily trust any single source for information but rather compares the information he receives from several different organizations and sources (apparently including the Internet). It is not unusual for him to order specialists and technocrats from throughout the government to appear before him so that he might directly question them concerning a particular matter. Finally, he believes that the decisions and choices he makes are better than those of the people around him. It is toward Kim Chong-il that all important information streams, and from him that all power, significant orders, and directions issue forth.[4] Ominously, much of the information and analysis he bases his decision making upon is fundamentally distorted by the strategic culture that his father established and he operates within.

The net effect of these factors is a strategic culture that is rudimentary, familial, and possessing few, if any, objective internal checks and balances. It views the United States as the primary enemy, a duplicitous and deceitful enemy who, if it perceives any weakness, is likely to initiate a war of annihilation employing WMD against the DPRK. Internally it views any disagreement with policies or criticism of the Kim regime—no matter how insignificant—as a direct threat to Kim Chong-il and is dealt with harshly. Even loyal dissent amongst the highest levels of the military and power-holding elite is discouraged and constructive variations to the implementation of Kim Chong-il's thoughts on strategic issues are reported as being rare. In a very real sense Kim Chong-il's thoughts and desires are the DPRK's strategic domestic and international policies.

Profile of North Korea's Strategic Culture

To understand the basis for the strategic culture developed by Kim Il-sung it is necessary to go back to the pre–World War II period.[5] Following Japan's victory in the Russo-Japanese War of 1904–1905, it became the dominant power in Asia and annexed Korea in 1911. Japan would rule Korea with a cruel and often inhumane hand until the end of World War II. The Japanese were then, and still are, viewed by the majority of Koreans as foreigners and oppressors.[6] During the late 1930s, the

Japanese military developed a small chemical and biological warfare (CBW) capability that it used against the Chinese. The Japanese also conducted an exhaustive regime of experimentation on Allied prisoners-of-war, Russians, and Chinese civilians.[7] The general nature of these chemical and biological operations and experimentation were known to the Chinese government, the Allies, and, to a lesser degree, the general population. At that time Kim Il-sung and the majority of the DPRK future leadership were young peasant guerrillas who were sporadically fighting the Japanese, first with the Communist Chinese, and then with the Soviet Army. Although only fragmentary evidence is available, it is apparent that they were influenced by what they would learn of these chemical and biological operations.[8] At the time of the U.S. nuclear bombing of Hiroshima and Nagasaki in 1945, Kim and his fellow guerrillas had been fighting the Japanese for five–ten years. As the reality and the rumors of the events at Hiroshima and Nagasaki spread throughout the world, the nuclear bomb was viewed as the ultimate "doomsday" weapon. This attitude was reinforced by the experiences of those Koreans returning from Japan who had been in Hiroshima and Nagasaki at the time of the bombing.[9] This fear became even more pronounced among Communist guerrilla leaders such as Mao Zedong and Kim Il-sung. By the end of World War II, both Kim Il-sung and a number of soon-to-be influential Koreans had an uneducated appreciation of, and indirect exposure to, the effects of nuclear, chemical and biological warfare. This awareness shaped their developing views of the world, warfare, and politics.

Combined with these early appreciations of WMD, four additional factors during the subsequent Fatherland Liberation War (i.e., Korean War) would help coalesce both Kim Il-sung's worldview and form the foundations of the strategic culture then developing within the nation.

1. The U.S. intervention in the Fatherland Liberation War was interpreted by Kim and his contemporaries as the prime reason the war of reunification failed. From this point forward the United States would be viewed as the primary enemy and as a bully "kicking the door in" and interfering in the purely internal affairs of nations of which it did not approve.

2. During the war both the DPRK and People's Republic of China (PRC) suffered from repeated, and to them, unexplained outbreaks of infectious diseases such as influenza, Dengue fever, and cholera. These outbreaks caused large numbers of civilian and military casualties. While the leadership knew that it was untrue, they fabricated the story that the United States was employing biological, and to a lesser degree chemical, weapons against their units in Korea and against villages within the PRC itself.[10] Furthermore, they claimed that former Japanese soldiers were cooperating with the United States in perpetrating these attacks.[11] For the uninformed masses of the DPRK it became a bedrock of "truth" and these claims are still repeated.

3. The United States on numerous occasions (the earliest being President Harry S. Truman's public statements on November 30, 1950) threatened to employ nuclear weapons against Korean People's Army (KPA) and "Chinese People's Volunteers" (CPV) units in Korea, and if necessary against the PRC proper, to end the war.[12] These threats struck a raw nerve since the leadership of both nations remembered the bombing of Hiroshima and Nagasaki, and neither the PRC nor DPRK could withstand a nuclear attack or had the capability to respond in kind. In combination with other factors the desired effect was achieved and a truce agreement was reached, thus ending the hostilities.

4. While appreciative of all the support received from the Soviet Union and PRC, Kim expressed disappointment with the Soviet Union's pressure to sign the Armistice Agreement. This would provide a context for Kim to view future Soviet actions (e.g., the Soviets backing down during the Cuban Missile Crisis, etc.) and fostered the belief that the DPRK must become self-sufficient.

In the years that followed the Fatherland Liberation War, public statements by U.S. officials, the continued U.S. military presence on the Korean Peninsula, and the inclusion of the ROK within the U.S. nuclear umbrella have contributed to peace. To the DPRK leadership, this U.S. presence has also reinforced the belief that the DPRK has little choice but to comply with the 1953 Armistice Agreement or face devastation from nuclear attack.

In the immediate postwar years the DPRK possessed neither WMD, nor the capabilities to produce them. Combined with the perceived threat poised by the United States, this contributed to a DPRK belief that possession of such weapons was a requirement to deter U.S./ROK aggression and set the stage for reunification of the Fatherland.[13]

In a December 1955 speech Kim Il-sung set forth a new political ideology known as Chuche that would quickly change the nature of DPRK society.[14] While generally defined as meaning "self-reliance and national identity" it has developed into a unique belief system that permeates every aspect of life in the DPRK. It has been used by both Kim Il-sung and Kim Chong-il to justify almost anything: "major policy initiatives, including eliminating factional enemies, widening diplomatic activities, neutralizing attempts by China or Russia to exert influence over Korea, questioning the legitimacy of the South Korean government, and relentlessly attacking U.S. imperialism."[15]

Today Chuche is a national ideology with distinctly religious overtones, with Kim Il-sung and Kim Chong-il at the center of the universe, being omnipotent and incapable of doing wrong. Because of its pervasiveness throughout society the DPRK's strategic culture has become an emanation of the Kim's Chuche thoughts.

Kim Chong-il was raised in and, since the 1970s, participated in the subsequent incremental evolution of the strategic culture established by his father. In this, both he and his father were accompanied by a small group of military and power-holding elites. This group consisted of trusted friends and relatives (mostly men)—many of whom had fought either as partisans with Kim Il-sung against the Japanese during World War II or as officers during the Fatherland Liberation War. Since Kim Il-sung's death in 1994, the composition of this small group of older generation elites has changed considerably as members have died, become enfeebled with age, or were gradually replaced by Kim Chong-il's trusted contemporaries.[16] To date, neither Kim nor his appointees have deviated significantly from the basic worldview or strategic culture established by Kim Il-sung. Notably, however, the majority of these new power-holding elites possess even less exposure to international arena than their predecessors, and none have experienced the realities of war. What long-term effect this will have on DPRK strategic culture, especially when Kim Chong-il is eventually succeeded by one of his sons, is unclear.

Even with the possibility of Kim Chong-il soon appointing one of his sons to succeed him, for the foreseeable future, it is unlikely that there will be any significant changes to Kim Chong-il's worldview or the DPRK's strategic culture.

Military and Power-Holding Elite

The "keepers" of the DPRK's strategic culture are an extremely small group of military and power-holding elites. All power within the DPRK originates with Kim Chong-il, who is simultaneously Chairman of the National Defense Commission, General Secretary of the Korean Workers' Party (KWP), and Supreme Commander of the Korean People's Army (a unified armed force consisting of the ground, navy, and air forces). Therefore what really matters within the DPRK is not so much an individual's schooling, personal achievements, employment, position within society, rank within the KPA, KWP, and so on but how close—physically and emotionally—that individual is connected to Kim Chong-il.

To implement their rule the Kims have cultivated and mercilessly maintained a diminutive class of military and power-holding elites. The primary qualification for membership in this class is absolute allegiance to the Kims. Such allegiance is rewarded by access to the Kims and the attendant privilege and power that it conveys. Until the mid-1990s these elites were primarily contemporaries of Kim Il-sung who had repeatedly demonstrated their personal loyalties and shared his worldview. Since Kim's death in 1994 this older generation is being slowly supplanted—primarily through attrition—by contemporaries of Kim Chong-il. All current members of the military and power-holding elite owe their status, privilege, and literally their lives and the lives

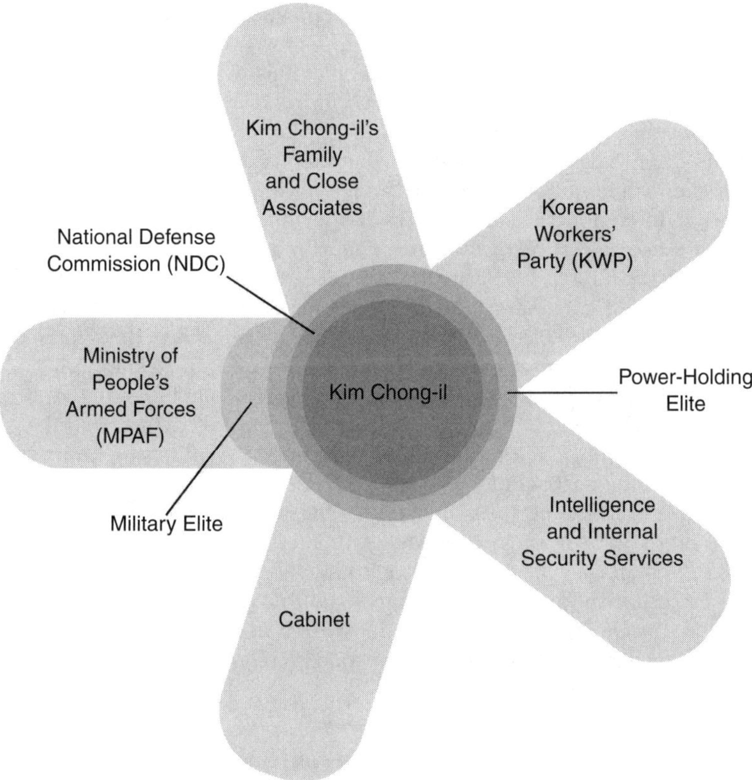

Figure 12.1 North Korea's Military and Power-Holding Elite.

of their families to the Kim clan. Any hint of disloyalty is dealt with harshly, with the offender—and often their extended family—being exiled from the capital P'yongyang to mountain work camps. In more extreme cases, offenders are executed.

This power structure can best be illustrated by viewing Kim Chong-il as the center—physically, politically, and socially—of the DPRK, as shown in figure 12.1. Immediately surrounding him are a group of individuals—primarily men—and their subordinates who come from five broad societal groupings: Kim Chong-il's extended family and close confidents,[17] Ministry of People's Armed Forces (MPAF), KWP, Cabinet, and intelligence and internal security services. The convergence of these groupings represents the power-holding elite within the DPRK. The pinnacle of the power-holding elite is the National Defense Commission (NDC), which consists of approximately ten individuals, most of whom hold military rank. Therefore, the military elite within the NDC should be understood to be among highest power-holders within the DPRK.

A noteworthy characteristic of the NDC specifically and the power-holding elite in general is that members occupy multiple leadership positions within the MPAF, KWP, and intelligence and internal security services. In fact, all the military members of the NDC are also members of the Central Military Committee. This cross-pollination and concentration of power within the hands of a few individuals enables Kim Chong-il, through the NDC, to easily maintain extremely firm control over all aspects of DPRK society and the flow of information. It also means that the decision-making process and poles of political power apparent in most nations are not present within the DPRK.

An additional aspect of the military and power-holding elite that has become an integral component of the DPRK's strategic culture is what would be termed in the West as corruption. In fact, this corruption should be viewed as being institutionalized and the means by which many of the military and power-holding elite have attained and maintained their positions. It is manifested in the access elites have to information, foreign manufactured goods, opportunity to have their children travel abroad for schooling, their own greater opportunities to travel, nepotism, and so on. Thus, favoritism and cronyism are endemic among the elite. Given this vortex of institutionalized corruption, fear of displeasing Kim Chong-il and a convoluted flow of information, it is certainly within the realm of possibility that Kim Chong-il is at times being deceived or misled at some level by subordinates. Exactly how this occurs is unclear, but it may manifest itself in a manner similar to the Iraqi regime under Saddam Hussein.[18] Thus, this may be manifested by managers or leaders of program exaggerating the achievements or potential capabilities of their programs or systems. This may account for some of the stories related by defectors concerning Kim Chong-il's surprise at times concerning the true conditions in military units or factories and the excessive remedies that he initiates to address these conditions.

Within such an environment of corruption it would serve an individual's interest (and by extension those who ally themselves with that individual) to have higher quality and greater diversity of information than a political rival. The corollary to this is that limiting a rival's access to information is of significant benefit to a member of the military and power-holding elite.

Lens of Self-Deception

One of the more notable aspects of the DPRK's strategic culture is that it is processed through a lens of self-deception. In what may be viewed as either "circular verification" or "self-fulfilling prophecy," this lens is both a product of Chuche and the strategic culture that it is filtering. This lens of self-deception is composed of four layers: historical worldview, political indoctrination, hatred for the United States, and authoritarian cultural rules. This lens is so darkly colored that instead of focusing and illuminating, it most often misrepresents and distorts the reality of the information.

As noted earlier, until the mid-1990s the real power within the DPRK rested within the hands of Kim Il-sung and a small group of military and power-holding elites. As a group these individuals possess a narrow and distorted worldview that is based not upon the free flow of ideas, questioning of facts, and exposure to different cultures and philosophies, but rather upon their limited personal experiences, Communist ideology, KWP propaganda, and Chuche. This worldview places world events and the actions of other nations within a distinctly historical context. In this view, Japan is not only a neighbor and important trading partner, it is also the nation that occupied Korea and brutally oppressed the Korean people for many years. Because of this, any action undertaken by Japan, benign as it might be, is viewed with suspicion.

The DPRK has never attempted to conceal the fact that it believes the United States is its principal enemy and the ROK its "puppet." In this view it was the United States that interfered in a purely internal dispute—the Fatherland Liberation War— and threatened to employ nuclear weapons. Since that time the United States has continued to both prevent the unification of Korea and threaten the existence of the DPRK with the use of nuclear weapons. Furthermore, it is the United States that "controls" the United Nations and directs world attention against the DPRK and other countries that it opposes. The DPRK leadership views U.S. actions in countries such as Grenada, Iraq, Panama, Somalia, and Vietnam as analogous to their own situation, with the United States acting as a bully "kicking the door in" and interfering in purely internal affairs. Therefore, all actions undertaken by the United States are viewed with distrust and as attempts to both prolong the division of the Korean people and directly threaten the existence of the Kim regime.

Korean society within both the ROK and DPRK has a strong underpinning of Confucian philosophy.[19] One notable aspect of this is the stringent authoritarian hierarchal rules. Within government organizations this is expressed by the fact that subordinates will rarely, if ever, disagree with their superiors. In fact, they are encouraged not to. Therefore, if a superior is known to possess a particular view on a subject their subordinates—whether they believe the view correct or not—will tend to work new information into that view. These authoritarian rules are also manifested in deep institutional loyalty that results in a frequent refusal to share information and detrimental inter-agency competition. While such submission to superiors and institutional loyalty are witnessed in some form throughout the business, military, and intelligence communities in the world it is quite evident within the DPRK they are taken to extremes under the umbrella of Chuche. The distinct possibility exists that this dynamic may manifest itself in a desire by the subordinates and support staffs to Kim Chong-il and the NDC to *not* present information that displeases them or is at variance to their stated opinions.

North Korea's Strategic Culture in Action

Whether consciously or subconsciously, the characteristics mentioned earlier suggest that the manner by which information is processed by individuals and institutions results in it passing through a lens of self-deception and exiting in a fundamentally flawed state. It is upon these assessments, however, that decisions within the DPRK are made. When combined with Kim Chong-il's apparent beliefs—that he "knows better" and can arrive at better decisions than those around him—this often leads to ill-advised courses of action and unanticipated outcomes. A prime example of this was evidenced by Kim Chong-il's public admission in 2003 that DPRK intelligence agencies had kidnapped Japanese civilians over the past thirty years. Kim's apparent analysis of the situation was that the Japanese would appreciate his magnanimous admission of guilt, view it as a sign of a new level of openness, and open themselves to the DPRK. It apparently never occurred to him that it would ignite deep emotions from a broad spectrum of the Japanese population and harden their feelings toward him and the DPRK. It should be anticipated that such a dynamic will be present during any future dealings with the DPRK—especially during times of crisis.

Within the military this dynamic can be illustrated by how the Military Training Bureau evaluated U.S. operations against Iraq during Operations Desert Storm and Iraqi Freedom. According to defectors international news broadcasts concerning Operation Desert Storm were taped and "Videos of the Gulf War were watched everyday in the Operations Office, and assessments of the military power of the United States and the multinational forces, and studies of their strategy and tactics, were re-assessed from new angles."[20]

In one of those paradoxes resulting from a flawed strategic culture that are so common when dealing with the DPRK the same defector indicates that what they witnessed in the videos was shocking and disturbing, yet the final analysis was

> the Gulf War was, in short, that it was "child's play." Should [the DPRK] face such circumstances, they concluded, it could easily deal with the United States and the multinational forces. The reasons for this were that: unlike in the past, a U.S.-led military block, even if it is formed, would be unable to act without the consent of its allies; in the event of another Korean war, neighboring powers would not go along with the U.S. position as they did in the Gulf War; [the DPRK's] asymmetry in conventional and high-tech weapons; and [the DPRK's] new confidence in electronic warfare.[21]

Other defectors recount that following Operation Desert Storm officers above regimental commander were required to watch videotapes of the war to familiarize themselves with U.S. tactics. The videotapes, however, had a negative effect upon the commanders who realized that modern war depends on modern weapons and that the weapons possessed by the KPA were obsolete.

During the 2003 buildup to and early combat phases of Operation Iraqi Freedom Kim Chong-il is reported to have gone into seclusion for fifty days beginning in mid-February and extending to the end of March. He even missed the traditional opening ceremonies of the Supreme People's Assembly in P'yongyang. The general assessment of this behavior was that Kim and the intelligence community interpreted media reports concerning U.S. attempts to decapitate the Iraqi leadership and the subsequent deployment of additional U.S. combat aircraft to East Asia as indications that he might also be the target of a similar decapitation attack. Yet, no such attack was contemplated by the United States.[22]

A recent example containing many of the elements of the strategic culture established years ago under Kim Il-sung remains valid under Kim Chong-il can be seen in the February 10, 2005, statement issued by the DPRK Foreign Ministry:

> We have already resolutely withdrawn from the NPT and have manufactured nuclear weapons for self-defense to cope with the Bush administration's policy of isolating and crushing the DPRK, which is becoming stronger. Our nuclear weapons will remain a

self-defensive nuclear deterrent under any circumstances. Today's reality shows that only strong power can protect justice and defend the truth. As the United States' imprudent rash acts and hostile attempts become more blatant, we only feel great pride in having strengthened, in every way from early on, the single-hearted unity of the entire army and all the people and self-defensive national defense capability while holding high the military-first banner.[23]

SUMMARY

More than any other nation today, the DPRK is the product of the personal dreams and ambitions of a single individual—Kim Il-sung. Kim was the world's longest reigning leader, having assumed power in the northern portion of the Korean Peninsula during 1948 and maintained that position until his death in 1994. The DPRK is an extension of Kim's thoughts, ideas, strengths, weaknesses, and fears. The net effect of this is a worldview and strategic culture built upon six central and interrelated principles:

1. Survival of the Kim clan;
2. elimination of all domestic threats;
3. reunification of the Fatherland;
4. establishment and maintenance of overwhelming conventional military strength;
5. acquisition of WMD and ballistic missiles; and
6. deterrence of the United States and ROK.

These six principles are themselves processed through the DPRK's political ideology known as Chuche and what has been termed as a lens of self-deception. In what may be viewed as either "circular verification" or "self-fulfilling prophecy" this lens is itself a product strategic culture that it is filtering. The four elements of this lens are,

1. Historical worldview;
2. political indoctrination;
3. hatred for the United States; and
4. authoritarian cultural rules.

This lens of self-deception is so darkly colored that instead of focusing and illuminating, it most often misrepresents and distorts real-world reality.

The repeated threats by the United States over the past fifty-plus years have contributed to the maintenance of peace on the Korean peninsula, but they have also fostered a strategic culture within the DPRK that it must absolutely possess WMD (especially nuclear weapons) as a means of countering the U.S. nuclear threat and thus ensuring their national existence.[24] This belief is rooted not only in strong emotions, but also in years of political, military, and intelligence analysis. When raised within the strategic culture developed by Kim Chong-il the 1994 statements by Kang Myong Do, a defector and son-in-law of then DPRK Prime Minister Kang Song-san, provide relevant insight into this conviction.

North Korea's nuclear development is not intended as a bargaining chip as seen by the Western world, but for the maintenance of its system under the circumstances in which it is faced with economic difficulties and a situation following the collapse of Eastern

> Europe...There is a firm belief that the only way to sustain the Kim Chong-il system is to have nuclear capabilities.[25]

According to defectors, Kim believes that if the KPA is weak, the state cannot exercise its power in international affairs and its survival will be in jeopardy. He emphasizes that "only when our military force is strong, can we take the initiative in a contact or dialogue with the United States or South Korea."[26]

The DPRK's strategic culture not only views nuclear weapons as "decisive weapons" and its primary means of deterring U.S. aggression, but as also providing the DPRK with international prestige, allowing them to take their rightful place among a select few world powers with all the respect and political power commensurate to such a position.

From Kim's perspective U.S. actions, unilaterally and through the UN, are attempts to impinge upon his ability to rule the DPRK, threats to his complete authority and autonomy, and are ultimately designed to overthrow him. These attempts directly affront the strategic culture developed by his father and embraced by him. The strategic culture that surrounds him fosters the idea that the DPRK is morally stronger than the United States and that by resolutely standing firm and threatening America he can outlast each administration.

The net effect of these factors is a strategic culture that is rudimentary, familial, and possesses few—if any—objective internal checks and balances. It views the United States as the primary enemy, one that is deceitful in practice, and willing to use WMD against the DPRK. Internally it views any disagreement with policies or criticism of the Kim regime—no matter how insignificant—as a direct threat to Kim Chong-il and are dealt with harshly. No constructive criticism is allowed, even from loyal members of the military and power-holding elite.

Within such an environment the actions of the DPRK, which are routinely evaluated by outsiders as "unpredictable," "irrational," "illogical," or simply "crazy," if viewed from within the context of its strategic culture can be understood as being quite rational and understandable.

NOTES

1. See Joseph S. Bermudez Jr., *Information and the DPRK's Military and Power-Holding Elite* in Kongdan Oh Hassig, *North Korean Policy Elites*, IDA Paper P-3903 (Alexandria: Institute for Defense Analyses, June 2004), available at http://www.brookings.edu/views/papers/fellows/oh20040601.htm.
2. Merrily Baird, *Kim Chong-il's Erratic Decision-Making and North Korea's Strategic Culture* in Barry R. Schneider, and Jerrold M. Post, eds., *Know Thy Enemy: Profiles of Adversary Leaders and Their Strategic Cultures* (Maxwell Air Force Base, Alabama: USAF Counterproliferation Center, July 2003, 2nd ed.), available at www.au.af.mil/au/awc/awcgate/cpc-pubs/know_thy_enemy/cover.htm.
3. For two excellent analyses of the Kim family and power-holding elites, see Kenneth E. Gause, *The North Korean Leadership: System Dynamics and Fault Lines*; and Alexandre Y. Mansourov, *Inside North Korea's Black Box: Reversing the Optics*, both in Kongdan Oh Hassig, *North Korean Policy Elites*.
4. Peter Maass, "The Last Emperor," *New York Times Magazine*, October 19, 2003; "Interview with Defector Hwang Jong Yop [Hwang Jang Yop]: A Rare Portrait of North Korea," *Time [Asia]*, September 7, 1999, Vol. 152, No. 9, www.time. com/time/asia/; "DPRK's Kim Chong-il's Position on Retaliation," *Choson Ilbo*, October 17, 1996, pp. 8–11, as cited in FBIS-EAS-96–231; "Defector to ROK on Kim Chong-il's Control of DPRK Military," *Win*, June 1996, pp. 161–67, as cited in FBIS-EAS-96–197; "Articles

by Defector Kang Myong-to Reported," *Chungang Ilbo*, April 21, 1995, p. 5, as cited in FBIS-EAS-95–097; "North Korean Defectors 27 July News Conference," *Choson Ilbo*, July 28, 1994, pp. 3–4, as cited in FBIS-EAS-94–145; and "Newspaper Profiles Kim Chong-il's Supporters," *Sindong-a*, February 1994, pp. 421–39, as cited in FBIS-EAS-94–050.

5. Adrian Buzo, *The Guerrilla Dynasty* (Boulder: Westview Press, 1999); Dae-Sook Suh, *Kim Il-sung: The North Korea Leader* (New York: Colombia University Press, 1988); and Sydney A. Seiler, *Kim Il-song 1941–1948* (New York: University Press of America).

6. These sentiments have been repeatedly expressed to the author in private conversations, during the past twenty-five years, with ambassadors, ministers, representatives, and private citizens from both the ROK and DPRK. It does, however, appear to be moderating among the younger generations in the ROK.

7. Peter Williams and David Wallace, *Unit 731: Japan's Secret Biological Warfare in World War II* (New York: The Free Press, 1989), p. 45; and Sheldon H. Harris, *Factories of Death: Japanese Biological Warfare 1932–45 and the American Cover Up* (New York: Routledge, 1994), pp. 67–73.

8. Author interview data.

9. Peter Hayes, *Pacific Powderkeg* (Lexington: Lexington Books, 1991), pp. 241–46.

10. John Cookson and Judith Nottingham, *A Survey of Chemical and Biological Warfare* (New York: Monthly Review Press, 1969), pp. 57–63 and 297–308; and U.S. Army, "Bacteriological Warfare Charges Against the United States: A Strategic Weapon in the Communist Propaganda Warfare," *FEC Intelligence Digest*, No. 32, October 2, 1952, pp. 6–10.

11. Author interview data; Cookson and Nottingham, *A Survey of Chemical and Biological Warfare*, pp. 57–63 and 297–308; and U.S. Army, "Bacteriological Warfare Charges," pp. 6–10; and David Tharp, "The Brutal Secret of Japan's WWII Unit 731," *United Press International*, August 8, 1995.

12. *San Diego Tribune.* "Papers Show Eisenhower Weighed Nuclear Attack," March 26, 1988, A5; and *San Diego Union.* "Nuclear Attack Reportedly Would Have Taken Week," March 29, 1988, A29.

13. John Wilson Lewis and Xue Litai. *China Builds the Bomb* (Palo Alto: Stanford University Press, 1988), chapters 1 and 2. These two chapters present an insightful discussion of the origins and effect of the PRC's fear of U.S. nuclear weapons usage.

14. Kongdan Oh and Ralph C. Hassig, *North Korea: Through the Looking Glass* (Washington, D.C.: Brookings Institute Press, 2000), chapter 2 provides an excellent and understandable explanation of Chuche (Juche). See also Bruce Cummings, "The Corporate State in North Korea," in Hagen Koo, ed., *State and Society in Contemporary Korea* (Ithaca: Cornell University Press, 1993), pp. 197–230.

15. Defense Intelligence Agency. *North Korea: The Foundations for Military Strength—Update 1995* (Washington, DC: Government Printing Office, December 1995), p. 1.

16. For the most part this was done in a manner consistent with traditional Confucian values of respect and honor for elderly and powerful individuals. See Paul S. Crane, *Korean Patterns* (Seoul: Hollym Corp., 1968).

17. Information on the Kim family may be found in Sarah Buckley, "North Korea's Secretive 'First Family,'" *BBC News*, October 29, 2003, accessed October 30, 2003, at http://news. bbc.co.uk/1/hi/world/asia-pacific/3203523.stm; and Peter Carlson, "Sins of the Son; Kim Chong-Il's North Korea Is in Ruins, But Why Should That Spoil His Fun?" *Washington Post*, May 11, 2003, p. D1. See also, Gause, *The North Korean Leadership*; and Mansourov, *Inside North Korea's Black Box*, both in Kongdan Oh Hassig, *North Korean Policy.*

18. James Risen, "Ex-Inspector Says C.I.A. Missed Disarray in Iraqi Arms Program," *New York Times*, January 26, 2004.

19. Crane, *Korean Patterns.*

20. "Ex-DPRK Major Unveils KPA Military Plan," *Pukhan*, February 1, 2000, pp. 92–99; and "Anti-Kim Front: DPRK Military May Revolt," *Chugan Choson*, December 2, 1993, pp. 32–34, as cited in FBIS-EAS-94–028.

21. Ibid.

22. "Kim Chong-II Reportedly Feared Being Next Target," *Houston Chronicle*, May 12, 2003, p. 12.
23. "DPRK 'Manufactured Nuclear Weapons,' To 'Suspend' 6-Way Talks for 'Indefinite Period,'" *Korean Central Broadcasting System*, February 10, 2005, as cited in FBIS.
24. Paul Shin, "Korea-Defection," *The Associated Press*, September 13, 1991.
25. "North Korean Defectors 27 July New Conference," *Choson Ilbo*, July 28, 1994, pp. 3–4, as cited in FBIS-EAS-94–145, July 28, 1994, pp. 59–63; James Sterngold, "Defector Says North Korea Has 5 A-Bombs and May Make More," *The New York Times*, July 28, 1994, p. A7; and Don Kirk, "Defector: N. Korea Eyes 10 A-Bombs," *Newsday*, July 28, 1994, p. A14.
26. "Defector to ROK on Kim Chong-il's Control of DPRK Military," *Win*, June 1996, pp. 161–67, as cited in FBIS-EAS-96–197.

13

Does Al Qaeda have a Strategic Culture?

Jerry Mark Long

An analyst writing for a prominent counterterrorism think tank recently offered a "primer" on the world's most feared terrorist network and the potential employment of weapons of mass destruction (WMD).[1] Saying that an al Qaeda attack using these weapons is "inevitable," the analyst held that such employment "would serve all the traditional purposes of terrorism: symbolism, propaganda, and psychological impact, irrespective of the failure or success of the mission." Then, in a sweeping conclusion, the analyst averred, "What matters is to cause mass casualties...In this context discussions about motives to deploy WMD are irrelevant. No matter how complex the deep principles or incentives behind WMD terrorism, the *only reliable motive is an unflinching desire to slay blindly.*"[2]

"Irrespective of success or failure." "Slay blindly." Unfortunately, the analyst's views seem to be as common as they are categorical and reductionistic. Al Qaeda's true aim, despite the spectacular assault on the World Trade Center, has never been simply indiscriminate slaughter. Indeed, its long-term goals have been articulated in a multitude of venues and with remarkable consistency. Although its ideologues have vigorously debated methods of achieving them, blind slaying has not numbered among them, whether as means or end. In studying al Qaeda documents, something else emerges: a view of the world and a strategic code more richly textured, nuanced, calculating, even deadly. Al Qaeda may indeed someday use WMD, but it will do so having calibrated its aims and—despite our author's assertion—success *will* count.

But the account given earlier falls short in another way, and it is this: we can no longer speak of a single al Qaeda, a vertical organization with a *shura* council rigorously controlling a top–down structure. It is better viewed as an ideology metastasizing through multiple "al-Qaedas," franchises that import the original message of the proto-al-Qaeda and adapt it to local and national exigencies. Increasingly, "al Qaeda" must be taken as a political metonymy, an expression to indicate an array of global Islamic organizations, operating with varying levels of autonomy, but generally subscribed to a salafist religious narrative that stipulates a political order that will be achieved through the use of controlled violence. The original al Qaeda remains, but it is no longer simply the hierarchical structure developed in the 1990s following the mujahideen triumph in Afghanistan. Al Qaeda is now an idea spread throughout the blogosphere, and that is where the greater threat lies.

The question of jihadist use of WMD must therefore be put in a double context. First, one must examine al Qaeda as a violent non-state, *non-national* actor (VNSNNA) whose ideology posits a nexus of strategic principles and suggests an operational code. Then, one must examine particular al Qaedas, violent non-state *national* actors (VNSNA), which may import that ideology, tailor it to local exigencies, and develop specific national operational codes. In taking this two-tiered approach, we are not discounting that Osama and the original al Qaeda may attempt to acquire and use WMD, but we are asserting that multiple jihadist groups are now deliberating possible use in their respective national settings. Thus, the question Western analysts face is considerably more complex than simply, "What is the likelihood al-Qaeda will employ WMD?"

This chapter takes only an initial step in the complex task of trying to determine whether and under what circumstances al Qaeda and its affiliates may use WMD. It will confine itself to examining the ideology, approached as narrative, of the *original* al Qaeda, not particular franchises. It will ask what its views are with respect to the acquisition and employment of WMD, and it will do so by using strategic culture as an analytic concept. What emerges is a contested ideology, but also one of substantial nuance, and—as we shall see—something considerably advanced beyond a simple desire to employ WMD to slay blindly.

AL QAEDA AND STRATEGIC CULTURE AS ANALYTIC TOOL

As an analytic concept, strategic culture studies developed in the 1970s, following the earlier idea of a political culture among elites, a "culture" amenable to critical analysis. Once the culture was understood, analysts could then make predictions about political behavior. As the idea developed, analysts applied the idea of strategic culture to the Soviet Union. In its usual formulation, the Soviets were seen as developing specific operational codes based on a long-developing culture that stemmed from centuries of Russian history and the wars that swept across Eastern Europe to the Russian heartland. Thus, analysts ascribed operational doctrines such as "defense in depth" and "correlation of forces" to facets of a deeper strategic culture, a set of factors that made for a kind of historically imposed inertia on present actions.[3]

Analysts of violent non-state actors have recently revived the concept, looking for a more insightful way of describing (and, where possible, predicting) strategic behaviors than simply positing them to a given actor's forward-looking calculation of maximum utility. That is especially important when looking at al Qaeda, for game theory is unable to take adequate account of suicide bombing. In such a case, of course, the actor does nothing to maximize his utility, but quite the opposite. And yet the rationality of the bombers seems intact, from a psychological point of view,[4] and when examined within a religious and historical context—the very thing strategic culture analysis compels us to do—the sacrifice the bombers make is both explicable and consistent. To use Hedrick Smith's apt phrase from another context (that of Soviet political behavior), what one confronts in the Middle East today is the weight of the salafist past upon the Islamist present. Strategic culture helps us read al Qaeda's past and offers an interpretation of present actions.

At the outset, one must acknowledge a special consideration in seeking to use strategic culture as a tool to examine al Qaeda. Heretofore, it has been used with respect to *state* actors. Al Qaeda, despite its dreams of a renewed caliphate, is not a state. Moreover, in the parlance of international relations, it isn't even a nation.

It is transnational. But the ostensible weakness of strategic culture as a tool may be its very strength, if prudently applied. "Nation" is a protean concept. One way of approaching it is to see a nation as a group of people who strongly identify with an overarching, shared cultural narrative, a key focus in strategic culture analysis. Indeed, a state has effective political cohesion to the degree it is coterminal with that nation and its narrative.

Thus, in many ways the nation is the unit more susceptible of strategic culture analysis, an analysis appropriate to the state only to that degree the state comprises those who share a national narrative. The Moro Islamic Liberation Front, the Tamil Tigers, the Basque separatists, the Chechen rebels, and Hamas would be amenable to this analysis, for while they are violent non-state actors, they are yet national actors within a state setting. The same could be said for particular al Qaedas within a local setting, whether in Bali, Morocco, or "Londonistan." This conceptualization would seem especially pertinent to national groups in Iraq. Rather than attempt to analyze violence in the Iraqi state as a whole, a more fruitful approach would see Iraq as an artificial state that comprises three nations. With respect to its creation after World War I, Sir Anthony Parsons, long a British diplomat in the Middle East, observed, "Woodrow Wilson had disappeared by then, and there wasn't much rubbish about self-determination. We, the British, cobbled Iraq together. It was always an artificial state; it had nothing to do with the people who lived there."[5] Strategic culture takes account of that crucial historical dimension. It would approach the Iraqi Sunni and Shia militants, not merely as combatants in a *state's* civil war, but as two *nations* who battle each other. Each side has its own deep cultural narrative, and each side has its account about The Other and the threat the other poses to its own values and very existence. Strategic culture, in approaching the state of Iraq, must analyze multiple narratives—just as it must for any non-homogenous state. And to the degree that a state is markedly pluralistic (i.e., differing national groups vying for advantage within a given government structure), strategic culture loses focus as an analytic tool, unless it allows for multiple narratives.

Which brings us to the question of whether al Qaeda, transnational as it is, would be amenable to such analysis. The answer is a qualified "yes." Religion can serve as a powerful ethnic marker,[6] a critical element constitutive of identity. In the case of Islam, the appeal that salafi jihadists make is that the bond of religion trumps state identification. This replicates the pattern of early Islam, wherein loyalty to the *ummah*, the Islamic community, was to supersede *asabiyya*, loyalty to the kinship group. In support, jihadists frequently cite Q 2:143, "Thus we have made of you/ an Ummat justly balanced/that ye might be witnesses/over the nations [al-nas, lit., 'the people' or 'the multitudes']." For al Qaeda, the organization is simply a tangible expression of this larger *ummah*.[7] And the *ummah* is not so much transnational as it is that nation that is trans-global. In contradistinction, say, to the Tamil Tigers who see themselves as a nation operating within the state context of Sri Lanka, al Qaeda members view their imagined *ummah* as that nation that is larger than any state. From the Western perspective, those from other countries who travel to Iraq as suicide bombers represent *different nationalities* that have converged on a failed state. From the Islamist perspective, these are members of the *one nation* who have traveled to the region to defend their religion *bi amwal wa anfusihim*, with their possessions and their lives. The brilliance of Osama and others is in the crafting of a religious narrative that gives a thick account of this nation, the *ummah*, and thus makes it a cultural reality for which men and women are willing to die. It is that nation and its narrative that we analyze here using the tools of strategic culture.

<table>
<tr><td colspan="3" align="center">Strategic Culture
(Ideational milieu; assumptions about war)</td></tr>
<tr><td>Metanarrative</td><td>Strategic Preferences</td><td>Behavior</td></tr>
<tr><td>(Community story >>>
about culture)</td><td>(Rank-ordered options >>>
about appropriate defense
measures)</td><td>(Operationalized
defensive measures
constrained by culture and
exigency)</td></tr>
</table>

Figure 13.1   Real-life Decision Making.

In this approach, as shown in figure 13.1, we will take "strategic culture"[8] to indicate an ideational milieu, one that makes important assumptions about the fundamental values of the community, the nature of the enemy that threatens those values, and the role of war in defending the same. These fundamental values coalesce in what we will term a meta-narrative, the overarching story that situates individuals in a distinct community, provides a cognitive roadmap by which they are to live, and that motivates members to protect the community against its enemies, even in the face of death. Within this larger narrative, elites rank order strategic options about how best to defend and promote the community through warfare. Then, in the messy details of contingent circumstances, decision makers act to achieve those valued ends.

The remainder of this chapter will focus especially on the second step of this diagram, the meta-narrative of al Qaeda and its concomitant preferences. Following that, it will then suggest what behaviors may arise within that "national" and trans-global entity.

THE CLASSICAL NARRATIVE

The classical view in Islam about the world and the role of jihad arose during the Abbasid caliphate. This doctrine developed following a series of stunning and quite rapid victories over rival tribes in the Arabian Peninsula, and the larger but effete empires of the Byzantines and Persians.[9] The story was retrospective, providing a justification for warfare, an explanation for its victories, and a justification for the ethical dimension of Islam's actions. This narration rendered the world thus:

dar al-Islam   *ahl al-kitab*   *dar al-harb*
(house of Islam)   (people of the book)   (house of war)

In this formulation, there was a categorical divide between the believers and the unbelievers, yet it provided an intermediate space for *ahl al-kitab*, people of the book, generally Christians, Jews, and other monotheists. Between the two houses there is perennial war. There may be occasional periods of *sulh*, a cessation of hostilities, or a *hudna*, a truce, but not *salaam*, true peace. Eventually, Islam will triumph, despite whatever setbacks it may suffer in the meantime. And that is a key point, for this inevitable victory requires faith, calculation, and long-term patience.

Despite representations in modern art, as Islam spread geographically, the aim was not forced conversions, but insuring that conquered peoples recognized the supremacy of Islam. Moreover, Islamist jurists formulated rules of warfare that parallel the West's ideas about *jus ad bellum* and *jus in bello*; for example, what constitutes a threat against Islam, who should be considered combatants, the permissibility of collateral damage, and what intentional damage might be inflicted on an enemy's territory.[10] It is important to note that this was not a monolithic formulation; there was a great deal of debate among Muslim scholars about how these questions ought to be answered.[11] It was also true of the principle of *dacwa*, the appeal that Muslims were to make to non-Muslims to embrace Islam. Scholars debated ways in which *dacwa* ought to be promulgated. They also debated who could live in tributary status: no one at all, monotheists only, or polytheists as well.

Refashioning the Narrative

Al Qaeda's formulation draws from this classical doctrine, as well as from a number of medieval and modern thinkers and movements (Ibn-Taymiyya, wahhabism, Maududi, Qutb, Abdullah Azzam, and many others). In this reformulation, Osama functions as a kind of lay mujtahid, one who gives independent interpretation to Islamic texts. But it is critical to understand that Osama is not free to give just any interpretation, or else he would have no legitimacy. Rather he functions within a historical and religious tradition that has set the parameters within which he must move. Moreover, he is clearly influenced by his mentors and by those other ideologues in al Qaeda with whom he interacts. In this regard, it is better to see Osama as a kind of Homer who does not invent his story but must refashion what has come to him in his cultural context. And it is equally important to see that al Qaeda is not monolithic. Osama is iconic and even something of a *batil*, an Islamic hero, but he is not *imperator* whose ideas alone carry weight. Within al Qaeda, as is true of Islam more generally, there is sharp contestation, and those who read the primary materials will see the degree to which that is true. And a critical corollary merges here. A single fatwa does not constitute the definitive al Qaeda position on an issue, nor is al Qaeda's doctrine frozen in ahistorical time. It is dynamic.[12]

Yet one may describe al Qaeda thinking in *broad* terms with relative accuracy. It begins with the dichotomy of the house of war and the house of Islam. Osama and others have appealed to this division on countless occasions. Osama's statement several weeks after 9/11 is typical. "These events have divided the whole world into two camps, the camp of the faithful and the camp of the infidels. May God shield us and you [i.e., other Muslims] from them."[13] But al Qaeda's use significantly attenuates the intermediate space for people of the book, and Jews are almost never offered any consideration for this category. On the other hand, the category *dar al-harb*, pretty much an undifferentiated mass in classical thinking, is particularized in contemporary thinking. It posits a trifecta of enemies: the West, The Jews, and traitorous Arab leaders.

Each of those may be further differentiated, using either secular or religious terms. For instance, the West may become either the "crusaders" or the "imperialists." Often it is simply "America." A particularly important term in their lexicon for the West is *kafirun*, unbelievers, and President Bush is designated "head of the unbelievers." The Jews generally are "Zionists" or the "Zionist entity." And the traitors among Arab leaders (usually heads of state in the Gulf Cooperation Council and virtually all senior members of the Saudi royal family) are "agents," intermediaries who do the bidding of the West and who fail to implement Islamic law, the *sharica*.[14] More significantly, al Qaeda terms them *murtadun*, apostates. That is significant, for classical Islam stipulated harsher treatment for those who had left the faith than for simple unbelievers. Palestinian President Mahmoud Abbas is a "layman" who "bartered away the true religion." And among non-Arab, Muslim leaders lumped in that category is President Musharraf of Pakistan, the "traitor" of Islam. Moreover, these categories sometimes get blended. Israel, for instance, is frequently accused of having formed a

"Crusader–Zionist alliance" with the West. Great Britain and the United States have formed "armies of unbelief" and "the Crusader West."[15] Ibrahim al-Ja'fari, the former prime minister of Iraq, was the "servant of the cross" who had declared war on his Muslim co-religionists. And so on, in seemingly endless permutations.

KEY DATES

Al Qaeda's contemporary doctrinal reformulation has, of course, taken place within a specific historical context, and several dates are critical to the Islamists. Apart from the obvious deeper history that al Qaeda often cites (the loss of the Iberian Peninsula, the crusades, etc.), several more recent events of the last century stand out, and al Qaeda ideologues frequently reference them. Here are five of those key dates.

1916—Sykes–Picot

Radicals (and indeed most Arabs) view this as the date of the great betrayal, when Britain secretly pursued its imperialist aims in the region, at the expense of the Arabs.[16] It is a strongly evocative date and seen as contributing to the end of the caliphate (1923) and the implementation of an "imperialist" mandate system. Immediately after 9/11, Osama released an audio tape in which he claimed that the attack on the WTC was retaliation for a series of Western assaults on the region, beginning with the critical era in World War I.

1948—Establishment of Israel

May 1948 is read as part of a Western plot to establish a beachhead on Muslim lands, and most Muslims and Arabs generally call this *al-nakba*, the disaster. Al Qaeda is more specific. This "loss of Palestine" is not merely loss of territory. It represents the loss of Jerusalem, the third holiest site in Islam and the first *qibla* (direction of prayer). Even Saddam, in his Machiavellian way, sought to leverage the religious aspect of Jerusalem as legitimation for his invasion of Kuwait. Many al Qaeda pronouncements, as with the 1998 fatwa, list the recovery of Palestine and the first *qibla* as a key war aim.

1967—The June War

Often referred to in the region as another *nakba*, Islamists highlight it as the failure of secular Arab nationalism and, indeed, the judgment of God. From this point, Islamists propounded their own alternative, what they have termed *al-Hal al-islami*, the Islamic solution. That has proved a paradigm, of sorts. Hezbollah, Hamas, the Muslim Brotherhood, and al Qaeda have seized on any sort of disaster as an opportunity to show—by rhetoric and practice—the superiority of the Islamic solution, mobilizing the aid that feckless Arab governments cannot, then exploiting the public relations moment.[17]

1973—The Ramadan/Yom Kippur War

Arabs view this as the war that restored the nation's honor (after the debacle of 1967) and demonstrated the vulnerability of the Zionist enemy.[18] Indeed, it made possible—at least in Sadat's view—a trip to Jerusalem to address the Knesset and participate in the Camp David talks. But it is important with respect to the history of al Qaeda. Osama has pointed to this as the beginning of his return to Islam. Because of the massive U.S. airlift to reinforce Israel after its initial setbacks in the Sinai, the war indicated to Osama the unalterable commitment of the West to support the Zionist entity, a formative event in the development of al Qaeda's view of the real nature and structure of the house of war. Not incidentally, this was underscored again in July 2006 when the United States resupplied Israel in its war with Hezbollah.

1990—The Gulf War

It is difficult to overstate the importance of this period. Osama, flush from victory in Afghanistan, offered to employ his *mujahideen* to repel Saddam. The Saudis turned instead to the West. But more important than United States *intervention* was the continued U.S. *presence* in the peninsula, a "defilement" that radicals compared to that of a woman ritually unclean during her monthly cycle.[19] This was the final validation, to Osama and others, of the West's intent to overrun the house of Islam, and provocation (jus ad bellum) to launch a "defensive" war, on their view.[20]

DOCTRINES OF WAR AND WMD

It is this meta-narrative, a key component of al Qaeda's strategic culture, selectively derived from classical doctrine and reshaped through historical contingency, that forms the basis for al Qaeda's strategic preferences and operational code. Al Qaeda, in fact, has made no secret of its strategic views, even if it practices reasonably good security with respect to operational employment. It is possible to "read al-Qaeda's playbook," as a recent publication of the Combating Terrorism Center at the United States Military Academy puts it.[21] And to read it is to be immediately struck by how thorough al Qaeda ideologues have been in deliberating war-fighting doctrine in light of the larger worldview of radical, salafist Islam. The reductionistic approach of reading al Qaeda as simply an undifferentiated group of terrorists seeking spectacular effects by indiscriminately killing massive numbers of Americans is a serious misreading indeed. Here, then, are three key points of al-Qaeda's culturally endowed doctrine.

A Long War

The war al Qaeda fights will be a long war, requiring patience and careful calculation. The authoritative source here is the writing of Sayyid Qutb, and he merits quoting at length on this critical point.

> [T]he growing bankruptcy of western civilization makes it necessary to revive Islam. The distance between the revival of Islam and the attainment of world leadership *may be vast*...but the first step must be taken...The Muslim community [i.e., the umma] today is neither capable of nor is required to present before mankind great genius in material inventions, such as would make the world bow its head before its supremacy and thus re-establish once more its world leadership. Europe's creative mind is far ahead in this area, and *for a few centuries* to come we cannot expect to compete with Europe.... How to initiate the revival of Islam? A vanguard must set out with this determination and then keep going, marching through the vast ocean of *jahiliyyah* [ignorance of the true

faith] which encompasses the entire world... The Muslims in this vanguard must know the landmarks and the milestones on the road to this goal so that they would know the starting point as well as the nature, the responsibilities, and the ultimate purpose of *this long journey.*[22]

In his statement the month after the attack on the World Trade Center, Osama used precisely this term—"vanguard"—which Qutb had used, claiming that it was they who had struck a blow against America. He finished his statement claiming, "The wind of change is blowing to remove evil from the peninsula of Muhammad."[23] In the ideological trajectory of his doctrinal mentor, Osama was stating the vanguard had set out on its long journey with this major blow against the *dar al harb*, and that winds of change had begun to stir, *not* that the task was completed nor even near completion. And al Qaeda understands that the fight is lengthy precisely because its fight is asymmetric, despite the dramatic success on 9/11. In fact, in a moment of candor after his "period of solitude," al Qaeda ideologue Abu Musʿab al-Suri declared, "It is inconceivable to imagine the defeat and destruction of America, with all the military and economic power that it has reached, except through natural disasters."[24] Hence the comment of al Qaeda on its al-Nidaa website about the necessity of unconventional warfare in 2003: "We expected that the method of defense of regular or semi-regular [Iraqi forces] would collapse...[Thus] we have focused on the modus operandi of guerilla warfare. This is the most powerful method Muslims have...[for] there is no chance that in the years to come we will be allowed to possess the elements of strength."[25]

This is not to indicate despair on the part of the Islamists but the realization that theirs is a long battle to gain the supremacy of Islam. In fact, the al-Nidaa statement emphasizes that guerilla warfare proved successful against the Americans in Vietnam and the Russians in Afghanistan. While it will occasionally be able to launch major operations, increasingly much of its focus must be on what Abu Bakr Naji calls "vexation and exhaustion operations" in his *Management of Savagery.*[26] Similarly, al Qaeda understands it must constantly evaluate and recalibrate its plans, based on careful study of jihads, past and present, and their relative success. Al-Suri is especially pertinent here as an al Qaeda intellectual who has produced a critical study on earlier experiences of jihads that failed, especially in Syria and the Hama Uprising in 1982.[27]

A Defensive War

The war al Qaeda fights will generally be couched as a defensive war, and therefore morally and culturally legitimate. That was clearly the case after 9/11 when al Qaeda pronouncements repeatedly described the attack as a justified retaliation for Western aggression against Muslims. The point is important, for it shows al Qaeda's sensitivity to international condemnations. Describing it as defensive has an additional benefit with respect to Islamic jurisprudence. Classical thinking differentiated jihad as *fard kifayah* or *fard ayn*, a collective obligation or an individual obligation. In the former case, the community was responsible for mustering a contingent that could conduct an offensive jihad. But the latter obtained when the Islamic community came under attack, and every individual must come to its defense.

Osama's (et al.'s) famous February 1998 fatwa uses exactly this approach. The Arabian Peninsula, with its sanctities, had come under attack. All Muslims, therefore, must come to its defense. Some months later, Osama gave an interview with al-Jazeera in which he commented on the jihadists who had carried out attacks against Riyadh (1995), Khobar (1996), and the US embassies in Africa (1998). "I look at these men with much admiration and respect, for they have removed the shame from the forehead of our umma."[28] Osama's comment reflects both Arab culture, as well as Islamist conviction. In his view, Arab honor had been besmirched by the colonialist West, and a reprisal attack, after the pattern of *ghazw*, was necessary to restore the honor and remove the shame. But Osama also cast this in Islamic terms: shame had come to the Islamic nation, and God had given authorization to defend the community:

> To those against whom
> War is made, permission
> is given to fight,
> because they are wronged—and verily,
> God is most powerful
> For their aid. Q 22:39

This same pairing of culture and religion may be found in *Military Studies in the Jihad against the Tyrants*, captured by British authorities in Manchester, England, in May 2000. Note that the title itself implies that this is defensive; this is preparation to turn back tyranny. The book opens with a "pledge" to "the sister believer whose clothes have been stripped off...whose hair the oppressors have shaved...whose body has been abused by the human dogs."[29] The imagery is striking, for it depicts violation of a woman's *cirdh*, honor. The humiliation that takes place (stripping, shaving) is indicative of violating a major cultural taboo, and the reference to dogs, generally seen as unclean in Arab culture, compounds the sense of previous violation. This violation mandates a response. For the Islamists, therefore, jihad is morally warranted, both culturally and religiously.

Abu Bakr Naji gives a much more nuanced analysis. In *The Management of Barbarism* (2004), Naji presents jihad as necessary to reverse moral entropy. In his view, jihad is a merciful gift from heaven:

> Before God sent down the law of jihad, He wanted to show humanity what would happen without jihad so that they would see the complete wisdom of the Lawgiver, praised and exalted be He. The result was terrible: stupid, stubborn opposition from most of the people and the followers of Satan...[T]he generations become corrupt upon the earth and spread unbelief and corruption among humans. They even work to create a fitna [chaos, dissension] for the believing few, either by direct pressure or by the fitna of exalting unbelief and its people in the eyes of the weak few among the believers...[In the gift of jihad, God shows the] completeness of [his] mercy to humanity, for this restores justice and averts eternal punishment for those who believe.[30]

This idea of jihad as a moral reprisal because of infidel attacks has been publicly articulated on numerous occasions. Abu Gheith, for instance, used it to describe 9/11. "Why were millions of people astounded by what happened to America on September 11?" Gheith asked. "America is the reason for all oppression, injustice, licentiousness, or suppression that is the Muslims' lot." It was therefore appropriate to "punish a Harbi infidel in the same way he treated a Muslim."[31] Similarly, Islamists depicted the London bombings in July 2005 as reprisal for earlier attacks against Muslims. On the first anniversary of the bombings, al Qaeda released a martyr video of Shehzad Tanweer, one of the London bombers. The British government had "declared war on Islam," he said, attacking without cause "mothers, children, brothers and sisters…in Palestine, Afghanistan, Iraq, and Chechnya." Non-Muslim British were guilty, by extension, for they had voted in the government that was responsible for those depredations. Zawahiri added a voiceover, saying these men were motivated by love of God and of his prophet.[32] And later in the month, Zawahiri released another tape after Israel invaded Lebanon. In this, Zawahiri justified Hezbollah, calling for retaliation against the "Zionist–Crusader war [that] is without conscience" and that had torn "Muslim bodies in Gaza and Lebanon," as well as in Chechnya, Kashmir, Afghanistan, and Iraq.[33] The pattern is consistent: al Qaeda's view of war is one in which it is taking morally defensible action against Western assaults against Muslims worldwide.

An Intelligent War

The war al Qaeda fights will be an intelligent one, predicated on their own strategic cultural analysis and perceptual lens. This has two components. The first is that al Qaeda has and will continue to study Western history, institutions, management principles, military doctrine, and so on. Moreover, it has also studied Western open-source counterterrorism doctrine. Captured al Qaeda documents, as well as al Qaeda pronouncements, show a remarkable knowledge of everything from the American political process and economic concerns, to the U.S. military's pre-positioning of supplies in the lower Persian Gulf and its disposition of forces. The second component is al Qaeda's ability to show flexibility with respect to its own methods, doing a fairly rigorous analysis of its failures and adapting new approaches. One such is al-Suri's *Observations Concerning the Jihadi Experience in Syria*.[34] Another is *The Story of the Arab Afghans from the Entry to Afghanistan until the Final Departure with the Taliban*, serialized in *Al-Sharq Al-Awsat* in December 2004. Among other observations, Abu Walid al-Masri, putative author of *The Story*, recalls Osama's false assumption that the United States could withstand only two or three decisive blows and that 9/11 should prove decisive.[35]

Of particular interest is al Qaeda ideologue Abu Bakr Naji, especially in light of his clear commitment to a strategic culture analysis of the West. He merits quoting at length.

> We urge that most of the leaders of the Islamic movement be military leaders or have the ability to fight in the ranks, at the very least. Likewise, we also urge that those leaders work to master political science just as they would work to master military science…Political action is very important and dangerous, such that one of them said: "A single political mistake (leads to) a result that is worse than one hundred military mistakes." Despite the hyperbole in this statement, it is true to the extent that it clarifies the seriousness of a political mistake…*The interest in understanding the rules of the political game and the political reality of the enemies and their fellow travelers* and then mastering disciplined political action through sharia politics and opposing this reality is not less than the importance of military action, especially if we consider that the moment of gathering the fruit—a moment which is considered the recompense for the sacrifices offered by the mujahids during long decades—is a moment resulting from a political strike and a decisive political decision. Thus, the most important of their political principles is the principle of (self) interest. Their principle absolutely does not submit to any moral value; rather, all the other principles are subordinate to it—friendship or enmity, peace or war—and are all determined according to (self) interest. The politicians of the West summarize that in a slogan which says, "There is no eternal enmity in politics and no eternal friendship; rather, there are eternal interests."[36]

Naji's closing paraphrase of Lord Palmerston's dictum from the mid-nineteenth century should come as no surprise. Al Qaeda, it seems, is determined to follow Sun Tzu's nonnegotiable principle of victory through knowledge, and it has done its homework rather thoroughly, to include reading primers of international relations.

On some level, al Qaeda has sought to formalize strategic analysis, as the *Encyclopedia of Jihad* makes clear. "The mission of [al-Qaeda's strategic intelligence unit] is gathering, organizing, and distributing military information on the strategic level of the [target] country. Its goal is to know the country's military, political, economical and social capabilities and to predict its intentions, in order to work confronting all possibilities."[37] In application, the knowledge so gained can have implementation at the strategic or tactical level, and may be used in lethal or nonlethal ways. One example that reflects multiple applications of strategic intelligence is al Qaeda's tracking of the Bush administration's awarding of Iraqi reconstruction contracts, announced in December 2003.[38] Within a day, one publication, *Al-Quds al-Arabi*, editorialized

> When we warned that US aggression against Iraq was aimed at achieving two important goals, to loot Iraq's economy and wealth and to serve Israeli interests and remove any real Arab threats to the racist Jewish state, there were those who accused us of exaggeration...Yesterday the US president, George Bush, announced that bids for contracts in Iraqi reconstruction will first be given to US companies, then other companies affiliated to allied countries which sent their forces to Iraq, risked the lives of their people, and served in the US project...The US decision will...increase the world's hatred for the current arrogant US administration.[39]

Osama noted how the issue of the contracts awards could be exploited, and he responded to the wedge moment with nonlethal propaganda:

> This war makes millions of dollars for big corporations, either weapons manufacturers or those working in the reconstruction [of Iraq], such as Halliburton and its sister companies...It is crystal clear who benefits from igniting the fire of this war and this bloodshed: They are the merchants of war, the bloodsuckers who run the policy of the world from behind the scenes.[40]

And the al-Quds Brigade, an al Qaeda unit in Saudi Arabia, formed quite lethal plans. It spent some months reconnoitering a Western housing compound where Halliburton employees lived, then attacked it in May 2004 with a small team, killing twenty-two persons. The next month, the leader of the mission, Fawwaz al-Nashami, described the "Battle of Khobar" in an interview with *Sawt al-Jihad* (Voice of Jihad). The battle was, Fawwaz said, part of the larger plan to purge the Arabian Peninsula of ritual impurities by attacking Western contractors. It also provided the occasion to appeal to Muslims working in the compound to embrace a salafist vision of Islam.[41]

As part of this intelligent war, al Qaeda understands its words and actions have multiple audiences. Its methods in war will be guided, to some degree, by an appreciation for and an adherence to classical Islamic strictures about *jus ad bellum* and *jus in bello*. As we note earlier, al Qaeda routinely positions itself as fighting a defensive war. But even if one considers all such elaborations as tendentious, al Qaeda is keenly aware of its public image. In an undated letter to Mullah Omar, Osama averred that gaining the upper hand in the "information war" (al-Harb al-iᶜlamiyah) represents 90 percent of the preparation for battle.[42] And Abu Musᶜab al-Suri has underscored the importance of propagandists to articulate the movement's objectives and legitimate use of violence.[43]

Much of al Qaeda literature is, therefore, quite taken with examining the reactions of various Muslim publics. For instance, al Qaeda attacks in Saudi Arabia that caused extensive casualties among Muslims (the Battle of Khobar did not) proved counterproductive, and after a year of harrowing attacks, they suddenly ceased. Al Qaeda clearly noted the negative public reaction, one that the Saudi royal family was quick to exploit, and it curtailed its attacks. Another example is the November 2005 hotel attacks in Amman that killed over fifty, to include members of a wedding party. Zarqawi offered an extensive apologia, saying that the hotels were a den of crusaders and Zionists, and that members of the wedding party were emphatically not the target. He then added,

> The obscenity and corruption spread [by the Jordanian government] have turned Jordan into a quagmire of utter profanity and debauchery, and anyone who has seen the hotels, the houses of entertainment, the dance parties, the wine bars, and the tourist resorts in Aqaba, in the Dead Sea [region], and in other places is wrenched with sorrow over what this family [i.e. the Jordanian royal family]—both its men and its women—has done to this country, whose people are good.[44]

In part, the concern about the violence is doctrinally driven. Naji has written,

> One should note that violence and coarseness must not transgress the limits of the Sharia and that one must pay heed to the benefit and harm (that results from) it, which the Sharia considers to be, in the rules of jihad, as one of the most important subjects for the guidance of creation, if not the most important subject.[45]

But al Qaeda is also intelligent and pragmatic. It wants to avoid what Jarret Brachman and William McCants term the "Shayma effect" after the botched assassination attempt on Egyptian Prime Minister Atif Sidqi. In the event, a young school girl (Shayma) was killed, and—as Zawahiri later noted—caused a propaganda debacle for Egyptian Islamists. In brief, al Qaeda is not blinded by zeal. It will formulate plans carefully calibrated to exploit perceived weaknesses of the enemy *and* that will play well with Islamic audiences.

AL QAEDA'S STRATEGIC CULTURE AND WMD

When we turn to al Qaeda's doctrine of WMD, the most salient factor is that there is none. This is not to say there are not *references* to acquisition and use. There certainly are a number of adversions. Typical are comments such as these from Suleiman abu Gheith, al Qaeda spokesman, in June 2002: "It is our right to fight them [the Americans] with chemical and biological weapons, so as to afflict them with the fatal maladies that have afflicted the Muslims because of [their] chemical and biological weapons."[46] Or this from Abu 'Abdullah Al-Kuwaiti: "If the American people are ready to die as we are ready to die, then our combat groups along with our military, nuclear, and biological equipment will kill hundreds of thousands of people we don't wish to fight."[47] But measured against the very large output of al Qaeda pronouncements, references are comparatively infrequent, as Reuven Paz points out, and when they do occur, it is most often to chemical munitions.[48] Significantly, manuals such as *Military Studies in the Jihad against the Tyrants* fail to mention them at all.[49]

There has also been vigorous deliberation within the al Qaeda shura about the utility of WMD. Perhaps the most important source is Abu Walid al-Masri, putative author of "The Story of the Arab Afghans from the Time of Arrival in Afghanistan until their Departure with the Taliban."[50] By his account, hawks within al Qaeda's shura have pushed for authorization. Most prominent among them was Abu Hafs al-Masri, until he was killed in a U.S. airstrike in November 2001. Abu Hafs had served as the organization's minister of defense and potential successor to Osama. He and others in al Qaeda argued they should try to obtain whatever they could of WMD for defense in a kind of Islamic MAD doctrine.[51] But others were deeply concerned about what they termed the "genie in the bottle," and they urged against acquisition. They feared pulling heaven down upon their heads in a retaliatory strike by the West. And thus what followed was extensive debate about ROE, targets, and jurisprudential questions concerning collateral damage. Also notable is that even the hawks described use in terms of deterrence, not first strike. Moreover, according to Abu Walid, the majority agreed that use of WMD is a sensitive and very dangerous issue. And in any event, he reported, al Qaeda could likely obtain only quite primitive weapons.[52]

Osama's own position seems ambiguous. On the one hand, Abu Walid reported that the al Qaeda leader had wanted to obtain dirty bombs from the Russian arsenal. Yet he also describes Osama as having blocked Abu Hafs from pursuing a WMD program.[53] When asked directly about chemical, biological, and nuclear weapons in an al-Jazeera interview in December 1998, Osama temporized, saying Israel and Christians had nuclear weapons capability. He then added, "America knows today that Muslims [i.e., Pakistan] are in possession of such a weapon."[54] Osama responded similarly in an interview that *Time* published the following month. Asked about chemical and nuclear weapons, he replied,

> Acquiring weapons for the defense of Muslims is a religious duty. If I have indeed acquired these weapons, then I thank God for enabling me to do so. And if I seek to acquire these weapons, I am carrying out a duty. It would be a sin for Muslims not to try to possess the weapons that would prevent the infidels from inflicting harm on Muslims.[55]

Clearly, Osama did make some attempt to acquire such weapons. One especially notable testimony about Osama and al Qaeda's interest in nuclear (or radiologic) weapons in particular is that of Jamal Ahmad al-Fadl, the Sudanese national who defected from the organization in 1996 and now lives under protective custody in the United States. Al-Fadl had served as the money man in al Qaeda's 1993 attempt to purchase uranium in Sudan. In the end, however, this deal, like others, proved unsuccessful.[56] It is also important to note that in February 2002, after swift defeat of Taliban, U.S. officials searched military camps that Osama and al Qaeda had used. They found no WMD.[57]

What should be apparent is that, despite its deliberations and even its attempts to obtain weapons materiel, al Qaeda has not elaborated a consistent *doctrine* with respect to the use of WMD and nuclear weapons in particular. Instead, where Western analysts do find discussions about WMD, they discover contestation on the issues of acquisition and employment, a contestation that is carried on within the parameters of a salafist Islamic narrative. Moreover, al Qaeda discussions also proceed within a framework of certain perceptions about the character and operational code of the West. None of this argues that al Qaeda will not again seek to acquire and employ WMD. Unlike Fahd's 2003 fatwa authorizing use, there has been no counter-fatwa among al Qaeda leaders or clerics proscribing use. *Use is clearly permissible.*

But indiscriminate employment, merely for spectacular effect, is highly unlikely. Al Qaeda's aim is not operational effect. It is to secure victory, and a victory with a legitimacy understood in religious terms. Because it is fighting an intelligent war, al Qaeda does consider the attitude continuum among fellow Muslims. Indiscriminate slaughter would multiply the "Shayma effect" among their co-religionists. That is true even when the victims are non-Muslim, for jurists have long argued against the deliberate targeting of noncombatants. And there is scant evidence that al Qaeda's argument that noncombatants are responsible for state actions, simply on the basis of having voted, has found traction among Islamic publics.

Additionally, al Qaeda has shown a pragmatic side. On the one hand, al Qaeda has authorized suicide attacks, for it can justify them as "martyrdom operations." But it realizes that indiscriminate use of WMD would likely bring devastating retaliation, and Afghanistan is a case in point. On the other hand, U.S. successes in physically attacking the Taliban and al Qaeda bases and in information warfare assaults on al Qaeda communications networks, as well as freezing al Qaeda financial assets—all have limited the panoply of weapons the organization can acquire or develop. Thus, al Qaeda is existentially limited in what it can acquire or develop, and jurisprudentially limited in what it would use and in what manner, if acquired. A jihadist attack, like politics, is the art of the possible. Based, then, on al Qaeda's history and strategic doctrine, and in view of pragmatic limits on what may be acquired and/or weaponized, the following summary of al Qaeda's WMD use seems warranted.

Limited employment of radiologic or chemical weapons, outside Muslim countries, is clearly possible and, if acquired, may even be probable. Employment within Muslim countries is much less likely. Use of weapons that could be characterized as causing indiscriminate mass slaughter seems implausible, both for pragmatic and jurisprudential reasons.

But the debate about al Qaeda and WMD cannot end there. What "al-Qaeda prime" may do and what al Qaeda franchises may do are separate questions. The threat from the former, in many ways, is decreasing; threats from the latter, increasing. In the future, we should expect al Qaeda's function to move more toward providing ideology, encouragement, and a kind of perverse legitimacy to field units that are operating with increasing autonomy. We ought, then, to be speaking of the WMD threat from al Qaedas. It is they, far away from the destruction of the mountainous hideaways of Afghanistan, who will be importing both a salafist ideology and new weapons to confront their enemies. Yet that was the original vision inspired by Shaykh Abdullah Azzam, in any event. Al Qaeda would be only a base. He never intended that the jihadists remain there. Today, his vision is being fulfilled. Al Qaeda is no longer the chief threat. Al Qaedas are. It is they, in their local contexts, that could more easily threaten the West with WMD, and it is their own adapted narratives the West must more rigorously study.

NOTES

1. The author would like to thank Dr. James Smith, Director of the Institute for National Security Studies, for making possible participation in the "Violent Non-State Actors, Strategic Culture, and WMD: The al-Qaeda Case" conference, held in McLean, VA, June 26–27, 2006. Many of the ideas presented here reflect the vigorous and open dialogue of the conferees. More especially, the author is grateful to the Institute and its host organization, the United States Air Force Academy, for providing a home during sabbatical leave from Baylor University, fall 2005. Additionally, profound thanks to Dr. Barry Harvey, associate professor of theology at Baylor University, who listened carefully

to arguments about the function of cultural narratives and offered a number of constructive comments, as well as bibliographic leads. Thanks, too, for the close reading and numerous critical suggestions of Amanda Mitchell, a very perceptive student of international relations and Middle East politics at Baylor University. As generally happens with academic papers, any merits this study possesses must be attributed, at least in part, to the suggestions, encouragement, and critique of others; any flaws, to the author himself.

2. Tiina Tarvainen, "Al-Qaeda and WMD: A Primer," *Terrorism Monitor*, June 2, 2005. Emphasis added.

3. An earlier and useful overview of this analytic approach may be found in Colin Gray, "Comparative Strategic Culture," *Parameters* (Winter 1984): 26–33. A recent attempt to assess the current status of the field of strategic studies is found in "Comparative Strategic Culture: Conference Report" issued by the Center for Contemporary Conflict and available at http://www.ccc.nps.navy.mil/events/recent/ComparativeStrategicCultureSep05_rpt.asp. An exceptionally vigorous critique of the approach is that of Alastair Johnston, "Thinking About Strategic Culture," *International Security* (Spring 1995): 33–64. While not discounting the concept as an analytic tool, Johnston does look to specify the term and to suggest ways of making its methodology more rigorous and its hypotheses falsifiable. My approach here is indebted to his discussion, as will be readily apparent.

4. The intact psychology of al Qaeda members is a key conclusion of the work of Marc Sageman. See particularly his *Understanding Terror Networks* (Philadelphia: University of Pennsylvania, 2004).

5. A number of sources may be cited for this background on Iraq's creation. To cite only two, Glenn Frankel gives a concise account in his "Lines in the Sand" in Micah Sifry and Christopher Cerf, eds., *The Gulf War Reader* (New York: Random House, 1991), pp. 16–20. David Fromkin, *A Peace to End All Peace* (New York: Holt, 1989) gives a superb review, focusing especially on Churchill, passim, but particularly pp. 191–92. On the orchestration of Feisal's "popular" selection and reception, see Fromkin, *A Peace to End All Peace*, pp. 506–8. The Parsons quote is in Frankel, "Lines in the Sand," p. 18.

6. On the concept of ethnic markers, see Sami Zubaida, *Islam, the People, and the State* (New York: Tauris, 1993).

7. An important self-description that salafists use is "vanguard," a term made popular by Sayyid Qutb in his major work *Milestones,* first published in Arabic in 1964 (Indianapolis: American Trust, 1990); it is also available online at http://www.islamistwatch.org/texts/qutb/Milestones/. The idea here is that Islam has fallen into moral decay, and a committed group of true believers (the vanguard, *talica*) will restore it to its early purity.

8. The idea of narrative as cognitive roadmap, I develop more fully in "From Gilgamesh to Fatwas," *War, Literature, and the Arts*, Vol. 18 (2007): 1–2.

9. An older but still useful exposition of the classical doctrine is Majid Khadduri, *War and Peace in the Law of Islam* (Baltimore, Johns Hopkins Press, 1955), passim. For a discussion of the origins and nuances of jihad, see Jerry M. Long, "Jihad," in Catherine Cookson, ed., *The Encyclopedia of Religious Freedom* (New York: Routledge, 2003), pp. 241–46.

10. For a good overview of the topic, see John Kelsay, *Islam and War* (Louisville: Westminster, 1993). Also valuable is Ann Elizabeth Mayer, "War and Peace in the Islamic Tradition and International Law," in John Kelsay and James T. Johnson, eds., *Just War and Jihad* (New York: Greenwood Press, 1991), pp. 195–226.

11. For an indication of the scope of that discussion among Islamic scholars, see the primary documents collected in Rudolph Peters, *Jihad in Classical and Modern Islam* (Princeton: Marcus Wiener, 1993).

12. This is especially important to note in connection with the fatwa issued by Nasir al-Fahd in May 2003 on the permissibility of WMD. The lengthy and carefully constructed fatwa follows the traditional pattern of posing and answering objections, drawing on the Quran, the hadith, and the writings of other scholars. But the claims of some Western analysts notwithstanding (to include the writer quoted at the start of this article), Fahd's pronouncement does not settle all. On an issue of this magnitude, several prominent and respected scholars would have to concur if the community were to have consensus.

But that hasn't happened, and there is a curious lack of reference among other leading Islamists to Fahd on this point. To see the degree of contestation there may be on critical issues, see Yvonne Haddad, "Operation Desert Storm and the War of the Fatwas" in Muhammad Khalid Masud et al., eds., *Islamic Legal Interpretations: Muftis and their Fatwas* (Cambridge, MA: Harvard University Press, 1996), pp. 297–309.

13. The full text is in "The Sword Fell," *New York Times*, October 8, 2001.

14. Zawahiri forwarded this theme again in late July 2006. After discussing the "Zionist–Crusader War" against Lebanon and Hezbollah, he concluded, "My Muslim nation, without a doubt it is clear to you now that the governments of the Arabic and Islamic countries are inefficient and conniving…You are all alone in the field." Cited in "In Zawahiri's Words: 'We Will Unite,'" *New York Times*, July 28, 2006. Several weeks later, on the fifth anniversary of the 9/11 attacks, Zawahiri continued the theme, accusing Egypt, Saudi Arabia, and Jordan of supporting Israeli hostility against Lebanon. Cairo, he said, had made a "graveyard" of the Arab's joint defense pact. *Al-Jazeera* online (Arabic), September 12, 2006.

15. Notably, on the first anniversary of the London train bombing, al Qaeda released a new tape with commentary and voiceover, which included the martyr statement of Shehzad Tanweer recorded prior to the attack. In his voiceover, Zawahiri pointed out, "The names of the station [*sic*] that were targeted have significance, both symbolically and in terms of morale, for the Crusader West," apparently referring to the bombing of the King's Cross—Tavistock line. The statement is in MEMRI, July 11, 2006.

16. An obvious example is the 1996 "Ladenese Epistle," in which the assault of the West on Islam is made the foundation of the argument that follows for defensive war. It is even more explicit in Osama's declaration in October 2001 in which he argued that 9/11 was simply retaliation for "80 years of humiliation" (see "The Sword Fell," cited earlier). Zawahiri and others share that analysis. What is lacking, however, is the sort of capacity for critical self-reflection that one finds in the writings of, say, Qutb and Mawdudi, who offer Muslim jeremiads. Self-reflection seems to have returned in Abu Mus'ab al-Suri, however, whose "Observations Concerning the Jihadi Experience in Syria" is remarkable on this account. See the summary available in Jarret Brachman and William McCants, *Stealing al-Qaeda's Playbook*, http://www.ctc.usma.edu/Stealing%20Al-Qai%27da%27s%20Play book%20--%20CTC.pdf.

17. Zawahiri writes of the impact of the 1967 defeat in his *Knights Under the Banner of the Prophet*. "The jihad movement realized that the woodworm had begun to eat the idol [Nasser, as leader of secular Arab nationalism] until he became weak because of the effects of the setback and he fell to the ground amid the bewilderment of his priests and the horror of his worshippers…The death of [Nasser] was not the death of one person but also the death of his principles, which proved their failure on the ground of reality, and the death of a popular myth that was broken on the sands of Sinai." *Al-Sharq Al-Awsat*, December 4, 2001 (FBIS-NES-2001–1204). Thereafter, Zawahiri writes, an invigorated militant Islam developed in the void.

18. It is significant, in this context, that the Egyptian military's successful plan to breach the Bar Lev defensive barrier and cross into the Sinai was code-named Operation Badr, explicitly referencing an early Muslim victory over the Makkans in 624 CE.

19. See, for instance, the striking use of this imagery in the al Qaeda attack on Western compounds in Saudi Arabia in May 2004, dubbed the "Khobar Operation." The text describing the assault is available at MEMRI, June 15, 2004.

20. This postwar period, we will argue, is the single most important precursor to Osama's attack on 9/11. His reading was that the house of war had overrun the house of peace. His fatwa in 1998 can only be understood against this backdrop. For more background on Osama's appeal to the Saudi royal family, see Yossef Bodansky, *Bin Laden: The Man Who Declared War on America* (New York: Random House, 2001), pp. 28–31; and reporting in *The Jordan Times*, November 8, 2001. For a coolly reasoned and powerfully stated Arab view on the U.S. presence and how provocative it might be, see Mohamed Heikal, *Illusions of Triumph: An Arab View of the Gulf War* (London: HarperCollins, 1992), pp. 333–34.

21. I am indebted here and in much of the discussion that follows to Brachman and McCants' *Stealing al-Qa'ida's Playbook*, and to the collection of primary materials in the "Harmony" database on the Combating Terrorism Center's website, http://www.ctc.usma.edu/.

22. Qutb, *Milestones*, pp. 7, 8, 9. Emphasis added.

23. "The Sword Fell."

24. *Al-sharq al-Awsat*, January 23, 2005 (World News Connection 20050123).

25. Cited in MEMRI, April 11, 2003.

26. Available on the Combating Terrorism Center's website, http://www.ctc.usma.edu/.

27. His *Observations Concerning the Jihadi Experience in Syria* is excerpted in CTC's *Stealing al-Qaeda's Playbook*, http://www.ctc.usma.edu/.

28. Cited in Bruce Lawrence, ed., *Messages to the World* (New York: Verso, 2005), p. 74.

29. Jerrold Post, ed., *The Military Studies in the Jihad against the Tyrants: The al Qaeda Training Manual* (Maxwell AFB, AL: USAF Counterproliferation Center, n.d.), p. 15. The anonymous and undated *Encyclopedia of Jihad* is even more direct: "Islam permits the killing and assassination of those who have wronged Allah, his Prophet, or Muslims, from among his worst enemies, without dispute" p. 514. I am grateful to the Combating Terrorism Center at West Point for access to this (formally) unpublished work. As per authorship, it is signed simply, "Office of Services/military bases and battle fronts." The multivolume work deals with a number of topics, from bomb-making to small arms use to assassination techniques

30. Naji, *Management of Savagery*, pp. 242–43, available at the Olin Institute, Harvard University (2006) at the following web address, http://www.wcfia.harvard.edu/olin/images/Management%20of%20Savagery%20-%2005–23-2006.pdf

31. MEMRI, June 12, 2002.

32. MEMRI, July 11, 2006.

33. "We Will Unite to Fight," *New York Times*, July 28, 2006.

34. See fn. 27 above.

35. *Al-Sharq Al-Awsat*, December 8, 2004. This is available in FBIS-NES-2004–1208.

36. Naji, *Management of Barbarism*, pp. 85–88, passim. Emphasis added.

37. *Encyclopedia*, 120. Once again, my thanks to the Combating Terrorism Center for access to this unpublished work. See also fn. 29 above.

38. The Bush administration's decision to award contracts to key members of the "coalition of the willing" is described in "Bush Defends Barring Nations from Iraq Deals," *New York Times*, December 12, 2003.

39. Cited in the BBC online, December 12, 2003.

40. MEMRI, April 15, 2004.

41. The story is reported in MEMRI, June 15, 2004.

42. The Arabic original is at http://www.ctc.usma.edu/aq/AFGP-2002–600321-Orig.pdf. Interestingly, the anonymous author of *The Story of the Arab Afghans* considered Osama to be "maniacally obsessed with the international media," a disaster for the Taliban. *Al-Sharq Al-Awsat*, December 10, 2004 (FBIS-NES-2004–1221).

43. Brachman and McCants, *Stealing al-Qaeda's Playbook*, p. 17.

44. MEMRI, December 8, 2005.

45. Naji, *Management of Barbarism*, p. 76.

46. MEMRI, June 12, 2002.

47. See http://www.ctc.usma.edu/aq/AFGP-2002–001120-Trans.pdf. The Center for Nonproliferation Studies has done a commendable yeoman's task in compiling an extensive list of references to WMD, the preponderance being to CBW. It is available at http://cns.miis.edu/pubs/other/sjm_cht.htm The difficulty, of course, is verifying the reliability of the sources and many prove simply chimerical—as with the allegation in al-Majalla in 2002 that Osama had purchased forty-eight "suitcase nukes" from the Russian mafia. After the successful U.S. attack on al Qaeda strongholds in Afghanistan, the number of reported attempts to obtain nuclear or radiologic materials for a dirty bomb dropped precipitously. See the chart referenced earlier.

48. See Reuven Paz, "Global Jihad and WMD," in Hillel Fradkin, Husain Haqqani, and Eric Brown, eds., *Current Trends in Islamist Ideology*, Vol. 2 (Washington: Hudson Institute, September 2005), pp. 80, 81.

49. Post, *Military Studies*

50. *Al-Sharq al-Awsat* serialized "The Story" beginning December 8, 2004. Authorship is not certain, but I will refer to the author as "Abu Walid," with that caveat. For an important examination of conflict within al Qaeda leadership more generally, see Montasser al-Zayyat, *The Road to al-Qaeda*, trans. Ahmed Fekry and ed. Sara Nimis (London: Pluto Press, 2004).

51. *Al-Sharq al-Awsat*, December 8, 2004. In his 2003 fatwa authorizing use of WMD, al-Fahd makes something of the same point: "If the infidels can be repelled from the Muslims only by using such weapons, their use is permissible, even if you kill them without exception and destroy their tillage and stock." More recently, Abu Muscab al-Suri has averred that WMD would offer "strategic symmetry." Cited in Paz, "Global Jihad and WMD," p. 83. The author wishes to express gratitude to Dr. Jarrett Brachman and the Combating Terrorism Center at West Point for supplying a copy of the full fatwa of al-Fahd.

52. *Al-Sharq al-Awsat*, December 9, 2004 (FBIS-NES-2004–1210).

53. *Al-Sharq al-Awsat*, December 8, 2004.

54. The interview is available in *Messages to the World*, pp. 65–94. This comment found on p. 72.

55. January 11, 1999. Accessed online.

56. A useful catalog of several attempts is found at http://cns.miis.edu/pubs/reports/binladen.htm.

57. "U.S. Analysts Find no Sign bin Laden Had Nuclear Arms," *NYT*, February 26, 2002.

Part III

The Way Ahead

14

Out of the Wilderness: Prime Time for Strategic Culture

Colin S. Gray

Introduction: Eyes on "The Plot"

Scholars are rightly suspicious of, or disdainful of and actually hostile to, common sense. After all, common sense is not really common, rather is it value-charged by culture, the subject of this essay. Nonetheless, we discard and despise common sense at our peril. Among other points, I will suggest that one can explain strategic culture and its associated concepts (public culture and military or organizational culture), what they are, how they work, and why they are important, both simply and accurately enough. Accurately enough for what? Accurately enough to grasp the essentials of "the plot" concerning strategic culture. And that, after all, is all that a defense community needs to achieve. I might proceed further, if pressed, and argue that the bare outlines of the plot are the most that can be achieved. By way of a thought-provoking analogy, you might care to consider the practical inutility of the nearly ninety years of scholarship that have been devoted to that highly scholar-unfriendly subject, the causes of war. Just about everything that has been written on the subject with a view to developing a general theory of the causes of war has been a thorough waste of effort. The reason is not hard to find. The job cannot be done. The relevant history is too complex, contexts are too rich and contingent. If you attempt the impossible, settle upon the wrong organizing question, you will accomplish nothing of much value, save by serendipity. I suspect that scholarship on strategic culture, albeit for a different reason, similarly is bound to fail when it ventures far beyond our culture-bound common sense and positivistically seeks a certain general wisdom. Strategy does not yield to the scientific method; nor does the study of culture.

A powerful, even compelling, idea like strategic culture easily is reduced to something far less compelling when it is adopted as the concept of the month, or even the period, by scholars and soldiers and officials. Both groups have their professional biases, even their *deformations professionelles*. For another analogy, a new religion will likely burst upon an astonished and delighted populace with a rather simple, yet powerfully persuasive, story. But once that story is interpreted and systematized into doctrine by professional theologians, much of the original message, the essential plot even, is apt to be watered down or lost. So, this chapter has much to say, not all of it friendly, about the way strategic culture is being studied and prospectively employed.

My purpose, though, is entirely constructive. I will endeavor to adhere to what I am calling the plot. If you prefer, and with some apologies to Jeremy Black who for some good reasons detests this notion, I will always try to keep in mind a master narrative.[1] That narrative, or plot, explains what we are talking about and, by plain implication, at least, why we are talking about it.

This study advances first by specifying some general points on our subject. Next, it bows to convention and offers judgments on definitions and methodology, notwithstanding the criticisms that have been offered, and will be offered in more detail later, of scholars who overindulge in the heady delights of theory. The author cannot deny that he too is a theorist. The tale then proceeds to explore the reasons why culture matters greatly. Finally, since cultural analysis has become so popular, it is necessary to outline the principal perils and pitfalls that await the overenthusiastic culturalist. But, first, let us stake out a position, and perhaps fortify it a little, by way of registering some general points.

SOME GENERAL POINTS

I will begin by anchoring the chapter with, perhaps to, five general judgments. These are discussed and developed in more detail in later sections.

Culture Comes of Age

After decades of wandering in the wilderness, the few scholars who wrote about strategic culture have recently been joined by, so it seems, just about everyone else. It seems as if the case for cultural analysis has been made and now is widely accepted. Exactly how such analysis should be performed, and on what, precisely, is another matter. Also, the anticipated benefits of cultural analysis remain somewhat uncertain. But, in the U.S. defense community you cannot keep a big, and possibly good, idea down; not once it has secured official adoption. When Army transformation documents refer to an intention to "transform its culture ..."[2] you know that both the noun and the verb are words that are much in favor. Ever since 1973, I have been quoting two wonderful sentences from Bernard Brodie's final book, *War and Politics* (1973). He wrote: "Whether with respect to arms control or otherwise, good strategy presumes good anthropology and sociology. Some of the greatest military blunders of all time have resulted from juvenile evaluations in this department."[3] Brodie cited the deadly facts that both Napoleon and Hitler despised the Russians. Were he alive today, he might well have cited the case of those who invade Iraq without understanding that the country—I speak loosely in that regard—is a multicultural society, which sometimes is controlled by a highly authoritarian central government.[4] Destroy that central government and the country reverts to control by its enduring tribal power structure. When Brodie offered his advice on the value of anthropology and sociology in 1973, he was conveying a message that the strategic studies community had not been hearing. One would like to believe that today his claim is generally accepted, in principle, if not necessarily much in practice, as yet.

Methodology and Understanding

Strategy is a practical business.[5] Scholars who lack experience in government, let alone in war itself, are apt to forget this. Also, of course, strategic studies typically is regarded as a subfield within the broad tent of international relations (to mix my metaphors). International relations, the multidiscipline, was kick-started as an academic pursuit in horrified reaction to World War I. What I am claiming is that strategic studies and its scholarly contextual master has always been intended to be useful to the society within which it is practiced and possibly to all humankind. It is not a fine art. Since all professions protect themselves with specialized language known only to initiates, it is not surprising that theorists of international relations have invented their own code words and, like all bodies of theologians, have fractured into competing schools of belief. Should I lose sleep worrying about whether I am a neoclassical realist or a constructivist? Could I possibly be both? Does it matter? The reason for this seeming digression is that scholars of international relations, most especially those of a marked social scientific bent, are now hot on the trail of that elusive quarry, strategic culture. So, their assumptions, methods, and goals are of some relevance to this essay. The trouble is, I suspect, that the industrious and methodologically innovative theorist is overreaching both what is possible and what is useful. For a helpful analogy, I draw your attention to an article written by Hedley Bull in 1968, "Strategic Studies and its Critics." Bull addressed, and supported, a charge leveled by some strategists at their own profession. The charge was that in their pursuit of "technical rigor and precision," many strategists have "lost touch with political variety and change."[6] This strategist, for one, cannot avoid the conviction that strategic cultural analysis sometimes is guilty of the same character of error that Bull identified. The demands of rigor and precision in theory construction are allowed to triumph over the substance of the subject. The writings of Alastair Iain Johnston on the strategic culture(s) of China are a classic example of what I mean.[7] He cannot include behavior in his definition of culture because to do so would torpedo his exercise in theory building. It would be difficult, not to say impossible, to assess the influence of strategic culture if it is both input and already is inherent in the output. I sympathize with him over his dilemma, though not with his solution. While a rigorous method is admirable, it ought not to take precedence over an inconvenient reality.

Jomini, Sun Tzu, and the Philosopher's Stone

Culture matters deeply, as is explained in a later section. But, it is not all that matters in strategy and security. Alas the spirit of Baron Antoine Henri de Jomini is alive and well and inhabits Washington, D.C. It was the spirit of his theory that gave us a technical and utterly apolitical understanding of strategic stability during the Cold War. Although Jomini said that strategy was an art, I doubt if he really believed it.[8] Rather, did he believe that there was a science of war, a science the mysteries of which he was the first to present coherently, if not to unlock? If you read liberal commentaries in opposition to ballistic missile defense or to the *Peacekeeper* (MX) intercontinental ballistic missile (ICBM), you will be in Jominian territory, intellectually. The Swiss colonel tells us in his best-known book, *The Art of War* of 1838, "that there is one great principle underlying all the operations of war—a principle which must be followed in all good combinations."[9] The maxims that follow are keyed to the principle of overwhelming an inferior portion of the enemy's army with a superior quantity of yours. In Jomini's words, "[e]very maxim relating to war will be good if it indicates the employment of the greatest portion of the means of action at the decisive moment and place."[10] The confused, if not baffled, soldier of today, can hardly help but be cheered by Jomini's claim, advice is too weak a term, that "[c]orrect theories, founded upon right principles, sustained by actual events of wars, and added to accurate military history, will form a true school of instruction for generals."[11]

But since Jomini's "one great principle" does not sit comfortably with the character of irregular warfare, our leading contemporary concern—for a while, at least—we can look to ancient China for a more suitable great principle. Not only do we find such help in Sun Tzu, we discover that it blesses cultural understanding. Indeed, it all but mandates cultural study. Despite its overfamiliarity, I am obliged to quote the well-known formula.

> Thus it is said that one who knows the enemy and knows himself will not be endangered in a hundred engagements. One who does not know the enemy but knows himself will sometimes be victorious, sometimes meet with defeat. One who knows neither the enemy nor himself will invariably be defeated in every engagement.[12]

Good advice, and it is at least half true. Self and other knowledge is important, even vitally so, but it does not guarantee success. There is a danger that Sun Tzu's excellent formula, reinforced by a Jominian spirit, will encourage the fallacious conviction that in understanding culture we have stumbled across the answer to, the correct great principle for, our strategic dilemmas. Thus, a secure grasp of the strategic cultures of friends and foes can serve as the Philosopher's Stone that transmutes the lead of mere information into the gold of a comprehension that is strategically usable.

Fashion Rules, Briefly

The American defense community has a history of intellectual, and even policy, capture by the big idea of the moment, perhaps even the decade. Not so long ago, the magic concept was Revolution in Military Affairs (RMA). RMA gave way to transformation, which, to be generous, one could interpret as the logical and practical consequence of RMA. Today it seems, at long last, culture either is, or is in serious danger of becoming, the big idea of the moment. In some ways this is good news. After all, this theorist, for one, has been advocating cultural analysis for thirty years. But, it is a law of life that fashion changes. It changes because American culture favors novelty and innovation, even if it is the rediscovery of the blindingly obvious, and because it is in the very nature of fashion to change. People, including defense theorists, get bored composing briefings on the same subject, time after time. Also, any subject eventually exhausts the imagination of theorists. Furthermore, as America's security problems shift, so does the focus of debate on suitable responses. Nonetheless, it is to be hoped that when the current modest level of official enthusiasm for cultural understanding ebbs away, some nuggets of lasting value will be left on our intellectual and institutional beaches. To venture a speculative thought, the most likely reason why strategic culture will lack staying power as a potent idea in the U.S. defense community will be because of its inherent difficulty.

Strategic cultural understanding is difficult to achieve and even more difficult to operationalize. The fact that it is an important concept, robust in its essentials against challenge, is irrelevant. The practical implications of the promotion of culture to intellectual and doctrinal leading edge status may well, indeed probably will, prove to be unduly demanding. For example, as the global superpower, determined to drain swamps anywhere in the global war on terror (GWOT, a now dated, but still attractive, acronym), America's need for cultural expertise is all but unbounded.[13] It takes years, even decades, to grow a body of Americans who are truly local experts.

All things are possible, but this strategic theorist is skeptical that culture, strategic and other, has the horsepower to stay the course in official U.S. policy focus, let alone in troop training and interagency cooperation. More to the point perhaps, it is by no means self-evident that the job is doable.

It is useful to change the question when the original question can produce only a negative answer. In reply to the question, can we achieve good cultural understanding of most of our likely friends and probable foes, one is obliged to say, almost certainly not. So, let us change the question. In answer to the reframed question, can we achieve good enough cultural understanding of some of our likely friends and most probable foes, we can say perhaps, albeit only with the application of a great deal of sustained effort. As much to the point is the issue of just how one uses cultural understanding. Who uses it, and how important is such use? That thought bears directly upon the core concern of this chapter, the significance of culture relative to other influences upon decisions and behavior. If culture is a variable intervening between stimulus and decision and action, a conception that this author does not endorse, what else intervenes?

Culture Matters

Given the critical tone and content of some of this section thus far, it is necessary that it be concluded on a strongly positive note. None of the criticisms leveled thus far and in the sections to come are intended to suggest that culture is of minor, let alone no, importance. This theorist has long been persuaded that culture is a significant, and can even be a determining, influence upon strategic decisions and behavior. The doubts expressed here pertain to the ways in which culture is conceptualized and, of much greater moment, to the practical difficulties that inhibit even culturally well-educated performance.

WHAT IS CULTURE AND WHAT DOES IT DO?

This chapter opened with an unscholarly endorsement of that old unreliable virtue, common sense. Unreliable though it is, it has much to offer to the would-be user of the concept, and perhaps the theory, of strategic culture. Before we delve into some of the dimmer and rococo regions of academic discourse, let us see if we can describe the essence of our subject in language that is simple and clear, yet that is not, as a consequence, misleading. When we refer to Russian strategic culture, for example, what we are claiming is that there is a "Russian way" both of thinking about the threat or use of force for political purposes, and of acting strategically. In the latter regard, so this statement maintains, there is a Russian "way of war." This Russian way is a distinctive product of Russia's history and geography, as interpreted for guidance by Russians. Stated thus, a host of critical questions beg for answer. Let me pre-empt at least a few of them. Whatever one's scholarly credo on research methodology, as I keep saying, it is necessary not to lose the plot. The plot, please remember, the master narrative, is the disarmingly elementary, even commonsensical, idea that a security community is likely to think and behave in ways that are influenced by what it has taught itself about itself and its relevant contexts. And that education, to repeat, rests primarily upon the interpretation of history and history's geography (or should it be geography's history?) My geopolitical friends favor the aphorism that "geography is destiny." Perhaps the dedicated culturalist will offer the rival dictum that "culture is destiny."

Let us clear some underbrush. However one chooses to define culture in general, and strategic culture in particular, those of us who wear the badge of the "culturalist" are not claiming that culture is always, or even necessarily often, the prime determinant of decision and action. Strategic decision and behavior typically is influenced by many factors, not least by those dynamics of executive action that ensure outcomes are negotiated among competing interests. However, it is well to remember that virtually whatever the mix of factors that we believe have produced a decision and its consequent strategic behavior, all of the people and the organizations within which they function are more or less distinctively encultured. This fact is more than a little inconvenient for some would-be theory builders. It would be helpful if one could postulate stimuli entering a decision-making process, with culture expediently confined to the role of intervening variable, among other intervening variables, between stimuli and decision. Alas, the world is not like that. Culture is not an intervening variable. We are all encultured. But to state that obvious point is not to claim that culture, understood as preference, necessarily has the last word on our decisions or our actions. Culture doesn't usually program us to think and behave like automata, though one can find cases where an approximation to such a malady appears to have occurred.

After reading a few pages of tortuous scholarly theorizing one longs for a return to basics. Having come perilously close to scholarly pathology, I will now be as basic as I know how in describing our subject. Strategic culture is of interest because the concept suggests, perhaps insists, that different security communities think and behave somewhat differently when it comes to strategic matters. Those differences stem from communities' distinctive histories and geographies. We can, and should, add many caveats and qualifications to the basic statement just offered. But, what I have just stated in the spirit of back to basics is *the plot*. It is deceptively simple. One would think that it is so elementary, commonsensical even, as to be banal. And yet, time after time, strategic history reveals belligerents who either believed that strategic culture was common and universal, or who simply chose to ignore the distinctive cultural dimensions of their adversaries. Of course, if one is ignorant of that dimension, it is difficult to do anything other than to assume that the enemy's strategic preferences will be broadly familiar.

I would like to suggest that there is rather less of substance, and of value, to some of the scholarly debate than meets the eye. We should not take our definitions or our theories too seriously.[14] A little theory goes a long way; more often than not it goes too far. I commend to you this anarchic comment by the anthropologist Leslie A. White: "Culture is not basically anything. Culture is a word concept. It is man-made and may be used arbitrarily to designate anything, we may define the concept as we please."[15] That is a little extreme, but his point is valid. Definitions are arbitrary and can be neither right nor wrong. Nonetheless, some definitions of culture are less defensibly arbitrary than are others. Rather than offering my own definition, I will endorse Jack Snyder's 1977 offering from the Rand study, which triggered the modern debate about strategic culture. Snyder's definition is good enough to provide focus and to help keep us glued to the plot. Snyder wrote, with one minor amendment, for the changed strategic context:

> Strategic culture can be defined as the sum total of ideas, conditioned emotional responses, and patterns of habitual behavior that members of a national strategic community have acquired through instruction or imitation and share with each other

with regard to [nuclear] strategy. In the area of strategy, habitual behaviour is largely cognitive behavior.[16]

Although I have done scholarly battle with Alastair Iain Johnston over the definitional issue of whether or not strategic culture should be understood to include behavioral as well as ideational phenomena, I am less and less persuaded that that debate had, or has, any real significance.[17] The ability of scholars to make a necessarily opaque concept such as strategic culture even less penetrable is truly amazing. Of course, it is the professional drive of the social scientist for theory that is largely to blame. I admit that it is more than moderately difficult to design a theory of strategic culture if the elusive beast, culture, is both input and output, presumed cause and presumed consequence. But, so what! The sins of the would-be cultural theorists pale by comparison with the nonsense that we know as neorealism. That theory, family of theories, or approach—take your pick—is relevant to this discussion since it is often contrasted with culturalism. On a personal note, when I first encountered neorealism, back in 1979 in Kenneth Waltz's *Theory of International Politics*, I thought it was so absurd that no one would, or should, take it seriously.[18] Obviously, I was wrong, with respect to its popularity, but not to its merit. Defense professionals understand that defense policy, strategy, and force planning are all made at home. Also, we understand that home differs radically from security community to security community. So the neorealist proposition that strategic history, past, present, and future, can be explained strictly by reference to the relations among political entities, with no regard paid to their domestic processes, is, frankly, preposterous. I thought this in 1979 and, being deeply conservative, I still think the same way today. A pure neorealist view of strategic history is as flawed as would be an unmodified belief in cultural dominance. I shall argue in this chapter that culture must always be a potential influence upon decision and action. But that potential is not uniformly, or necessarily, realized.

Useful work has been done by scholars of recent years in sorting out different segments of our subject. Specifically, there is now widespread agreement that although strategic culture has long been, and remains, the umbrella concept, in fact we need to distinguish among: (i) public culture; (ii) strategic culture; and (iii) military (organizational) culture. Relatively little work has been performed as yet in attempts to connect the three. Among the many virtues of recognition of these minimal, but essential, distinctions is the discouragement they should give to those who might be inclined to look for a neatly unitary strategic culture. There may be a body of strategic beliefs and attitudes to which, say, most Americans would sign up. But, the many organizational players in policymaking and policy implementation will each have their unique take on how those common beliefs and attitudes should be expressed in actual strategic behavior. In effect, I am going back a decade even from Kenneth Waltz, to Graham Allison and the theory of bureaucratic politics.[19] Remember the old maxim: "where you stand depends on where you sit." I do not wish to reject one rational choice model only to endorse another. Nonetheless, to study strategic culture it is necessary to disaggregate the subject somewhat. In addition to identifying community-wide strategic nostrums and the like, it is necessary also to consider the institutional preferences of self-interested organizations with their career structures. It may make sense to think in terms of multiple cultural identities.

Where does culture come from? As indicated already, it comes from history and geography. However, one must qualify that general claim by noting that culture is not static. It can evolve, it can adapt, and it can even change radically if battered by traumatic shock. Isobel V. Hull, in her study of the military culture of Imperial Germany, observes intriguingly that "[o]ne might say that militaries are in the trauma business."[20] World War I itself may not have changed public and eventually the strategic and military cultures of Russia and Germany. But it was the principal enabler of the cultural revolution wrought by the Bolsheviks. Also, with much assistance from the Great Depression, 1914–1918 eventually bears a major responsibility for another cultural revolution, that effected by Hitler and his Nazis. Historians argue about whether the Third Reich was the culmination of, or the exception to, German history, and a similar argument occasionally flourished with reference to tsarist Russia and Stalin as the new Red Tsar. My point, simply, is that public and strategic culture can change dramatically. Unsurprisingly, the most usual cause of such change is the traumatic effect of war and its consequences.

We must insist that culture in its several identities—public, strategic, military-organizational—should consist of assumptions and ideas that are strongly held. Its roots may not be very deep, and the plant might be a recent development, but it has to be hardy to be worthy of the description, cultural. Culture does not refer to mere opinions, to fashionable attitudes, or to shifting patterns of behavior. However, to claim that it, this somewhat opaque, mysterious "it" of culture, is more permanent than opinion is not to suggest that it is permanent; it is not. Culture changes, adapts, sometimes adapts poorly, and, as an effect of societal shock, can alter radically.

Like strategy, culture is a difficult concept to explain, let alone portray convincingly.[21] You know you are in trouble when our culture specialists, the cultural anthropologists and sociologists, cannot agree on a definition. Culture is among the most contested of concepts. Fortunately, as sensible people, in desperation we are at liberty to enlist common sense in our column. Since culture, like love and honor, for other examples, cannot be captured and photographed directly, the best we can manage is to identify evidence, at least probable evidence, of its presence. In that respect, following the formula suggested by sociologist Raymond Williams, I look for culture in a community's ideals, in its ideas as revealed by its documents and other artifacts, and in its behavior.[22] In order to outflank methodologically the long-running scholars' dispute over whether or not behavior should be included in the preferred definition of culture, it is helpful to ask, "what does culture do?"

Today, most, though certainly not all, strategic commentators and senior defense officials agree with the proposition that culture is important. That now popular, even fashionable, opinion is broadly correct. Such doubts as I have, which are explained later in this chapter, pertain not to the issue of culture's importance, but rather to finding useful answers to the quintessential strategist's question, "so what?" In fact, culture is much easier to explain than it is to define. What does culture do? It enables us to make sense of our world. Culture provides us with the assumptions, largely unspoken and unwritten, that are the foundation for, though not the sole determinants of, our judgments.[23] Culture yields us the truths, small and large, that we know should guide our decisions and actions. In practice, we will often ignore those truths and behave expediently. Our strategic culture is likely to educate us with quite powerful preferences. But in a world that contains competing interests at home, in short a political process, and external menaces, we must do the best we can.

A culturalist perspective is not at odds with a realist one, at least it is not provided one thinks clearly and files some of the more theoretical literature somewhere appropriate. To quote Isobel V. Hull again, we are all "cultural creatures."[24] This insight has come as something of a revelation to the devotees of universal rational choice. And, as Keith Payne has argued convincingly with respect to deterrence, the principal pillars of modern Western strategic theory, which is to say the dominant theories of deterrence, limited war, and arms control, were all of them constructed on the false assumption of a common rationality.[25] Such an assumption is acultural. There may well be a fairly common rationality among security communities, in fact it is highly probable that all such communities make decisions and act upon them in a rational manner. The trouble lies with the content of that rationality, with its reasonableness in our encultured view, not with the process that purposefully connects means with ends. The suicide bomber is a rational person. But, to us, he or she is not a reasonable one.

Realism and culturalism are not in opposition, except in some fictional universe that should not detain us. Since we are all encultured, whether we like it or not, we are obliged to pursue our interests with our values and preferences as a more or less powerful influence upon our decisions and behavior. As often as not, our world is one of necessity wherein we must simply do our best to realize as many of our desires as the relevant context permits. Culture need not imprison us and command us to behave in ways that are dysfunctional. Of course, it may do, in which case we risk entering a pathological decision-making and behavioral condition. I can conceive of behavior motivated by urges that are strongly cultural in origin, but scarcely at all "realist" as that much abused term should imply. But, it is literally impossible for there to be behavior of a realist character that is utterly bereft of cultural influence. French statecraft, for example, is justly celebrated for its cynical and realistic expediency. Those useful characteristics are not acultural, rather are they integral to French public and strategic cultures.

The scholarly debate that contrasts realism with culturalism inadvertently encourages us to forget that we are encultured with strategic nostrums and other assumptions that derive from interpretation of our security community's historical experience. Culturalists do not need to be unworldly idealists, to be despised and ignored by allegedly hard-headed realists. To repeat: we are all cultural creatures. Moreover, strategic cultures are by and large functional, not dysfunctional, for their bearers. The dedicated owners of truly dysfunctional strategic cultures have a way of vanishing from the history books.

In common with its close relatives, public and military cultures, strategic culture is not an optional extra. All security communities have belief systems, assumptions, and preferences for behavior that play as one, among many, factor or dimension in their strategic histories. On many strategic issues, distinctive cultural influence may scarcely be a player, while on others it will all but command policy. One size in theory does not fit every historical case.

WHY CULTURE MATTERS

Strategic culture and geopolitics are no rivals, and neither are strategic culture and *realpolitik*. While citing a caveat with respect to some religious contributions to the ideational, it is plausible to claim that culture is not free floating, offering a range of options to communities in need of a little guidance. Rather culture is grounded, even rooted, in the geopolitical history, the unique experience, of a people. When I say that strategic culture is grounded in the historical experience of a particular geopolitically located, if in some cases, mobile, people, I mean that it is that people's interpretation of their history. But, that claim, as just stated, should not be understood as endorsement of a pure version of the constructivist creed. It is not. Despite the many warnings about the perils and pitfalls that await the unwary culturalist that this chapter specifies in the next section, let no one doubt that a close to maximalist claim for the importance of culture is going to be advanced here.

Do not forget the core of our subject; what we are really talking about. Regardless of the precise definition of culture, and strategic culture in particular, that you most favor, our subject functions on two levels. First, it can be the prime mover of thought, judgment, policy, and all that follows therefrom. Second, it must always be present as an actual, or potential, influence on our decisions and behavior. The reason, if, yet again, I dare restate the obvious, is that we are all cultural creatures. In his recent Adelphi Paper *The Transformation of Strategic Affairs*, Lawrence Freedman makes much use of, and has interesting things to say about, the concept of "narratives." In Freedman's words, narratives are "compelling story lines which can explain events convincingly and from which inferences can be drawn ..."[26] I must register some, but only some, dissent from Freedman, though, when he claims that "[n]arratives are designed or nurtured with the intention of structuring the responses of others to developing events. They are strategic because they do not arise spontaneously but are deliberately constructed or reinforced out of the ideas and thoughts that are already current."[27]

That can be so, but it understates the role of culture. It is true to claim that culture, including strategic culture, can be molded purposefully into a narrative cunningly contrived for the purpose of popular persuasion. One thinks immediately, almost reflexively, of the powerful ideologies, indeed the political quasi-religions, of Marxism and Nazism. However, excepting such extreme cases that have been historical outriders of our subject, albeit outriders of extraordinary significance, communities do not deliberately construct their cultures, strategic and other. Those cultures emerge and change as a kind of natural phenomena. They are the ever evolving product of the many efforts peoples make to explain their past, understand their present, and anticipate their future.

So opaque is the concept of culture, so hard is it to capture and quantify for analysis, that it lends itself all too easily to exaggeration or near dismissal. I suggest that the problem lies not so much with the concept of culture, but rather with our failure to think with sufficient clarity about what it is and how it works. There is too much unhelpful binary analysis. Culturalism or realism, and so forth. Consider Hitler or Stalin, or possibly Osama bin Laden: dedicated ideologues, culturalists in the fullest meaning of the word. Those men simultaneously were (and are) sincere ideologues, yet were able to behave tactically in ways that appeared to contradict their deepest beliefs when it was expedient to do so. Hitler, of course, was far less adaptable than was Stalin. To hold firmly to a master historical narrative that explains the process of change, and who should be history's winners and who its losers, does not disable one from being agile and adaptable as to means and methods. In practice, a distinguishable national strategic culture is likely to act as a holding company over a number of subsidiary military and other related cultures. Strategic culture will have a stronger or weaker influence from issue area to issue area. Also, the overall strategic culture should be considerably forgiving of those expedient and opportunistic decisions and behaviors that circumstances appear to command.

Despite the judgments just offered, it is well not to forget what our subject is about: what is the plot? If we think schematically and hierarchically, for the sake of this illustration, it is commonplace to postulate a significance tree that has political vision at the top, with the succeeding levels downward comprising policy, grand strategy, military strategy, operations, and tactics. But whence cometh political vision? The answer, of course, is that it comes from what we call culture, strategic culture in this case. It is from our culture that we find the vision of the good or better life for ourselves and for our security community. And it is from that vision that policy draws what it is able to, given real-world constraints. Truly, culture must reign, sometimes it rules, while it is ever present, so well integrated as to be unlabeled, in our thoughts and judgments, because we cannot prevent it being so.

There are many reasons one can cite in praise of strategic cultural analysis. I select just five among them to support my claim that such analysis is not only important, it is close to essential. One cannot quite claim that it is essential in the sense of being a *sine qua non* for victory or for the avoidance of defeat. The culturally ignorant can, and do, win wars. Also, the culturally educated will not necessarily be reliably victorious as a reward for their anthropological expertise. But those caveats are not of great significance. After all, as the Prussian grand master tells us, "[w]ar is the realm of chance."[28] Nothing can guarantee victory. However, there are ways of loading the dice in one's favor. Cultural comprehension is one such way. So, why does culture matter to the strategist?

Culture and Moral Factors

Culture matters greatly because it is the most important source of the moral factors that are central to the nature of war as well as to the character of wars. On its first page, *On War* declares, without equivocation, that "[w]ar is thus an act of force to compel our enemy to do our will."[29] And what is this "will"? Clausewitz informs us that "the will is itself a moral quality."[30] He proceeds to explain that

> most of the matters dealt with in this book [*On War*] are composed in equal parts of physical and moral causes and effects. One might say that the physical seem little more than the wooden hilt, while the moral factors are the precious metal, the real weapon, the finely-honed blade.[31]

The object in war is not usually to destroy the enemy physically, rather it is to subordinate his will to ours. It is not much of an intellectual stretch to argue that war, coercion and deterrence are all intercultural struggles. They are contests between independent wills, the content and strength of which are very much, though not exclusively, the products of culture. But, deterrence, coercion, and war cannot be reduced conveniently simply to intercultural strife. The physical dimension matters also. The Germans and Japanese did not lack potent strategic cultures and the will to win in 1944–1945. Rather were they short of men, material, and sound strategy. However, few wars are waged for the proximate purpose of completely destroying the enemy's strategic strength. Rather are they usually conducted for limited purposes and by military and other means roughly proportional to those goals. The salience of culture is revealed most clearly with respect to deterrence. For deterrence to succeed, the intended deterree has to decide he is deterred. He has a choice. And success or failure in deterrence is never attributable strictly to presumed calculations of the material balance. Much, if not most, of the abstract modeling of stable deterrence in which defense analysts used to indulge, was, of methodological necessity, innocent of the vital ingredient of political velocity. Rational choice has difficulty with powerful feelings. Culture, cultural understanding or its lack, is apt to be the key to deterrence success or failure.[32]

Know Yourself

As usual, Sun Tzu was right. It is important to know ourselves. Unfortunately, it is extraordinarily difficult to know oneself in terms of strategic culture. In principle, we should perform far better, be more consistently successful, if we were able to look in the strategic mirror and see ourselves without significant distortion. In practice, of course, we tend to see ourselves as we would like to be. So deep is a security community's vested interest in its version of its own master strategic historical narrative that one should not expect objective self-assessment. Perhaps in the aftermath of strategic trauma, a measure of objectivity may creep in. The Germans achieved this under the inspired leadership of Chief of Staff Hans von Seeckt after World War I, with their fifty-seven study committees.[33] After Vietnam, the Americans assuredly did not. The official U.S. response to the protracted disaster of the Vietnam project was to ignore it for more than a generation.

It is necessary to emphasize that countries do not pick their strategic cultures at random, or because of intellectual or other fashion. Particular strategic cultures are adopted, accepted, and digested as "cultural assumptions," to quote Professor Black,[34] because they fit the characters and contexts of the relevant societies. It is true that they evolve, and that they can alter radically as a result of traumatic shock. But, it is not true that a strategic culture can be discarded by an act of will, at least not rapidly and thoroughly, save in circumstances of direst necessity. Remember that societies, security communities, do not choose their strategic cultures. Rather it is their strategic cultures that choose them. There is a marriage between a society's strategic need and the culture that seems best to meet that need. Of course, this is an oversimplification. However, the culture of a nation, the American for example, is not acquired by rational choice, certainly not by a single such choice. The country behaved in as strategically effective a way as it was able. That historical experience came to be all but codified in what today we are calling strategic culture.

Behind strategic culture is a historical record, past, present, and prospectively future, in which material relations among political entities are vitally significant. Strategic culture is likely to be a highly important factor, positive or negative, perhaps some of each, contributing to overall strategic effectiveness. A cultural paradigm is a construction, and as such it can be deconstructed and reconstructed, at least in theory. In practice, even a cultural paradigm that is having a dysfunctional influence upon decision making and actual strategic behavior, may not be changeable. One might not recognize the problem with one's organizing assumptions, and even if one does, the requirements and implications of change may be unduly formidable. Strategic culture certainly can be adaptable, but it is not infinitely so. It is not acquired lightly and casually, and neither can it be discarded and replaced promptly at will from a catalogue of alternative strategic cultures. An interesting question that has yet to attract any noteworthy scholarship address is the extent to which a security community is able to choose its strategic culture. In most regards we acquire our public, strategic, and military cultures, without any exercise of conscious choice. Given the pervasive influence of strategic culture, generally silent and invisible, it is not obvious that we would know how to go about changing it, even should we wish to do so. After all, culture is a part of us. As I have argued elsewhere, we inhabit a more or less distinctive strategic context, and we are a functioning part of the context.[35]

There is probably some merit in Americans, Britons, Russians, and so forth, being more culturally self-aware. But, we have to pose the classic strategist's question, "so what?" Americans, Britons, and Russians are what they are. While they are not locked into strategic cultures that are static and eternal in all respects, they are to an important degree captives of the cultures with which local interpretations of their distinctive histories have armed them. Even if you recognize some significant dysfunctionality in your strategic and military cultures, you may not be able to take effective corrective action. This is very much a live issue at present with respect to the official U.S. commitment to transform its armed forces, the Army most especially, of course, into an instrument of excellence in the conduct of irregular warfare of all kinds. Success is possible, but unlikely. If one compares what we used to call the traditional American way of war with the style required for the countering of insurgency and terrorism, one discovers an almost perfect mismatch.[36]

Better self-knowledge is desirable, but it can offer no magical solution to the problems of a maladaptive military instrument. Strategic culture is the product of a centuries-long dialogue between a people and its history. It is not going to yield readily, painlessly, and comprehensively to a would-be revolutionary drive from the policymakers of the moment.

Know Others Again

Sun Tzu was correct, at least he was substantially so. One cannot make a virtue of cultural ignorance. Before striking a cautionary note, let us endorse the commonplace belief that it is highly desirable to understand as much about the adversary as possible. Cultural intelligence is particularly valuable because it explains the intellectual and moral context within which decisions will be made. Needless to say, perhaps, it is far easier to count tanks and missiles than it is to grasp the cultural assumptions of an alien society, let alone comprehend the cognitive psychology of enemy leaders. How do their brains work? Physiologically like ours, of course. But, does our anatomical commonality conceal radical differences in values, preferences, and goals?

Sun Tzu makes much of the utility in understanding the enemy, and rightly so. However, his wise words need to be read with reservations. His good advice identifies a standard that is rarely met, and probably is rarely attempted. How seriously do belligerents strive to understand each other, let alone themselves? Far more often than not crises and wars erupt and one or perhaps both sides have no choice other than to function in cultural ignorance as best they are able. The classic "Principles of War" provide a partial solution to the perils of strategic cultural ignorance. At least they do if the object in the war is the complete overthrow of the enemy. One of those "principles" asserts the utility of maintaining the "initiative."[37] In other words, keep the enemy dancing to your tune. Operate within his decision cycle, his OODA loop if you prefer, so that he is never able to wage the kind of war he might prefer.[38] In practice, this would-be solution to the problem of ignorance is not likely to be very fruitful. The reasons are because most wars are not conducted for unlimited goals, and most wars last long enough for military initiatives to run out of logistic steam, even if only briefly. Also, we know from experience as well as from Clausewitz that friction, chance, indeed the whole "climate of war" can embarrass even the wisest of nostrums and maxims.[39]

Just suppose that the leaders of Imperial Japan understood themselves and, unimaginably, came also to understand the United States by, say, June 1944, the month of the fatal Battle of the Philippine Sea off Saipan. Such cultural comprehension would have been of zero value. Tokyo could not have used such anthropological insight to any strategic purpose. They were doomed. The United States was an implacable foe, totally untroubled in 1944–1945 by considerations of collateral damage, and was still considerably ignorant of relevant Japanese culture. But it did not matter for the outcome of the war. Even had Americans grasped fully the importance of the Japanese notion of honor, they could not have used that understanding, save with respect to the vital importance to the enemy of the preservation of the Imperial office. On a much more constructive note, had Americans read their Thucydides carefully in 1940–1941, they should have been impressed by the middle item in his famous tryptich of motives for war: fear, honor, and interest. U.S. efforts to coerce Japan posed lethal threats both to Japanese interests and, above all else, to its honor. On the Japanese side, had Tokyo studied American public and strategic cultures, it ought to have realized that the Imperial Navy's Pearl Harbor preference must guarantee the onset of a total war that it could not possibly win. Indeed, the only scenario that might yield success for Tokyo would be one wherein Germany defeated the Soviet Union. However, even that happy, if increasingly improbable, prospect would fall short of guaranteeing U.S. acquiescence in Japanese aggression. The mutual cultural mis-assessments of Japan and the United States in 1940–1941 illustrate clearly just how important it can be to achieve cultural understanding of the foe.[40]

THE PERILS AND PITFALLS OF CULTURAL ENQUIRY

In the judgment of this strategic theorist there is, and can be, no productive debate between those who favor study of the cultural dimension to war, peace, and strategy, and those who do not. The claim that cultural study has not yielded insights superior to those attainable by realist investigation is misguided on several counts.[41] It is wrong in that it postulates a realist project that is somehow, strangely, culture free. Frankly, that is absurd. Also, it flies in the face of an overwhelming weight of strategic historical evidence. Indeed, the case, not for a culturalist approach, but rather for the study of culture, including cognitive psychology, is so strong that the caveats cited in this section are only that, caveats not showstoppers.

Everyone will have their own favorite list of doubts and problems with cultural enquiry. Just eleven of these are cited here for brief analysis. Each could benefit from essay-length treatment.

Explaining Too Much

Since all humans are encultured, most of us multiply so, culture begins to look like a theory of everything. Such a theory, alas, is a theory of nothing. If everything we think and do has to be influenced by culture, and is in a vital sense a cultural manifestation, inter alia, there is no noncultural space at all. Since this peril has some empirical merit, theorists of culture need to consider it more seriously than they have to date. Scholars have to acknowledge that that which is theoretically inconvenient is not necessarily, as a consequence, untrue. Common sense can be of assistance.

The Problem of Evidence

What is the evidence? Well, it rather depends on how one defines culture. If we suppose, for the sake of argument, that there are wholly extra-cultural influences on policy and strategy, such factors should not be considered outside of their cultural context. The sensible culturalist does not assert that culture invariably rules. Rather is the claim to the effect that culture is usually, perhaps always, a factor, one dimension among many. Unpicking a decision, deconstructing a strategy and style in warfare, for clear evidence of cultural footprints, is always going to be a contestable endeavor. The somewhat irritating truth is that all of us, our institutions, and our processes of governance, have been shaped, at least influenced, by what we understand as culture. This claim is, I believe, methodologically devastating. Nonetheless, it is true. And it does not in any way detract from the proposition that cultural matters are vitally important.

Culture as Panacea

Politicians and soldiers are problem-solvers. Truth is what works. Strategy, and strategic studies, is a pragmatic undertaking.[42] As a consequence, defense communities typically are vulnerable to ambush and capture by almost any new sounding big idea that is touted as the solution to the overwhelming problem of the moment. Strategic culture is just such a big idea. It is ironic that it always was a good idea. It was good when this author and others wrote about it in the 1970s and 1980s, and when Sun Tzu praised its virtues 2,400 years ago. Better late than never, one should observe. Context is all. Culture has become popular, even fashionable, all of a sudden, because the United States and its allies today are engaged in transcultural warfare.[43] There is nothing whatsoever novel about transcultural warfare, but it does happen to be different from the rough symmetry that characterized the Soviet–American strategic standoff for forty-plus years, as well as the two world wars. It is understandable that Washington will lend an ear, and provide some money, to almost anyone who is selling a patent medicine to cure its contemporary problems. "Culture" is one such patent medicine, in the minds of many. This is unfortunate, because, as this chapter has argued, there is an excellent case for cultural study. We can only hope that a sensible regard for the cultural dimension to war and strategy will not be tainted unduly by association with the belief that cultural mastery is the path to strategic salvation.

Cultural Essentialism

One suspects that in most cases, most of the time, it is impractical to seek to distinguish the cultural from the unarguably noncultural among the influences upon decisions. Indeed, as this chapter has suggested tentatively and somewhat dangerously, it is not obvious that a meaningful distinction between the cultural and the extra-cultural can or should be drawn. A brute force way to bulldoze this difficulty is by having resort to the wonderful word, "essentially." The determined, not to say dogmatic, culturalist, scores with his or her great essentialist simplification. All the while, a nod is given to other, lesser influences. The hunt for essential truth is never ending, as scholars strive to penetrate to the heart of the matter. Whether or not there is such an animal is a troubling question.

Culture Can and Does Change

Culture does not change frequently or, usually, radically. If it did, it would not be culture. Definition has its uses. Culturalist enquiry is subject to the temptation to assume a relatively static character to strategic and military cultures. The same pathology afflicts those among us who write about "the American (or other) way of war." *Mea culpa*, I believe.[44] Strategic culture both evolves and can shift seismically if it is assaulted by a traumatic shock of sufficient awesomeness.

Culture Is Diverse

A security community may have more than one strategic culture, at least at the level of a traditional way of war. Britain has been the exemplar of a maritime power, and for a long while it was the proud owner of a global empire acquired for profit and defended by maritime supremacy. But, strange to note, in the twentieth century, as in the high Middle Ages for England, Britain was as much, if not more, a continental, as a maritime power. In World War I, after August 19, 1915, Britain made an open-ended commitment to continental warfare, a decision that eventually resulted in General Haig commanding a BEF of sixty divisions.[45] In 1939–1940, Britain planned to contribute at least forty divisions to a recreation of the Western Front, a development mercifully ambushed by the Germans' westward strike on May 10, 1940. While, lastly, from the late 1940s until the end of the 1980s, aside from the campaigns of imperial devolution, and the domestic nuisance of the IRA, the British armed forces prepared assiduously for continental warfare on the North German plain. There was always a significant maritime dimension to British strategic thought and effort; how could there not be for an insular power? But, it is not much of an exaggeration to claim that the twentieth was Britain's continental century. The point of the British illustration is to suggest that reasonably well-led states have strategic cultures that are adaptable to change, and often deeply unwelcome, political and strategic contexts.

Not only can strategic culture accommodate the diversity needed to meet unexpected threats, also, of course, it has more than one sword arm. Military culture will vary both among the geographically specialized services, and within those services among their separate branches. With some good reason, it may be argued that a country's strategic culture does exist and function as a cohesive whole, notwithstanding the diversity just cited. In fact, I believe this generally, though only generally, to be the case. For reasons of history and geography, to restate the mantra of this essay, communities do have preferred ways in defense preparation, and of war. Their three, or more, services will not be of equivalent combat prowess or national strategic importance. Most, if not all, countries will be more formidable in some, rather than other, forms of warfare. The United States, for example, has been preeminent as an air power; indeed it has been the world's first such.[46]

Strategic Culture Is Not Entirely Exclusive

The largely American theorists who created modern strategic thought in the 1950s were unwise to assume that a common logic and rationality would inform Strategic Persons everywhere. Nonetheless, much of the lore of statecraft, strategy, operations, and tactics is recognized universally as best practice, *ceteris paribus*. People will behave differently not only because they are culturally distinctive, but also because their circumstances will differ. To the best of my knowledge, there is no rule of strategic history or cognitive psychology that requires people to follow their dreams and desires, regardless of context. Culture is an influence, it is not a drug that produces all but mindless strategic behavior. There is a danger that in hunting for evidence of strategic and military cultures, scholars will both privilege the apparently eccentric and neglect the ideas and habits that communities share, especially if they occupy the same cultural space.[47]

Strategic Cultures Borrow and Adapt

If one is in hot pursuit of an elusive strategic culture, one is unlikely to be overly friendly to the ideas of cultural borrowing and adaptation. It is frustrating to succeed in corralling a country's strategic culture, only to learn that that culture is willing and able to borrow what its bearers recognize to be contemporary best practice from abroad. In short, strategic and military cultures may be quite adaptable. They will not be infinitely so. As we suggested earlier, truly radical change in culture occurs only as a result of seismic political, social, or military shock. But, it can and does occur. However, recent historical scholarship shows that when security communities benefit from the diffusion of useful strategic ideas and technologies, they are likely to choose to benefit in ways distinctive to themselves.[48] Historical examples abound, but the cases of national diversity in armored and air forces in World War II provide near perfect illustration of the triumph of culture.

Cultural Empathy Does Not Ensure Victory

It is always a good idea to understand both the enemy and one's friends. But, understanding alone, no matter how accurate, has only limited value. Someone, or something, at the military end of the strategy bridge actually has to do strategy, operationally and tactically. The most characteristic feature of warfare is violence. War entails the threat to use force, and the actual breaking of things and killing of people. As our studies of strategic and military culture advance, we must never forget, to repeat, that strategy is a pragmatic enterprise. It is not hard to identify weaknesses, in principle, in an adversary's strategic culture. But, can we exploit them? Understanding and consequential effective behavior may be two very different things. As often as not, one suspects, the achievement of a much deeper cultural comprehension will simply reinforce the conviction that the enemy inhabits another intellectual and emotional planet.

Policy and Strategy Are Negotiated Outcomes

Scholars may succeed in teasing out what they believe to be the core elements of a country's strategic culture, only to forget that their subject is, dare we repeat, a practical one. Academics do not inhabit a world of intellectual compromise and expedient decisions. Instead, they are, or should be, committed to the search for truth. Had such scholars functioned in government they would know that the pure flame of strategic culture is certain to be dimmed by the constraints imposed by scarce resources and competing agencies. In short, policy and strategy are always negotiated outcomes. The negotiation is unlikely to negate the influence of a general strategic culture entirely, but it is certain to ensure that that culture will be mediated by financial constraints and by competing organizational interests and cultures.

Beware of the Methodological Bog

This final peril and potent source of pitfalls was mentioned early on in this chapter. Some social scientists, theorists of International Relations to be precise (names withheld to protect the guilty), are wont to commit the same fundamental mistake that mars a great deal of official American defense analysis. In the apposite words of John J. Weltman, and I admit to quoting him out of context, the development of nuclear strategy "represent[ed] an attempt at a Jominian solution to a problem that was essentially Clausewitzian."[49] The theorists in question seek a certainty of understanding that is not attainable. For a contemporary illustration of this phenomenon, official military enthusiasm for EBO (Effects Based Operations) is the latest example of an attempt to turn the art of war into the science of war.[50] Of course, it is folly. But, the quest for calculable certainty is never ending.[51] Given the hazards of warfare, such a search is easily understandable. Alas, warfare cannot be reduced to a quantifiable problem. Similarly, many of the worthy efforts by scholars to uncover the secrets of a country's strategic culture, and especially the influence of that culture on behavior, are triumphs of misplaced methodological ingenuity. Methodologically elaborate and rigorous historical case studies of strategic culture, not that there have been many, have a way of being obliged to do great violence to the nuances and complexity of their subject. I doubt if I am the only person to notice that sophistication, at least ambition, in methodology is rarely rewarded with plausible sophistication in knowledge gained. I suggest, as I have before, that in common with the causes of war, the scholarly challenge presented by strategic culture resides primarily in the highly resistant nature of the subject, rather than with deficiencies in our research.

CONCLUSIONS

Five claims serve to conclude this chapter. First, our analysis supports and affirms the view that culture in its several guises—public, strategic, and military organizational—is vitally important. The "cultural thoughtways" of friends, foes, and, of course, ourselves can have a directive or a shaping effect upon decisions and behavior.[52] In 1979, Ken Booth argued that "[s]trategic studies divorced from area studies is largely thinking in a void. The general neglect of area studies is one of the biggest criticisms which can be levelled against strategists."[53] Booth was correct then, while just about everybody interested in security policies and strategy has come, very belatedly, to realize that he is correct for today and tomorrow.

Second, hard experience should tell us that a little theory for the probing of strategic culture goes a long way, usually too far. The needs of theory building and the reality of culture's ubiquitous contextuality, are, alas, severely at odds. This does not matter for our understanding of strategic culture, but it can be deadly for the practicality, let alone the utility, of theory. I suggest that since we are all necessarily encultured, everything that we think strategically, and that subsequently we seek to do for strategic reasons, may be influenced by the cultural dimension.

Third, cultural awareness and understanding can only be helpful, but they are not a panacea for strategic dilemmas. Even a genuine cultural expertise is not *the* answer, the magic key to strategic success. There are many reasons why policy and strategy can succeed or fail, and cultural empathy or blindness is only one of them. Those among us who are recent converts to culturalism, or even just to a new respect for the cultural anthropology of conflict, should hasten to reread our Clausewitz. Such factors as chance, friction, fear, the fog of war, and sheer incompetence may well be more important in the shaping of events than is strategic and military culture.

Fourth, cultural change, even cultural transformation, can and does happen, but do not hold your breath waiting for it. There are serious reasons, rooted in local perceptions of historical experience and in a community's geopolitical context, why a country's strategic culture is what it is. To recognize the need for change, as in the United States today with reference to the challenge posed by irregular enemies, is not necessarily to ensure that the needed change will occur. Such change may meet with too much resistance.

Fifth and finally, the new culturalism is in danger of becoming fashionable; indeed, it may be fashionable already. For those of us who have long touted the virtues of cultural study for strategists, it is most satisfying to note that the subject of our belief is now a prime-time issue area. But, the trouble with fashion is that it has to change. We should worry, lest the current enthusiasm for cultural study and culturally informed strategic behavior fade into history. They may join the other inherently brief fashions that have marked the passage of recent American strategic history. New, or more often, rediscovered, concepts can be discarded because they are soon intellectually exhausted, at least at a fairly elementary level. Strategic culture may well cease to find widespread favor once officials, soldiers, and sensible scholars come to appreciate just how difficult a subject it is. More to the point, perhaps, political and military executives will be discouraged by mature recognition of the difficulties that must hinder prudent efforts to operationalize cultural knowledge and understanding. Practical people, a category that should include strategists, will ask that most brutally direct of questions, "so what?" So what do we do with greater self-, and other-, cultural understanding? Culture matters greatly, but so do the other dimensions of war, peace, and strategy.

NOTES

1. Jeremy Black, *Rethinking Military History* (London: Routledge, 2004), p. 1. For an opposing point of view, see Lawrence Freedman, *The Transformation of Strategic Affairs*, Adelphi Paper 379 (London: IISS, March 2006), pp. 22–26.
2. U.S. Army, *Army Campaign Plan* (Washington, DC: Office of the Deputy Chief of Staff, G-3, Department of the Army, April 12, 2004), p. 10.
3. Bernard Brodie, *War and Politics* (New York: Macmillan, 1973), p. 332.
4. See Montgomery McFate, "The Military Utility of Understanding Adversary Culture," *Joint Force Quarterly*, No. 38 (3rd qtr. 2005), pp. 42–48.
5. Brodie, *War and Politics*, p. 453. "Strategic thinking, or 'theory' if one prefers, is nothing if not pragmatic. Strategy is a 'how to do it' study, a guide to accomplishing something and doing it efficiently."
6. Hedley Bull, "Strategic Studies and Its Critics," *World Politics*, Vol. 20, No. 4 (July 1968), p. 600.
7. Alastair Iain Johnston, *Cultural Realism: Strategic Culture and Grand Strategy in Chinese History* (Princeton, NJ: Princeton University Press, 1995).
8. Baron Antoine Henri de Jomini, *The Art of War* (1838; reprinted London: Greenhill Books, 1992), p. 321.
9. Ibid., p. 70.
10. Ibid., p. 323.
11. Ibid., p. 325.
12. Sun Tzu, *The Art of War*, trans. Ralph D. Sawyer (ca. 400 BC; reprinted Boulder, CO: Westview Press, 1994), p. 179.
13. See Donald H. Rumsfeld, *Quadrennial Defense Review Report* (Washington, DC: U.S. Department of Defense, February 6, 2006), esp. pp. 21–22.
14. For a useful guide to the scholarly debate, see Stuart Poore, "Strategic Culture," in John Glenn, Darryl Howlett, and Poore, eds., *Neorealism Versus Strategic Culture* (Aldershot, UK: Ashgate, 2004), pp. 45–71.

15. Leslie A. White, *The Concept of Cultural Systems: A Key to Understanding Tribes and Nations* (New York: Columbia University Press, 1975), p. 4n.

16. Jack L. Snyder, *The Soviet Strategic Culture: Implications for Limited Nuclear Operations*, R-2154-AF (Santa Monica, CA: Rand, September 1977), p. 8.

17. Colin S. Gray, *Modern Strategy* (Oxford: Oxford University Press, 1999), Chapter 5.

18. Kenneth Waltz, *Theory of International Politics* (New York: Addison-Wesley, 1979).

19. Graham Allison, *Essence of Decision: Explaining the Cuban Missile Crisis* (Boston, MA: Little, Brown, 1971).

20. Isobel V. Hull, *Absolute Destruction: Military Culture and the Practices of War in Imperial Germany* (Ithaca, NY: Cornell University Press, 2005), p. 96.

21. For an unrestrained and politically incorrect portrayal of the importance of culture, see Victor Davis Hanson, *Why the West Has Won: Carnage and Culture from Salamis to Vietnam* (London: Faber and Faber, 2001).

22. Raymond Williams, "The Analysis of Culture," in John Storey, ed., *Cultural Theory and Popular Culture: A Reader* (Hemel Hempstead, UK: Harvester-Wheatsheaf, 1994), p. 56.

23. I am indebted to Black, *Rethinking Military History*, pp. 13–22.

24. Hull, *Absolute Destruction*, p. 329.

25. Keith B. Payne, *The Fallacies of Cold War Deterrence and a New Direction* (Lexington, KY: University Press of Kentucky, 2001).

26. Freedman, *Transformation of Strategic Affairs*, p. 22.

27. Ibid.

28. Karl von Clausewitz, *On War*, trans. Michael Howard and Peter Paret (1832; reprinted Princeton, NJ: Princeton University Press, 1976), p. 101.

29. Ibid., p. 75 (emphasis in original).

30. Ibid., p. 184.

31. Ibid., pp. 184–85.

32. Payne, *Fallacies of Cold War Deterrence*.

33. See James S. Corum, *The Roots of Blitzkrieg: Hans von Seeckt and German Military Reform* (Lawrence, KS: University Press of Kansas, 1992). Despite this praiseworthy and probably historically unique exercise, it is interesting to note that the Wehrmacht revealed some lethal weaknesses in World War II that had a long history behind them and therefore may warrant ascription as cultural.

34. Black, *Rethinking Military History*, p. 13.

35. Gray, *Modern Strategy*, chapter 5.

36. I have argued this thesis in *Irregular Enemies and the Essence of Strategy: Can the American Way of War Adapt* (Carlisle, PA: Strategic Studies Institute, US Army War College, March 2006).

37. See John I. Alger, *The Quest for Victory: The History of the Principles of War* (Westport, CT: Greenwood Press, 1982); and Anthony D. Mc Ivor, ed., *Rethinking the Principles of War* (Annapolis, MD: Naval Institute Press, 2005).

38. OODA: Observation, Orientation, Decision, Action. This formula for (tactical) victory was invented by Col. John Boyd of the USAF. It was inspired by his experience of jet fighter combat over Korea. See Grant T. Hammond, *The Mind of War: John Boyd and American Security* (Washington, DC: Smithsonian Institution Press, 2001).

39. Clausewitz, *On War*, p. 104.

40. See Forrest E. Morgan, *Compellence and the Strategic Culture of Imperial Japan* (Westport, CT: Praeger, 2003).

41. As in Michael C. Desch, "Culture Clash: Assessing the Importance of Ideas in Security Studies," *International Security*, Vol. 23, No. 1 (Summer 1998), pp. 141–70.

42. "As in many other branches of politics, the question that matters in strategy is: Will the idea work? More important, will it be likely to work under the special circumstances under which it will next be tested? . . . *strategy is a field where truth is sought in the pursuit of viable solutions.*" Brodie, *War and Politics*, pp. 452, 453 (emphasis in original). I must confess to

being the person whom Brodie correctly criticized, by name, with his emphasis upon the pragmatic nature of strategy and strategic study.

43. For an outstanding recent historical analysis of transcultural warfare, see Hew Strachan, "A General Typology of Transcultural Wars—The Modern Ages," in Hans-Henning Kortum, ed., *Transcultural Wars: From the Middle Ages to the 21st Century* (Berlin: Akademie Verlag, 2006), pp. 85–103.

44. Colin S. Gray, "The American Way of War," in Mc Ivor, ed., *Rethinking the Principles of War* (Newport, RI: U.S. Naval Institute Press, 2005), pp. 13–40.

45. Michael Howard, *The Continental Commitment: The Dilemma of British Defence Policy in the Era of the Two World Wars* (London: Temple Smith, 1972), p. 57. Also see David French, *British Strategy and War Aims, 1914–1916* (London: Allen and Unwin, 1986), Chapter 6.

46. See Eliot A. Cohen, "The Mystique of U.S. Air Power," *Foreign Affairs*, Vol. 73, No. 1 (January/February 1994), PP. 109–24. In his *Storm over Iraq: Air Power and the Gulf War* (Washington, DC: Smithsonian Institution Press, 1992), Richard P. Hallion, the USAF's Official Historian, claims that "[a]s dominant land power characterized a *Pax Romana*, and dominant sea power a *Pax Britannica*, dominant air power is the characteristic of modern America," p. 267.

47. This danger was flagged many years ago in Gerald Segal, "Strategy and 'Ethnic Chic,'" *International Affairs*, Vol. 60, No. 1 (Winter 1983/84) pp. 15–30.

48. The case studies are excellent in Emily O. Goldman and Leslie C. Eliason, eds., *The Diffusion of Military Technology and Ideas* (Stanford, CA: Stanford University Press, 2003).

49. John J. Weltman, *World Politics and the Evolution of War* (Baltimore: Johns Hopkins University Press, 1995), p. 152.

50. Milan N. Vego, "Effects-Based Operations: A Critique," *Joint Force Quarterly*, No. 41 (2nd qtr., 2006), pp. 51–57, is a blistering condemnation that takes no prisoners.

51. The finest work of strategic theory since Clausewitz's *On War* warns that "planning for certitude is the greatest of all military mistakes, as military history demonstrates all too vividly." J.C. Wylie, *Military Strategy: A General Theory of Power Control* (1967; reprinted Annapolis, MD: Naval Institute Press, 1989), p. 72.

52. "Cultural thoughtways" is an inspired concept borrowed gratefully from Ken Booth, *Strategy and Ethnocentrism* (London: Croom Helm, 1979), p. 14.

53. Ibid., p. 147.

15

Conclusion: Toward a Standard Methodological Approach

Jeannie L. Johnson

In the spirit of Colin Gray's admonition that a "little theory goes a long way" in the discipline of strategic culture, our final effort in this volume is to provide those engaged in security studies a practical framework for pursuing strategic culture research. The framework presented here is an outcome of the lessons learned through the case study process, and the practical priorities emphasized by those who do the real work of national security.

A Proposed Framework

Our methodological direction to case study authors in this volume was purposefully flexible and culturally comprehensive. We cast the net widely to see which methodological patterns would surface with consistency and prove useful. This exercise provided the insights we were hoping for, but underlined the need to determine some common reference points for the study of strategic culture. A multitude of factors, and of actors, influence security policy in any given state. The next step in theoretical refinement is to make some decisions about which of these appropriately fall under the auspices of "strategic culture," and which do not.

It must be noted at the outset that no serious strategic culture scholar claims that cultural investigation will allow for pointed and certain predictive power about adversary behavior. Culture is but one component of a much larger equation. A full accounting of the factors contributing to any particular security decision might be described as follows: Elite agendas processed through national culture, the national policy process, and organizational cultures that are married to material capabilities, and inhibited or advanced by external actors. The model of strategic culture proffered here combines the central components of this larger outlay. National culture, national policy processes, and organizational cultures might reasonably set the research agenda for the domestic phenomenon termed strategic culture.

Professionals in the academic world typically study each of these three components separately. Anthropologists make their trade by delving into the mysteries of local and national cultures, comparativists in the field of political science amass and analyze data on the form and efficacy of various national policy processes, and the study of organizational culture—determining the outlines of institutions and their internal rules, doctrines, and incentive structures—has become a common mode of employ by international as well as domestic political theorists.[1]

A fair question then, is what the study of strategic culture hopes to add. The first point would be that strategic culture allows for a security lens to be placed on all of the aforementioned study. It points researchers to a specific task, and corrals data in a way particularly useful to foreign policy analysis. Second, strategic culture fills a much-discussed gap in international relations theory. It accepts that most actors are likely rational, but insists that "rationality" must be understood within a cultural context. The study of strategic culture plays a critical role in understanding a regime's "tendencies." It draws flexible outlines around behavior considered acceptable, and preferable, and offers a sounder understanding of decision parameters.

U.S. intelligence and policy analysts have traditionally provided solid information in assessing the national policy processes for states of interest regarding the interplay between agencies, formal and informal decision structures, relationships between civilian leadership and the military, levels of corruption, preferences for loyalty or merit, tolerance for dissent, levels of popular participation, issue ownership between competing institutions, power hierarchies, and a wealth of other regime-specific information. The two research areas in need of much greater strategic depth are national and organizational culture. To cover both is beyond the scope of this conclusion. The insights yielded from our case studies lend themselves primarily toward a more refined assessment of national culture. Therefore, the remainder of this chapter will focus efforts toward defining the aspects of national culture most relevant to security policy, and proposing some methods for its study.

A Word on Culture

Most practitioners advocating the inclusion of cultural nuance into foreign policy formation and analysis understand that a society's culture is not monolithic. Cultures are layered entities that might be better understood as "belief clusters."[2] Some of these beliefs may compete, and some widely held values or narratives may be drawn to the fore more prominently in one era than in another. Therefore, the study of culture requires a rather sophisticated and highly flexible approach that allows for human will and a dynamic operating environment.

Given the cobbled nature of "culture," significant subsets of culture within a society may need to be treated individually. For any particular region competing layers may include tribal, ethnic, religious, professional, gender differentiated, national and civilization level cultures.[3] Sometimes these norms coincide, sometimes they do not. A first exercise for the study of any society might be to draw up cultural "maps" highlighting the variety of cultural layers in play. Which layers provide dominant influence may depend on regional custom, generational preferences, or the specific issue at hand.

For security purposes, understanding the breadth of possibilities within a given society hedges against surprise. The cultural nurseries that schooled today's leadership may be somewhat different than those that socialize the group that replaces them. Beatrice Heuser uses the example of weapons of mass destruction (WMD) to warn:

> It is thus not possible to exclude the possibility that regimes will come to power within nuclear-weapons owning states whose attitudes to WMD will differ from those of the regimes that first procured them (e.g. the main procurement motivation may have been

more for deterrence or status reasons, the new regime might consider their actual use in a concrete military situation.) This is particularly easy to imagine in states where two or more significantly different cultures exist side by side, for example one close to that of the Western Liberal culture, one extremely focused on nationalism…, and one extremely focused on religion, to the point of basing arguments on the assumption of an afterlife, which can compensate for any human sacrifice in this life. Pakistan can serve as an example of such a mix of cultures.[4]

Keeping track of culture requires tenacity and a deep commitment to the subject matter. Although most of what we deem "cultural" must have enough staying power to merit the label, determining which cultural attributes are currently influencing policy and which are resting latent in the population is a messy business. Cultural change often comes about through the process of one group's interpretation of national identity becoming favored over another, either incrementally or by way of revolution.

Initial probes into a regime will reveal the extent to which it is appropriate to speak of, and examine, a "national" culture. In some cases, national cultures are quite intact, populations are homogeneous, shared history is lengthy, and national boundaries are clear. In these cases, methods for assessing our traditional sense of "national culture" prove quite useful. Regimes born of artificial boundaries, however, may still be struggling to forge common frames of reference. The visions of disparate groups will likely be competing for prominence in the national identity story. With this caveat in mind, the methods provided here will most often be cast in national culture terms, with the understanding that they need be applied to significant subcultures within the state when those subcultures have potential to influence security policy.

MODEL AND METHODS FOR EXAMINING NATIONAL CULTURE

A rubric as elastic as national culture captures a tremendous number of variables. Our first task is to determine which of these plays a significant role in contributing to the "rational" calculation of security policy for a particular regime. The aim of a parsimonious research model must be to narrow the world of variables to those that are most likely to have an effect on security policy, or are sufficient to understanding the pivotal components of a foreign society's cost/benefit analysis. Four variables that may provide such a baseline include: identity, values, norms, and perceptive lens. Each will be discussed in turn.

Identity

A nation-state's view of itself, comprising the traits of its national character, its intended regional and global roles, and its perceptions of its eventual destiny. Most international relations theorists agree that nation-states are self-interested, and seek net gain. Even economists, however, clarify that rationally self-interested actors are pursuing personal, not universal, goals: "Thus, the economic statement that man is thought to be rational is a fairly modest one. It merely means that he attempts to achieve his goals, and that he devote at least some thought, some of the time, to how to do it."[5]

Rather than accept the blanket assumption of absolute power-seeking offered by neorealism (primarily defined in military and economic terms), strategic culture analysis assumes that states form their interests, and their views of other actors, based on a normative understanding of who they are, and what role they should be playing. Theo Farrell makes the role of identities for security policy in its most kinetic form—war-fighting—more explicit: "Ideas of who we are tell us why we should fight. To be sure, wars are fought over material things—the occupation of territory, the acquisition of resources and to gain access to markets. But politics and people also go to war in order to enact particular identities."[6] In this volume, Murhaf Jouejati notes that Syria's self-identity as "champion of Arab rights" meant acting on interests that realism would have difficulty explaining:

> Although Syria could have stayed out of the war in 1948, the then small Syrian army rushed to the frontline in support of its Palestinian brethren in their conflict with the emerging Jewish state. In 1956, although Egypt alone was the target of the tripartite Israeli/British/French alliance, Syria joined the conflict—out of Arab solidarity…During the 1960s, although Israel's attempts to channel water from the Jordan River to the Negev desert did not affect Syria, the Syrian Government set out to divert the Jordan River's head waters—fueling tensions between Arabs and Israelis that culminated in the Six Day War.[7]

Thomas Mahnken also emphasizes the role of identity in his chapter on the United States. He notes that the strong identity marker of American "exceptionalism" means the United States "rejects the European tradition of power politics"; justifies its "impulse to transform the international system in the service of liberal democratic ideals"; and—in the words of George Kennan—produces excessive "moralism and legalism" in its foreign policy. The moralistic flavor of America's exceptionalism identity means that marches to war are most often framed as crusades against evil. While this approach serves to rally the necessary public support, it has also put policymakers in a difficult position when it is in America's national interest to pursue limited war aims. Strategies that do not seem to achieve a "fight to the finish" objective often suffer significant popular backlash.

War, and the weapons of war, is affected by a state's perceived identity. For example, Glenn Chafetz, Hillel Abramson, and Suzette Grillot explore the divergent paths, under similar circumstances, taken by Ukraine and Belarus with regard to nuclear policy. The authors present a strong correlation between four identity typologies and a "marked tendency toward nuclear acquisition."[8] They label these identities regional leader, global system leader, regional protector, and anti-imperialist.[9] According to their argument, leader states seek nuclear weapons as a necessary status symbol. Protectors seek the defensive insurance offered by a nuclear shield—both for themselves and for others; and anti-imperialists believe they must own the most powerful weapon available within the global system if they are to overturn it.

The method they suggest for coding role conception is readily duplicable. The authors provided six individual raters with a comprehensive sampling of general statements concerning "role, identity, or purpose, regardless of audience"[10] made by key policymakers over a two–four-year period. Raters were allowed to classify statements into as many of the fourteen available categories as they deemed appropriate. The authors used this data to track role "articulations" with behavior over time in order to claim a positive correlation.[11] Ukraine's leadership orientation caused it to waiver far longer on nuclear compliance than did Belarus's self-conception as "collaborator."

Identity and role conception may be the most telling barometer for regime receptivity to international pressure regarding nuclear weapons acquisition or proliferation. Those states that see themselves as "cooperators" or "mediators" are far more likely to fall in line with international norms than are regimes who wear their pariah status as a badge of honor, or who believe they are destined to be "victims" of the system. Notwithstanding material and security realities (as we may observe them), these self-imposed identities must be taken seriously as state platforms for action. As Lawrence Sondhaus sums up, "Encultured beliefs in the righteousness of one's own cause are the greatest obstacle to a harmonious world; to accept them as real (rather than dismiss them as a rhetorical cover for a rational reality) helps us better understand ourselves, our adversaries, and the world in general."[12]

Values

The issue of "values" may be approached in at least two distinct ways. One is defined as a society's notions of right and wrong, of good and evil, of proper and improper conduct. These notions are important, and intrinsic to the study of strategic culture, but, for the purposes of this research, will be examined under the next category—norms—which looks specifically at the behaviors that are accepted and expected within a society.

The notion of values proffered here is of a more calculus-oriented sort. Put simply, what sorts of goods—both material and immaterial—does this society value more highly than others? The French fiercely value the purity and international prominence of their language, adult *liberté,* and leisure time. The Navajo value corn pollen, the sacred number four, and their reputation as indispensable code-talkers during World War II. National resources, of course, are valued among all societies for the economic possibilities they offer, but might also be valued for powerful sentimental attachments driven by culture. Thomas Friedman, in his book *From Beirut to Jerusalem* (1995) makes a case for the value Israeli Jews place on the territories of the West Bank as regions of national biblical heritage—Judea and Samaria.[13] Hebron is not just a West Bank village, it is "the town where the Jewish patriarchs Abraham, Isaac and Jacob were buried, and where Abraham, the Father of the Nation, had purchased, for 400 shekels of silver, his first piece of land in Palestine (Canaan)."[14]

Values, therefore, might be best understood as highly prized features of a society, whether those are earth underfoot or notions of national honor. As it is awkward to speak of a piece of territory, a national landmark, or a holy site as a "value," a more calculus-oriented reference system may be in order. Our task is to ascertain value *placed* on an item. "Value assessments" of this nature might range along a scale from "nonnegotiable" to "low priority." These would apply whether the item in question is the Dome of the Rock or Latin notions of *machismo.* Understanding what is of little worth in a society is often as important for targeted policy as understanding the goods that are prized.

Value assessments must be understood with a healthy degree of accuracy in order to craft effective security policy and shape public diplomacy messages in ways that resonate with target audiences. Foreign populations may weigh foundational political concepts such as liberty and security in a significantly different balance than their Western counterparts. Suffering may be valued as necessary to form depth of character, and violence may be valued as an expression of manhood.

The Danish newspaper printing of unflattering cartoons of Muhammad illustrates the point of divergent social values. For Westerners viewing the situation, the value at stake was clearly freedom of the press and freedom of expression. By Western standards, civilized values require the "maturity" to handle offensive press. An act of violence in reaction to a printed cartoon was clearly childish and barbaric; in short, "irrational."

For Muslims, the value at stake was, instead, defense of the sacred. Muhammad comprises an essential part of the Islamic sacred sphere, and it is the clearly the duty of each Muslim to defend it, even at the cost of bloodshed. Certainly not all Muslims share this view at the same level, but enough did to cause an international uproar.

State decisions to move forward on a nuclear weapons program are often driven by motivations to protect, or showcase national values. Indians from the subcontinent, according to our chapter from Rodney Jones, place great value on intellectual achievements, specifically those in the technical fields. Jones points out that the value placed on proving mastery of the world's most sophisticated technologies played an important role in India's drive to achieve nuclear competence:

> This trait drove India's investment in modern science and engineering across the board, its acquisition of modern military technology and large standing military forces, its development of nuclear and missile capabilities—against international opposition, and its secret development of chemical weapons. [In addition,] this trait is conducive to Indian practitioners in strategic decision-making and negotiations being better informed and more analytically focused than most of their external interlocutors.[15]

Some precedent has been set in tracking value priorities within and between nations. Researcher Shalom Schwartz asked respondents in over fifty countries to evaluate a set of values according to their utility as "guiding principles of one's life."[16] Based on over 60,000 responses, Schwartz compiled 10 distinct value types. These types, as well as other polling data on value orientation,[17] may prove useful in providing negotiators with notions of general value orientation when approaching interlocutors from abroad.

More specific data on ideational and material values may be unearthed from a range of investigative methods. One young scholar, in order to better understand his own Iranian roots, traveled the country asking a diverse sampling of Iranian nationals the same question, "Tell me your story." He watched for patterns and repeated references in order to piece together, in his words, "the soul of Iran."[18] One might imagine a widely solicited survey based on the same informal, conversational methods, but more directly targeted at narratives highlighting values (What should I know about Iran? What is it to be Iranian? What are Iran's greatest assets? What aspects of your society do you most value?). Open-ended questions tend to produce more qualitative data than quantitative, and are often a necessary precursor to formalized polling methods as they allow themes to surface that a researcher raised outside the culture may not think to include. Question prompts, of course, would have to match the language and question style of the culture under examination.

When conversation with locals is difficult, then observing which aspects of the society are ritualized and celebrated, what sort of figures streets and primary schools are named for (military victors, poets, statesmen, etc.), which heroes are given monuments in the town square, and which privileges, when under attack, cause riots in the streets may all provide the observer with starting points for deeper value assessments.

Norms

Accepted and expected modes of behavior. An evaluation of norms may illuminate why some rational means toward an end goal are rejected as unacceptable, even though they would be perfectly efficient. Tannenwald and Price have explored the nonuse of nuclear, chemical, and biological weapons as a case in point. They cite numerous examples where use of chemical or nuclear weapons would have made sense, and been effective, from a pure realpolitik standpoint, but was refrained from nonetheless. Their claim is that the reluctance manifested by states in employing these weapons is a product of normative boundaries on action—in this case, global norms adopted and internalized at the domestic level.[19]

Greg Giles explores the power of national norms on security policy in a number of ways in his chapter on Israel. One particularly poignant example focuses on the Israeli Defense Forces (IDF) and its conclusions about engagement in the 1987 Intifada:

> Eventually, the IDF command publicly acknowledged that it could not engage in the types of operations needed to eliminate the Intifada without violating societal norms. In essence, IDF Chief of Staff Dan Shomron declared that there was no acceptable military solution to the uprising and that it had to be resolved politically.[20]

A second example highlights the limits on the power of elites to use societal norms to package controversial decisions. Judaic tradition transfers the sin of war to the party that initiates it. Thus, the distinction between wars forced upon the state (obligatory), and wars selected for (optional) is of profound ethical importance. "Ethically, the former are considered 'just' wars that require full public support, while the latter lack consensus and, by extension, moral clarity."[21]

The 1982 invasion of Lebanon put Israeli norms to the test. All prior wars had been cast as no-choice wars. The political and military leaders at the time tried various tactics at framing the 1982 confrontation in the same way. Their efforts failed.

> In contrast to all prior wars, the 1982 invasion of Lebanon was deemed [by the public] to be a "war by choice" and consequently at odds with traditional Jewish definitions of a just and legal war. This triggered a national debate that deepened the questioning of fundamental beliefs and assumptions at the core of Israeli strategic culture…As the goals of the operation expanded, and Israeli casualties mounted, initial public support for the war dissipated.[22]

The term "norms" is a bit problematic definitionally (a case that might be made for all cultural variables) as authors writing on culture and policy have used it to mean both a set of *practices,* and also the world of *beliefs* that inform those practices. Theo Farrell homes in on the beliefs side when he defines his use of the term: "Norms are intersubjective beliefs about the social and natural world that define actors, their situations, and the possibilities of action."[23] Peter Katzenstein in *The Culture of National Security,* favors a slightly more behavior-oriented approach. He defines norms as, "Collective expectations for the proper behavior of actors with a given identity."[24]

These two definitions fit the essence of what Geert and Gert Jan Hofstede describe as hardwired notions of "evil versus good, dirty versus clean, moral versus immoral, ugly versus beautiful, unnatural versus natural," and so on.[25] Behaviors cast as clearly corrupt in one society may be perfectly admissible in another. In his chapter on Iran, Willis Stanley points out that the Iranian leadership follows moral tenets that include

> [t]he cultural and religious sanction of deception and façade when necessary to preserve the faith, one's life or, most importantly, the regime. The roots of this flexibility are

not difficult to intuit: living as Shia in a sea of Sunnis, and as Iranians in a sea of Arabs, required developing the survival skills of the often weak and powerless. Indeed, the degree to which Iranian elites were able to co-opt their conquerors through application of the administrative skills developed over centuries speaks to the flexibility that has kept Iran's unique cultural identity alive through the present day.

The concept of norms captures the wide range of human behavior. The spectrum extends from those practices informed by a deeply ingrained sense of right and wrong to surface practices that are social habit, but not connected to a terribly profound belief system. Not all norms are absorbed, or informed, equally. Kevin Avruch makes the point:

> [C]ultural representations—images and encodements, schemas and models—are internalized by individuals. They are not internalized equally or all at the same level, however. Some are internalized very superficially and are the equivalent of cultural clichés. Others are deeply internalized and invested with emotion or affect.[26]

As pointed out later in his book, norms infused with strong sentiment or informed by a dedicated belief system may persist over long periods of time despite the fact that the practices they produce do not progress lifestyles toward ends we would consider "optimal." He warns against

> the excessively optimistic presumptions of classical functionalism—that somehow the solutions found or used by a culture are always the right ones or the best ones. On the contrary, cultural solutions at the level of local knowledge and practice can be and very often have been (to use the locution of some colleagues) severely "suboptimal."[27]

What this means for policymakers is that, depending on the level of internalization of the norm in question, efforts toward demonstrating improved practices through public diplomacy messaging or hands-on training may result in peripheral, if any, progress. Humans are perfectly capable of pursuing norms they believe in, whether they "make sense" or not.

In order to determine which sorts of beliefs and behaviors are likely to play a strong role in security policy, methods that enable us to rank, in some fashion, the salience of norms are required. At the far end of the spectrum are norms informed by dearly held, hardwired beliefs. These norms are internalized and will persist without supervision, even in the face of more "logical" recommendations. At the other end are those practices that are widely observed socially, but fit Avruch's notion of "cultural clichés." These may be forced practices passed down by government—complied with by citizens but quickly abandoned as soon as the supervising power is removed, or may be something as simple as habit carried forward by social inertia, long severed from its original raison d'etre, or any sincere belief system.

An example of widespread, but superficial cultural habit might help illustrate the point: the frequent Anglo-Saxon practice of "knocking on wood." A completely uniformed observer to British and American society might conclude through discursive content analysis that both societies are deeply superstitious about the fortune-enhancing qualities of wood and are loathe to make decisions without invoking it. He would note the frequency of the practice (breadth) and the fact that it permeates all social and economic classes (depth) to support this conclusion. This does not necessarily equate with the reality of a norm's strength, however. Frequency of practice and permeability of social class are not sufficient indicators of norm strength. Quantitative data must be informed by a strong dose of qualitative expertise.

Another type of often widespread, but thinly founded normative practice is norms that are being "tried out"—perhaps adopted from abroad, from media, or from pressure within the international community. These surface practices may persist for a very decent length of time and seem nearly ingrained into the community, but are, in fact, dependent on stable, fairly contented, highly supervised environments in order to persist. When significant economic, political, or social insecurity is introduced into the equation, these norms break down. Formerly cooperative citizens pull back to "bedrock" norms associated with the core levels of their primary culture cluster. Sectarian relations in Lebanon and ethnic relations in the former Yugoslavia both serve as examples of this phenomenon.

Keeping these caveats in mind, observers of security policy must be interested in understanding internalized practices in as many areas as possible, but certainly a few in particular. One essential area would be diving as deeply and as thoroughly as possible into a society's notions of morality. War-making and the weapons used to do it are essentially moral considerations. Heuser cites Germany as an example:

> In the culture of the Bonn Republic, the use of force was from its creation regarded an absolute evil, and anything symbolizing this use of force, above all nuclear weapons, has been thought of, literally, as diabolical. Throughout the Cold War, nuclear weapons were thus rejected as totally immoral by an important section of the West German population, to the point where it would have been out of the question for any government to procure nuclear weapons—their own population would not have allowed them to.[28]

Advancing our comprehension of another's morality requires, first, identifying a set of what seem to be moral guides, and, second, testing these for robustness. The first task is not as impossible as it may appear. The notions of morality we are concerned with are shared, societal level mores, and must be transmitted from one generation to the next. As this occurs they are expressed orally, repeatedly, and/or are codified and recorded.[29] Two areas of public discourse where this occurs most overtly are in the teaching of children, and in justifying public policy.

Because children must be taught overtly, and repeatedly, the way to properly behave within their society, discourse aimed at them is a rich source of societal morality. Elementary school texts,[30] fables that point out right behavior from wrong, songs that teach accepted principles, media characters that demonstrate proper attitudes and actions, and discipline exerted by teachers in classrooms and parents in parks, grocery stores, church, and the home, all are a wealth of morality code information. Hero legends ought to be given particular attention. Although very few parents expect their children to emulate folk heroes in practical form, the stories told represent the ideal "moral types" of a society.[31]

Public discourse between rulers and the ruled represent a second area where normative codes seem most accessible. In order to justify public acts and policy choices, statesmen reference common frames of right and wrong, of appropriate and inappropriate. Tracking the frequency of reference to particular frames provides some indication of norm strength.[32] Huiyen Feng's chapter is an excellent example of this technique. She analyzes the speeches of two separate Chinese leaders (Mao and Deng) in order to track the consistency of normative frames for action over time—Confucian versus Parabellum. Her findings indicate that normative frames used to legitimate foreign policy are affected both by the personal beliefs of key leadership figures, and by the threat-level context of the times. Tracking these patterns early on will suggest to policymakers which normative frame is in play, and the "template for action"[33] that frame suggests.

Rhetoric going the opposite direction proves useful for tracking norm salience as well. Where a reasonably free press exists, reporters act as watchdogs for norms violations among public officials.[34] The discourse back and forth will unveil a portion of the belief systems used to rationalize, or cast as appropriate, the behavior in question. Justifications that calm the populace during a time of uproar should be given special attention.

When the press is not allowed this role, public mutterings may prove the best guide. Tracking complaints about official behavior, and probing for the "why" behind behaviors deemed inappropriate, might be the task of a new sort of intelligence officer on the ground. Disaffection with state leadership may come in the form of protest, critical blogging,[35] or biting humor pointed at political officials, while congruence might manifest itself through strong turnout for state events and parades, voluntary displays of state insignia, or healthy membership in state-related organizations.[36] Attention should be paid to proverbs and quips that are used in justifying behavior or explaining events.

Once extant norms have been identified, they ought be tested, to the extent possible, for robustness. Jeffrey Legro has written extensively on measurement of norm strength.[37] He proposes that a norm be evaluated according to three criteria: how clearly it is recorded in the rules of society (specificity), how long it has existed within this society and its strength in standing up to normative competitors (durability), and how widely it is accepted and referenced in discourse (concordance).[38] Verbal content analysis of educational texts, legal forms, and political rhetoric may prove a useful starting point for conducting Legro's tests.

Perceptive Lens

Beliefs (true or misinformed) and experiences or the lack of experience that color the way the world is viewed. As is widely understood, behavior is based on the *perception* of reality, not reality itself. Perceptions of "fact," of our own histories, of our image abroad, of what motivates others, of the capabilities of our leadership and our national resources, and other security-related ideas, all play a strong role in forming what each regime believes to be rational foreign policy.

A number of distressing examples of the policy implications of a powerful and highly controlled national perceptive lens are evident in Bermudez's chapter on North Korea. He points out that within Kim Chong-Il's hermit kingdom the United States is portrayed as the primary enemy, and one that is perfectly willing to use WMD against North Koreans:

> During the [Korean] war both [North Korea] and People's Republic of China suffered from repeated, and to them, unexplained outbreaks of infectious diseases such as influenza, Dengue fever, and cholera. These outbreaks caused large numbers of civilian and military casualties. While the leadership knew that it was untrue, they fabricated the story that the United States was employing biological, and to a lesser degree chemical, weapons against their units in Korea and against villages within the PRC itself.[39]

Bermudez' analysis indicates that North Korea sees itself as morally stronger than the United States, and, in some areas, more militarily proficient. President

Kim Chong-Il reportedly characterized U.S. tactics in the Gulf War as "child's play." The erroneous beliefs Kim holds, and perpetuates, are rarely challenged by subordinates who fear to raise any issues that may be perceived as negative. This results in a misinformed perceptive lens sustained by circular verification.

National myths represent an important layer on a regime's cultural lens. Helmut Lotz notes that whether a myth is fact or fiction is of little consequence. Its value lies not in historical accuracy, but in its ability to "produce a common interpretation of the world in a situation where many individuals possess little information."[40] He classifies myths as "cognitive maps"[41] and demonstrates their utility as the "means that consume the least amount of resources to rally people behind a common cause."[42] Perhaps most damning for rational choice theorists, Lotz concludes that "Pure rationality would not be strong enough to produce the sacrifice every state must enforce on the individual in order to survive a crisis such as war." Myth, with its attendant emotional bonds, is required.[43]

Myths often define for a society the standards of victory and what entails defeat. These are not universal notions. U.S. analysts vastly underestimated the projected duration of the 1999 bombing campaign on Serbia due, in part, to an information gap concerning Serbian myths of victory and defeat. Serbia's national holiday is not a celebration of a past battlefield victory, but of a glorious defeat in 1389 at the hands of the Ottoman Turks. Serbs celebrate the bravery and valor of national hero Prince Lazar who received a heavenly visitation on the eve of battle and was told that he faced certain defeat the next day. Given the choice, Lazar declared that it was better to die in battle than to live in shame. He did precisely that, and became cemented in Serbian legend.

This tale permeates Serbian society. It is taught to youngsters in school, celebrated as the national holiday, and is represented in homes and offices in the renowned painting "Kosovo Girl." The message of the myth for Serbs is that victory may be found in standing up to a hegemonic bully and going down in flames of valor. This may go a good distance in explaining why Serbs exited their homes wearing targets on their heads during the heat of U.S. bombing. It was a moment of Serbian victory.

Effective coercion depends on accurately forecasting an adversary's reaction to the sticks threatened their direction. Kerry Kartchner cautions that absent a sound understanding of adversary culture, threats issued "may not even be considered threats, or…may be considered challenges to be confronted, thus having the exact opposite effect of that desired."[44]

Because plural myths exist within any society, one may be tempted to imagine myth morphing and myth wielding as a tool of elites. The assumption would be that rather than being influenced and constrained by culture, elites manipulate it for their own ends. To some extent this is true. Leaders who know their audience and are skilled in pushing cultural buttons are certainly in a position to march national emotion to their own tune.

Myths are not without a life of their own, however. Once invoked, myths form soft boundaries around action. The justification for action heralded by the myth is often married to appropriate means and end goals. A leader may succeed in getting popular consent for a grand strategy by casting it in a common framework, but then will be held to the standards represented there. Contravention of those standards would make that leader vulnerable to attacks from domestic opponents, or perhaps even skilled messengers from outside the regime. Hellmut Lotz characterizes domestic political competition in these terms, and emphasizes that rhetoric as an important starting point for investigations into culture's essentials:

> [I]t is imperative for the political actor who attempts to manipulate public opinion to identify those myths that are the core of a society's beliefs…The struggle to define an issue in one's own terms is a race to link the issue to the core values of a society. It is imperative to beat opponents to the high ground of core beliefs.[45]

An interesting place to start one's study of perceptive lens might be the foreign policy gaffs committed by the regime in question. A country's misreading of the intentions or values of other actors is often a product of mirror-imaging, and can therefore tell us much about that regime's own perspective.[46]

THE VARIABLES EVALUATED

Selecting identity, values, norms, and perceptive lens as our core variables in examining WMD decisions from a strategic culture perspective presents several advantages. First, each has a specific security dimension. Among other things, identity tells us the global role a nation-state intends to play and its likely aspirations. Values determine which principles, and material goods, are negotiable and which are not. A study of norms will help us understand which means are more likely to be employed than others in attaining state goals. And examining a nation's "perceptive lens" may contribute significantly to understanding the character of bounded rationality operating within a state. Data perceived as fact by a national population need not have any semblance to the truth.

A second advantage of these particular variables is that each remains expansive enough to capture much of what is important about national culture. Inputs such as geography, history, access to technology, political experience, religious traditions, education, demographics, common texts, and so on *create* identity, values, norms, and a group's perceptive lens. In some ways these four variables can be viewed as security-related outputs of national culture. As such, each of the four may be treated as starting points for queries into the wide range of human societies. The categorizations are not meant to be exclusive, but should be assumed to overlap. The Serbian myth of Prince Lazar, for instance, plays a role in defining Serbian identity, in establishing norms of warfare, in contributing to a perceptive lens that regards external powers as hostile, and in imbuing Kosovo's Field of Blackbirds (where the battle took place) with high national value.

As scholarship continues to expand and experiment, it may reach to include significant non-state actors. Jerry Mark Long makes an excellent case for the application of concepts normally reserved for "nations" to non-state actors. If a nation is defined as "a group of people who strongly identify with an overarching, shared cultural narrative," then groups such as al Qaeda and others who share a meta-narrative—"the overarching story that situates individuals in a distinct community, provides a cognitive roadmap by which they are to live, and that motivates members to protect the community against its enemies"—may be analyzed with many of the same research tools that have served to unearth cultural data for nation-states.

The motivation for this volume is to move forward efforts toward filling the information gaps presented by foreign societies. In doing so, we are well advised to survey the spectrum of social science methods and, in our analytical and intelligence institutions, apply significantly more resources, and creativity, to the collection, and coordination of culture-based intelligence.[47] One effort toward this end is to provide a common framework for research. Future case studies conducted through a common framework, and with common notions regarding the parameters of strategic culture, will allow for hypotheses to surface concerning the influence of strategic culture on security policy, and mark the beginning stages of theory-building in this field. This volume does not complete that journey, but aims to inspire work in that vein. In the words of Colin Gray, "One cannot make a virtue of cultural ignorance."[48] As complicated and time intensive as the study of strategic culture may be, it remains in our national interest to pursue it.

Notes

1. For a particularly good example of this type of research, see William C. Mitchell and Randy T. Simmons, *Beyond Politics* (Boulder, CO: Westview Press, 1994).
2. Term coined by Beatrice Heuser, "Beliefs, Culture, Proliferation and Use of Nuclear Weapons," *Journal of Strategic Studies: Special Issue on Preventing the Use of Weapons of Mass Destruction*, Vol. 23, No. 1 (March 2000), p. 77.
3. Theo Farrell has completed a paper on the effect of "professional" norms on military organizational cultures across nation-states. These norms are established at the global level and are so influential that they are often pursued by national military institutions even when it makes very little strategic sense. Theo Farrell, ed., *The Norms of War: Cultural Beliefs and Modern Conflict* (London: Lynne Rienner, 2005).
4. Heuser, "Beliefs, Culture, Proliferation," p. 94.
5. Gordon Tullock and Richard McKenzie, *The New World of Economics: Explorations into the Human Experience* (Homewood, IL: Richard D. Irwin, 1981), p. 9.
6. Farrell, *The Norms of War*, p. 1.
7. See chapter ten, "The Making of Syria's Strategic Culture," by Murhaf Jouejati in this volume.
8. Glenn Chafetz, Hillel Abramson, and Suzette Grillot, "Culture and National Role Conceptions: Belarussian and Ukrainian Compliance with the Nuclear Proliferation Regime," in Valerie Hudson *Culture and Foreign Policy*, ed. (Boulder, CO: Lynne Rienner, 1997), p. 175. The authors also offer a list of seven typologies unlikely to engage in illegal proliferation.
9. The authors note that these National Role typologies are slightly modified versions of those proposed by Kal Holsti in "National Role Conception in the Study of Foreign Policy," *International Studies Quarterly*, Vol. 14 (1970), pp. 233–309.
10. Chafetz, Abramson, and Grillot, "Culture and National Role Conceptions," p. 184.
11. Ibid., pp. 184–91.
12. Lawrence Sondhaus, *Strategic Culture and Ways of War* (New York: Routledge, 2006), p. 130.
13. Thomas L. Friedman, *From Beirut to Jerusalem* (New York: Anchor Books, 1995), p. 257.
14. Ibid., p. 260.
15. See chapter 8, "India's Strategic Culture and the Origins of Omniscient Paternalism," by Rodney Jones in this volume.
16. Schwartz's work is referenced in Stephan Dahl, "Intercultural Research: The Current State of Knowledge" (Middlesex University Business School), p. 16. Shalom Schwartz, "Universals in the Content and Structure of Values: Theoretical Advances and Empirical Tests in 20 Countries," in Mark P. Zanna, ed., *Advances in Experimental Social Psychology*, (San Diego: Academic Press, 1992), pp. 1–65; Schwartz, "Beyond Individualism/Collectivism: New Dimensions of Values," in Uichol Kim et al. eds., *Individualism and Collectivism: Theory, Method and Applications*, (London: Sage, 1994), pp. 85–122.

17. Anthropologist Anne Clunan, of the Naval Post Graduate School, brought to my attention World Values Survey data that has accumulated over the course of two decades. This research may be found at http://www.worldvaluessurvey.org/. The website includes a list of the books that have been published based on the findings.
18. Afshin Molavi, *The Soul of Iran: A Nation's Journey to Freedom* (New York: W.W. Norton, 2002).
19. Richard Price and Nina Tannenwald, "Norms and Deterrence: The Nuclear and Chemical Weapons Taboos," in *The Culture of National Security: Norms and Identity in World Politics,* Peter J. Katzenstein, ed., (New York: Columbia University Press, 1996), pp. 114–52.
20. See chapter 7, p. 109, in this volume.
21. Giles, quoting Charles Ben-Dor, "War and Peace: Jewish Tradition and the Conduct of War,"*Israeli Defense Forces Journal,* Vol. 3, No. 4 (Fall 1986), pp. 47–50.
22. Giles, chapter 7.
23. Theo Farrell, "Constructivist Security Studies: Portrait of a Research Program," *International Studies Review,* Vol. 4, No. 1 (2002), p. 49.
24. Katzenstein, *The Culture of National Security,* p. 5.
25. Geert Hofstede and Gert Jan Hofstede, *Culture and Organizations: Software of the Mind* (New York: McGraw-Hill, 2005), p. 8. Although they use the term "values" to represent this group of beliefs, the Hofstedes acknowledge that the two words "norms" and "values" are often used interchangeably, so will likely not object to our placing their concepts within the norms category. See footnote 17, p. 378.
26. Kevin Avruch, *Culture and Conflict Resolution* (Washington, DC: United States Institute of Peace Press 1998), p. 19.
27. Ibid., p. 20.
28. Heuser, "Beliefs, Culture, Proliferation," p. 89.
29. Farrell, "Constructivist Security Studies," p. 60.
30. Jeremy Moyes, interview (April 2006).
31. Bernard Lewis argues that these ideal types provide influence so strong that they often represent national identity. He uses the figure of Saladin as Muslim hero as a case in point. Lewis, *The Multiple Identities of the Middle East* (New York: Schocken Books 1998), p. 21.
32. Andrew P. Cortell and James W. Davis, Jr., "Understanding the Domestic Impact of International Norms: A Research Agenda," *International Studies Review,* Vol. 2, No. 1 (Spring 2000), pp. 65–87; and Paul Kowert and Jeffrey Legro, "Norms, Identity, and Their Limits: A Theoretical Reprise," in *The Culture of National Security,* pp. 451–97.
33. Hudson, *Culture and Foreign Policy,* p. 9.
34. Greg Giles, interview (May 2006).
35. Matthew Berrett, interview (July 2007).
36. Gentri Lawrence, interview (2006).
37. For example, Jeffrey W. Legro, *Cooperation Under Fire: Anglo-German Restraint During World War II* (New York: Cornell University Press 1995); Legro, "Which Norms Matter? Revisiting the 'Failure' of Internationalism," *International Organization,* Vol. 51, No. 1 (1997), pp. 31–63. Paul Kowert and Jeffrey Legro, "Norms, Identity and Their Limits," in *The Culture of National Security,* pp. 451–97.
38. Legro, *Cooperation Under Fire.*
39. See chapter 12, p. 191, this volume.
40. Helmut Lotz, "Myth and NAFTA: The Use of Core Values in U.S. Politics," in *Culture and Foreign Policy,* p. 73.
41. Ibid., p. 74.
42. Ibid., p. 79.
43. Ibid.
44. See chapter 4, p. 57, this volume.

45. Lotz, "Myth and NAFTA," p. 92.

46. Beatrice Heuser, interview (November 2007).

47. Captain Stephanie Kelly demonstrated the importance of "creativity" during her stay in Iraq, where she organized the systematic collection of RUMINT (rumors intelligence). Her research produced surprising, and extremely useful, results. Stephanie Kelley, "Rumors in Iraq: A Guide to Winning Hearts and Minds," *Strategic Insights* Vol. 4, No. 2 (February 2005).

48. See chapter 14, p. 233, this volume.

Appendix: Recommended Readings

Almond, Gabriel A., R. Scott Appleby, and Emmanuel Sivan. *Strong Religion: The Rise of Fundamentalisms around the World*. Chicago: University of Chicago Press, 2003.

Asante, Molefi Kete, and William B. Gudykunst, eds. *Handbook of International and Intercultural Communication*. Newbury Park: Sage, 1989.

Augsburger, David W. *Conflict Mediation across Cultures*. Louisville: Westminster John Knox Press, 1992.

Avruch, Kevin. *Culture & Conflict Resolution*. Washington, DC: United States Institute of Peace Press, 1998.

Avruch, Kevin, Peter W. Black, and Joseph A. Scimecca, eds. *Conflict Resolution: Cross-cultural Perspectives*. New York: Greenwood Press, 1991.

Barnouw, Victor. *Culture and Personality*. Homewood, IL: Dorsey Press, 1963.

Basrur, Rajesh M. "Nuclear Weapons and Indian Strategic Culture." *Journal of Peace Research*, Vol. 38, No. 2 (March 2001): 181–98.

Becker, Miriam D. "Strategic Culture and Ballistic Missile Defense: Russia and the United States." *Aerospace Power Journal*, Special Edition 1994.

Binnendijk, Hans, ed. *National Negotiating Styles*. Washington, DC: U.S. Department of State, Foreign Service Institute, April 1987.

Blank, Stephen J. et al. *Conflict, Culture, and History: Regional Dimensions*. Maxwell Air Force Base, Alabama: Air University Press, 1993.

Bluedorn, Allen. *The Human Organization of Time: Temporal Realities and Experience*. Stanford: Stanford Business Books, 2002.

Booth, Ken. "American Strategy: The Myths Revisited," in Ken Booth and Moorhead Wright, eds. *American Thinking about Peace and War*. New York: Harper and Row, 1978, pp. 1–35.

———. *Strategy and Ethnocentrism*. London: Croom, Helm, 1979.

———. "The Concept of Strategic Culture Affirmed," in Carl G. Jacobsen, ed. *Strategic Power: The United States of America and the USSR*. London: Macmillan Press, 1990, pp. 121–28.

Booth, Ken, and R. Trood, eds. *Strategic Cultures in the Asia–Pacific Region*. New York: St. Martin's Press, 1999.

Booth, Ken, and Moorhead Wright, eds. *American Thinking about Peace and War*. New York: Harper and Row, 1978.

Botti, Timoth J. *Ace in the Hole: Why the United States Did Not Use Nuclear Weapons in the Cold War, 1945–1965*. Westport, CT: Greenwood Press, 1996.

Boyer, Paul. *By the Bomb's Early Light: American Thought and Culture at the Dawn of the Atomic Age*. New York: Pantheon Books, 1985.

Bozeman, Adda. *Politics and Culture in International History*. Princeton, NJ: Princeton University Press, 1960.

Brooks, Risa, and Elizabeth Stanley, eds. *Creating Military Power: The Sources of Military Effectiveness*. Stanford: Stanford University Press, 2007.

Builder, Carl H. *The Masks of War: American Military Styles in Strategy and Analysis*. Baltimore and London: Johns Hopkins University Press, 1989.

Bunn, Elaine. "Can Deterrence Be Tailored?" *Strategic Forum*, No. 225, Washington, DC: Institute for National Strategic Studies, National Defense University (January 2007): 3–5.

Burles, Mark, and Abram N. Shulsky. *Patterns in China's Use of Force: Evidence from History and Doctrinal Writings.* Santa Monica: RAND, 2000. MR-1160-AF.

Cahoone, Lawrence E. *Cultural Revolutions: Reason versus Culture in Philosophy, Politics, and Jihad.* University Park, PA: Pennsylvania State University Press, 2006.

Cain, Anthony C. "Iran's Strategic Culture and Weapons of Mass Destruction: Implications for U.S. Policy." *The Maxwell Papers, Maxwell Paper No. 26,* Air War College, April 2002.

Cassidy, Robert M. *Russia in Afghanistan and Chechnya: Military Strategic Culture and the Paradoxes of Asymmetric Conflict,* U.S. Army War College, Strategic Studies Institute, February 2003.

Chay, Jongsuk, ed. *Culture and International Relations.* New York: Praeger, 1990.

Chubin, Shahram. *Iran's Nuclear Ambitions.* Washington, DC: Carnegie Endowment for International Peace, 2006.

Clark, Mark T. "Nuclear Deterrence for Small Nuclear Powers (South Africa, Israel, India, Pakistan)," in Bradley A. Thayer, ed. *American National Security Policy: Essays in Honor of William R. Van Cleave.* Fairfax, VA: National Institute Press, 2007, pp. 35–51.

Clawson, Patrick, and Michael Eisenstadt. *Deterring the Ayatollahs: Complications in Applying Cold War Strategy to Iran.* The Washington Institute for Near East Policy, Policy Focus #72, July 2007.

Cohen, Raymond. *Negotiating across Cultures: Communication Obstacles in International Diplomacy.* Washington, DC: United States Institute of Peace, 1991.

Cortell, Andrew P., and James W. Davis, Jr., "Understanding the Domestic Impact of International Norms: A Research Agenda." *International Studies Review,* Vol. 2, No. 1 (Spring 2000): 65–87.

Cromartie, Michael, ed. *Religion, Culture, and International Conflict: A Conversation.* Lanham: Rowman and Littlefield, 2005.

Dalgaard-Nielson, A. "The Test of Strategic Culture: Germany, Pacifism and Pre-emptive Strikes." *Security Dialogue,* Vol. 36 (2005): 339–59.

Davis, Alex, and Dan Fu. "Culture Matters: Better Decision Making through Increased Awareness." Stottler Henke Associates, Interservice/Industry Training, Simulation, and Education Conference, 2004.

Deibel, Terry L., and Walter R. Roberts. *Culture and Information: Two Foreign Policy Functions.* Washington Paper No. 40, Beverly Hills: Sage, 1976.

Desch, Michael. "Culture Clash: Assessing the Importance of Ideas in Security Studies." *International Security,* Vol. 23, No. 1 (Summer 1998): 141–70.

DeSutter, Paula A. *Denial and Jeopardy: Deterring Iranian Use of NBC Weapons.* Washington, DC: National Defense University Press, 1997.

Dror, Yehezkel. *Crazy States: A Counterconventional Strategic Problem.* Milwood, NY: Kraus Reprint, 1971.

Duffield, John S. "Germany Confounds Neorealism." *International Organization,* Vol. 53 (1999): 765–803.

Duffield, John S., Theo Farrell, Richard Price, and Michael C. Desch. "Isms and Schisms: Culturalism versus Realism in Security Studies." *International Security,* Vol. 24, No. 1 (Summer 1999): 156–80.

Elkins, David, and Richard Simeon. "A Cause in Search of Effect, or What Does Political Culture Explain?" *Comparative Politics* (January 1979): 127–45.

Ellis, Richard, and Michael Thompson. *Culture Matters: Essays in Honor of Aaron Wildavsky.* Boulder, CO: Westview Press, 1997.

Ermarth, Fritz. "Contrasts in American and Soviet Strategic Thought," in P. Edward Haley et al., eds. *Nuclear Strategy, Arms Control, and the Future.* Boulder, CO: Westview Press, 1985, pp. 159–65.

Farrell, Theo. "Culture and Military Power." *Review of International Studies,* Vol. 24 (1998): 407–16.

———. "Constructivist Security Studies: Portrait of a Research Program." *International Studies Review,* Vol. 4, No. 1 (2002): 49–72.

———. "Strategic Culture and American Empire." *SAIS Review* (Summer–Fall 2005): 3–18.

————. *The Norms of War: Cultural Beliefs and Modern Conflict*. Boulder, CO: Lynne Rienner, 2005.

Gannon, Martin J. et al. *Understanding Global Cultures: Metaphorical Journeys through 17 Countries*. Thousand Oaks, CA: Sage, 1994.

Geert, Hofstede. *Culture's Consequences: Comparing Values, Behaviors, Institutions, and Organizations across Nations*, 2nd ed. Thousand Oaks: Sage, 2001.

Geertz, Clifford. *The Interpretation of Cultures: Selected Essays*. New York: Basic Books, 1973.

Gelfand, Michele J., and Jeanne M. Brett, eds. *The Handbook of Negotiation and Culture*. Stanford: Stanford University Press, 2004.

Gell, Alfred. *The Anthropology of Time: Cultural Constructions of Temporal Maps and Images*. Providence: Berg, 1992.

Giles, Gregory, F. "The Islamic Republic of Iran and Nuclear, Biological, and Chemical Weapons," in Peter Lavoy, Scott Sagan, and James Wirtz, eds. *Planning The Unthinkable: How New Powers Will Use Nuclear, Biological, and Chemical Weapons*. Ithaca, NY: Cornell University Press, 2000, pp. 79–103.

————. "The Crucible of Radical Islam: Iran's Leaders and Strategic Culture," in Barry R. Schneider and Jerrold M. Post, eds. *Know Thy Enemy: Profiles of Adversary Leaders and Their Strategic Cultures*, 2nd ed. Maxwell Air Force Base, Alabama: USAF Counterproliferation Center, July 2003, pp. 141–62.

Glenn, John, Darryl Howlett, and Stuart Poore, eds. *Neorealism versus Strategic Culture*. London: Ashgate, 2004.

Gray, Colin S. "National Style in Strategy: The American Example." *International Security*, Vol. 6, No. 2 (Fall 1981): 21–48.

————. "Comparative Strategic Culture." *Parameters*, Vol. 14, No. 4 (Winter 1984): 26–33.

————. *Nuclear Strategy and National Style*. Lanham, MD: Hamilton, 1986.

————. "Strategy in the Nuclear Age: The United States, 1945–1991," in Williamson Murray, MacGregor Knox, and Alvin Bernstein, eds. *The Making of Strategy: Rulers, States, and War*. Cambridge: Cambridge University Press, 1994, pp. 579–613.

————. "Strategic Culture as Context: The First Generation of Theory Strikes Back." *Review of International Studies*, Vol. 25 (1999): 49–69.

————. "The American Way of War," in Anthony D. Mc Ivor, ed. *Rethinking the Principles of War*. Annapolis: Naval Institute Press, 2005, pp. 13–40.

Gries, Peter Hays. *China's New Nationalism: Pride, Politics, and Diplomacy*. Berkeley: University of California Press, 2005.

Hanson, Victor Davis. *Carnage and Culture: Landmark Battles in the Rise of Western Power*. New York: Doubleday, 2001.

Harris, Marvin. *The Rise of Anthropological Theory: A History of Theories of Culture*. New York: Columbia University Press, 1968.

Harrison, Lawrence E., and Samuel P. Huntington, eds. *Culture Matters: How Values Shape Human Progress*. New York: Basic Books, 2000.

Heuser, Beatrice. "Beliefs, Culture, Proliferation and Use of Nuclear Weapons," in Eric Herring, ed. *Preventing the Use of Weapons of Mass Destruction*. London: Frank Cass, 2000, pp. 74–100.

Hopf, Ted. *Social Construction of International Politics: Identities and Foreign Policies*. Ithaca, NY: Cornell University Press, 2002.

Howlett, Darryl. "Strategic Culture: Reviewing Recent Literature." *Strategic Insights*, Vol. 4, No. 10 (October 2005). http://www.ccc.nps.navy.mil/si/2005/Oct/howlettOct05.asp (accessed November 19, 2007).

Hudson, Valerie M., ed. *Culture and Foreign Policy*. Boulder, CO: Lynne Rienner, 1997.

Hudson, Valerie M., and M. Sampson. "Culture Is More Than Static Residual: Introduction to Special Section on Culture and Foreign Policy." *Political Psychology*, Vol. 20, No. 4 (December 1999): 667–75.

Huntington, Samuel. *The Clash of Civilizations and the Remaking of World Order*. New York: Touchstone, 1997.

Hymans, Jacques E.C. *The Psychology of Nuclear Proliferation.* Cambridge: Cambridge University Press, 2006.

Jablonsky, David. *Strategic Rationality Is Not Enough: Hitler and the Concept of Crazy States.* Carlyle: U.S. Army War College, Strategic Studies Institute, August 8, 1991.

Jervis, Robert. *Perception and Misperception in International Politics.* Princeton, NJ: Princeton University Press, 1976.

Jervis, Robert, Richard Ned Lebow, and Janice Gross Stein. *Psychology and Deterrence.* Baltimore: Johns Hopkins University Press, 1985.

Johnston, Alastair Iain. *Cultural Realism: Strategic Culture and Grand Strategy in Chinese History.* Princeton, NJ: Princeton University Press, 1995.

———. "Thinking about Strategic Culture." *International Security,* Vol. 19, No. 4 (Spring 1995): 33–64.

Jones, David R. "Soviet Strategic Culture," in Carl G. Jacobsen, ed. *Strategic Power: USA/ USSR.* New York: St. Martin's Press, 1990, pp. 35–49.

Kartchner, Kerry M. "American Diplomacy and the Arms Control Imperative," in Bradley A. Thayer, ed. *American National Security Policy: Essays in Honor of William R. Van Cleave.* Fairfax, VA: National Institute Press, 2007, pp. 102–11.

Katzenstein, Peter J., *Cultural Norms and National Security: Police and Military in Postwar Japan.* Ithaca, NY: Cornell University Press, 1996.

———. ed. *The Culture of National Security: Norms and Identity in World Politics.* New York: Columbia University Press, 1996.

Kennan, George F. "The Sources of Soviet Conduct." *Foreign Affairs,* July 1947.

Kier, Elizabeth. *Imagining War: French and British Military Doctrine between the Wars.* Princeton, NJ: Princeton University Press, 1997.

Kimmerling, Baruch. "The Social Construction of Israel's 'National Security,'" in Cohen Stuart, ed. *Democratic Societies and Their Armed Forces: Israel in Comparative Context.* London: Frank Cass, 2000, pp. 215–53.

———. *The Invention and Decline of Israeliness: State, Society, and the Military.* Berkeley: University of California Press, 2001.

Kincade, William. "American National Style and Strategic Culture," in Carl G. Jacobsen, ed. *Strategic Power: USA/USSR.* New York: St. Martin's Press, 1990, pp. 10–34.

Klein, Yitzhak. "A Theory of Strategic Culture." *Comparative Strategy,* Vol. 10, No. 1 (1991): 3–23.

Krause, Keith, ed. *Culture and Security: Multilateralism, Arms Control and Security Building.* London: Frank Cass, 1999.

Kux, Stephan. *Language and Strategy: A Synoptic Analysis of Key Terms in the Strategic Doctrines of the Nuclear Powers.* Bern: Peterlang, 1990.

Lantis, Jeffrey. "Strategic Culture and National Security Policy." *International Studies Review,* Vol. 4, No. 3 (2002): 87–101.

Lavoy, Peter R. "Nuclear Myths and the Causes of Nuclear Proliferation." *Security Studies,* Vol. 2 (Spring–Summer 1993): 192–212.

Lefebvre, Vladimir A. *Algebra of Conscience: A Comparative Analysis of Western and Soviet Ethical Systems.* Dordrecht, Holland: D. Reidel, 1982.

Legro, Jeffrey. *Cooperation under Fire: Anglo-German Restraint during World War II.* Ithaca, NY: Cornell University Press, 1995.

Leites, Nathan. *The Operational Code of the Politburo.* New York: McGraw-Hill, 1951.

———. *A Study of Bolshevism.* New York: Free Press, 1953.

Levine, Robert. *A Geography of Time: The Temporal Misadventures of a Social Psychologist.* New York: Basic Books, 1997.

Lewis, John Wilson, and Litai Xue. *Imagined Enemies: China Prepares for Uncertain War.* Stanford: Stanford University Press, 2006.

Lind, Michael. *The American Way of Strategy: U.S. Foreign Policy and the American Way of Life.* Oxford: Oxford University Press, 2006.

Linn, Brian M. "The American Way of War Revisited." *Journal of Military History,* Vol. 66, No. 2 (April 2002): 501–33.

Lock-Pullan, Richard. *US Army Innovation and American Strategic Culture after Vietnam.* London: Routledge, 2005.

Longhurst, Kerry. "The Concept of Strategic Culture," in G. Kummel and A.D. P:Prufert, eds. *Military Sociology: The Richness of a Discipline.* Baden-Baden: Nomos, 2000, pp. 301–10.

Lord, Carnes. "American Strategic Culture." *Comparative Strategy*, Vol. 5 (Fall 1985): 273–74.

Mahbubani, Kishore. *Can Asians Think? Understanding the Divide between East and West.* Southroyalton, VT: Steerforth Press, 2002.

Mahnken, Thomas G. "The American Way of War in the Twenty-First Century," in Efraim Inbar, ed. *Democracies and Small Wars.* London: Frank Cass, 2003, pp. 73–84.

Mahnken, Thomas G., and James R. FitzSimonds. *The Limits of Transformation: Officer Attitudes toward the Revolution in Military Affairs.* Newport: Naval War College Press, 2003.

Mazarr, Michael J. "Culture in International Relations." *The Washington Quarterly*, Vol. 19, No. 2 (Spring 1996): 177–97.

Mazrui, Ali A. *Cultural Forces in World Politics.* New York: James Currey, 1990.

Merrily, Baird. "Kim Chong-il's Erratic Decision-Making and North Korea's Strategic Culture," in Barry R. Schneider and Jerrold M. Post, eds. *Know Thy Enemy: Profiles of Adversary Leaders and Their Strategic Cultures*, 2nd ed. Maxwell Air Force Base, Alabama: USAF Counterproliferation Center, July 2003, pp. 109–40.

Moore, Carmella C., and Holly F. Mathews, eds. *The Psychology of Cultural Experience.* Cambridge: Cambridge University Press, 2001.

Morgan, Forrest E. *Compellence and the Strategic Culture of Imperial Japan.* Westport, CT: Praeger, 2003.

Morrison, Terri, Wayne A. Conaway, and George A. Borden. *Kiss, Bow, or Shake Hands: How to Do Business in Sixty Countries.* Avon, MA: Adams Media Corporation, 1994.

Mott, William H., and Jae Chang Kim. *The Philosophy of Chinese Military Culture: Shih vs. Li.* New York: Palgrave Macmillan, 2006.

Mousseau, Michael. "Market Civilization and Its Clash with Terror." *International Security*, Vol. 27, No. 3 (Winter 2002/3): 5–29.

Munch, Richard, and Neil J. Smelser, eds. *Theory of Culture.* Berkeley: University of California Press, 1992.

Murray, Douglas J., and Paul R. Viotti, eds. *The Defense Policies of Nations: A Comparative Study.* 2nd edition. Baltimore: Johns Hopkins University Press, 1989.

Nagy, George. "Nuclear Deterrence and the American Way of War," in Owen C.W. Price and Jenifer Mackby, eds. *Debating 21st Century Nuclear Issues.* Washington, DC Center for Strategic and International Studies, 2007, pp. 203–25.

Nathan, A.J. "Is Chinese Culture Distinctive?—A Review Article." *Journal of Asian Studies*, Vol. 52 (1993): 923–36.

Nisbett, Richard E. *The Geography of Thought: How Asians and Westerners Think Differently…and Why.* New York: Free Press, 2003.

Ortner, Sherry B., ed. *The Fate of "Culture": Geertz and Beyond.* Berkeley: University of California Press, 1999.

Palmer, Dave R. *Provide for the Common Defense: America, Its Army, and the Birth of a Nation.* Novato, CA: Presidio Press, 1994.

Patai, Raphael. *The Arab Mind.* Revised Edition. New York: Hatherleigh Press, 2002.

Payne, Richard J. *The Clash with Distant Cultures: Values, Interests, and Force in American Foreign Policy.* Albany: State University of New York Press, 1995.

Perkovich, George. *India's Nuclear Bomb: The Impact on Global Proliferation.* Berkeley: University of California Press, 1999.

Post, Jerrold M. *Leaders and Their Followers in a Dangerous World: The Psychology of Political Behavior.* Ithaca, NY: Cornell University Press, 2004.

Press, Daryl G. *Calculating Credibility: How Leaders Assess Military Threats.* Ithaca, NY: Cornell University Press, 2005.

Quester, George H. "Cultural Barriers to an Acceptance of Deterrence," in Roman Kolkowicz, ed. *The Logic of Nuclear Terror*. Boston: Allen and Unwin, 1987, pp. 82–108.

Rosen, Stephen Peter. "Military Effectiveness: Why Society Matters." *International Security*, Vol. 19, No. 4 (Spring 1995): 5–31.

Rossi, M.L. *What Every American Should Know about the Rest of the World*. New York: Plume Books, 2003.

Rudesill, Dakota S. "Paper Tiger or Waking Dragon? Considering Nuclear Change in China," in Owen C.W. Price and Jenifer Mackby, eds. *Debating 21st Century Nuclear Issues*. Washington, DC: Center for Strategic and International Studies, 2007, pp. 102–16.

Russell, James A., ed. The Proliferation *of Weapons of Mass Destruction in the Middle East*. New York: Palgrave Macmillan, 2006.

Sagan, Scott D., and Kenneth N. Waltz. *The Spread of Nuclear Weapons: A Debate*, 2nd ed. New York: W.W. Norton, 2002.

Schivelbusch, Wolfgang. *The Culture of Defeat: On National Trauma, Mourning, and Recovery*. New York: Picador, 2003.

Schneider, Barry R., and Jerrold M. Post, eds. *Know Thy Enemy: Profiles of Adversary Leaders and Their Strategic Cultures*. USAF Counterproliferation Center, Maxwell Air Force Base, Alabama, November 2002.

Scobell, Andrew. *The Chinese Calculus of Deterrence: India and Indochina Michigan Studies on China*. Ann Arbor: University of Michigan Press, 1975.

———. *China and Strategic Culture*. Carlisle Barracks, PA: Strategic Studies Institute, U.S. Army War College, 2002.

———. *China and Strategic Culture*. Honolulu: University Press of the Pacific, 2004. Reprint of 1998 edition.

———. "Is There a Chinese Way of War?" *Parameters*, Vol. 35, No. 1 (2005): 118.

Shaffer, Brenda, ed. *The Limits of Culture: Islam and Foreign Policy*. Cambridge, MA: MIT Press, 2006.

Simpson, John, and Ian Kenyon. *Deterrence and the New Global Security Environment*. Abingdon, UK: Routledge, 2006.

Slocombe, Walter B. *Democratic Control of Nuclear Weapons*, Geneva Centre for the Democratic Control of Armed Forces. DCAF, Policy Paper No. 12, Geneva, April 2006.

Smith, Long Johnson, "Strategic Culture and Violent Non-State Actors." Occasional Paper #64, U.S. Air Force Institute for National Security Studies, February 2008.

Snowman, Daniel. *Britain and America: An Interpretation of their Culture 1945–1975*. London: Harper Torchbooks, 1977.

Snyder, Jack L. *The Soviet Strategic Culture: Implications for Limited Nuclear Options*. Santa Monica: RAND, R-2154-AF, September 1977.

———. "The Concept of Strategic Culture: Caveat Emptor," in Carl G. Jacobsen, ed. *Strategic Power: The United States of America and the USSR*. London: Macmillan Press, 1990, pp. 3–9.

Snyder, Scott. *Negotiating on the Edge: North Korean Negotiating Behavior*. Washington, DC: U.S. Institute of Peace, 1999.

Sokolski, Henry, and Patrick Clawson. *Checking Iran's Nuclear Ambitions*. University Press of the Pacific, 2004.

Solomon, Richard H. *Chinese Negotiating Behavior Pursuing Interests through "Old Friends."* Washington, DC: United States Institute of Peace Press, 1999.

Sondhaus, Lawrence. *Strategic Culture and Ways of War*. New York: Routledge, 2006.

Steiner, Barry H. *Bernard Brodie and the Foundations of American Nuclear Strategy*. Lawrence, KS: University of Kansas Press, 1991.

Stuart, Cohen. "The Scroll or the Sword? Tensions between Judaism and Military Service in Israel." *Israel Studies*, Vol. 12, No. 1 (Spring 2007): 103–126.

Tanham, George K. "Indian Strategic Culture." *Washington Quarterly*, Vol. 15, No. 1 (Winter 1992): 129–42.

Twing, Stephen W. *Myths, Models, and U.S. Foreign Policy: The Cultural Shaping of Three Cold Warriors*. Boulder, CO: Lynne Rienner, 1998.

Vlahos, Michael. *Strategic Defense and the American Ethos.* SAIS Papers in International Affairs, Number 13. Westview Press/Foreign Policy Institute, School of Advanced International Studies, Johns Hopkins University, 1986.

———. "Culture and Foreign Policy." *Foreign Policy* No. 82 (Spring 1991): 59–78.

Weigley, Russell F. *The American Way of War: A History of United States Military Strategy and Policy.* Bloomington: Indiana University Press, 1973.

Weldes, Jutta, Mark Laffey, Hugh Gusterson, and Raymond Duvall, eds. *Cultures of Insecurity: States, Communities, and the Production of Danger.* Minneapolis: University of Minnesota Press, 1999.

Williams, Michael C. *Culture and Security: The Reconstruction of Security in the Post–Cold War Era.* London: Routledge, 2006.

Williams, Michael J. *On Mars and Venus: Strategic Culture as an Intervening Variable in U.S. and European Foreign Policy.* Berlin: Lit Verlag, 2005.

Wolfe, Alvin W., and Honggang Yang. *Anthropological Contributions to Conflict Resolution.* Athens, AL: University of Georgia Press, 1994.

Zaman, Rashed uz. "India's Strategic Culture." Unpublished PhD dissertation, Reading University, 2006.

Zhan, Shu Guang. *Deterrence and Strategic Culture: Chinese–American Confrontations, 1949–1958.* Ithaca, NY: Cornell University Press, 1992.